THE END OF THE POEM

THE END OF THE POEM

OXFORD LECTURES **PAUL MULDOON**

FARRAR, STRAUS AND GIROUX

NEW YORK

FARRAR, STRAUS AND GIROUX
19 Union Square West, New York 10003

Distributed in Canada by Douglas & McIntyre Ltd.
Printed in the United States of America
Published in 2006 by Farrar, Straus and Giroux
First paperback edition, 2007

The Library of Congress has cataloged the hardcover edition as follows:
Muldoon, Paul.
    The end of the poem / Paul Muldoon.— 1st ed.
        p.   cm. — (Oxford lectures)
    ISBN-13: 978-0-374-14810-2 (hardcover : alk. paper)
    ISBN-10: 0-374-14810-4 (hardcover : alk. paper)
        1. Poetry, Modern—20th century—History and criticism. 2. Poetry,
Modern—19th century—History and criticism.   I. Title.   II. Oxford
lectures (New York, N.Y.)

PN1271.M85 2006
809.1'04—dc22

                                                    2005028125

Paperback ISBN-13: 978-0-374-53100-3
Paperback ISBN-10: 0-374-53100-5

Designed by Gretchen Achilles

www.fsgbooks.com

1   3   5   7   9   10   8   6   4   2

FOR TOM PAULIN

CONTENTS

THE END OF THE POEM

ALL SOULS' NIGHT

W. B. YEATS

Midnight has come, and the great Christ Church Bell
And many a lesser bell sound through the room;
And it is All Souls' Night,
And two long glasses brimmed with muscatel
Bubble upon the table. A ghost may come;
For it is a ghost's right,
His element is so fine
Being sharpened by his death,
To drink from the wine-breath
While our gross palates drink from the whole wine.

I need some mind that, if the cannon sound
From every quarter of the world, can stay
Wound in mind's pondering
As mummies in the mummy-cloth are wound;
Because I have a marvellous thing to say,
A certain marvellous thing
None but the living mock,
Though not for sober ear;
It may be all that hear
Should laugh and weep an hour upon the clock.

Horton's the first I call. He loved strange thought
And knew that sweet extremity of pride

That's called platonic love,
And that to such a pitch of passion wrought
Nothing could bring him, when his lady died,
Anodyne for his love.
Words were but wasted breath;
One dear hope had he:
The inclemency
Of that or the next winter would be death.

Two thoughts were so mixed up I could not tell
Whether of her or God he thought the most,
But think that his mind's eye,
When upward turned, on one sole image fell;
And that a slight companionable ghost,
Wild with divinity,
Had so lit up the whole
Immense miraculous house
The Bible promised us,
It seemed a gold-fish swimming in a bowl.

On Florence Emery I call the next,
Who finding the first wrinkles on a face
Admired and beautiful,
And knowing that the future would be vexed
With 'minished beauty, multiplied commonplace,
Preferred to teach a school
Away from neighbour or friend,
Among dark skins, and there
Permit foul years to wear
Hidden from eyesight to the unnoticed end.

Before that end much had she ravelled out
From a discourse in figurative speech
By some learned Indian
On the soul's journey. How it is whirled about,
Wherever the orbit of the moon can reach,
Until it plunge into the sun;

And there, free and yet fast,
Being both Chance and Choice,
Forget its broken toys
And sink into its own delight at last.

And I call up MacGregor from the grave,
For in my first hard springtime we were friends,
Although of late estranged.
I thought him half a lunatic, half knave,
And told him so, but friendship never ends;
And what if mind seem changed,
And it seem changed with the mind,
When thoughts rise up unbid
On generous things that he did
And I grow half contented to be blind!

He had much industry at setting out,
Much boisterous courage, before loneliness
Had driven him crazed;
For meditations upon unknown thought
Make human intercourse grow less and less;
They are neither paid nor praised.
But he'd object to the host,
The glass because my glass;
A ghost-lover he was
And may have grown more arrogant being a ghost.

But names are nothing. What matter who it be,
So that his elements have grown so fine
The fume of muscatel
Can give his sharpened palate ecstasy
No living man can drink from the whole wine.
I have mummy truths to tell
Whereat the living mock,
Though not for sober ear,
For maybe all that hear
Should laugh and weep an hour upon the clock.

Such thought—such thought have I that hold it tight
Till meditation master all its parts,
Nothing can stay my glance
Until that glance run in the world's despite
To where the damned have howled away their hearts,
And where the blessed dance;
Such thought, that in it bound
I need no other thing,
Wound in mind's wandering
As mummies in the mummy-cloth are wound.

Oxford, Autumn 1920

I WANT TO SAY A WORD OR TWO about my choice of this somewhat booming, perhaps even slightly bumptious phrase, "the end of the poem," for the general title of this series of lectures. To begin with, the idea of delivering fifteen lectures over five years is an extremely resistible one—matched only in its resistibility, I dare say, by the idea of *receiving* fifteen lectures over that same period. Who in his or her right mind would commit to a relationship that lasts longer than many marriages, and where one party in the contract, the aforesaid receiver of the lectures, is assigned much more favourable terms than the other? Whereas the receiver of lectures can always come up with some pressing, prior engagement to excuse his or her absence—for ten or twelve of the lectures, say—it's a little more tricky for the deliverer. Not only must the poor deliverer show up—which, despite what Woody Allen says, accounts for about eight rather than eighty per cent of the success of any venture—he must positively shine, maybe even scintillate. And he must scintillate, be there three hundred in the Examination Schools or three. I have to confess that I had this latter figure of three quite firmly in mind when I hit on the idea of the general title, *The End of the Poem*, for, while I was confident that the three most perspicacious readers in the audience—you know who you are—would continue to find it rich and resonant over the entire five years, I was less confident of being able to persuade anyone else that the phrase might be rich and resonant for more than about five seconds.

When I began to think of where I might find a little toe-hold on the slippery slope of this huge subject, particularly in the context of an inaugural lecture, it struck me that "All Souls' Night" by W. B. Yeats was tailor-made for the occasion. I use the words "context" and "tailor-made" advisedly because, as we'll see, the poem turns out to be in part a shuttling, as it were, between the words "textual" and "textile," words that this notoriously poor speller might well have mistaken one for the other, though neither appears in the poem. (I'm reminded, with regard to the spelling, of the occasion on which Yeats misspelt the word "professor" in his letter of inquiry about a professorship at Trinity College, Dublin.) It's clear that Yeats was very conscious of an appropriateness of the slippage between these two words, "textual" and "textile," conscious that they share the Latin root *texere*, "to weave," just as he's very conscious of the etymology of the word "line," and that there's an etymological "line" running through the poem that is quite at one with, and mimetic of, its material. I'll also be looking at other invisible threads through the poem, mostly having to do with proper names, including the name of at least one other poet who looms large in "All Souls' Night."

The poem comes to mind most immediately, of course, as being tailor-made by virtue of the occasion and the setting, this being All Souls' Day in Oxford, the city where Yeats wrote the poem in the autumn of 1920—perhaps, as Richard Ellmann suggests in *The Identity of Yeats*, beginning it on this very date. That the poem was written in Oxford in the autumn of 1920 might not ordinarily be of any great significance to anyone other than a literary critic, except that Yeats does indeed assign this information a significance, placing it, literally, at the end of the poem. There it is, in small italics: *Oxford, Autumn 1920*. Now, one of the unlikely, generally overlooked, aspects of reading a poem is that one may begin, as I just have, at the end. One may scan the poem as a shape on the page, taking in aspects of its geometry, well before one embarks on what we think of as a conventional line-by-line reading. Since I've begun at the end, let me continue by taking that piece of information, the dating and placing of the poem, and folding it back into the title "All Souls' Night." At first sight, the information that the poem was written in Oxford in the autumn of 1920 can hardly be seen to extend the meaning of the poem. It's self-evident that All Souls' Night falls in autumn. And, as the poem begins, the setting is also self-evident:

> Midnight has come, and the great Christ Church Bell
> And many a lesser bell sound through the room;
> And it is All Souls' Night.

Now, I suppose that some of the first readers of "All Souls' Night" might have had a momentary sound-picture of the great bell of the twelfth-century Augustinian priory church in Christchurch, Hampshire, or the great bell of the Anglican cathedral in Christchurch, New Zealand, when they came upon something along the lines of the poem, either in *The London Mercury* of March 1921, or in its simultaneous appearance in the United States in *The New Republic* of March 9, 1921, when they did not have the benefit of the date and place. I speak of "something along the lines of the poem." I should say, "what passed for what we now take to be 'All Sŏuls' Night.' " For, as we know from Allt and Alspach's *The Variorum Edition of the Poems of W. B. Yeats*, the poem began thus in *The New Republic*:

> It is All Souls' night and the great Christ Church bell . . .

while in *The London Mercury*, where a little smidgin of good old-fashioned poetic diction didn't raise an eyebrow, it read

> 'Tis All Souls' Night and the great Christ Church bell . . .

with a version of what is now the opening line, "For it is now midnight," appearing as line 3. It's worth pondering what might have been going on in Yeats's mind when he made these revisions, and to judge what might have been gained, or lost, in the process. One gain would have been the mimesis of the tolling of the bell in the predominantly spondaic metre of what is now the first line:

> Midnight has come, and the great Christ Church Bell
> And many a lesser bell sound through the room;

For what it's worth, one may divine (particularly if one's predisposed to hearing them) twelve stresses or bell-tolls in those first two lines before the release of

And it is All Souls' Night.

Another consideration that Yeats would have weighed, in the revision of the opening lines of the poem, would have been his urge to avoid the stress falling on the wrong foot, resulting in a loss of balance of sound and sense in the iambic "For it is now mid*night*." "And it is All Souls' Night" is an altogether more effective rounding out of the spondaic pattern, with almost equal stress on each of those five syllables. The word "spondee," if you recall, has at its heart the idea of duration, the duration of the pouring of a drink-offering or libation to the gods or, as it turns out in this poem, the ghosts of the dead.

And two long glasses brimmed with muscatel
Bubble upon the table.

The recurrence of the word "and" at the beginning of three consecutive lines results in an extraordinary combination of the incantatory and the carefree, the negligence which in Yeats is often merely apparent, sometimes massively real. (It's always worth remembering that we're dealing here with a man who was ignorant of which side his ancestors had fought on at the Battle of the Boyne, as is evidenced by an early version of the "Introductory Rhymes" to his 1914 volume *Responsibilities*, when he names James II as the "bad master" of his "old fathers.")

I seem to recall a critical discussion of these present lines centering on whether muscatel is indeed a wine in which we could decently expect to meet a bubble, the implication being that it's introduced here to meet what commentators used to refer to as "the exigencies of rhyme." This question of whether muscatel, not to be confused with muscadet, does indeed "fume" is one on which I propose to do a great deal of research over the next five years, and I'll report back to you when I have a finding, though, as I'm sure you'll realise, the likelihood of my making any finding will depend largely upon funding. For Yeats's purposes, it's vital that this particular bottle of muscatel exhibit a certain sparkle, given that it announces the contiguous spirit-world associated with All Souls' Night.

As the *Encyclopaedia Britannica* reminds us, this is

> the day appointed in the Roman Catholic church for a special commemoration of all the faithful departed, those baptized Christians who are believed to be in a state called purgatory because they have died with the guilt of lesser sins on their souls. Catholic doctrine holds that the prayers of the faithful on earth will help cleanse these souls in order to fit them for the vision of God in Heaven . . . The institution of a day for a general intercession on November 2 is due to Odilo, abbot of Cluny (d. 1048). The date, which became practically universal before the end of the thirteenth century, was chosen to follow All Saints' Day, November 1st . . . The feast was abolished in the Church of England at the Reformation but has been revived in Anglo-Catholic churches.

In the *Britannica* entry for "All Saints' Day" we're reminded that "in medieval English usage the festival was known as All Hallows, and its eve is still known as Halloween." It's as "Halloween" that Yeats would have known, as a child, the November 1 festival, though by the turn of the century he's more likely than not to have come to think of it by another term, Samhain, the Celtic New Year. The word "Samhain" means "summer's end" (from the Old Irish *sam*, summer, and *fuin*, end), and it was, as James MacKillop reminds us in his very handy *Dictionary of Celtic Mythology*, "the most important of the four great calendar feasts of Celtic tradition . . . The antiquity of Samhain is attested to by the Coligny Calendar [the series of bronze tablets dating from the first century B.C. unearthed in 1897 at Coligny, in eastern France] which cites the feast of *Samonios* . . . Samhain's equivalents on the Christian calendar are All Saints' Day (introduced by Pope Boniface IV in the 7th cent. to supplant the pagan festival of the dead) and Halloween." *Samhain* was, if you recall, the name of the house magazine of the Irish Literary Theatre, which appeared intermittently between the years 1901 and 1908 and was, of course, edited by Yeats.

Another of the unlikely, generally overlooked aspects of reading a poem has to do with the intermittent quality of our reading, so that having begun it, and proceeded a little into it, one may now leap back to the beginning, now again leap forward. This is particularly true of poems with which we're familiar, as Walter Fenno Dearborn pointed out in *The Psychology of Reading* (1906):

> That which we ordinarily do when we run over in "our mind's eye" the lines of a page which we have just been reading or of a passage which we have committed to memory offers an instance of a movement of attention over a field that is not present in the visual sense, except as a memory image . . . As is well known, many can recall during the recitation of a memorized passage a pretty constant image of the general appearance of the page and of an occasional word or group of words.

Now, one group of words that leaps off Dearborn's yellowed page is the phrase "mind's eye," which we also meet in line 33 of "All Souls' Night," an allusion to the best-known usage of the phrase, by Shakespeare, in *Hamlet*, where the prince sees the ghost of his father—"In my mind's eye, Horatio"—a not inappropriate allusion in the context of this poem about familiar spirits.

But I'm getting ahead of myself. Let me go back to the line

And two long glasses brimmed with muscatel

There's a great deal of data packed into these seven words. To begin with, these "two" glasses take the place of "two" people, two people who have had an intimate dinner, perhaps, and are about to toast each other in a strong, sweet dessert wine. The glasses are "brimmed," about to overflow, just as the line itself flows over, the verse *turns*, into the next, with the violent enjambment on "muscatel/bubble." The last syllable of "muscatel" most certainly sends us back to "bell" and signals that we have entered what might be described as a restricted area. For it's only now, as we come to where the fourth line ends on "muscatel," that we fully understand that we are in a stanza, or "room," through which "the great Christ Church Bell / And many a lesser *bell* sound," the internal perfect rhyme now defining the very chamber through which its chime echoes and reechoes. When I say "perfect" in this instance I mean the rhyme of "bell" and "bell," and I'd remind you of Yeats's bold use of perfect rhyme in two consecutive stanzas of "Byzantium," a poem thematically linked to "All Souls' Night," though written ten years later, in 1930:

Before me floats an image, man or shade,
Shade more than man, more image than a shade;

Miracle, bird or golden handiwork,
More miracle than bird or handiwork

I'll come back to the question of perfect rhyme in just a moment. For now, let me direct you to a near-perfect rhyme, the rhyme between Yeats and Keats. I'm reminded immediately of the occasion when Yeats read at Colgate University in Hamilton, New York, and the university president, who'd insisted on making the introduction and had obviously boned up big-time, introduced Yeats as the author of "Ode to Psyche," "Ode to a Nightingale" and "Ode on Melancholy." This is not only an honest mistake, of the sort that anyone who stands up to speak is likely to make, but it's not entirely without basis. For this very line, on which we've lingered quite a while, includes at least two words that Yeats has borrowed from Keats. The words are "brimmed" and "bubble" and they come directly from "Ode to a Nightingale":

O for a beaker full of the warm South
   Full of the true, the blushful Hippocrene,
      With beaded *bubbles* winking at the *brim*.

"Ode to a Nightingale" also includes the line "The coming musk-rose, full of dewy wine," and I've no doubt—though some will say I should—that the *musk* ghosts the *musc*atel just as, towards the end of the Keats poem, we have

Forlorn! The very word is *like a bell*

Which brings us back to "the great Christ Church Bell." Now, if I were still involved in my Clarendon Lectures on Irish literature I'd be inclined to say something about this scene conforming to the convention of a *feth fiada*, where the sound of a bell is often a signal of a moment of interface between this world and some other, but I'm not, so I won't. I will, however, quote a few sentences from Yeats's brief treatise, collected in *The Celtic Twilight*, "Concerning the Nearness Together of Heaven, Earth, and Purgatory":

> In Ireland this world and the world we go to after are not far apart . . . A lady I knew once saw a village child running about in a long trailing petticoat upon her, and asked why she did not have it cut short. "It was my grandmother's," said the child; "would you have her going about up yonder with her petticoat up to her knees, and she dead but four days?"

Then I'll go back to James MacKillop, who writes:

> Standing between the two halves of the Celtic year, Samhain seemed suspended in time, when the borders between the natural and the supernatural dissolve and the spirits from the Otherworld might move freely into the realm of mortals.

It's the possibility of this free movement of a spirit into the mortal realm that the speaker anticipates in these last lines of the first stanza of "All Souls' Night":

> A ghost may come;
> For it is a ghost's right,
> His element is so fine
> Being sharpened by his death,
> To drink from the wine-breath
> While our gross palates drink from the whole wine.

By the time we get to the end of this predominately spondaic line there's a realisation that we've arrived at a stopping-place, what with the length of line 10 now back in sync with 1, 2, 4 and 5, not to speak of its being complete emphasised by the word "whole." That awareness would have been underlined for readers of both *The New Republic* and *The London Mercury* by the fact that each of the ten stanzas appeared under a Roman numeral.

There's a realisation, too, that this being line 10, the stanza is somewhat outside Yeats's normative *ottava rima*, the form of most of his big poems of the previous ten years. That "All Souls' Night" should make its way into the world in ten-line units reintroduces the idea of Yeats being visited by Keats, since a ten-line unit (though not with the same rhyme-scheme) is employed in both "Ode to a Nightingale" and "Ode on Melancholy," each of which has very specific connections with this first stanza of "All Souls' Night." In "Ode on Melancholy" we find the occurrence, again within one line, of two key words, "palate" and "fine":

> Aye, in the very temple of Delight
>   Veiled Melancholy has her sov'reign shrine,
>   Though seen of none save him whose strenuous tongue
>   Can burst Joy's grape against his *palate fine*.

In "Ode to a Nightingale," meanwhile, we have:

> My heart aches, and a drowsy numbness pains
>   My sense, as though of hemlock I had drunk,
> Or emptied some dull opiate to the drains
>   One minute past, and Lethe-wards had sunk.

Now, I want to make the first of several suggestions which may strike some of you, including the three most perspicacious among you, as being quite outlandish. This has to do with a term for what would be offensive to a "palate fine," a synonym for the "drains" in what has been "emptied . . . to the drains," a term which, in his simultaneous recognition of, and resistance to, its appropriateness, would have presented Yeats with a problem. The term is "lees," which *Webster's* defines as "dregs, grounds, residue," and it's an indicator of what lies under the surface of these lines which centre on his wife, Georgie Hyde-*Lees*. It's the unnamed Georgie Hyde-Lees, after all, who is the presiding spirit not only of the poem but of *A Vision*, the prose work to which it is "an epilogue," a reference which I glossed over as I embarked on this close reading of the first stanza of "All Souls' Night," beginning as I did at the end of the poem.

I WANT TO CHANGE PACE for a moment to try to understand one aspect of Yeats's dating and placing of the poem—probably the most obvious aspect of it—which is, of course, more about the dating and placing of Yeats. And the dates are somewhat more significant than the mischievous W. H. Auden suggested in "Academic Graffiti":

> To get the last poems of Yeats
> You need not mug up on dates;
>   All the reader requires
>   Is some knowledge of gyres
> And the sort of people he hates.

We should remember that in November 1920, Yeats was fifty-five years of age. Only three years earlier, in 1917, he had married Georgie Hyde-Lees, twenty-five years his junior, in a Register Office in Paddington. Yeats was even then perceived as a major poet. A report of his wedding in the *Freeman's Journal* in Dublin had described him as "perhaps the greatest figure in Anglo-Irish literature, and . . . by general consent of his literary critics first among the poets of the time." Georgie Hyde-Lees had now borne Yeats a daughter, Anne, in 1919, while his son, Michael, would be born in the village of Thame, just outside Oxford, the following year, in 1921. Georgie Hyde-Lees had also been a party to an extraordinary outpouring of images and symbols through her "automatic writing." Richard Ellmann's account of, and accounting for, her contribution—in *The Identity of Yeats*—remains the most succinct:

> A few days after their marriage, Mrs. Yeats tried to distract her
> preoccupied husband by "faking" automatic writing, and then
> discovered, to her astonishment, that she could write it without
> meaning to. The writing continued sporadically over several years,
> but had to be sorted, organized, and completely revised before it
> could be published. A reader of *A Vision* may have difficulty in
> accepting this account, even though masses of automatic writing
> exist to authenticate it, because the ideas in the book are not novel in
> Yeats's work . . . That Georgie Hyde-Lees Yeats's automatic writing
> should have assumed so Yeatsian a form is not surprising. She had
> belonged to the same or similar occult organizations as her husband

and had read many of the same books. She knew his work thoroughly, especially the most recent, such as *Per Amica Silentia Lunae* (1917), a long essay which discusses the mask, the anti-self, and their supernatural counterpart, the daimon. And she spoke on these matters every day with a talkative husband.

That "talkative husband," whom she dubbed "William *Tell*," was the main source for the revelation that Georgie had been a medium for the "unknown writer," a revelation made by Yeats in his introduction to *A Vision*:

> I persuaded her to give an hour or two day after day to the unknown writer, and after some half-dozen such hours offered to spend what remained of life explaining and piecing together those scattered sentences. "No," was the answer, "we have come to give you metaphors for poetry."

Yeats goes on to describe the chief among those metaphors, the aforementioned "cone or gyre":

> On December 6th [1917] a cone or gyre had been drawn and related to the soul's judgement after death; and then just as I was about to discover that incarnations and judgements alike implied cones or gyres, one within the other, turning in opposite directions, two such cones were drawn and related neither to judgement nor to incarnations but to European history.

This idea of the "gyre" or "cone" may be traced partly to Swedenborg, who mentions "double cones" in his *Principia rerum naturalium*, partly to Hegel's ideas about "the continuous unification of opposites," but also, I want to suggest, partly to a source that was much nearer home for Yeats, Arthur O'Shaughnessy's (1844–81) very popular "The Poets," which begins:

> We are the music makers,
>   And we are the dreamers of dreams,
> Wandering by lone sea-breakers,
>   And sitting by desolate streams . . .

And ends:

> We, in the ages lying
>   In the buried past of the earth,
> Built Nineveh with our sighing,
>   And Babel itself with our mirth;
> And o'erthrew them with prophesying
>   To the old of the new world's worth;
> For each age is a dream that is dying,
>   Or one that is coming to birth.

These last two lines are a paraphrase of what will become Yeats's system. The very phrase "each age" is picked up by Yeats in one of the most famous passages from *A Vision*:

> *Each age* unwinds the thread another age had wound, and it amuses me to remember that before Phidias, and his westward moving art, Persia fell, and that when full moon came round again, amid eastward moving thought, and brought Byzantine glory, Rome fell; and that at the outset of our westward moving Renaissance Byzantium fell; all things dying each other's life, living each other's death.

The image of the "gyre" followed hard on the heels of the idea of "the phases of the moon," Yeats's madcap system for categorising human nature. A visitor to the Yeats house at 4 Broad Street, now Wendy News, in October or November 1920 could have expected to find him- or herself coming under the fierce scrutiny not only of a green parrot (one of a host of caged birds in which Yeats delighted), but of Yeats himself, before being classified and assigned a position in the appropriate phase of the moon. "The power to classify," Ellmann writes in *Yeats: The Man and the Masks*,

> is the power to control, and a new sense of strength comes into his writing. The ideal phase in *A Vision*, the phase "where Unity of Being is more possible than at any other phase," is shortly after the full moon, phase 17, and here Yeats classifies himself along with Dante, Shelley and Landor . . . In the Yeats household at Oxford in 1920 and

1921, as L.A.G. Strong has described it, the poet would often shoot some searching question at an unsuspecting guest whose answer would reveal where he could be typed in the lunar cycle. Mrs. Yeats and John Butler Yeats belonged to phase 18, where unity is beginning to break up, though a "wisdom of the emotions" is still possible. Lady Gregory was in phase 24, where codes of conduct must dominate; and George Russell, in spite of his vigorous objections, was put in phase 25, where the self accepts "some organized belief." Ezra Pound was originally in the highly subjective phase 12, but Yeats moved him among the humanitarians of the late objective phases after seeing him feed all the cats at Rapallo.

In Yeats's system, the particular "phase" into which an individual fell might be quite out of sync with the "gyre" of history, as Yeats found himself out of sync with the era which he believed was about to end seven years later, in 1927. As Frank Kermode puts it in his unfortunately entitled *The Sense of an Ending*:

> One of the assumptions prevalent in sophisticated apocalyptism was what Yeats called "antithetical multiform influx"—the forms assumed by the inrushing gyre as the old one reaches its term. The dialectic in Yeats's gyres is simple enough in essence; they are a figure for the co-existence of the past and future at the time of transition. The old narrows to its apex, the new broadens towards its base and the old and new interpenetrate.

I have to confess that it was only when I read this description by Kermode that I recognised in his description of the "gyres" the "two long glasses" on the table on this liminal night. Kermode continues:

> Actually, on Yeats's view of the historical cycle, there were transient moments of perfection, or what he called Unity of Being; but there was no way of making these permanent, and his philosophy of history is throughout transitional. In this he is not, of course, original; but his emphasis on the traditional character of our own pre-apocalyptic moment, in contrast with those exquisite points of

time *when life was like the water brimming beautifully but unstably over the rim of a fountain,* seems, for all the privacy of the expression, characteristically modern.

Yeats will be revisited by this image of the vessel "brimmed" to over-flowing in a related poem written in the apocalyptic year itself, between July and December 1927:

Such fullness in that quarter overflows
And falls into *the basin of the mind*

The poem is "A Dialogue of Self and Soul" and it ends with the lines:

We are blest by everything,
Everything we look upon is blest.

Let me try now to "ravel out," to use a term Yeats uses in line 51, the complex skein of imagery in "All Souls' Night," beginning with the word "blest" or "blessed." You'll notice it there on line 6 of the last stanza. The word is double-edged, not only in the context of "A Dialogue of Self and Soul," a poem centering on a Japanese sword, but in "All Souls' Night" itself. The etymological sense of "bless" is given by the *OED* as "mark so as to hallow with blood." Another meaning of the word "bless" is "to wound." Now, while that second meaning of the word is obsolete and comes, supposedly, from a different root, the two meanings are, according to the entry, "often associated, either humorously or in ignorance." I think Yeats associates them, neither humorously nor in ignorance, for the simple reason that the word "wound" appears as the very last word of the poem, though we correct our reading of it immediately to have it rhyme with "bound" and mean something else, the past participle of "wind." We've been wrong-footed on this same word earlier in the poem, in line 3 of the second stanza, where one is tempted to pronounce it as *woond* rather than *waund.* That's partly because, now that the stanzaic pattern has been established, we expect a rhyme for "sound" at the *end* of the fourth line and are somewhat taken aback when we meet the word "wound" as the first word of the third line, and are inclined to pronounce it w$\overline{oo}$nd. That's compounded by some of the vocabulary of the preceding two lines—"cannon," "quarter"—words that have violent associations. We revise our reading of "quarter" from the "hanging, drawing and quartering" association to the sense in which it's also used in "A Dialogue of Self and Soul":

> Fix every wandering thought upon
> That *quarter* where all thought is done.

The fact that the word "wound" appears at both the beginning of line 13 and the end of line 14 is not without its significance and underlies the idea that there is no beginning and no end. In that sense, the line is mimetic of what it describes, and what must be "ravelled out" of the poem is the line itself. The first definition of "line" in the *OED* is "a rope, cord, string," relating to its root in the word *linum*, meaning "flax." (We have to wait for definition 23e of "line" to meet "the portion of a metrical composition which is usually written in one line.") Now, there are two words having to do with flax that are relevant here. One is "linen," the material of the "mummy-cloth" in which the mummy is bound, the material no doubt of the petticoat worn by the child and her grandmother in "Concerning the Nearness Together of Heaven, Earth and Purgatory." In his essay on "Swedenborg, Mediums, Desolate Places," written in 1914 and collected in *Explorations I*, Yeats comments:

> If our terrestrial condition is, as it seems, the territory of choice and of cause, the one ground for all seed-sowing, it is plain why our imagination has command over the dead and why they must keep from sight and earshot. At the British Museum at the end of the Egyptian room and near the stairs are two statues, one an august decoration, one a most accurate-looking naturalistic portrait. The august decoration was for a public site, the other, like all the naturalistic art of the period, for burial beside a mummy. So buried it was believed, the Egyptologists tell us, to be a service to the dead . . . A shepherd at Doneraile told me some years ago of an aunt of his who showed herself after death stark naked and bid her relatives to make clothes and give them to a beggar . . . Presently she appeared again wearing the clothes and thanked them.

The central imagery of this passage overlaps with the central imagery of "A Coat," a poem published in this same year, 1914, but written in 1912, in which "my song" is identified specifically with "a coat," while there's an aesthetic tension between the formal "embroideries / out of old mythologies" and the naturalistic "walking naked." There is, in other words, a connection in Yeats's mind between the "line" of verse, "linen," and the line between "this world and the world we go to after" that becomes the true subject, insofar as one may determine such a thing, of the poem. For, by the end of the poem, the summoning up of the actress Florence Farr Emery and Yeats's fellow members of the Order of the Golden Dawn, MacGregor Mathers and William Horton, seem incidental to the poem's summoning up of itself, incidental to its own coming into being:

> Such thought, that in it bound
> I need no other thing,
> Wound in mind's wandering
> As mummies in the mummy-cloth are wound.

This is "the marvellous thing" Yeats has to say, "a certain marvellous thing," as he has it in the second stanza. In the deliberate repetition of that "marvellous" I'm pointed towards a very specific Marvell—Andrew of that ilk—to whose "A Dialogue between the Soul and Body" Yeats is indebted for the title and structure of "A Dialogue of Self and Soul." (As is clear from the revised typescript of "All Souls' Night," held in the Bodleian, the word "marvellous" once appeared *three* times in the poem, until Yeats changed, in line 86, "I have a marvellous thing to tell" to "I have mummy truths to tell.") I think, moreover, that Yeats is influenced here by some of the core imagery of "A Dialogue between the Soul and Body"— the indivisibility of body and soul that has the Body cry out:

> Oh who shall me deliver whole,
> From bonds of this Tyrannic Soul?

Yeats again fixes on two words in the last stanza of "All Souls' Night"— "thought" and "wandering"—and carries them over to those two lines from the first stanza of "A Dialogue of Self and Soul" which I quoted earlier:

Fix every wandering thought upon
That quarter where all thought is done.

I'll fall in with my notoriously poor-spelling friend and spell that "done" with two *n*'s, as in John of that ilk. For, to go back to the first line of the poem as readers of *The London Mercury* read it—" 'Tis All Souls' Night and the great Christ Church bell"—Yeats echoes both the cadence and vocabulary of the first line of Donne's "A Nocturnall upon St. Lucy's Day":

'Tis the yeares midnight, and it is the dayes

Part of Yeats's decision to revise the line might have been based on an urge to avoid not only such a direct quotation of Donne, particularly when the poem turns out to be in essence a metaphysical conceit, but also an echo of Keats, the ghost of the structure of the first line of "The Eve of St. Agnes": "St. Agnes' Eve—Ah, bitter chill it was." When he repositions the phrase in what is now line 3 he manages to take the curse off the overt reference while retaining what one might call its covert operation.

In other respects, Yeats was keen to be in touch with Keats. A year earlier, lodged in the same house at 4 Broad Street, Yeats had inquired of his Communicators about the origin of the image of Keats's nightingale. The response was that it had come "from a previously existing transference." Yeats now became exercised by the idea that he might be able to partake of Keats's mental processes, particularly if they were accessible through the "general mind," or *Spiritus Mundi*," as he terms it in "The Second Coming." In addition to the references to "Ode to a Nightingale" to which I've already referred, my attention is drawn to stanza 6:

Darkling I listen; and for many a time
    I have been half in love with easeful Death,
Called him soft names in many a mused rhyme,
    To take into the air my quiet breath . . .

The word "breath" occurs twice in "All Souls' Night," in stanzas 1 and 3 (in both cases rhymed with "death"). In the case of stanza 3, the sentiments of Keats's lines are carried over wholesale and are recognisable in Horton's death-wish. The idea of the phantom "breath" is one that Yeats would experience a year later, in 1921:

> While we were staying at a village near Oxford we met two or three nights in succession what seemed a sudden warm breath coming up from the ground at the same corner of the road.

In stanza 1 of "All Souls' Night," meanwhile, two key words—"midnight" and "soul"—are borrowed from Keats's next lines in "Ode to a Nightingale":

> Now more than ever seems it rich to die,
> > To cease upon the *midnight* with no pain,
> > > While thou art pouring forth thy *soul* abroad
> > > > In such an ecstasy!

That "ecstasy," meanwhile, shows up in the penultimate stanza in "The fume of muscatel / Can give his sharpened palate *ecstasy*." (If I weren't running out of time, I'd want to make a case for seeing in that word "sharpened" [we've already come across it once in the first stanza—"being *sharpened* by his death"] the shadowy figure of a certain William *Sharp*, better known by his pseudonym "Fiona Macleod," to whom Yeats had written in 1901 that "she" should strive in her writing for the clarity of "a tumbler of water rather than *a cup of wine*." If Yeats's description of him in a letter to his widow after his death in 1905, which I quote from R. F. Foster's *W. B. Yeats: A Life*—"he was very near always to the world where he now is & often seemed to me *to deliver its messages*"—is anything to go on, Sharp/Macleod might easily have appeared somewhat more formally in "All Souls' Night.")

I want now to try to link the ghost of this "immortal Bird," the nightingale, to another, the linnet. For in addition to the connection between the poetic "line" and "linen," there's a connection in Yeats's mind between the "line," both in the sense of the "poetic line" and the "line of descent," and the "linnet," the bird that is indivisible from the flax-seeds upon which it feeds, and from which its name derives through French. Insofar as the linnet might be said to have a symbolic function in Yeats, it stands, I think, partly for peace and contentment. We remember that evening on "The Lake Isle of Innisfree" would be "full of the linnet's wings." I mentioned earlier Yeats's predilection for keeping cage-birds, and we know, indeed, from his "Hodos Chameliontos," written in 1922, that he associates keeping birds with the security of family life ("Now that I am a settled man and have many birds—the canaries have just hatched out five nestlings—I have before me the problem that Locke waved aside"), while in an extraordinary description of his son, Michael, in a 1921 letter to John Quinn, he writes that he is "better looking than *a newborn canary.*" In section VII of his introduction to *A Vision*, meanwhile, he reports:

> A little after my son's birth I came home to confront my wife with the statement "Michael is ill." A smell of *burnt feathers* had announced what she and the doctor had hidden.

Now, no canary appears in "All Souls' Night," except perhaps in the guise of the meaning of that word as "a light sweet wine from the Canary Isles," a wine not unlike "muscatel," which Yeats has borrowed yet again from Keats. This comes from "Lines on the Mermaid Tavern," a poem which shares its central theme with "All Souls' Night":

> Souls of Poets dead and gone,
> What Elysium have ye known,
> Happy field or mossy cavern,
> Choicer than the Mermaid Tavern?
> Have ye tippled drink more fine
> Than mine host's *Canary* wine?

Yeats's intertwining of assorted cage-birds with a sense of his own lineage is already evident from "A Prayer for My Daughter," written between February and June of 1919, where the relationships of poetic "line," "lineage" and "linnet" are fused:

> If there's no hatred in a mind
> Assault and battery of the wind
> Can never tear the linnet from the leaf.

Earlier in the poem, Yeats has associated the linnet with the intellectual life—"May she become a flourishing hidden tree / That all her thoughts may *like the linnet* be"—and I think this strand connects with "All Souls' Night" in at least one significant way, having to do, once again, with the indivisibility of "linnet" and "leaf." It's hard, in this context, not to read "leaf" as a leaf of paper, particularly when it's associated with the word "tear," but it connects also with the idea of "winding"—Yeats pronounces "wind" (*wĭnd*) as *wīnd*—and it reappears in the last lines of "All Souls' Night":

> Such thought, that in it bound
> I need no other thing,
> Wound in mind's wandering
> As mummies in the mummy-cloth are wound.

There's not only a faint echo of William Blake's "winding-sheet" from *Auguries of Innocence* but a distinct reference to Yeats's own "Swedenborg, Mediums, and the Desolate Places" (1914), in which, referring directly to Blake's description of "a robin redbreast in a cage," he describes him as being *"put into a rage* by all painting where detail is generalised away," before asserting:

> Born when Swedenborg was a new excitement, growing up with a
> Swedenborgian brother . . . and having, it may be, for nearest friend
> the Swedenborgian Flaxman with whom he would presently quarrel,
> he answered the just-translated *Heaven and Hell* with *The Marriage of
> Heaven and Hell*. Swedenborg was but "the linen clothes folded up" or
> the angel sitting by the tomb, after Christ, the human imagination,
> had arisen.

This passage is remarkable for several reasons, not least for the coincidence of the "flax" in the reference to John *Flax*man (1755–1826), the neo-classical sculptor and draftsman, and the "linen" in the allusion to Blake's categorisation of Swedenborg's writings in *Heaven and Hell* as "the *linen* clothes folded up." In "All Souls' Night," Yeats is striving for an image of wholeness—"the whole wine"—that's based on this phrase from *The Marriage of Heaven and Hell*, just as the image of the vessel "brimmed" goes back, with the sideways glance to Keats, to another image in Blake's text:

The cistern contains: the fountain overflows
One thought. fills immensity.

That comes from the section entitled "Proverbs of Hell" and it's telling, I suggest, that Yeats uses neither the words "Heaven" nor "Hell" in "All Souls' Night," opting instead for the circumlocution "To where the damned have howled away their hearts, / And where the blessed dance."

I have a final suggestion about another word Yeats doesn't use here, that has to do with his motivation for dating and placing "All Souls' Night," which will, I'm certain, strike some as being totally off-the-wall, but which falls into a way of reading which I find useful, certainly in this poem. It has to do with being alert to another resisted usage—a word, like "lees," which simply does not find its way onto the page but which is central to a poem that is prefaced by the opening of a bottle of wine. The word I'm thinking of is "cork," and it's a word that would have been much in Yeats's mind at the beginning of November 1920, given that the mayor of the city of Cork, Terence MacSwiney, had died in Brixton Prison only a few days earlier, on October 24, 1920, after being on hunger-strike for seventy-four days. The death of MacSwiney occurred in the context of the Anglo-Irish War, a war which prompted Yeats to publish "Easter 1916," a poem he had kept under wraps for four years. On November 1st, the day before "All Souls' Night" was probably begun, the eighteen-year-old Kevin Barry, an IRA volunteer also from County Cork, was hanged in Dublin, shortly thereafter to enter the folk memory through the ballad named after him. The dating and placing of "All Souls' Night" is a very deliberate contextualising of its occasion, a context and an occasion from which, however much we might like to believe otherwise, it's hard to entirely disentangle the poem, however freestanding a structure it may appear. That MacSwiney, or Barry, might be spectre at the feast is an idea that Yeats is quite determined not to allow, and which he manages almost successfully. The political context, the context in which MacSwiney or Barry might be a walking *wound*, would have been all too well understood by many of the first readers in *The London Mercury*, if not *The New Repub-*

lic. But it had to be signposted, or neonised, in subsequent publications, including the appearance of "All Souls' Night" in its critical position as the last poem in Yeats's 1928 volume, *The Tower*, where "*Oxford, Autumn 1920*" signalled not only the end of the poem but the end of a book and indicated Yeats's relationship, geographical and historical, to the material of the moment. My sense is that it's part of our responsibility as readers to try, insofar as it's possible, to psych ourselves into that moment, as well as into the mind through which it made its way into this world, not only in terms of placing a text in its social context, but in terms of its relation to other texts.

As I've tried to suggest, the text or texts to which "All Souls' Night" might stand as an epilogue is not so much *A Vision* but a selection of poems by Keats, a writer whom Yeats categorised in a 1913 letter to his father as the "type of *vision*," and from whom he conglomewrites key words and images. These poems include not only those to which I've already referred but "The Fall of Hyperion," from which Yeats borrows the ideas of drinking from "a cool vessel of transparent juice / Sipped by the wandering bee, the which I took" (42–43) and "the tall shade, in drooping linens veiled." At the heart of "Lamia," a poem in which Keats rhymes "bees" and "lees" (Book I, lines 141–42), is a similar notion of the shift from "when the wine has done its rosy deed / And every soul from human trammels freed" (II, 219–20) through "as it erewhile made / The tender-personed Lamia melt into a shade" (II, 237–38) to the last word of the last line, "And, in its marriage robe, the heavy body wound," echoed by Yeats in the last word of his last line, "As mummies in the mummy-cloth are *wound*."

That still leaves us with "*Oxford, Autumn 1920*." The "*Autumn*" is such an astonishingly direct reference to "To Autumn" that one's inclined to ignore it until it can no longer be ignored. Again, Yeats has ventriloquized Keats in his vocabulary—"o'er-*brimmed*," yet again, and "conspiring with him how to load and *bless* / with fruit the vines that round the thatch-eves run"—those vines as likely as not to bear muscatel grapes, which were common in England on account of their ability to withstand the cold and wet of the climate. Elsewhere we have a version of the "lees" cryptocurrent in "the last oozings" of the "cider-press," while "drowsed with the fume of poppies" appears in "the *fume* of muscatel" itself. We might re-

mind ourselves that the subject matter of "To Autumn" is cyclical movement and the fact that autumn, a season associated with oncoming death,
has a "music" every bit as stirring as that of spring. The cyclical movement
of things is much in Yeats's mind here and it accounts largely for the reference back to the conventional dating of "To Autumn," written in 1819 but
published in 1820, in his *Autumn, 1920,* the centennial aspect underscored by the fact that the poem is precisely one hundred lines long.

CHAPTER 2

THE LITERARY LIFE

TED HUGHES

We climbed Marianne Moore's narrow stair
To her bower-bird bric-à-brac nest, in Brooklyn.
Daintiest curio relic of Americana.
Her talk, a needle
Unresting—darning incessantly
Chain-mail with crewel-work flowers,
Birds and fish of the reef
In phosphor-bronze wire.
Her face, tiny American treen bobbin
On a spindle,
Her voice the flickering hum of the old wheel.
Then the coin, compulsory,
For the subway
Back to our quotidian scramble.
Why shouldn't we cherish her?

You sent her carbon copies of some of your poems.
Everything about them—
The ghost gloom, the constriction,
The bell-jar air-conditioning—made her gasp
For oxygen and cheer. She sent them back.
(Whoever has her letter has her exact words.)
"Since these seem to be valuable carbon copies

(Somewhat smudged) I shall not engross them."
I took the point of that "engross"
Precisely, like a bristle of glass,
Snapped off deep in my thumb.
You wept
And hurled yourself down a floor or two
Further from the Empyrean.
I carried you back up.
And she, Marianne, tight, brisk,
Neat and hard as an ant,
Slid into the second or third circle
Of my Inferno.

A decade later, on her last visit to England,
Holding court at a party, she was sitting
Bowed over her knees, her face,
Under her great hat-brim's floppy petal,
Dainty and bright as a piece of confetti—
She wanted me to know, she insisted
(It was all she wanted to say)
With that Missouri needle, drawing each stitch
Tight in my ear,
That your little near-posthumous memoir
"OCEAN 1212"
Was "so wonderful, so lit, so wonderful"—

She bowed so low I had to kneel. I kneeled and
Bowed my face close to her upturned face
That seemed tinier than ever,
And studied, as through a grille,
Her lips that put me in mind of a child's purse
Made of the skin of a dormouse,
Her cheek, as if she had powdered the crumpled silk
Of a bat's wing.
And I listened, heavy as a graveyard
While she searched for the grave
Where she could lay down her little wreath.

IN MY DISCUSSION of W. B. Yeats's "All Souls' Night," a poem written in Oxford in *"Autumn 1920,"* I tried to suggest that it was difficult to read it without a proper regard for its intertextual relations, in particular the links between it and a series of poems by John Keats, including "To Autumn," published one hundred years earlier, in 1820. This centennial aspect of "All Souls' Night" is underscored by the fact that it's exactly one hundred lines long. I also suggested that while "All Souls' Night" is billed by Yeats as being an "Epilogue to *A Vision*," it stands less as an addendum to that text than a coda to events in Yeats's life, including his involvement with the "automatic script" of his wife, Georgie Hyde-Lees. That eternal triangle between husband, wife and a spirit world keen to be in touch is one replicated by Ted Hughes and Sylvia Plath, as Plath notes in her description of a Ouija board session in her journal entry of Friday, July 4, 1958:

> Last night Ted and I did Pan for the first time in America . . . There are so many questions to ask it. I wonder how much is our own intuition working, and how much queer accident, and how much "my father's spirit."

Like Yeats's "Communicators," Pan is not shy about offering some literary commentary:

> Pan informed us my book of poems will be published by Knopf . . . Also: fifty poems for my book. Pan stated his favorite poem of Ted's is "Pike" ("I like fish") and of mine is "Mussel Hunter" ("Kolossus likes it"). Kolossus is Pan's family god . . . Among other penetrating observations Pan said I should write on the poem subject "Lorelei" because they are my "own kin." So today for fun I did so . . .

In a letter to her mother written the following day, July 5th, Plath covered much of the same territory:

> We did our Ouija board for the first time in America, and it was magnificent fun—responsive, humorous, and very helpful. It seems to have grown up and claims it is quite happy in America, that it likes "life in freedom," that it uses its freedom for "making poems."

That Plath should muse on "life in freedom" is scarcely surprising on the day after Independence Day. Two days later, in her journal entry for July 7, 1958, the idea of independence, or its opposite, was still much on her mind:

> My danger, partly, I think, is becoming too *dependent* on Ted. He is didactic, fanatic . . . It is as if I were sucked into a tempting but disastrous whirlpool. Between us there are no barriers—it is rather as if neither of us—or especially myself—had any skin, or one skin between us and we kept bumping into and abrading each other.

I want to concentrate in this chapter on that aspect of the phrase "the end of the poem" connected to the notion of there being "no barriers" between the poem and the biography of its author—including the hinterland of the letter, the journal, the gossip column—paying particular attention to "The Literary Life," the breathtakingly barbed, perhaps even rebarbative poem by Ted Hughes which appeared in his best-selling 1998 volume, *Birthday Letters*. I'll try to make sense of why Hughes takes such an extraordinarily hostile view of Marianne Moore, and I'll try to connect that hostility to the fact that there's "one skin" between several poems by Hughes and Moore (as well as poems by Plath and Moore) that keep "bumping into and abrading each other."

LET'S BEGIN WITH THE TITLE, "The Literary Life," a phrase which, even before we turn to the first line of the poem, sets off a great fizzing and ticking of the irony-meter. For Hughes and Plath, in the summer of 1958, the idea of "the literary life" must have seemed not only desirable but, in Hughes's case at least, a done deal. They'd spent the previous academic year, 1957–58, at Smith College in Northampton, Massachusetts. Though Plath had been overwhelmed by preparation for her classes and worked only intermittently on a novel and short stories, she had nonetheless published a significant number of poems in the book originally entitled *The Earthenware Head*, then *The Bull of Bendylaw*, then *The Devil of the Stairs*, which would finally appear as *The Colossus*, named partly after Pan's family god, of whom more later. As for Hughes, his first collection had been off to a flying start since as long ago as February 1957. In a journal entry for the 27th of that month, Plath had reported:

> Ted's book of poems—*The Hawk in the Rain*—has won the first *Harper's* publication contest under the three judges: W. H. Auden, Stephen Spender & Marianne Moore! Even as I write this, I am incredulous. The little scared people reject. The big, unscared practicing poets accept.

The logical outcome of this award had been a triumphant visit to New York, some of the highlights of which were described by Plath in a letter to her mother of June 10, 1958:

> We saw the Bowery "bums" and the Harlem negroes and the Fifth Avenue tycoons and, best of all, Marianne Moore, who was lovely at her home in Brooklyn and admires Ted very much and served us strawberries, sesame-seed biscuits and milk and talked a blue streak. Can we reserve tickets and take you to see her this Sunday?

This, then, is the scene set in the opening lines of "The Literary Life":

> We climbed Marianne Moore's narrow stair
> To her bower-bird bric-à-brac nest, in Brooklyn.

These opening lines of the opening stanza—the opening stanza on which I'll concentrate here today—establish almost everything of the tone of what ensues. The term "tone" covers a vast amount, as we know from *The New Princeton Encyclopedia of Poetry and Poetics*:

> Word choice, syntax, imagery, metaphors, or other figurative devices can contribute to tone as expressing the attitude of the speaker . . . But one must keep distinct the tone of the poem's speaker and that of the poem itself.

This last distinction is appropriate in the case of many poems, I'm certain, where one of our first tasks as readers is to determine who's speaking the poem. In the case of "The Literary Life," the "We" of the first line refers to two historical characters, Plath and Hughes, and the conceit of the poem is that there's almost no distinction between those historical characters and the characters who appear in the poem. I write "almost" because, in any account, formal or informal, there is necessarily an element of invention, of construction and reconstruction of the self, including what looks very much like a revision of the first impressions made on Plath and Hughes. One of the difficulties facing readers not only of this poem but any poem in *Birthday Letters* is an odd one. It is, simply, that we run the risk of knowing too much about the identities of the main characters. We know too much from sources extraneous to the poem, not least of which is the immediate context of other poems featuring the same characters and exhibiting much the same tone. This tonal consistency—some would say "monotony"—does suggest to me that many, if not most, of the poems in *Birthday Letters* were written within one time-frame. The jacket copy for the Faber and Faber edition describes them as being "written over a period of more than twenty-five years," from which some might suppose that they were written here and there along the way over the entire span of those years. Again, my own supposition is that, other than the one we know to have been published ("You Hated Spain," included in *Selected Poems 1957–81*), most if not all of these poems were written at the same time, long after the events they describe, perhaps even at one sitting. This hunch is borne out by the fact that Emory University, where almost all of the Hughes papers are held, has nothing whatsoever in the way of manuscripts from *Birthday Letters*. I use the term "one *sitting*" and it brings me back to the séance described in an earlier poem in the collection, "Ouija":

> Once, as we bent there, I asked:
> "Shall we be famous?" and you snatched your hand upwards
> As if something had grabbed it from under.
> Your tears flashed, your face was contorted,
> Your voice cracked, it was thunder and flash together:
> "And give yourself to the glare? Is that what you want?
> Why should you want to be famous?
> Don't you see—fame will ruin everything."
> I was stunned. I thought I had joined

Your association of ambition
To please you and your mother,
To fulfill your mother's ambition
That we be ambitious.

This kind of writing is "literary" in the sense of "carried on by letter," in that it partakes of a tone—chatty, catty, half condescending, half conciliatory—we might meet in a letter from someone we know well about someone else we know well. Again, this presents a difficulty to us as readers, as we're brought up and taken aback again and again by the realisation that what we know well about the subject matter and its treatment derives from that aforementioned wide range of extraneous sources. It's hard, for example, to draw a line between *Birthday Letters* and *Letters Home*, both rather blatantly sharing the word *"Letters"* and, less blatantly, much of the same information. As Anne Stevenson puts it in her preface to a new edition of *Bitter Fame*, without a sense of the wider context, the poems in *Birthday Letters* are "at the least opaque, at the most meaningless." However problematic this regard for the wider context may be for us, it's surely no less problematic for Hughes himself as he kicks off here with what is virtually the royal "We" and revisits the scene already familiar to many readers from that letter of June 19, 1958, in which Plath mentions the "Bowery bums" in the same breath as "Marianne Moore." I suspect, indeed, that Hughes has so recently read *Letters Home* that he retains the word "Bowery" and carries it over as the *"bower"* component of "bower-bird."

But I'm getting ahead of myself. Let me go back to my assertion that much of the tone of the poem is established in that first line:

We climbed Marianne Moore's narrow stair

The word "narrow" brings with it not only the pejorative connotations having to do with a failure of intellect, with rigidity or lack of openness— "narrow-mindedness"—that prefigure Moore's failure to respond appropriately to Plath's poems, but also a sexual innuendo that will be picked up later in the word "nest." There's a faint echo of Wordsworth's "Nuns fret not at their convent's narrow room" that carries with it a comment on what seems to have been Marianne Moore's barely perceptible sexuality, a sexuality that nonetheless exhibited itself in her common use of the image of a "wedge," or *cuneus*, to represent the female part, the wedge itself defined as an object "narrow" at one end. The idea of the "stair" that is "climbed" as a metaphor for sexual activity (or, in this case, an ironic comment on Moore's seeming *in*activity) would have been much in Hughes's mind in 1958, the year of the publication of *The Hawk in the Rain*, since it was a concluding image in a poem collected in 1955 by the writer with whom he would already have seen himself as being in serious contention:

> For you would hardly care
> That you were less deceived, out on that bed,
> Than he was, stumbling up the breathless stair
> To burst into fulfilment's desolate attic.

There's not exactly anything of Larkin's "bursting" into the attic here, but there is surely an alliterative overload on the "bower-bird bric-à-brac nest, in Brooklyn," its "stumbling" and "breathless" tongue-twisting pointing yet again to the ironic undercutting of its subject, Marianne Moore set up in her ivory tower only to be knocked down. One might note, by the way, that Hughes prevents the poem from collapsing into a mere log-jam of alliteration by the shrewd use of a comma before "in Brooklyn."

I use the word "tower" here, and I use it advisedly, since Yeats is another presence, a presence to which we're alerted by the proximity of the words "stair" and "nest," not to speak of all those buzzing *b*s, all sending us back to "The Stare's Nest by My Window," section VI of "Meditations in Time of Civil War," a poem from Yeats's 1928 volume *The Tower*:

> We have fed the heart on fantasies,
> The heart's grown brutal from the fare;
> More substance in our enmities
> Than in our love; O honey-bees,
> Come build in the empty house of the stare.

The appearence of the "stare" (in this case a starling, though echoic of a "winding *stair*") prepares the way for the "birds" later in the poem. The "bower-bird," it turns out, is itself a member of the starling family. The allusion to "Meditations in Time of Civil War" also signals that there's considerable "substance" in Hughes's "enmities," particularly this one for Marianne Moore, and that Marianne Moore's poetic house, her "nest," is "empty," her poetic enterprise bogus and bankrupt. Not only is Moore's poetry bric-a-brac, she herself is described as a curiosity:

> Daintiest curio relic of Americana.
> Her talk, a needle
> Unresting—darning incessantly
> Chain-mail with crewel-work flowers,
> Birds and fish of the reef
> In phosphor-bronze wire.

The "needle / Unresting" of Marianne Moore's "talk" is corroborated by Plath's account of how she "talked a blue streak," just as her being a "curio" is recognisable already in Plath's suggestion that she might be a theatre- or museum-attraction ("Can we reserve tickets and take you to see her this Sunday?"). The word "curio" comes from the last line of "The Camperdown Elm," a Moore poem set in Brooklyn, in which the tree is described as "our crowning *curio*," and that phrase is used as a section heading in the final chapter of Charles Molesworth's 1990 biography of Moore, a book with which I suspect Hughes was familiar. The "needle" "in line 4 also suggests a nasty, pointed aspect of Moore's personality, particularly when we meet it again in line 42—"that Missouri *needle*"—the repetition mimetic of the repetitive action of sewing which dominates the poem. We see other examples of such repetition in the poem— "Daintiest" and "Dainty," "Americana" and "American," "bowed" and "bowed," "face" and "face." The inversion, meanwhile, of "darning incessantly / Chain-mail with crewel-work flowers" suggests the artificiality of the "flowers" and their subjects "Birds and fish of the reef / In phosphor-bronze wire." It turns out that a description of one of those very birds of which Moore writes, the ostrich, includes the word "needle":

> he
> whose comic duckling head on its
> great neck revolves with compass-*needle* nervousness
> when he stands guard.

This "needle" also darts in the direction of *Heart's Needle*, the 1959 collection by W. D. Snodgrass, a poet admired by Plath who was credited by Robert Lowell as being the first "confessional" poet, a tradition to which this poem surely belongs. There is, indeed, a humorous nod in the direction of the more conventional "confessional" in lines 47–50, where Moore and Hughes adopt the poses of priest and penitent respectively and conduct their conversation "as through a grille." That "grille" is just one of the distancing, self-protective devices associated with Moore, beginning with the "Chain-mail" here in line 6. Her own poems abound in images of armor and armor-plating, as in the case of "Armor's Undermining Modesty," with its description of a moth:

> It was a moth almost an owl,
> its wings were furred so well,
> with backgammon-board wedges interlacing
> on the wing—
>
> like cloth of gold in a pattern
> of scales with a hair-seal Persian
> sheen.

Meanwhile, in "His Shield," we come upon:

> The pin-swin or spine-swine
> (the edgehog miscalled hedgehog) with all his edges out,
> echidna and echinoderm in distressed-
> pin-cushion thorn-fur coats, the spiny pig or porcupine,
> the rhino with horned snout—
> everything is battle-dressed.

Let's concentrate for a moment on the fact that Moore's "Chain-mail" is embroidered with "crewel-work flowers." The term "crewel-work" refers to "work done with crewels or worsted yarns," but two other words come to mind, two near versions of "crewel." The first, "cruel," is pretty obvious in the context of a cruel poem concerning itself with Moore's cruelty. The second, less obvious, is much more significant. It's the word "accrual," a word describing perfectly the most common method employed in the "work" of Marianne Moore, that's to say the method of accretion—of image heaped upon image, trophy upon trophy in the "bower-bird bric-à-brac nest." This word "accrual," I want to suggest, also describes perfectly the most common method employed in the "work" of Ted Hughes, with its breathless piling on of significant detail upon significant detail. I quote from "Dehorning," a poem collected in Hughes's 1979 volume, *Moortown*:

> The needle between the horn and the eye, so deep
> Your gut squirms for the eyeball twisting
> In its pink-white fastenings of tissue. This side and that.
> Then the first one anaesthetised, back in the crush.
> The bulldog pincers in the septum, stretched full strength,
> The horn levered right over, the chin pulled round
> With the pincers, the mouth drooling, the eye
> Like a live eye caught in a pan, like the eye of a fish
> Imprisoned in air. Then the cheese-cutter
> Of braided wire, and stainless steel peg handles,
> Aligned on the hair-bedded root of the horn, then leaning
> Backward full weight, pull-punching backwards,
> Left right left right and the blood leaks
> Down over the cheekbone, the wire bites
> And buzzes, the ammonia horn-burn smokes
> And the cow groans, roars shapelessly, hurls
> Its half-ton commotion in the tight cage. Our faces
> Grimace like faces in the dentist's chair. The horn
> Rocks from its roots, the wire pulls through
> The last hinge of hair, the horn is heavy and free,
> And a water-pistol jet of blood
> Rains over the one who holds it—a needle jet
> From the white-rasped and bloody skull-crater.

This is surely an enactment of Hughes's exhortation to Plath, reported by her in a journal entry, that you should "get hold of a thing and shove your head in it." Hughes would insist that poetry should come, or be seen to come, as Keats put it in his 1818 letter to Benjamin Bailey, "as naturally as leaves to the tree," an idea in marked contrast with the "treen" aspect of Moore:

> Her face, tiny American treen bobbin
> On a spindle,
> Her voice the flickering hum of the old wheel.

Hughes uses this archaic word "treen," meaning "made of tree," to point up what he would propose to be the archaic, the wooden, in Moore's work, including the urge to turn animals into furniture, as she does "The Jerboa":

> Its leaps should be set
> to the flageolet;
>   pillar body erect
>   on a three-cornered smooth-working Chippendale
>   claw—propped on hind legs, and tail as third toe,
>   between leaps to its burrow.

It's from this same poem, "The Jerboa," that Hughes borrows the "bower-bird":

> Looked at by daylight,
> the underside's white,
>   though the fur on the back
>   is buff-brown like the breast of the fawn-breasted
>   bower-bird.

And it's from a sister poem to "The Jerboa," "Logic and 'The Magic Flute,' " which also associates animal and musical movement, that Hughes has derived, I propose, some aspect of the opening line of "The Literary Life":

> Up winding stair,
>   here, where, in what theater lost?
>   was I seeing a ghost—

a reminder at least
> of a sunbeam or moonbeam
that has not a waist?
> By hasty hop
> or accomplished mishap,
the magic flute and harp
somehow confused themselves
> with China's precious wentletrap.

At the risk of going "by hasty hop / or accomplished mishap," I'll suggest that Hughes, in "The Literary Life," is alluding to Yeats mediated through Moore—the "wentletrap" is the "*winding stair*" of a spiral seashell, a neighbour of the "fish of the reef / In phosphor-bronze wire." In the course of two lines, Hughes points to the two main metaphors for poetry-making used by Yeats—poetry as metal-working in the "*birds* . . . in phosphor-bronze wire" and poetry as spinning and weaving in these images of the "bobbin," the "spindle," the unabashedly Yeatsian "old wheel." Hughes picks up on this thread in lines 42 and 43—"drawing each stitch / Tight in my ear," with its echo of Yeats's "Adam's Curse":

I said, "A line will take us hours maybe;
Yet if it does not seem a moment's thought,
Our *stitching and unstitching* has been naught.

In the midst of all these images of sewing and working at the loom, I'm struck by the fact that Hughes simply cannot bring himself to use that word "loom," though he comes close to it a little later on. In this instance of a phenomenon we might call "poetic recusancy," Hughes points to the subject, if we may call it such, of his poem. That subject is less "The Literary Life" than literary influence, and the combination of the unspoken "loom" and the "crewel-work flowers" are clear indications of Hughes's acknowledgement of a near version of the word "loom." I refer to Harold B*loom*, the author of *The Anxiety of Influence*, his great 1973 study which remains one of the most illuminating contributions to our understanding of the working of poets and poetry.

I'll leave off this close reading of the first stanza of "The Literary Life" to remind myself of Bloom's thesis. As he states in his introduction:

Poetic history, in this book's argument, is held to be indistinguishable from poetic influence, since strong poets make that history by misreading one another, so as to clear imaginative space for themselves. My concern is only with strong poets, major figures with the persistence to wrestle with their strong precursors . . . But nothing is got for nothing, and self-appropriation involves the immense anxieties of indebtedness, for what strong maker desires the realization that he has failed to create himself? Poetic influence, or as I shall more frequently term it, poetic misprision, is necessarily the study of the life-cycle of the poet-as-poet.

Bloom goes on to expound on this life-cycle, which he sees as falling into six parts, having to do with (1) *Clinamen*, or "poetic misreading," which suggests a failure in the original; (2) *Tessera*, the "completion" by the poet of his precursor, where that failure is in some way rectified; (3) *Kenosis*, "a movement towards discontinuity with the precursor"; (4) *Daemonization*, where "the later poet opens himself to what he believes to be a power in the parent-poem that does not belong to the parent proper"; (5) *Askesis*, where the later poet embarks on "a movement of self-purgation which intends the attainment of a state of solitude"; and (6) *Apophrades*, "the return of the dead," in which "the later poet, in his own final phase, holds his own poem so open again to the precursor's work that at first we might believe the wheel has come full circle and that we are back in the later poet's flooded apprenticeship . . . But the poem was once *held* open to the precursor, where once it *was* open, and the uncanny effect is that the new poem's achievement makes it seem to us, not as though the precursor were writing it, but as though the later poet himself had written the precursor's characteristic work."

I suggest that this is precisely what's happening in the case of this poem, to the extent that it seems almost written to Bloom's order, what with "the old *wheel*" immediately preceding the "return of the dead" from what must be a version of Hades, complete with the obol for the ferryman:

Then the coin, compulsory,
For the subway
Back to our quotidian scramble.
Why shouldn't we cherish her?

That "cherish" sends me back to Act III, Scene ii, of Shakespeare's *King Henry VIII*, a play with which Hughes deals very briefly in *Shakespeare and the Goddess of Complete Being*, to the injunction by Cardinal Wolsey to Thomas Cromwell, "Love thyself last: *cherish* those hearts that hate thee." I suspect that Hughes is using the word "cherish" as a marker of the crypto-current of hatred running under these lines, including those "enmities" that have "more substance" than "*love,*" the "fantasies" that have "fed the *heart*" in "The Stare's Nest by My Window" from "Meditations in Time of Civil War."

You notice, by the way, how Hughes resists what would be the obvious word to fill out the syntax of lines 12–14:

Then the coin, compulsory,
For the subway [*fare*]
Back to our quotidian scramble.

He resists that "fare" partly because it would rhyme with "stair" from line 1, partly because it would then conjure up Yeats's "the heart's grown brutal on the fare" in a way that would be much too overt, perhaps so overt as to raise a smile. The "coin" has to carry the weight by itself. The fact that it is "compulsory" is corroborated by Elizabeth Bishop's "Efforts of Affection," her memoir of Moore and her apartment at 260 Cumberland Street:

On the end of the bookcase nearest the front door sat the famous bowl of nickels for subway fare (nickels for years, then dimes, then nickels *and* dimes, and finally quarters). Every visitor was made to accept one of these upon leaving; it was absolutely *de rigueur*. After one or two attempts at refusing, I always simply helped myself to a nickel as I left, and eventually I was rewarded for this by Marianne's saying to a friend who was protesting, "Elizabeth is an *aristocrat*; she *takes* the money."

The "coin" in "the coin, compulsory" does indeed sustain considerable pressure per square inch, deriving as it does from *cuneus*, the "wedge" used to strike the blank metal, so that it could be said to be "characteristic" of Moore in the Bloomian sense, "as though the later poet himself had written the precursor's characteristic work." Hughes has alluded to Moore's "wedge" before now, of course, as long ago as his poem "An Otter," collected in his 1960 volume, *Lupercal*. This poem was written at the behest of Pan, in the course of that same Ouija communication of Independence Day 1958, as Plath mentions in her journal entry of July 5th:

> The Ouija board also told Ted to write about "Otters," so he is doing so, and the beginnings sound quite good.

The "wedge" appears there in two guises. The first is in the description of the otter as an implement which "cleaves the stream's push." The second instance of the "wedge" is typographical, in that the poem is indented on the page, a visual allusion to Moore's stepped patterns, familiar to us from any number of poems including "The Jerboa." The two-part structure of "The Jerboa" is picked up in "An Otter," as is the very irregular syllabic prosody of the first part of the poem, irregular because Hughes is determined to subvert what was probably a much stricter syllabic template so as to throw the reader off the trail and almost completely lose him. Like the animal he's describing, he's involved "in double robbery and concealment." For the very subject matter of the poem derives, I propose, less from the exhortations of Pan than from a reading of Moore's poem "The Wood-Weasel," which includes the image of "that otter-skin," the image with which "An Otter" concludes:

> Yanked above hounds, reverts to nothing at all,
> To this long pelt over the back of a chair.

There's a connection between this otter and "Wodwo," the eponymous speaker of the title poem of Hughes's 1967 collection, each coming and going out of "nothing":

> I seem
> separate from the ground and not rooted but dropped
> out of nothing casually

Earlier in the poem the "Wodwo" has inquired:

> What am I to split
> The glass grain of water

The answer to that question is surely "Another wedge." In an introduction to a reading of "Wodwo," Hughes described this speaker of the poem as "some sort of satyr or half-man or half-animal," a description which sounds remarkably like that of the conventional Pan, the goat-man who is an emblem of fertility, including poetic fertility, though he also has it within his power to cause "panic" in flocks of sheep and herds of cattle. I quote again from "Dehorning":

> Then tweezers
> Twiddle the artery nozzle, knotting it enough,
> And purple antiseptic squirts a cuttlefish cloud over it.
> Then the other side the same. We collect
> A heap of horns. The floor of the crush
> Is a trampled puddle of scarlet. The purple-crowned cattle,
> The bullies, with suddenly no horns to fear,
> Start ramming and wrestling.

In addition to Hughes's use of her method of accrual, the subject matter of this poem is quintessential Moore—the "battle-dressed" animal. Elsewhere in *Moortown* there are descriptions of cows "mailed with dung, a rattling armour." I won't belabour the point, but I will repeat it, that "Dehorning" comes from a book in which the very word "Moore" is an element of the title, as clear an indicator as one might find of Hughes's desire to simultaneously include and occlude her influence.

LET ME BEGIN to *con*clude here by reminding you that on July 17, 1958, twelve days after Hughes had begun "An Otter," Plath would record in her journal:

> Marianne Moore sent a queerly ambiguous spiteful letter in answer
> to my poems and request that she be a reference for my Saxton
> [*grant application*]. So spiteful it is hard to believe it: comments of

absolutely no clear meaning or help, resonant only with great unpleasantness: "don't be so grisly," "I only brush away the flies" (this for my graveyard poem), "you are too unrelenting" (on "Mussel Hunter"), and certain pointed remarks about "typing being a bugbear," so she sends back the poems we sent. I cannot believe she got so tart and acidy simply because I sent her carbon copies ("clear," she remarks). This, I realize, must be my great and stupid error— sending carbons to the American lady of letters.

Hughes's version of the sending of the "carbon copies" of Plath's poems to Marianne Moore (I'm struck by the humorous repetition of this term "carbon copies" in line 22) is consistent with Plath's account in some respects ("I took the *point* of that 'engross'" may be drawn from Plath's description of Moore's "*pointed* remarks"), inconsistent in others (the copies are "Somewhat smudged" in Hughes, "clear" in Plath). What's absolutely clear, I think, is Hughes's continuing sense of the Bloomian underpinning of what he's describing. Immediately following the idea of one strong poet sending "carbon copies" to another is a description of the contents of those "carbon copies," first among which is "the ghost gloom," a near version of "the ghost *Bloom*." That "Mussel Hunter at Rock Harbor" should have been a poem thought by Moore to be "too unrelenting" is perhaps less odd than it must have seemed to Plath, and raises questions about one aspect of the anxiety of influence on which Harold Bloom does not dwell—namely the attitude of the precursor to the later poet when their lifetimes and careers overlap. My suggestion is that what Moore recognised in "Mussel Hunter at Rock Harbor" was the beginning of the attempt by Plath to render her obsolete. In a journal entry of March 20, 1957, Plath had set down her sense of where she stood in relation to the competition:

Arrogant, I think I have written lines which qualify me to be The Poetess of America (as Ted will be The Poet of England and her dominions). Who rivals? Well, in history Sappho, Elizabeth Barrett Browning, Christina Rossetti, Amy Lowell, Emily Dickinson, Edna St. Vincent Millay—all dead. Now: Edith Sitwell and Marianne Moore, the aging giantesses.

A few sentences later in this same entry, Plath writes of how her "most close" rival, Adrienne Rich, "will soon be eclipsed" by Plath's new poems. The idea of eclipsing Moore, of cutting this "aging giantess" down to size, is already on Plath's mind, just as it's on Hughes's here. Part of Hughes's method is to distort the perspective on Moore. We've already seen "her face, *tiny* American treen bobbin." By lines 49–50 we meet "her upturned face / That seemed *tinier than ever.*" As I suggested earlier, Moore is presented here as a penitent, appealing for absolution, for forgiveness for the sin of not responding appropriately to the "carbon copies." That "Mussel Hunter at Rock Harbor" was indeed a "carbon copy" of Moore was acknowledged by Plath herself in a letter to her brother Warren, dated June 11, the day after her description to her mother of the visit to Moore in Brooklyn:

> Here is a poem I made about the fiddler crabs we found at Rock Harbor when we went to get mussels last summer for fish bait . . . This is written in what's known as "syllabic verse," measuring lines not by heavy and light stresses, but by the *number* of syllables, which here is 7. I find this form satisfactorily strict (a pattern varying the number of syllables in each line can be set up, as M. Moore does it) and yet it has a speaking illusion of freedom (which the measured stress doesn't have) as stresses vary freely.

This consideration of "freedom" comes just a few days before the July 5 letter I quoted earlier, the one in which "We did our Ouija board for the first time in America," in which Pan is quoted as liking "life in freedom." That Plath associates Pan with "freedom" is clear from a journal entry of May 1, 1957, in which she writes of the tension between her academic and creative work:

> My prophetic Pans and Kevas are *free* already and their impatient tugs toward writing at every itch applied by reading Marianne Moore, Wallace Stevens, etc., disturb my equilibrium—suddenly I no longer care—let *The Waste Land* run how it may—I am already in another world—or between two worlds, one dead, the other dying to be born.

These last phrases faintly echo that passage from Yeats's *A Vision* which begins "Each age unwinds the thread another age had wound" and ends "all things dying each other's life, living each other's death." Plath is here appealing to Yeats because of her association of *A Vision* and her own spiritualist ventures, but her indebtedness to Yeats was longstanding, evident as early as her 1956 poem "Pursuit":

> Entering the tower of my fears,
>   I shut my doors on that dark guilt,
>   I bolt the door, each door I bolt.
> Blood quickens, gonging in my ears:
>
> The panther's tread is on the stairs,
> Coming up and up the stairs.

This last image of the "stairs," whereby Yeats is mediated through Plath, is yet another source for the opening of "The Literary Life." We know that the "panther" in question is largely symbolic of Hughes, though it's somewhat symbolic of Yeats. The two poets are deeply connected in Plath's mind, as her journal entry of February 25, 1957, makes clear:

> Ted is an excellent poet, full of blood & discipline, like Yeats.

It was this same entry in which she recorded how *The Hawk in the Rain*—the "*Hawk*" that had barely escaped the pull of the "widening gyre" in which "the falcon cannot hear the falconer"—had won the *Harper's* contest "under the 3 judges: W. H. Auden, Stephen Spender & Marianne Moore!" I want to suggest that, for Plath, a version of the "panther" comes to stand for the poetic influence, not so much of Yeats, or Hughes, but Moore herself. I want to suggest that the name of the Ouija board communicator, "Pan," is an abbreviated form, a pet name, of the very same "*panther*." You may recall Plath's questioning the extent to which Pan might be a manifestation of "my father's spirit," which may explain why, in his communication of Independence Day 1958, Pan "also told Ted to write about 'Otters,'" since a near version of that word, *Otto*, is the given name of Plath's father, "Prince Otto" being another regular guest at the Ouija board. The Oedipal drama set down by Bloom, in which a father figure must be obliterated by a son who is possessed of love and admiration along with envy and fear in almost equal measure, would account for Plath and Hughes's susceptibility to Pan's statement, in this same communication, that "his favorite poem of Ted's is 'Pike,'" adding that "I like fish." This is a communication, I suggest, of the fact that the "accrual-work" method of "Pike" is, yet again, based on Moore's poem, "The Fish," so much so that Hughes has carried over several words from Moore's poem. Moore's "The water drives a wedge / of iron through the iron edge / of the cliff" is picked up in the wedge-image of

> One jammed past its gills down the other's gullet;
> The outside eye stared: as a vice locks—
> The same *iron* in this eye
> Though its film shrank in death.

Moore's "crabs like / green lilies, and submarine / toadstools" is echoed in Hughes's description of how the pike move "over a bed of *emerald*, silhouette / Of *submarine* delicacy and horror" and the pond "whose *lilies* and muscular tench / Had outlasted every visible stone / Of the monastery that planted them." The idea of what survives as it "grows *old*"—this last word another instance of shared vocabulary—might indeed be said to be the subject of both poems. As for Pan's enthusiasm for Plath's "Mussel Hunter at Rock Harbor," Plath must surely have hoped that her precursor poet might still hold her, the later poet, in high regard. What the real Marianne Moore, rather than Marianne/Pan, would have recognised in "Mussel Hunter" would have been a number of "carbon copies" of images drawn not only from "The Fish"—Plath has taken over both the vocabulary and the subject matter of "the crow-blue mussel-shells" and the "crabs like green lilies"—but Moore's general image-field of "claws," "one / Claw swollen to a shield large / As itself," "mottled mail," not to speak of the tendency toward the exotic miniaturism of

> The crab-face, etched and set there,
>
> Grimaced as skulls grimace: it
> Had an Oriental look,
> A samurai death mask done

On a tiger tooth, less for
Art's sake than God's.

No wonder the real Marianne Moore found this "too unrelenting,"
no wonder she would "not engross" the "carbon copies." When Hughes
writes that "I took the point of that 'engross' / Precisely" he sends me to
the OED to check on the precise meaning of the word. It means "to write
in large letters; chiefly, and now almost exclusively, to write in a peculiar
character appropriate to legal documents; hence, to write out or express in
legal form." I suspect that what Hughes is driving at here is Moore's reluc-
tance to legitimise Plath as an heir. That critical imprimatur would have to
wait, at least in this version of events, until Moore's visit to England in
1964, a year after Plath's death. So far as I know, this 1964 visit was the last
for Moore, which makes Hughes's throwaway "a decade later," with the
suggestion that the visit might have taken place in 1968, precisely that—
throwaway. Hughes is determined, though, to allow a decent interval to
elapse so that Plath's star will have risen sufficiently to force Moore to reverse her initial poor judgement.

> Holding court at a party, she was sitting
> Bowed over her knees, her face,
> Under her great hat-brim's floppy petal,
> Dainty and bright as a piece of confetti—
> She wanted me to know, she insisted
> (It was all she wanted to say)
> With that Missouri needle, drawing each stitch
> Tight in my ear,
> That your little near-posthumous memoir
> "OCEAN 1212"
> Was "so wonderful, so lit, so wonderful"—

Like the other repetitions in the poem, this double dose of "so wonderful" successfully renders the bloated nature of much of what is conventionally perceived as "The Literary Life," embracing as they do the
word "lit." Here Hughes is parodying the very blurb-speak which Moore
provided for the U.S. edition of The Hawk in the Rain ("The work has fo-

cus, is aglow with feeling, with conscience; sensibility is awake, embodied in appropriate diction") by substituting "lit" for "aglow." Amusingly, the piece by Plath which Moore is now applauding, "Ocean 1212-W," to give it its full title—it's a reference to Plath's grandmother's telephone number in Winthrop, Massachusetts—is chockablock with Mooreana, what with the sea likened to "some huge, radiant animal" full of "egg stones, fan shells, colored glass" and "tea-sets—tossed in abandon off liners, or consigned to the tides by jilted brides." The piece was written in 1962 and broadcast in that year by the BBC. It was published in *The Listener* in 1963, but remained uncollected until 1977, when it appeared in *Johnny Panic and the Bible of Dreams*. In other words, the chances of Moore ever having read this piece, be it by 1964, or 1968, are quite slender, which is why I suggest that Hughes is doing a little "embroidering" of the facts.

Not surprisingly, given that "Ocean 1212-W" was written in 1962, after Hughes had left her Plath's true subject here is the sense of "the separateness of everything," the sense of "violence," the sense of her being one of those "jilted brides." In the context of this poem, she is a bridesmaid to whom the precursor bride has not thrown her nosegay, her posy. I use this word "posy" advisedly because it is, if you recall, a version of "poesie," "a collection or 'bouquet' of 'flowers' of poetry or rhetoric."

In addition to being identified as "darning incessantly / Chain-mail with crewel-work *flowers*," Moore's face appears now "Under her great hat-brim's floppy *petal*, / Dainty and bright as a piece of confetti." These images of Moore involve a wilful distortion of both her physical and her poetic presence in a way that, once again, seems written with Harold Bloom somewhere near the front of the mind, an idea reinforced, as I suggested earlier, by what by now has become a super-abundance of flower imagery, not to speak of the nod in the direction of "lit crit" also embedded in that "so wonderful, so *lit*, so wonderful." "A piece of confetti" is something left over after a wedding, and Hughes's implication is that, despite the fact that she's "holding court at a party," the party's over for Marianne Moore. Despite the question usually raised of a bride—"Why shouldn't we *cherish* her?"—Moore is less a bride than a maiden aunt, or as line 31 would suggest, a maiden "*ant*." The word "court" itself sets off another furious spluttering in the old irony-meter, since "The Literary Life" is written by the Poet Laureate to the *Court* of Elizabeth II, who lived in a house called *Court* Green. Hughes, rather than Moore, is now the "aging giant." Even in 1964, if 1964 it is, when he has to kneel to be on level terms with her, he has already shrunk her poetic garland to "her *little* wreath."

This transmogrification of Moore points to another central aspect of the poem—the fact that it is a charm, perhaps even a curse. The "bristle" in the "bristle of glass, / Snapped off deep in my thumb" connects with Hughes's "Thistles," a poem which refers to "splintered weapons" of Viking warriors who are motivated by the "revengeful" and engaged in a "feud." The "bristle" also connects with Hans Christian Andersen's *The Snow Queen*, in which a splinter of glass is lodged in the heart of Kai, so that Kai, Gerda and the Snow Queen are replicated by Hughes, Plath and the wicked Moore. The "bristle . . . in my thumb," meanwhile, is reminiscent of the weird sister's incantatory "By the pricking of my thumbs" in *Macbeth*, while some of the ingredients likely to show up in a respectable witch's brew—"the skin of a dormouse," "a bat's wing"—are to be found in lines 52–54. I might mention that, like Yeats, Hughes had a strong interest in numerology, and I suspect it's no accident that this poem has fifty-seven lines, appropriate to a subject who first made an impact on Hughes and Plath in 1957, particularly if, as I suggest, this poem is a spell against Marianne Moore. "The Literary Life" is not only an extraordinarily unabashed account of a particularly strong attack of the anxiety of influence, but it's impossible to read without a sense of the biographies of the main characters, without a regard for information available only well beyond the bailiwick of the poem, including such information about times, dates and places.

CHAPTER 3

THE MOUNTAIN

ROBERT FROST

The mountain held the town as in a shadow.
I saw so much before I slept there once:
I noticed that I missed stars in the west,
Where its black body cut into the sky.
Near me it seemed: I felt it like a wall
Behind which I was sheltered from a wind.
And yet between the town and it I found,
When I walked forth at dawn to see new things,
Were fields, a river, and beyond, more fields.
The river at the time was fallen away,
And made a widespread brawl on cobblestones;
But the signs showed what it had done in spring:
Good grassland gullied out, and in the grass
Ridges of sand, and driftwood stripped of bark.
I crossed the river and swung round the mountain.
And there I met a man who moved so slow
With white-faced oxen, in a heavy cart,
It seemed no harm to stop him altogether.

"What town is this?" I asked.

            "This? Lunenburg."

Then I was wrong: the town of my sojourn,
Beyond the bridge, was not that of the mountain,
But only felt at night its shadowy presence.
"Where is your village? Very far from here?"

"There is no village—only scattered farms.
We were but sixty voters last election.
We can't in nature grow to many more:
That thing takes all the room!" He moved his goad.
The mountain stood there to be pointed at.
Pasture ran up the side a little way,
And then there was a wall of trees with trunks;
After that only tops of trees, and cliffs
Imperfectly concealed among the leaves.
A dry ravine emerged from under boughs
Into the pasture.

                    "That looks like a path.
Is that the way to reach the top from here?—
Not for this morning, but some other time:
I must be getting back to breakfast now."

"I don't advise your trying from this side.
There is no proper path, but those that *have*
Been up, I understand, have climbed from Ladd's.
That's five miles back. You can't mistake the place:
They logged it there last winter some way up.
I'd take you, but I'm bound the other way."

"You've never climbed it?"

                        "I've been on the sides,
Deer-hunting and trout-fishing. There's a brook
That starts up on it somewhere—I've heard say
Right on the top, tip-top—a curious thing.
But what would interest you about the brook,
It's always cold in summer, warm in winter.

One of the great sights going is to see
It steam in winter like an ox's breath,
Until the bushes all along its banks
Are inch-deep with the frosty spines and bristles—
You know the kind. Then let the sun shine on it!"

"There ought to be a view around the world
From such a mountain—if it isn't wooded
Clear to the top." I saw through leafy screens
Great granite terraces in sun and shadow,
Shelves one could rest a knee on getting up—
With depths behind him sheer a hundred feet—
Or turn and sit on and look out and down,
With little ferns in crevices at his elbow.

"As to that I can't say. But there's the spring,
Right on the summit, almost like a fountain.
That ought to be worth seeing."

       "If it's there.
You never saw it?"

      "I guess there's no doubt
About its being there. I never saw it.
It may not be right on the very top:
It wouldn't have to be a long way down
To have some head of water from above,
And a *good distance* down might not be noticed
By anyone who'd come a long way up.
One time I asked a fellow climbing it
To look and tell me later how it was."

"What did he say?"

      "He said there was a lake
Somewhere in Ireland on a mountain top."

"But a lake's different. What about the spring?"

"He never got up high enough to see.
That's why I don't advise your trying this side.
He tried this side. I've always meant to go
And look myself, but you know how it is:
It doesn't seem so much to climb a mountain
You've worked around the foot of all your life.
What would I do? Go in my overalls,
With a big stick, the same as when the cows
Haven't come down to the bars at milking time?
Or with a shotgun for a stray black bear?
'Twouldn't seem real to climb for climbing it."

"I shouldn't climb it if I didn't want to—
Not for the sake of climbing. What's its name?"

"We call it Hor: I don't know if that's right."

"Can one walk around it? Would it be too far?"

"You can drive round and keep in Lunenburg,
But it's as much as ever you can do,
The boundary lines keep in so close to it.
Hor is the township, and the township's Hor—
And a few houses sprinkled round the foot,
Like boulders broken off the upper cliff,
Rolled out a little farther than the rest."

"Warm in December, cold in June, you say?"

"I don't suppose the water's changed at all.
You and I know enough to know it's warm
Compared with cold, and cold compared with warm.
But all the fun's in how you say a thing."

"You've lived here all your life?"

> "Ever since Hor
Was no bigger than a ———" What, I did not hear.
He drew the oxen toward him with light touches
Of his slim goad on nose and offside flank,
Gave them their marching orders and was moving.

AS I WAS TRYING to make some sense of the complex relationship between Marianne Moore and Ted Hughes in my discussion of Hughes's "The Literary Life," I happened upon "The Buffalo," a poem in which Moore describes the animal as being

> no white-nosed Vermont ox yoked with its twin
>> to haul the maple-sap,
> up to their knees in
>> snow;

We recognise this "Vermont ox" as having been led by its white nose from lines 16–18 of "The Mountain":

> And there I met a man who moved so slow
> With *white-faced* oxen, in a heavy cart,
> It seemed no harm to stop him altogether.

In her review of Reuben A. Brower's 1964 *The Poetry of Robert Frost: Constellations of Intention*, Moore comments on these three lines:

> Is not "Time Out," also, about another mountain, so similar in feeling as to be its twin?

> The mountain he was climbing had the slant
> As of a book held up before his eyes
> (And was a text albeit done in plant).

I want to suggest, in my close reading of this "text" of the mountain itself, that Moore's insight into Frost's method of "twinning"—she uses the word of the "Vermont ox yoked with its twin"—is profound. It is associated with what Moore describes elsewhere as Frost's "complementarity," by which I take it she means the tendency for one poem, such as "The Mountain," to flow into, to fill out or be filled out by, another such as "Time Out." The sense of the phrase "the end of the poem" on which I'll focus here has to do with the influence of one poem on another within the body of work of a single poet, whereby the "gaps" or "blanks" in one poem are completed or perfected by another—whereby what is missing in "The Mountain," for example, is also bodied out in "Directive"—and that the "body" of the work is indivisible from the "body" of the poet.

That this consideration of what is missing might be one of the "subjects" of "The Mountain" is signalled from the outset:

The mountain held the town as in a shadow.
I saw so much before I slept there once:
I noticed that I *missed* stars in the west

The very first line contains another clue to the secret life of "The Mountain," part of which has to do with Frost's own name. We'll meet the poet's name more obviously in lines 50–54, where the "man who moved so slow" is describing a stream:

One of the great sights going is to see
It steam in winter like an ox's breath,
Until the bushes all along its banks
Are inch-deep with the *frosty* spines and bristles—
You know the kind.

In line 1, there is already an intimation of Frost's name, missing like the "stars in the west," since another way of rendering the first image would be "The town was in the lee of the mountain," an idea substantiated by lines 5–6:

I felt it like a wall
Behind which I was sheltered from a wind.

The speaker of the poem, a speaker not unlike the historical character Robert Lee Frost, named after the historical character, General Robert E. Lee, is announcing from the outset that a major concern of this poem will be one thing being overshadowed by, or sheltering behind, another—town overshadowed by mountain, writer overshadowed by writer, poem overshadowed by poem.

Let's look again in detail at those first two lines. The first thing to be said about the opening words "The mountain" is that we've just had them, in the title of the poem. The second thing is that these two words don't quite mean the same thing to the reader who meets them in this somewhat similar, but slightly different, context of the opening line. What has happened? At least two events have taken place, I suggest. To begin with, the repetition of the title confirms its significance *as* the title, that this title belongs to that class of titles which act as signposts, pointing as this one does towards the significance of "The Mountain" as the central focus of the poem, a significance underscored by line 28:

The mountain stood there to be pointed at.

The second thing that has happened is that the phrase "The mountain" has a new context in terms of rhythm. You'll notice that line 28 falls into what will, by the time we reach it, have emerged as the dominant metrical pattern of the poem, the unrhymed iambic pentameter, what we term blank verse. As usual, I appeal to the *Princeton Encyclopedia of Poetic Terms* for the scuttlebutt on "blank verse":

> Blank verse first appeared in Italian poetry of the Renaissance as an unrhymed variant of the *endecasillabo*, then was transplanted to England as the unrhymed decasyllabic or iambic pentameter . . . "Blank" as used of verse (the earliest *OED* citation is by Nashe in 1589) suggests a mere absence (of rhyme) . . . One associates rhyme with symmetries and closures. Omission of rhyme, by contrast, encourages the use of syntactic structures greater and more various than could be contained strictly within the line, and so makes possible an amplitude of discourse, a natural-seeming multiformity, not easily available to rhymed verse.

So spiny and bristling is Robert Lee Frost that, rather than establish a pattern in line 1, say, and break with it in line 2, he prefers to do the opposite, so that it's only in lines 2–3 that the iambic pentameter is set up:

> I saw so much before I slept there once:
> I noticed that I missed . . .

Now, I want to try to connect two of the key elements mentioned in that definition of blank verse—"absence" and "omission"—with the "absences" and "omissions" which are the subject matter of the poem, and to suggest that the "blank" form of the poem is indivisible from its "blank" content. As Elizabeth Shepley Sergeant reports in *Robert Frost: The Trial by Existence*, Frost avers:

> In making a poem you have no right to think of anything but the subject matter; after making it no right to boast of anything but the form.

To make a connection between "blank" verse and "blank" subject matter is one—perhaps the only—way of making sense of Frost's further contention that "The Mountain" "has no equal of mine *in form* but 'Stopping by Woods' and 'An Old Man's Winter Night.' " The phrase "before I slept" in line 2 of "The Mountain" has already pointed us in the direction of the last two lines of "Stopping by Woods on a Snowy Evening":

> And miles to go before I sleep,
> And miles to go before I sleep.

Despite the fact that they were published almost ten years apart, in 1914 and 1923 respectively, these two poems are in dialogue with each other, one "barking backwards" at the other. In his aphoristic essay "Poetry and School," published in 1951, Frost himself suggests that

> The way to read a poem in prose or verse is in the light of all the other poems ever written. We may begin anywhere. We *duff* into our

first. We read that imperfectly (thoroughness with it would be fatal), but the better to read the second. We read the second the better to read the third, the third the better to read the fourth, the fourth the better to read the fifth, the fifth the better to read the first again, or the second if it so happens.

A little later in the same passage Frost comments:

The same people will be apt to take poems right as know how to take a hint when there is one and not to take a hint when none is intended.

Let's try to take a hint—an intended one, I trust—from Frost's assertion that "Stopping by Woods on a Snowy Evening" be the "equal" of "The Mountain" in form. The poem, while it's not written in blank verse, is nonetheless concerned with the perfect embodiment of another form of "blankness," the *whiteness* which again connects it to Frost's own name and to Frost's own personage:

Whose woods these are I think I know.
His house is in the village, though;
He will not see me stopping here
To watch his woods fill up with snow.

I think that one reason why Frost may consider this a formal triumph has to do, once again, with the idea of mimesis, of the *stanza* finding its "standing" or "stopping place" on four successive occasions to coincide with a unit of sense, the last of which, despite its suggestion of sallying forth, coincides also with stasis:

And miles to go before I sleep,
And miles to go before I sleep.

In other words, despite the suggestion of action or forward motion, the repetition embodies inaction, a freeze-frame for which Frost has prepared the way with another of those plays on his own name:

My little horse must think it queer
To stop without a farmhouse near
Between the woods and *frozen* lake
The darkest evening of the year.

There's yet another sense, I suspect, in which "Stopping by Woods on a Snowy Evening" is mimetic of what it describes, a sense that once again has to do with a play on Frost's name, or a word that's a near version of it. That virtual anagram is "forest," a synonym for the "woods" of the title and the "woods" near the "frozen lake." It's in the clearing, or blank space, "between the woods and frozen lake" in which the poem operates, an echo, I suggest, of lines 6–8 of "The Mountain":

And yet *between the town and it* I found,
When I walked forth at dawn to see new things,
Were fields, a river, and beyond, more fields.

This space between the town and the mountain is a metaphysical one, a very present absence. I want to suggest that "The Mountain" might have "no equal in form" for yet another reason having to do with Frost's name. The word I'm thinking of is "rime," defined by the *OED* as meaning "hoar-*frost*; *frozen* mist," not to be confused—or very much to be confused—with the word which, until about 1650, was also spelt "rime," now usually rendered as "rhyme," defined as meaning "metre; agreement in the terminal sounds of lines or words." If we think back to that definition of blank verse as having to do with "absence" or "omission of rhyme," then we may certainly delight in Frost's self-delighting claim, his "boast," about form, particularly since a central image of the poem has to do with an "absence of *rime*":

One of the great sights going is to see
It steam in winter like an ox's breath.

The content is, once more, indivisible from the form, the blank verse which has been the mode of so many of the great poems in English, by some of the greatest poets writing in the language. I'll concentrate here on two—Wordsworth and Milton. We might, for example, detect a hint of Milton in lines 7–8:

When I walked forth at dawn to see new things,
Were fields, a river, and beyond, more fields.

That "new" sends me back not only to the last—rhyming, as it turns out—couplet of "Lycidas" ("At last he rose, and twitched his mantle blue: / Tomorrow to fresh woods, and pastures *new*") but the blank verse final lines of *Paradise Lost*:

The world was all before them, where to choose
Their place of rest, and providence their guide:
They, hand in hand, with wandering steps and slow,
Through Eden took their solitary way.

That "slow" is carried over into "The Mountain" in the description of the "man who moved so slow," a man who turns out to be a guide of sorts, though almost as reliably unreliable as the speaker of "Directive," a poem published in 1946:

The road there, if you'll let a guide direct you
Who only has at heart your getting lost,
May seem as if it should have been a quarry—
Great monolithic knees the former town
Long since gave up pretense of keeping covered.

We'll meet another version of the "man who moved so slow" in "Directive":

Someone's road home from work this once was,
Who may be just ahead of you on foot
Or creaking with a buggy load of grain.

He may well be the speaker of "The Draft Horse":

With a lantern that wouldn't burn
In too frail a buggy we drove
Behind too heavy a horse
Through a pitch-dark limitless grove.

Not only is this figure familiar from a number of Frost poems, he seems to have strayed from Wordsworth's central casting:

> And there I met a man who moved so slow
> With white-faced oxen, in a heavy cart,
> It seemed no harm to stop him altogether.

Let me stop altogether, at the stanzaic stopping place, to remind myself of "The Old Cumberland Beggar," a man so slow "him even the *slow-paced waggon* leaves behind," a man whom we find "seated, by the highway side / On a low structure of rude masonry / Built *at the foot of a huge hill.*" I stop to remind myself of the leech-gatherer in "Resolution and Independence," who's described "As a huge stone is sometimes seen to lie / Couched on the bald top of an eminence," whose voice was "like a stream / Scarce heard." I stop to remind myself of "Michael":

> Near the tumultuous brook of Greenhead Ghyll,
> In that deep valley, Michael had designed
> To build a Sheepfold; and, before he heard
> The tidings of his melancholy loss,
> For this same purpose he had gathered up
> A heap of stones, which by the streamlet's edge
> Lay thrown together, ready for the work.

I stop to remind myself of the episode in Book I of the 1850 version of *The Prelude* in which one night the young Wordsworth borrows, or steals, a boat:

> When, from behind that craggy steep till then
> The bound of the horizon, a huge peak, black and huge,
> As if with voluntary power instinct,
> Upreared its head. I struck and struck again,
> And growing still in stature the grim shape
> Towered up between me and the stars, and still,
> For so it seemed, with measured motion, like a living thing,
> Strode after me.

It's tempting not to see this "huge peak, black and huge" which "towered up between me and the stars" as the template for the mountain defined by the "missed stars in the west," particularly if we recall Frost's 1913 letter to Thomas Mosher, written while he was at work on the poems of *North of Boston*:

> If I write more lyrics it must be with no thought of publication. What I *can* do next is bring out a volume of blank verse that I have already well in hand and won't have to feel I am writing to order. I had some character strokes I wanted to get in somewhere and I chose a sort of eclogue form for them. Rather I dropped into that form. And I dropped to an everyday level of diction that even Wordsworth kept above. I trust I don't terrify you. I think I have made poetry. The language is appropriate to the virtues I celebrate. At least I am sure I can count on you to give me credit for knowing what I am about. You are not going to make the mistake that Pound makes of assuming that my simplicity is that of the untutored child. I am not undesigning.

It's precisely because of his appetite, and aptitude, for a readily available surface, a "level of diction that even Wordsworth kept above," that Frost's depth and durability tend to be "missed." In my discussion of this poem, I'll want not "to make the mistake that Pound makes" and overlook the fact that Frost is "not undesigning," that he is, in the phrase he uses in "Two Tramps in Mud Time," "the lurking frost in the earth beneath." I'll want not to misconstrue the leisurely, laid-back tone of the description of the effect of what the river "had done in spring" for something akin to lassitude or laxity, not to misconstrue the throwaway for the trite when, as a reader, "I walk(ed) forth at dawn to see new things."

Two things about the "things" in line 8. The first is that it's a further underpinning of the Wordsworthian, sending us back to, among other instances, "Lines Composed a Few Miles Above Tintern Abbey" ("A motion and a spirit, that impels / All thinking *things*, all objects of all thought, / And rolls through all *things*") and "Intimations of Immortality" ("The *things* that I have seen I now can see no more"). The second thing about "things" has to do with its chiming with the word "spring" in line 12, not undesigningly, "if design govern in a thing so small," since the word "spring" is used on two further occasions in the poem, at the end of lines 63 and 77, two "rhyming" lines in the midst of "a fusillade of blanks." This last phrase derives from Frost's poem "A Loose Mountain," another of the poems with which this one is twinned, and to which I'll return a little later when I consider various other lacunae in this text, notably the dash, followed by yet another kind of blank, in line 106.

For the moment, I'm going to swing round the blank wall of "The Mountain" to consider the "man who moved so slow," with his blank-faced oxen and his relation to that "spring." This is the man who identifies the "town that is no more a town," as the speaker of "Directive" might have it, as "Lunenburg," a place-name of German origin. Even a passing knowledge of German, such as my own, will give some clue to one aspect of the identity of this drover, particularly if we leap ahead to line 96:

Hor is the township, and the township's Hor

In other words, if we take our cue from the German place-name, the "burg," or "township" (literally a "castle"), is indivisible from, synonymous with, the "berg," or "mountain," which the locals know as Hor.

I use the word "clue" advisedly, because as Gerard Quinn, my old teacher and friend of forty years, with whom I've been in conversation on the subject of Robert Frost for a good twenty-five of those, has pointed out in a recently published article on "Robert Frost and Ireland," there's a crossword-puzzle aspect to this poem. You'll know immediately why I've bothered to spend twenty-five years in conversation with Gerard Quinn when I point you, as he pointed me, to a riddle in lines 75–76:

"What did he say?"

"He said there was a lake
Somewhere in Ireland on a mountain top."

Gerard Quinn suggests, with all the reserve of a well-brought-up academic, that embedded in the word "Ireland" is the word "élan," which might refer us to the *élan vital* central to the 1907 work *L'évolution créatrice*, published in 1911 as *Creative Evolution*, of Henri Bergson (1859–1941), the philosopher within whose name the aforementioned *berg* is itself embedded. As a very badly brought-up nonacademic, I'd want to go the whole hog and say that Frost is indeed involved in such a playful stratagem having to do with Bergson. I quote from a 1907 letter to Bergson from another of Frost's heroes, William James:

> O my Bergson, you are a magician, and your book is a marvel . . . In
> finishing it I found . . . such a flavor of persistent *euphony*, as of a rich
> river that never foamed or ran thin, but steadily and firmly
> proceeded with its banks full to the brim.

I'm tempted, once again, to think that Frost has this passage in mind, particularly the phrase "that never foamed or ran thin," when he writes in "Directive":

> Your destination and your destiny's
> A brook that was the water of the house,
> Cold as a spring as yet so near its source,
> Too lofty and original to rage.

Some version of this image-cluster of stream, brook, spring or lake occurs in a number of Frost poems which complement "The Mountain." One thinks immediately of "West-Running Brook," with its rhapsodic description of *élan vital*:

> The universal cataract of death
> That spends to nothingness—and unresisted,
> Save by some strange resistance in itself,
> Not just a swerving, but a throwing back,
> As if regret were in it and were sacred.
> It has this throwing backward on itself
> So that the fall of most of it is always
> Raising a little, sending up a little.

The phrase "most of it" points us in the direction, not surprisingly, of "The Most of It," which turns out, not surprisingly, to complement "The Mountain." "The Most of It" begins with images of "some tree-hidden cliff across the lake," echoing "the cliffs / Imperfectly concealed among the leaves" in lines 31–32, and "the boulder-broken beach," echoing "Like boulders broken off the upper cliff, / Rolled out a little farther than the rest" in lines 98–99. That image also brings to my mind Wordsworth's "Michael," if you recall that "heap of stones, which by the streamlet's edge / Lay thrown together." There's also an echo of the "peak" passage from *The Prelude* in "The Most of It," when a threatening "embodiment" of—what?—manifests itself to the speaker:

> As a great buck it powerfully appeared,
> Pushing the crumpled water up ahead,
> And landed pouring like a waterfall,
> And stumbled through the rocks with horny tread,
> And forced the underbrush, and that was all.

This "great buck" is, I propose, an eland—one of the African antelopes rather than North American, I know—but appearing anagrammatically there in "landed" and, for the crossword-puzzle solvers among us, another word in which "élan" is embedded, just as it's "embodied," to go back to Frost's term, in the creature itself. The fact that both "élan" and "eland" are to be found in "Ireland" is not without its reason, one which would further substantiate Gerard Quinn's argument. It is that Henri Bergson was of Irish extraction, both his parents being Irish-Jewish.

There's an Irish connection with two other thinkers who figure in this poem. I'm thinking of George Berkeley (1685–1753), whose presence is signalled in much the same way as is Bergson's, by a playful crossword-puzzle clue there in line 14, in which a stripped-down version of his name is embedded in "driftwood stripped of *bark*." I know this reading will seem like a stretch to some, but I'm inclined towards it because of a certain laborious quality in Frost's description in lines 28–30:

> The mountain stood there to be pointed at.
> Pasture ran up the side a little way,
> And then there was a wall of trees with trunks;

To which a reader might be inclined to respond, "Show me a tree *without* a trunk." The phrase "to be pointed at" reminds us of the teacherly aspect of much of Frost's writing and steers us towards a synonym which is "imperfectly concealed," as he has it in line 32, "among the leaves" of the "text albeit done in plant" of the mountain. What's imperfectly concealed in the phrase "trees with trunks" is, once again, the word "bark." It's followed in lines 29 and 34 by the occurrence of the word "pasture," not once but twice, picking up the occurrence, not once but twice, of "fields" in line 9 and the occurrence of "grass," not once but twice, in line 13. The common synonym for "pasture," "fields" and "grassland" is "lea," so filling out the homophone "bark lea." If I were feeling much friskier than I am today I might steer you in the direction of a synonym for "a dry ravine" in line 33. (Notice again the slightly cumbersome, slightly contorted phrasing of "A dry ravine emerged from under boughs / Into the pasture.") The synonym I'm thinking of is "gorge," a near version of Berkeley's given name. But I'm not feeling frisky today, so I won't bother. I will bother to guide, and goad, you in the direction of the guide with his goad in "The Mountain," and what he has to tell the speaker who "walked forth at dawn to *see* new things." Some version of the verb "see" occurs *eight* times in this poem, including the central exchange in lines 65–67 about the "spring / Right on the summit" of Hor:

"That ought to be worth seeing."

                       "If it's there.
You never saw it?"

                "I guess there's no doubt
About its being there. I never saw it."

This dialogue is a fairly obvious rehearsal of Berkeley's most famous dictum, "*Esse* is *percipi*" ("To see is to be perceived").

Another thinker with an Irish connection is the aforementioned William James (1842–1910), whose 1909 book *A Pluralistic Universe*, based on the Hibbert Lectures given in Oxford the previous year, included a chapter on Bergson in which he wrote:

What makes you call real life confusion is that it presents, as if they were dissolved in one another, a lot of differents which retrospective conception breaks life's flow by keeping apart. But *are* not differents actually dissolved in one another? Hasn't every bit of experience its quality, its duration, its extension, its intensity, its urgency, its clearness, and many aspects besides, no one of which can exist in the isolation in which our verbalised logic keeps it?

This passage resonates not only with the core of "The Mountain," accounting for why one might find "between the town and it" such a heap "of detail, burned, *dissolved*, and broken off," to borrow from line 3 of "Directive," with its "dissolved" inspired, I suspect, from its occurrence, not once but twice, in the James passage. The other key words borrowed from that passage into "Directive" are "presents," in the sense of the tense, and "confusion," versions of both of which are alluded to in the first line of the poem—"Back out of all this *now too much* for us," with its echo of Wordsworth's "The world is too much with us"—and the last, with its injunction to the reader to "Drink and be whole again beyond *confusion*." It's worth reminding ourselves that in 1898, while he briefly attended Harvard, taking courses in Greek, Latin and philosophy, Frost was thwarted in his ambition to study with James, who was on medical leave that year, though he would later write that "My greatest inspiration, when I was a student, was a man whose classes I never attended."

The water that the reader is being directed to drink comes from "a brook that was the water of the house," though this is "a house that is no more a house / But only a belilaced cellar hole." Let me focus on this "house that is no more a house"—this ruin of a house—to find a way into another influence on this poem, that of yet another thinker, Ralph Waldo Emerson (1803–82), whose essay on "Nature" includes the following:

The reason why the world lacks unity, and lies broken and in heaps, is because man is disunited with himself.

Two sentences before, we come upon the remarkable phrase "The *ruin* or the *blank* that we see when we look at nature, is in our own eye." Part of the project of "The Mountain" has to do, yet again, with an Emersonian reconciliation of "self" and "other" so that the "boundary lines" become indivisible, as the "blank" eye takes in the "ruin" of "Mont Blank."

This wordplay is less fanciful than one might imagine, I propose (particularly in a writer who has it, again in "Two Tramps in Mud Time," that "the work is play for mortal stakes"), since it sends us back to Wordsworth again, back to the description in Book VI of *The Prelude* of the crossing of the Alps, a description which connects it in turn to the passage in Emerson:

> That very day,
> From a bare ridge we also first beheld
> Unveiled the summit of Mont Blanc, and grieved
> To have a soulless *image on the eye*
> That had usurped upon a living thought
> That never more could be.

The following lines (from the 1850 version) refer to the landscape as "a *book* / Before our eyes," a metaphor to which I'll return. There's a "guide," of course, who deserts the travellers at a critical moment. The travellers "then paced the beaten downward way that led / Right to a rough stream's edge, and there broke off; / The only track now visible was one / That from the torrent's further brink held forth / Conspicuous invitation to ascend / A lofty mountain." This phrase "the only track now visible" is carried over, I propose, to "Directive" as "*The only field / Now left's* no bigger than a harness gall," while the "lofty" is carried over to the "spring as yet so near its source / Too *lofty* and original to rage."

The "source" points us in the direction of what I suspect is another source for both "Directive" and "The Mountain." It's Percy Bysshe Shelley's boldly titled "Mont Blanc," a poem which I simply don't have space to discuss in detail here but which is sometimes read as being "about" the relationship of the Universal Mind, as embodied by the "dark, deep Ravine" (note the familiar combination of "dark" and "deep") and the individual human mind, as embodied by a "feeble brook." Shelley's "Mont Blanc" and Frost's "The Mountain" are alike in at least one other, more obvious, respect in that what happens on the peak is mysterious, "snows" falling there that "none beholds." It's a mountain on which "Frost and the Sun in scorn of mortal power / Have piled: dome, pyramid, and pinnacle, / A city of death, distinct with many a tower / And wall impregnable of beaming ice. / Yet not a city, but a flood of ruin / Is there that from the boundaries of the sky / Rolls its perpetual stream."

I WANT TO ROLL TOWARDS A CONCLUSION of my very partial and imperfect reading of this dazzlingly complex poem by focussing on one or two further "blanks" in the "fusillade of blanks" I mentioned earlier. I'll try to connect them once more to Frost's name, the body of work to which it is attached, and the mountain of "The Mountain" itself. I'll begin with that "belilaced cellar hole" from "Directive," and I'll rewrite that crossword-puzzle clue having to do with "the lake in Ireland" to read "There is a lake in belilaced." Another example of precisely the same technique is to be found in lines 39–40 of "The Mountain," where "those that *have* / Been up, I understand, have climbed from Ladd's." The "Ladd" there is, I suggest, somewhere in "Aladdin," the character from *The Thousand and One Nights* who finds the lamp and its genie under a "marble slab" in the side of a mountain. We may recall how Frost appeals to the story of Ali Baba in "Directive":

> Nor need you mind the serial ordeal
> Of being watched from forty cellar holes
> As if by eye pairs out of forty firkins.

These stories from *The Thousand and One Nights* involve either violent shifts in scale from minuscule to huge or sudden appearances and disappearances. In the case of "Aladdin and His Enchanted Lamp," both ideas come into play, and they relate to line 106 of "The Mountain," to a time when " 'Hor / Was no bigger than a ———.' " Frost uses images having to do with shifts of scale in the size of two pearls in "How Hard It Is to Keep from Being King When It's in You and in the Situation," where a slave (a first cousin of Aladdin's genie, perhaps) remarks that "the small one's worth the price / But the big one is worthless." But let me leave the "Ladd" in "Aladdin" and go back to the *lac* embedded there in "a belilaced cellar hole," a line which points us again not only to Bergson, but to Bergson mediated by William James, as a sentence or two we find a little later in the passage of *A Pluralistic Universe* I quoted earlier make clear:

> Reality always is, in M. Bergson's phrase, an endosmosis or conflux
> of the same with the different: they compenetrate and telescope. For

conceptual logic, the same is nothing but the same, and all sames with a third thing are the same with each other. Not so in concrete experience. Two spots on our skin, each of which feels the same as a third spot when touched along with it, are felt as different from each other.

This image of the "two spots on our skin" is connected, I think, with the line immediately following, and modifying "a belilaced cellar hole" in "Directive"—"Now slowly closing like a dent in dough"—since "doughy" or "pasty" are often used of the colour and consistency of human skin. That conflux of the "same" with the "different" in the James passage is familiar to us from a number of Frost poems, including that favourite of illiterate admen, "The Road Not Taken." We see a version of it here in lines 101–4:

> "I don't suppose the water's changed at all.
> You and I know enough to know it's warm
> Compared with cold, and cold compared with warm.
> But all the fun's in how you say a thing."

A version of this last phrase is used again by Frost in a letter of January 1, 1917, to Louis Untermeyer:

> What I like about Bergson and Fabre is that they bothered our evolutionism so much with the cases of instinct they have brought up. You get more credit for thinking if you restate formulae or cite cases that fall in easily under formulae, *but all the fun is outside saying things* that suggest formulae that won't formulate—that almost but don't quite formulate. I should like to be so subtle at this game as to seem to a casual person altogether obvious.

Frost's positioning of himself on an "outside" and his use of the word "game" bring to mind two complementary couplet-poems—"It takes all sorts of in- and outdoor schooling / To get adapted to my kind of fooling" and "We dance round in a ring and suppose, / but the Secret sits in the middle and knows." The "middle" of that "ring" is the "blank" of a target, a moving version of which is offered by "The White-Tailed Hornet," a refugee from the work of the aforementioned French entomologist, Jean-Henri Fabre (1823–1915):

> The white-tailed hornet lives in a balloon
> That floats against the ceiling of the woodshed.
> The exit he comes out at like a bullet
> Is like the pupil of a pointed gun.

After mistaking a nailhead and a huckleberry for the fly on which he's bent, this hornet finally gets the real thing in its sights:

> At last it was a fly. He shot and missed;
> And the fly circled round him in derision.
> But for the fly he might have made me think
> He had been at his poetry, comparing
> Nailhead with fly and fly with huckleberry:
> How like a fly, how very like a fly.

I quote at length from "The White-Tailed Hornet" because its reference to finding similes and metaphors—or the *failure* to find one—brings us back to one of the major "blanks," or lacunae, in "The Mountain":

> "You've lived here all your life?"
>
> > "Ever since Hor
> Was no bigger than a ———" What, I did not hear.

And we don't ever hear for certain what this boulder "broken off the upper cliff" of "The Mountain" might be, what the other leg of that simile might be, what might make it "whole again beyond confusion." We get glimpses of it in other poems, I suspect, including the "nailhead," the "huckleberry" and the "fly" of "The White-Tailed Hornet." We glimpse another version of that Fabrean fly in "A Considerable Speck," where the speaker deals "plainly with the intelligence" of

A speck that would have been beneath my sight
On any but a paper sheet so white
Set off across what I had written there.

(The fact that "The Mountain" is "filling up" the "blank" page of itself is thrown into relief, as it were, by the generous clearings and gaps between the sections of direct speech. This provides further support of Frost's boast that the "blank" form and "blank" content are one.) The subtitle of "A Considerable Speck" is "*Microscopic*," and it connects, yet again, with that passage from William James in which he describes the essence of metaphor-making, whereby the "same" and the "different" might "compenetrate and *telescope*." The notion of a sudden and substantial shift in scale or perspective which a telescope, or microscope, is likely to render brings me back to "The Mountain" and what it was "no bigger than." We glimpse a possible answer to the puzzle in the description in "Directive" of the "belilaced cellar hole / Now slowly closing *like a dent in dough*." We seem to be getting warmer when we glimpse another possible answer in "Home Burial," a poem included, like "The Mountain," in Frost's 1914 volume *North of Boston*, where the husband describes "the little graveyard" in which the child is buried:

So small the window frames the whole of it.
Not so much larger than a bedroom, is it?

Such is the wholeness of Frost's work that this poem sends us immediately back to "Directive" and the injunction:

Then make yourself at *home*. The only field
Now left's *no bigger than a* harness-gall.

This image of the "harness-gall" connects with the William James passage, I want to suggest, in its attention to one of those "*spots on our skin*." James's image is itself echoic of the ubiquitous Wordsworth and "There are in our existence spots of time," the line in Book XII of *The Prelude* which ushers in an episode of "visionary dreariness" focussing on "a naked pool that lay beneath the hills, / The beacon on the summit." In another related passage, this time in Chapter V of *Pragmatism* (1907), James quotes Wordsworth's "central peace subsisting at the heart / of endless agitation" (*The Excursion*, Book IV, lines 1146–47) to give a concrete image for his sense of "the negatives that haunt our ideals here below" which "must be themselves negated in the absolutely Real. This alone makes the universe solid. This is the resting deep. We live upon the stormy surface; but with this our anchor holds, for it grapples rocky bottom." The paragraph in which these sentences occur is taken up with the idea of what "would tighten this loose universe," a metaphor which partly informs the title of "A Loose Mountain," a poem related to "A Considerable Speck" by its subtitle of "*Telescopic*." James has already used an astonishing metaphor on the previous page having to do with the rationalist mind. "The belly-band of its universe," he writes, "must be tight." And it's on this phrase that Frost draws, I suspect, for the "harness-gall" in "Directive," the "harness-gall" which would result from "the belly-band of the universe" being "tight," the "harness-gall" which our "guide" with his "goad" can't quite bring himself to voice here in "The Mountain." After this "blanking out," this gap in the text "substituted, for decorum's sake," as the *OED* has it, "for a word of execration":

He drew the oxen toward him with light touches
Of his slim goad on nose and offside flank,
Gave them their marching orders and was moving.

The word "flank" sends us in a couple of directions here. Its military connotations are supported by the phrase "marching orders," reminding us of the ghost of General Robert E. Lee in the name of the poem's maker, a poet whose weighty subject matter is managed with "light touches." An obvious, if unspoken, *rime*-word would be "blank," reminding us of the "form" of the poem. But there's another sense of "form" of which Frost was thinking, I suspect, when he made that boast of "The Mountain." It has to do with Bergson again, with a section of Chapter IV in *Creative Evolution*, entitled "Form and Becoming," in which he writes that "*form is only a snapshot view of a transition*." It's in this other sense, I suggest, that our understanding the surface of a poem like "The Mountain" might correspond to the "vision that a systematic intellect obtains of the universal becoming when regarding it by means of snapshots, taken at intervals, of its flowing." This poem is, in that sense, a representation of a "mountain interval," a phrase which just happens to be the title of Frost's next collection, published in 1916. Earlier in the same passage, Bergson writes:

> Now, in the continuity of sensible qualities we mark off the
> boundaries of bodies . . . The body pre-eminently—that which we
> are most justified in isolating within the continuity of matter,
> because it constitutes a relatively closed system—is the living body; it
> is, moreover, for it that we cut out the others within the whole.

This passage includes two words, "body" and "cut," which we find in line 4 of "The Mountain," and a third, "boundaries," the singular of which we find in lines 93–96:

> "You can drive round and keep in Lunenburg,
> But it's as much as ever you can do,
> The *boundary* lines keep in so close to it.
> Hor is the township, and the township's Hor—

Now, I've not said anything much about Hor as yet, though we've spent a great deal of time on its "flanks." We remember that Frost studied Greek at Harvard, so he's more likely than not to associate the name "Hor" with the Greek word *horos,* "a *boundary* or limit," which must surely account for why, in line 95, "The boundary lines keep in so close to it." We may recall that Hor is the name of the "mountain of mountains" in the Book of Numbers, the mountain on which Yahweh ordains Aaron will die without seeing the promised land because he disobeyed Yahweh's orders at the Waters of Meribah, causing water to gush from a rock with his magic rod. That rod appears here in the guise of the "goad" in the hand of the "guide," who might be giving "marching orders" to the Israelites. The term "marching orders" has another resonance, though, of an image used by Bergson in the passage I quoted earlier:

> Suppose we wish to portray on a screen a living picture, such as
> the *marching* past of a regiment . . . to take a series of snapshots of
> the passing regiment and to throw these instantaneous views on the

screen, so that they replace each other very rapidly . . . is what the cinematograph does.

This cinematographic system gives a new urgency to the last word of the poem, "moving," just as it forces us to read lines 57–62 in the light in which they're written:

> I saw through leafy *screens*
> Great granite terraces in sun and shadow,
> Shelves one could rest a knee on getting up—
> With depths behind him sheer a hundred feet—
> Or turn and sit on and look out and down,
> With little ferns in crevices at his elbow.

There's a "bookish" system of imagery in place here. We see it in the mountain having "the slant / As of a *book* held up before his eyes." We see it in the word "leafy." We see it in the word "shelves." We see it in a synonym for "granite terraces" and "shelves" which Frost can't quite bring himself to use here in "The Mountain," though we find it in line 15 of "Directive":

> The *ledges* show lines ruled southeast-northwest

That "ledges" is etymologically connected with the word "ledger," the first, obsolete, meaning of which is "a book that lies permanently in some place." There's a connection with the Mount Hor in Numbers, if only that Aaron's co-leader, Moses, was already famous for climbing a mountain and returning with a couple of ledge(r)s. Because of his not following Yahweh's directions, Moses was not allowed to enter the promised land but merely to glimpse it from Mount Pisgah. It probably won't come as too much of a surprise to most readers of Robert Frost that in Orleans County, Vermont, are two mountains, Mount Pisgah and Mount Hor. What did come as a surprise to this reader, however, was the discovery that Mount Hor is better known as Mount *Hoar*. This brings us back to the definition of "rime" as "hoar-*frost*" and is yet another instance of why the poet made his boast about the "form" of "The Mountain." His own hoar-frosty personage is indivisible from the hoar-frosty mountain which is indivisible from the hoar-frosty poem.

In my next chapter I'll be looking at Elizabeth Bishop's prose poem "12 O'Clock News," and trying to determine, insofar as I might manage it, where a poem ends and prose begins. In the meantime, I'll begin to end here with three or four prose pieces by Frost which suggest that, in his own case, everything he writes, however slight or frothy it might seem, is part of a substantial and far-reaching project. In "Petra and Its Surroundings," which came out in the December 1891 number of the *High School Bulletin* in Lawrence, Massachusetts, he writes:

> From Mt. *Hor* the *view* is one of magnificent sameness; but not until the *cliffs* have towered above, not until the storm has crowded its overwhelming torrents down the *ravines*, can the grand sublimity of the situation be felt. In its unstability, the region is like an ice-floe.

In addition to the subject matter and the instances I've already italicised, there are several further instances of vocabulary shared with "The Mountain," as Frost goes on to write of the *"cliffs* festooned with pale *fern"* and the *"open ground walled* for the most part by *sheer* precipices, falling for *hundreds of feet* into the city."

A version of that "fern" which appears here in line 62 as "little ferns in crevices at his elbow" also shows up in a July 4, 1916, letter to his friend John Haines, the Gloucestershire poet, botanist and barrister, in which he lovingly recalls "the *fern* we groped on the *little cliff* for by the light of a match in your English winter twilight." In his edition of the *Selected Letters of Robert Frost*, Lawrance Thompson describes how Frost "spent part of the hay-fever season at Lake Willoughby, Vermont, botanizing" for orchids and ferns. We should remember that Lake Willoughby lies between Mount Pisgah and Mount Hor, or Hoar.

As early as that 1891 essay on "Petra and Its Surroundings," Frost is likening the region in which Hor/Hoar stands to an "ice-floe," one of the first of the dozens of times some variant of "frost," "ice" or "snow" appear in his work, including the uncollected poem "Down the Brook . . . and Back," also written in 1891, in which the word "snow" appears once and some version of the word "ice" no less than *five* times within a mere twenty-three lines. Those five instances of "ice" are connected with the assertion in 1939's "The Figure a Poem Makes" that "like *a piece of ice* on a hot stove the poem must ride on its own melting," the perfect, most profound, linking of Hoar-poet with Hoar-poem, the berg of the poem with the berg of the mountain. It's precisely because of the widespread, deep-seated nature of this tendency that Marianne Moore couldn't help but envisage those white-nosed Vermont oxen "up to their knees in / snow." And it's why Frost gives us the little humorous nod there in line 54 when he follows up the fact that "the bushes all along its banks / Are inch-deep with the frosty spines and bristles—" with *You know the kind.*" We know it from "Fish-Leap Fall," another uncollected poem, of 1919:

> From further in the hills there came
> A river to our kitchen door
> To be the water of the house
> And keep a snow-white kitchen floor.

That "snow-white" image of domesticity contains hints of Frost's name ("snow") and the name of his wife, Elinor *White*. Frost has also associated "woman" and "mountain" in "The Birthplace":

> The mountain pushed us off her knees.
> And now her lap is full of trees.

These lines send us back to "Directive," yet again, to the "great monolithic *knees* the former town / Long since gave up pretense of keeping covered" and, another personification, "an enormous Glacier / That braced his feet against the Arctic Pole." That "Glacier" is once again poet and poem ("braced his *feet*"), just like the "piece of ice." The "piece of ice" sends us to "Some say the world will end in fire, / Some say in *ice*" ("Fire and Ice"). The phrase "the world will end" sends us to "Too Anxious for Rivers," the poem immediately following "Directive," which begins:

> Look down the long valley and there stands a mountain
> That someone has said is *the end of the world.*

Line 14 of "Too Anxious for Rivers," meanwhile, reads:

> The world as we know is an elephant's howdah

This sends us back to the "belly-band of the universe" that is too "tight"—
or is it too "loose"?—and the resulting "harness-gall." It connects with the
harnessed "oxen" and the "cow" in "The Milky Way is a Cowpath," which

> Had for the universe
> Left trivia behind;
>
> And gone right on astray
> Through let-down pasture bars
> Along the Milky Way
> A-foraging on stars.

These lines help make some sense of the otherwise strange notion in lines
85–86 of "The Mountain" of "when the cows / Haven't come down to the
bars at milking time." The "belly-band" sends us to the "guide" who, in
line 43 of "The Mountain," describes himself as being *"bound* the other
way." The notion of being "bound" sends us not only to Aaron and Moses
and the people whom they led "out of the house of bondage" but also to
"The Prophet" of Frost's 1936–59 uncollected poem of that title, a poem
which could have been written only by a poet confident of the "bound-
lessness" of his work:

> They say the truth will make you free.
> My truth will bind you slave to me—
> Which may be what you want to be.

CHAPTER 4

12 O'CLOCK NEWS

ELIZABETH BISHOP

gooseneck lamp

As you all know, tonight is the night of the full moon, half the world over. But here the moon seems to hang motionless in the sky. It gives very little light; it could be dead. Visibility is poor. Nevertheless, we shall try to give you some idea of the lay of the land and the present situation.

typewriter

The escarpment that rises abruptly from the central plain is in heavy shadow, but the elaborate terracing of its southern glacis gleams faintly in the dim light, like fish scales. What endless labor those small, peculiarly shaped terraces represent! And yet, on them the welfare of this tiny principality depends.

pile of mss.

A slight landslide occurred in the northwest about an hour ago. The exposed soil appears to be of poor quality: almost white, calcareous, and shaly. There are believed to have been no casualties.

typed sheet

Almost due north, our aerial reconnaissance reports the discovery of a large rectangular "field," hitherto unknown to us, obviously man-made. It is dark-speckled. An airstrip? A cemetery?

In this small, backward country, one of the most backward left in the world today, communications are *envelopes* crude and "industrialization" and its products almost nonexistent. Strange to say, however, signboards are on a truly gigantic scale.

We have also received reports of a mysterious, oddly shaped, black structure, at an undisclosed distance to the east. Its presence was revealed only because its highly polished surface catches such feeble moonlight as prevails. The natural resources of the country being far from completely known to us, there is the possibility that this may be, or may contain, some powerful and terrifying *ink-bottle* "secret weapon." On the other hand, given what we *do* know, or have learned from our anthropologists and sociologists about this people, it may well be nothing more than a *numen*, or a great altar recently erected to one of their gods, to which, in their present historical state of superstition and helplessness, they attribute magical powers, and may even regard as a "savior," one last hope of rescue from their grave difficulties.

At last! One of the elusive natives has been spotted! He appears to be—rather, to have been—a unicyclist-courier, who may have met his end by falling from the height of *typewriter* the escarpment because of the deceptive illumination. *eraser* Alive, he would have been small, but undoubtedly proud and erect, with the thick, bristling black hair typical of the indigenes.

From our superior vantage point, we can clearly see into a sort of dugout, possibly a shell crater, a "nest" of soldiers. They lie heaped together, wearing the camouflage "bat- *ashtray* tle dress" intended for "winter warfare." They are in hideously contorted positions, all dead. We can make out at least eight bodies. These uniforms were designed to be used in guerrilla warfare on the country's one snow-covered mountain peak. The fact that these poor soldiers are wearing them *here*, on the plain, gives further proof, if proof were necessary, either of the childishness and hopeless impracticality of this inscrutable people, our opponents, or of the sad corruption of their leaders.

ONE ASPECT OF THE PHRASE "the end of the poem" which I plan to consider here is that of the delineation of where verse ends and prose begins, a delineation somewhat blurred, if not obliterated, by the mode of the "prose poem." I'm reminded of the dangers and difficulties attending such a project by Robert Giroux's account, in his introduction to her *Collected Prose*, of his first meeting with Elizabeth Bishop:

> She was an extremely attentive listener, but scarcely spoke until I told her of my experience escorting Marianne Moore to the New York premiere of T. S. Eliot's *The Cocktail Party*, at his request (he was unable to leave London). After the performance, we had been caught in the aisle behind the Duke of Windsor, and heard him say (at which point Marianne gently poked me in the ribs): "They tell me Mr. Eliot wrote this play in verse, but I must say you'd *never* know it!"

It was Eliot himself, of course, who had weighed in on the subject of verse and prose in his 1917 *New Statesman* article on "The Borderline of Prose":

> Both verse and prose still conceal unexplored possibilities, but whatever one writes must be definitely and by inner necessity either one or the other.

While Eliot wrote at least one magnificent prose poem—I'm thinking of "Hysteria"—he was inclined to dislike, even to disallow, the term, all too aware that the borderline between verse and prose represented by the form was a minefield in which any hard-and-fast theory would almost certainly be exploded. In my musings on this subject, I'll also try to be mindful of the view of Owen Barfield, also expressed in an article in *The New Statesman*, this time in 1928, that "to regard concentrations on hybrids or borderline cases as a means of clearing up typical differences" is mistaken:

> Whereas in point of fact these borderline cases are the most likely ones of all to confuse our minds, inducing us to ask the wrong kind of questions, and to forget what we are inquiring for in the ardour of inquiry.

That Elizabeth Bishop's prose poem "12 O'Clock News" might itself be concerned with such "borderline cases" is suggested by the fourth paragraph/stanza, which describes a *typed sheet* as a "field" which is "dark-speckled" and "obviously man-made." The poem asks us to think of the *typed sheet* as being akin to an "airstrip" or "cemetery." I suppose that, in the overall context of the landscape of the writer's desk described in the prose poem, this typewritten page may itself be seen as either a rough-and-ready runway, a clearing dotted with tree stumps or, more persuasively, a cemetery covered with makeshift signs, the crossings-out of a work in progress. Within the smaller context of the *typed sheet* itself, the white expanses of the page margins, or the breaks between verse-stanzas or prose-paragraphs, are more likely to substantiate the "airstrip" than the "cemetery" interpretation. There is, in any event, the positing of a relationship between topography and typography.

In my attempt to read Robert Frost's "The Mountain," I was much concerned with any number of "blanks" in the poem, including the exaggerated stanza breaks in the typographical presentation of that poem. There I appealed briefly to Ralph Waldo Emerson's 1836 essay on "Nature" to try to make sense of one reading of those "blanks" in the "ruin or the *blank* that we see when we look at nature." I might also have appealed to Emerson for the provenance—or part of the provenance—of line 8 of "The Mountain," which reads "When I walked forth at dawn to see new things." In his essay "The Poet," published in book form in 1844, Emerson writes:

> For it is not metres, but a metre-making argument, that makes a poem—a thought so passionate and alive that like the spirit of a

plant or animal it has an architecture of its own, and adorns nature with a *new thing*.

I suspect that the spirit of Emerson's "new thing" lies somewhat behind the title of "12 O'Clock *News*," as do, more substantially, Ezra Pound's paired maxims that "literature is *news* that stays *news*" and that a poet must "make it *new*." This last injunction of Pound also lies somewhat behind Bishop's description of the field as *"hitherto unknown to us,"* or "new." The phrase "obviously man-made" refers directly to a "poem," I expect, since a "man-made" thing would be the outcome of the activity described by the Greek word *poiesis*. The objective of the poem itself to make metaphors (to find likeness in unlike things, to present, in the Emersonian sense, new ways of seeing the things of the world), is another aspect of the phrase "the end of the poem" I'd like to try to explore here. Yet another sense of the phrase I'll be focussing on, in my passes over the terrain of this prose poem, is that of the precise location of the surface of the poem, particularly when there seems to be a discrepancy between the surface and the subterranean—what we generally term "irony." Along the way I'll attempt to place "12 O'Clock News" in the context of some of Elizabeth Bishop's other writing, not only the poems appearing with it in her last collection, *Geography III*, a book which came out in 1976, three years before her death, but also some of her prose writings, including one or two of her prose poems. I'll also say a brief word or two about the impact of this prose poem on three or four subsequent writers of poetry and prose, including Seamus Heaney, Derek Mahon, Craig Raine and Salman Rushdie.

I USED THE WORD "margins" just a moment ago, and I'll come back to it now and linger over it a little while, not least because the notion of the margin, not to speak of the marginal, are particularly relevant to "12 O'Clock News." We notice that the body of the text is justified right, the conventional justification for prose, prose that springs forward rather than verse that falls back. The text is also justified left, of course, but with a much wider "airstrip" than usual running down the side of the page. This allows for an italicised legend on the left of the page—*"typed sheet,"* say—to point, like an anatomical term connected by a fine line, to a feature of the main body of the text on the right:

Almost due north, our aerial reconnaissance reports the discovery of a large rectangular "field," hitherto unknown to us, obviously manmade. It is dark-speckled. An airstrip? A cemetery?

By the time we've read this, we're already familiar with the process of defamiliarization in which the poem exults, so familiar indeed that we may have jumped a little ahead of ourselves and concentrated on the left-hand monitor, or stereophonic speaker, and got the bass-line of the poem from that series of "legends"—"gooseneck lamp," "typewriter," "pile of mss.," "typed sheet," "envelopes," "ink-bottle," "typewriter eraser" and "ashtray." These are not only things of the world but things of a writer's world, the view of, and from, a writer's desk which, as I've already mentioned, may be said to be the "subject" of "12 O'Clock News." One can imagine a circumstance in which this left-hand column might be seen as revealing too much, a circumstance in which we prefer to read the "answer" at the back of the book, or even upside down at the bottom of the page, rather than have it given simultaneously with, if not a little before, the question. Part of the delight, surely, of trying to make sense of a riddle from the *Exeter Book* lies in our not quite knowing what is being described. Is it a bird? Is it a plane? Is it a gooseneck lamp? Such questions are irrelevant, it would seem, when we know straightaway that it is most definitely a "*gooseneck lamp*." That the poem is concerned with this tension between knowing and unknowing is evident from the outset, since the promise of "News" in the title is immediately contradicted by the opening words of the poem, at once buttonholing and blasé:

As you all know, tonight is the night of the full moon, half the world over. But here the moon seems to hang motionless in the sky. It gives very little light; it could be dead. Visibility is poor. Nevertheless, we shall try to give you some idea of the lay of the land and the present situation.

It will become clear, as the poem proceeds, that Bishop's primary aim here is to mix and match—not necessarily smoothly and seamlessly, for reasons I'll come to later—three or four types of discourse. They are those of the anthropologist or sociologist ("It may well be nothing more than a *numen*, or a great altar recently erected to one of their gods"), the travel writer ("At last! One of the elusive natives has been spotted!"), the foreign, or war, correspondent ("There are believed to have been no casualties") and, allied to this last, the radio or television reporter ("We shall try to give you some idea of the lay of the land and the present situation"). The discourse of the television report is particularly significant in this respect since it accounts, at least partly, for the provenance of what I referred to earlier as the "legends" to the left of the page, which might be much more usefully viewed as "captions," or "titles," or "idents" on a television screen. The description, in the eighth paragraph/stanza of "12 O'Clock News" of the "*ashtray*" full of soldiers in "hideously contorted positions, all dead" owes something of its immediacy to television reportage of the Vietnam War, that most immediate, most media-mediated, of conflicts, which had finally come to some sort of end in 1975, the year before "12 O'Clock News" was collected. Insofar as anything may be said to come naturally to a writer, the discourse of the television report must have come fairly naturally to Elizabeth Bishop, since its three main features of clarity, conciseness and concreteness, combined with a certain coolness (in the sense of editorial detachment), had been the hall- or watermarks of her poetry from the very beginning.

Writing in *The Nation* of Bishop's first collection, *North and South*, which appeared in 1946, Marianne Moore had observed:

> Elizabeth Bishop is spectacular in being unspectacular. Why has no one ever thought of this, one asks oneself; why not be accurate and modest?

Moore knows of one or two poets who have "thought of this," of course, as is evident from her allusion both to the structure and substance of a celebrated sentence from Edward Thomas's celebrated review, one of three he wrote in quick succession, of Robert Frost's *North of Boston*:

> These poems are revolutionary because they lack the exaggeration of rhetoric, and even at first sight appear to lack the poetic intensity of which rhetoric is an imitation.

As we know to be so often the case with writers' comments on other writers, the very insight Thomas affords into Frost's poetic practice affords an even greater insight into his own. In Thomas's "Cock-Crow," for example, one can see, in the first seven lines, a mimicking of "the exaggeration of rhetoric" to which he refers:

Out of the wood of thoughts that grows by night
To be cut down by the sharp axe of light,—
Out of the night, two cocks together crow,
Cleaving the darkness with a silver blow:
And bright before my eyes twin trumpeters stand,
Heralds of splendour, one at either hand,
Each facing each as in a coat of arms:

The eighth and final line of the poem would appear, in Thomas's phrase, "to lack poetic intensity":

The milkers lace their boots up at the farms.

The tension between lines 7 and 8 of "Cock-Crow," the tension between the high-flown and the humdrum, is what makes Thomas "revolutionary."

So "spectacular in being unspectacular," so "revolutionary because they lack the exaggeration of rhetoric," are the poems of Bishop and Thomas that these two poets, for example, now occupy major rather than minor, dominant rather than diminished, positions in the history of twentieth-century poetry, displacing some of the more grandiloquent and garish cocks of the walk of their respective eras—Robert Bridges, say, or Robert Lowell—by dint of having looked long and hard:

At four o'clock
in the gun-metal blue dark
we hear the first crow of the first cock

just below
the gun-metal blue window
and immediately there is an echo

off in the distance,
then one from the backyard fence,
then one, with horrible insistence,

grates like a wet match
from the broccoli patch,
flares, and all over town begins to catch.

Elizabeth Bishop's long, hard look at "Roosters," with their "horrible insistence," is a poem, and a phrase, Marianne Moore must have had in mind when she wrote, in the same 1946 *Nation* review I quoted earlier:

> With poetry as with homiletics tentativeness can be more positive than positiveness; and in *North and South* a much instructed persuasiveness is emphasized by uninsistence.

The word "insistent" also occurs, in the phrase "insistent buttonholers," in Bishop's own 1941 prose piece "Mercedes Hospital." It "was because of Marianne Moore," as Bishop acknowledges in "Efforts of Affection," "that in 1935 [her] poems first appeared in a book." Her "older mentor" is more likely than not to have had the opportunity to read, and have her own critical terminology influenced by, the description in "Mercedes Hospital" of a certain Miss Mamie:

> Above all, there is her inquisitiveness and talkativeness and that childlike expression in her eyes when she takes hold of my shoulders and peers into my face and asks question after question—just as St. Anthony might have rushed out of his cell, and seized a traveler by the elbow and naively but determinedly asked him for news of the world. In fact, all the saints must have been insistent buttonholers, like Miss Mamie.

Let me go back now to the opening paragraph/stanza of "12 O'Clock News" ("*of the world*") and the opening phrase, which I described earlier as being "at once buttonholing and blasé":

As you all know, tonight is the night of the full moon, half the world over.

It's only by the time we get to the second phrase, "tonight is the night of the full moon," that we understand that the "12 O'Clock" referred to is midnight rather than noon, the time when writers "burn the *midnight* oil," an activity which sometimes leads their work to "smell of the *lamp*," as "12 O'Clock News" will—wittingly so, I believe—using vocabulary such as "glacis," "calcareous," "*numen*" and "indigenes." Only by the time we reach the word "moon" do we connect the italicised caption on the left with the text on the right, only on that word does what we ordinarily think of as a metaphor come into existence.

> The word "metaphor" is just a highfalutin description of a very common, ubiquitous process by which all of us try to increase our understanding of the world around us. You move from the familiar to the unfamiliar. You use what you know as a tool for trying to better understand what you don't know.

That, believe it or not, was Vice President Al Gore, quoted on the subject of metaphor in a profile in *The New Yorker* of July 31, 2000. According to my other favourite bathroom reading, *The New Princeton Handbook of Poetic Terms* (or, if I'm expecting to stay for a while, *The New Princeton Encyclopedia of Poetic Terms*), the term "metaphor" means "transference":

> Metaphor is a trope, or figurative expression, in which a word or phrase is shifted from its normal uses to a context where it evokes new meanings. When the ordinary meaning of the word is at odds with the context, we tend to seek relevant features of the word and the situation that will reveal the intended meaning . . . Following I. A. Richards, we can call a word or phrase that seems anomalous the "vehicle" of the trope and refer to the underlying idea that it seems to designate as the "tenor."

I'm afraid I never fail, when I hear these terms, to think of that dreadful old shaggy dog story which ends with the line about the tenor being

Pavarotti, the vehicle a stretch limousine. That's partly, I suspect, because I've never been able to get the terms straight in my mind and, if ever I do, find them less than revelatory, simply because in many poems it's not entirely clear if Pavarotti's carrying the limo or the limo's carrying him. That uncertainty is thrown into sharp relief by "12 O'Clock News," where the basic elements of the metaphors are at once joined and disjoined, the engine simultaneously souped up, supercharged, and stripped down, spread out all over the front lawn. The conventional reading of the metaphors in "12 O'Clock News" would propose that the "tenor" is, in each instance, what we find in the italicized left-hand column, the "underlying idea" of the *"ashtray,"* say, while the "vehicle," the idea that seems anomalous—"the nest of soldiers" who "lie heaped together"—appears to the right. Or is it the other way round? Isn't "the nest of soldiers" who "lie heaped together" as strong a contender for the status of "underlying idea," or "tenor," the *"ashtray"* as likely to be the "vehicle," the "idea that seems anomalous"? It depends very much on what one takes the "subject" of "12 O'Clock News" to be. I've already suggested that the poem would seem to be most immediately "about" a writer's desk, but it may well be just as effectively read as being "about" a "small, backward country" with an "inscrutable people" who are our "opponents"—in other words, as a poem of political engagement, perhaps even a poem calling for political action. The very *in*action described in the opening sentences, whereby the *"gooseneck lamp"* is compared, feebly, to the feeble "moon" (or the "moon," feebly, to the feeble *"gooseneck lamp"*), is indicative of a sense of stagnancy and stasis which continue to hang over "12 O'Clock News." This sense of being in some sort of doldrums suggests another part of the provenance of those italicised legends, a provenance encoded in the description of a "moon" that is "dead" and "motionless":

> All in a hot and copper sky,
> The bloody sun, at noon,
> Right up above the mast did stand,
> No bigger than the *Moon.*
>
> Day after day, day after day,
> We stuck, nor breath nor *motion;*

As idle as a painted ship
Upon a painted ocean.

This is not to speak of the nod and wink of the term *"gooseneck"* in the direction of another large seagoing bird yoked to another "neck":

Ah! well a-day! what evil looks
Had I from old and young!
Instead of the cross, the *Albatross*
About my *neck* was hung.

Directly to the left of that last stanza of "The Rime of the Ancient Mariner," in the exaggerated margin, Coleridge gives an "argument," often rendered in an italic typeface, of the narrative:

The shipmates, in their sore distress, would fain throw the whole guilt on the ancient mariner: in sign whereof they hang the dead sea-bird round his neck.

Though there's a comic side to the fact that this prose "argument," or précis, is made up of twenty-seven words, four more than the twenty-three of the verse stanza on which it comments, the very fact that the prose occupies a little more space in the world would seem to substantiate Coleridge's famous observation, recorded in *Table Talk*, that prose is made up of "words in their best order," while poetry is made up of "the *best* words in their best order."

WITH COLERIDGE'S less than helpful distinction in mind, let me try now to address the point at which "12 O'Clock News" stops being verse and becomes prose. It happens somewhere between the end of the third sentence and the beginning of the fourth, almost certainly between the words "dead" and "visibility." Maybe there's a way of testing it. One may imagine, for example, a free-verse poem in which the first two lines read:

As you all know, tonight is the night
of the full moon, half the world over.

There's an obvious line break after "night." That way, the phrase "of the full moon" may be withheld so that a discovery, admittedly modest, about the nature of the "night" may be made as the reader rounds the corner. This first line has nine syllables and four uneven stresses, as does the second. The end of this second line coincides with the end of a unit of sense, "half the world over." The repetition of a nine-syllable, four-stress line establishes a pattern, a set of expectations which the poem, were it written in verse, might build upon, either concurring with or, from time to time, running counter to them.

So far so good. Let's see how the next line might go, if we were attempting to take the present words in the present order and, as if such a thing were possible, convert them into lines of free verse. This third line might read as follows:

But here the moon seems to hang

There'd be a very clever enjambment there as we were left hanging on "hang," but the line seems a bit on the short side, with only seven syllables and three stresses. Let's try again:

But here the moon seems to hang motionless

That allows another modest play on the mimesis of the line coming to rest on that key word "motionless." We've ten syllables, four stresses. Not bad. Either of these two lines would support the idea, which I mentioned earlier, that it's only with the word "moon" that we begin to make sense of the *"gooseneck lamp."* Having admired the justice of the comparison, we may now go back and understand the physical verifiability of the "moon" and the *"gooseneck lamp"* lighting only "half the world," a somewhat more engaging prospect than the basic "moon"/*"gooseneck lamp"* nexus. The net is cast a little wider, and the note struck a little wittier, in this next sentence: "It gives very little light; it could be dead."

Let's go back now to the business of "translating" this "prose poem" into verse:

But here the moon seems to hang motionless

might be followed up by:

in the sky. It gives very little light; it could be dead.

So far, fairly good. But the halting effect of the sequence of three short (two- or three-stress) phrases combined in this sentence and the next brings the verse rhythm, such as the one I've been bold enough to impose, to just that: a halt. "It gives very little light; it could be dead. Visibility is poor." The "dead" there refers both to the everyday description of a lightbulb that no longer functions and the barren, reflective surface of the moon. It also refers, *self*-reflectively, to the precise moment in this prose poem where there's an acknowledgement that the rhythms are indeed those of prose rather than verse, where it is, in terms of the verse structure, "dead" in the water. It's a measure of Bishop's genius, as well as the "endless labor" she alludes to in the *typewriter* section, that she allows the poem a further commentary on itself by following up the crucially positioned "dead" with the crucially positioned "visibility," announcing the central concern of the poem to be what I described earlier as "looking long and hard," however adverse the conditions. After the lopped-off, fitful "It gives very little light; it could be dead. Visibility is poor," comes the leisurely, fluent "Nevertheless, we shall try to give you some idea of the lay of the land and the present situation."

Let me concentrate for a moment on that phrase "the lay of the land," which, redolent as it is of the double meaning of "lay" as "lie" and "a short lyric or narrative poem intended to be sung," might well be Elizabeth Bishop's motto. One need look no further than the titles of her books—*North and South*, *A Cold Spring*, *Questions of Travel*, *Geography III*—to see that topographical map-reading might be described as her major subject. The very first poem in her first book, *North and South*, is called "The Map," and it shows her at her understated best:

The names of seashore towns run out to sea,
the names of cities cross the neighboring mountains
—the printer here experiencing the same excitement
as when emotion too far exceeds its cause.

Bishop follows up this intellectually engaging metaphor with an even more physically engaging one:

> These peninsulas take the water between thumb and finger
> like women feeling for the smoothness of yard-goods.

Not only is this metaphor engaging, it is beautifully *gauged*—in the sense that it's as finely measured as the process of fine measurement it describes.

The idea of the gauge is related to the idea of scale, and the idea of scale, appropriate or inappropriate ("as when emotion too far exceeds its cause"), is central to any number of Bishop's poems. I think of "At the Fishhouses," a poem which refers to "scales" in another sense in its description of an old man:

> There are sequins on his vest and on his thumb.
> He has scraped the *scales*, the principal beauty,
> from unnumbered fish with that black old knife,
> the blade of which is almost worn away.

There's a reference to this secondary meaning of "scales" in the *typewriter* paragraph/stanza of "12 O'Clock News," complete with a little fish, a carp, glinting there just under the surface of "es*carp*ment," an instance of subliminality vastly more probable than that supposedly presented in George W. Bush's recent television advert in which the word "rats" appeared for a thirtieth of a second before filling out to become "bureau*crats*":

> The escarpment that rises abruptly from the central plain is in heavy
> shadow, but the elaborate terracing of its southern glacis gleams
> faintly in the dim light, like fish *scales*.

I think of "Crusoe in England," with its reference to a "scale" in yet another sense, where the speaker recalls how he "made home-brew":

> I'd drink
> the awful, fizzy, stinging stuff
> that went straight to my head

and play my home-made flute
(I think it had the weirdest *scale* on earth)
and, dizzy, whoop and dance among the goats.

In the case of both these poems, "At the Fishhouses" and "Crusoe in England," there's a subliminal connection between these "scales," musical or fishy, and a scale in the sense of a "graduated table" of relative largeness or smallness. In "At the Fishhouses," the poem moves from a close-up of the "sequins," through a medium shot of a seal described as being "interested in music; like me a believer in total immersion, so I used to sing him Baptist hymns," to a wide shot of a sea:

It is like what we imagine knowledge to be:
dark, salt, clear, moving, utterly free,
drawn from the cold hard mouth
of the world, derived from the rocky breasts
forever, flowing and drawn, and since
our knowledge is historical, flowing, and flown.

This movement in "At the Fishhouses" from the specifics of harvesting to a meditation on the big picture is reminiscent of Robert Frost's method in "After Apple-Picking," from the echoes of Frost's "long two-pointed ladder" in Bishop's "steeply peaked roofs / and narrow, cleated gangplanks [that] slant up / to storerooms in the gables"; of Frost's "barrel" in Bishop's "big fish tubs completely lined / with layers of beautiful herring scales"; of Frost's "ten thousand thousand fruit" in Bishop's "unnumbered fish"; of Frost's "My instep arch not only keeps the ache, / It keeps the pressure of a ladder-round" in Bishop's "If you should dip your hand in, / your wrist would *ache* immediately, your bones would begin to *ache*," its allusive aspect underlined by the repetition, lest we miss it first time around. "Crusoe in England" has a Frostian allusion, also, one which is already hinted at in that image in "At the Fishhouses" of the "black old knife" used to scrape the scales, whereby Crusoe's knife is an artefact emblematic of art:

The knife there on the shelf—
it reeked of meaning, like a crucifix.

It lived. How many years did I
beg it, implore it, not to break?
I knew each nick and scratch by heart,
the bluish blade, the broken tip,
the lines of wood-grain on the handle . . .

This last line refers to Frost's celebrated description of "The Ax-Helve" as poem:

He showed me that the lines of a good *helve*
Were native to the *grain* before the *knife*
Expressed them, and its curves were no false curves
Put on it from without. And there its strength lay
For the hard work.

The combination of aesthetics and erotics embodied by "The Ax-Helve" is clear from subsequent descriptions of how the French-Canadian, Baptiste, "chafed its long white body / from end to end with his rough hand shut round it." It's Baptiste who comments, in the last line of the poem, "See how she's *cock* her head!" A few lines earlier, the ax-helve is described as follows:

Erect, but not without its waves, as when
The snake stood up for evil in the garden—

There's a similar connection of a tool connected with writing, as the ax-helve most certainly is, in the *typewriter eraser* paragraph/stanza of "12 O'Clock News":

At last! One of the elusive natives has been spotted! He appears to be—rather, to have been—a unicyclist-courier, who may have met his end by falling from the height of the escarpment because of the deceptive illumination. Alive, he would have been small, but undoubtedly proud and erect, with the thick, bristling black hair typical of the indigenes.

This is a wonderful instance, I think, of Bishop's trademark tendency towards the corrective phrase "—rather, to have been—," particularly when it's mimetic, once again, of the activity it describes, that of "correction" by "erasure." This sense of Bishop's poems' being made up of erasure upon erasure, blank upon blank, reminds me of Robert Lowell's evocation of her work methods in "Calling":

> Do
> you still hang your words in air, ten years
> unfinished, glued to your notice board, with gaps
> or empties for the unimaginable phrase—

There's now something faintly unimaginable, given our politically correct era, about the phrase "with the thick, bristling black hair typical of the indigenes." Even as far back as the early to mid-1970s, it would surely have raised a question about the attitude of the speaker implicit in such a description, particularly when read in conjunction with the description in the *ashtray* paragraph/stanza of "the childishness and hopeless impracticality of this inscrutable people, our opponents." Even then, it would have been difficult to read such descriptions without questioning whether they were meant to be taken at face value, if it might not be necessary to read them as being ironized. The term "inscrutable," for example, now has a racist tinge when used straightfacedly of anyone of Asian background. As I suggested earlier, the Asians who would have come most immediately to mind as "our opponents" in the early to mid-1970s would have been the Vietnamese, this group "in hideously contorted positions, all dead" familiar from the daily news, or from the poems of Robert Lowell:

> "It was at My Lai or Sonmy or something,
> it was this afternoon . . . We had these orders,
> we had all night to think about it—
> it was to burn and kill, then there'd be nothing
> standing, women, children, babies, cows, cats . . .
> As soon as we hopped the choppers, we started shooting.
> I remember . . . as we was coming up upon one area
> in Pinkville, a man with a gun . . . running—this lady . . .
> Lieutenant LaGuerre said, 'Shoot her.' I said,
> 'You shoot her, I don't want to shoot no lady.'
> She had one foot in the door . . . When I turned her,

there was this little one-month-year-old baby
I thought was her gun. It kind of cracked me up."

Now I don't suppose that anyone is about to suggest that the views expressed here are those of Robert Lowell. We have lots of indicators—the fact that the poem's within quotation marks, that the speech is so idiomatic and ungrammatical—that there's a continental divide between the content of the poem and the contention of the author. The same applies to "12 O'Clock News," though it may not be quite so obvious. However much we may recognise elements of the poem as being Bishopian—I want to say "Episcopal"—the speaker of the poem is clearly *not* the archetypical Bishop speaker. No attempt is made here to synthesise the jostling modes of discourse I pointed to earlier—the modes of the anthropologist/sociologist, the travel writer, the foreign/war correspondent, the radio/television reporter. There is no attempt to synthesise the jangling imagery of a poem which appeals at one moment to the Vietnam War, at another to the Cold War, as in the *ink-bottle* stanza/paragraph:

The natural resources of the country being far from completely
known to us, there is the possibility that this may be, or may contain,
some powerful and terrifying "secret weapon."

There's a "secret weapon" of sorts deployed here by Bishop herself, since the text set down by the pen dipped in this ink-bottle has a subtext, one that's a lot more substantial than the cliché of "the pen is mightier than the sword." The tonal breaks in the surface of "12 O'Clock News" point to an underlying stress in the speaker, of whom it might as truly be said as of the speaker in the Lowell poem that the subject matter has "kind of cracked [her] up." This may not be so immediately recognisable here because of the playful aspect of the poem (I'm reminded that the term "lay," in the "poem" sense, is thought to be related to the Latin word *ludus*), but the extreme circumstances of Bishop's speaker are no less convincing, or full of conviction, than Lowell's. It's difficult not to see a certain passion and pity in Bishop's description of the soldiers "heaped together . . . in hideously contorted positions." I write "soldiers," though I may mean "cigarette butts." The confusion is similar to the one which

Bishop raises in "Poem," as the poem immediately following "12 O'Clock News" is tellingly entitled:

> A specklike bird is flying to the left.
> Or is it a flyspeck looking like a bird?

In any event, I come away with a sense of Bishop's own pain from one particular detail in this section, that of the white cigarette papers being reminiscent of "uniforms . . . designed to be used in guerrilla warfare on the country's one snow-covered mountain peak." The exposure of these "soldiers" is emblematic of Bishop's own sense of exposure, I think, one which has a poignancy that's all the more evident when we consider the place of the cigarette in her poems and letters. In "At the Fishhouses," for example, the speaker and the old man with "the sequins on his vest and his thumb" is emotionally connected to the speaker when he "accepts a Lucky Strike" from her. In "A Cold Spring," "Greenish-white dogwood infiltrated the wood, / each petal burned, apparently, by a cigarette-butt." In a letter written while she was an undergraduate at Vassar she reports:

> It is a wonderful cold night here. I live up in a tower (that isn't a figure of speech) and so have a fine view of the stars and the smokestacks of the power plant. A ladder goes up out of our living room or lobby onto the roof and once up among the elaborate Victorian iron railings, it's a very nice spot to smoke a dishonest cigarette. We are gradually filling the gutters with butts.

This positioning of the writer of the Vassar letter ("I live up in a tower . . . and so have a fine view") is echoed precisely by the speaker of the *ashtray* paragraph/stanza:

> From our superior vantage point, we can clearly see into a sort of dugout, possibly a shell crater, a "nest" of soldiers.

There's a complex psychodrama underlying these lines. The representation of the male organ as "proud and erect, with the thick, bristling black hair" in the *typewriter eraser* paragraph/stanza is followed here by a representation of the female organ as "a sort of dugout, possibly a shell crater, a 'nest.'" Several of these images are familiar to us from other Bishop poems, including this last "nest," recognisable from "Jeronimo's House," the poem immediately preceding "Roosters" in *North and South*, in which "my house" is described as "my gray wasp's *nest* / of chewed-up paper / glued with spit" and "my love-*nest*":

> At night you'd think
>   my house abandoned.
> Come closer. You
>   can see and hear
> the writing-paper
>   lines of light

The connection between "the writing-paper" and "lines of light" is an exact prefiguring of the method of "12 O'Clock News." The words "dugout" and "crater" point us back in the direction of "Crusoe in England." Now, the first of these, "dugout," doesn't actually appear in the poem, nor indeed in *Robinson Crusoe*, but Crusoe's intellectual failure in making what, after the early nineteenth century, would be known as a dugout, in the "canoe" sense, so far from the water, is surely one of the most revealing episodes in Defoe's novel, revealing both of Crusoe's resolve and resignation:

> This grieved me heartily, and now I saw, tho' too late, the folly of beginning a work before we count the cost, and before we judge rightly of our own strength to go through with it.

Happily, the word "crater(s)" does appear in "Crusoe in England," in connection with the "volcanoes," of which there are "fifty-two" on the island, "volcanoes dead as ash-heaps." The ash*tray* paragraph/stanza, with its panoramic view of the "*dead*" soldiers, sends me to that other sense of the term "dead soldiers"—to which Lowell surely refers, perhaps unconsciously, in his use of the word "empties" in "with gaps / or empties for the unimaginable phrase" for which Bishop might wait for "ten years." There's no mention in "12 O'Clock News" of the empty "drink-bottle"—

as likely, alas, to have been a fixture of Bishop's desk as the *"ink-bottle"* we do find here. The fact that a "bottle of ink" was one of the few items Defoe's Crusoe "would have given it all for" makes me want to try to substantiate my sense of the "complex psychodrama," as I described it, underlying not only these lines about the " 'nest' of soldiers" but the earlier assertion, in the *pile of mss.* stanza/paragraph, that "There are believed to have been no casualties." Yet again, the surface jauntiness of this phrase belies the subterranean disjuncture, whereby the speaker of the poem is, in a profound sense, a "casualty," whereby the "pain" and "exposure" I associated earlier with the speaker is reminiscent of aspects of Bishop's own personal life, her alcoholism and her lesbianism, which might have left her feeling exposed. Both these aspects of Bishop's life find their fairly obvious objective correlatives in the figure of Crusoe himself, Crusoe who'd "drink / the awful, fizzy, stinging stuff / that went straight to my head," Crusoe who writes of Friday:

> If only he had been a woman!
> I wanted to propagate my kind,
> and so did he, I think, poor boy.
> He'd pet the baby goats sometimes,
> and race with them, or carry one around.
> —Pretty to watch; he had a pretty body.

The single-sex nature of any possible relationship on Crusoe's island is echoed in the singularity of the other things of the world which he catalogues (that urge to itemize and tally of which Defoe's Crusoe is a master is carried over into the itemizing of both "Crusoe in England" and "12 O'Clock News"), be it the singularity of the sun ("there was one of it and one of me"), the "one kind of berry" used to make "the awful, fizzy, stinging stuff," or the "one tree snail, a bright violet-blue / with a thin shell" which "crept over everything, / over the one variety of tree." This snail reminds us of another sense of "scale" connected in Bishop's mind with the "graduated table" I touched on earlier, the extension of the fish-scale sense of "one of the small thin membranous or horny outgrowths or modifications of the skin" to "any of the thin pieces of metal composing scale-armour," a protection against the sense of exposure in the *ash-*

tray paragraph/stanza. The relationship between this sense of "scale" as "armour" and "graduated table" is clear from several other Bishop poems, including the erotic prose poem "Rainy Season; Sub-Tropics." In the "Giant Snail" section of that poem, for example, the snail-speaker describes her shell as having a "curled white lip" and its "inside" being "smooth as silk" but complains "O! I am too big. I feel it. Pity me." That combination of inappropriate emotional and physical scale is found once again in "Crusoe in England" with its "I often gave way to self-pity" and "if I had become a giant, / I couldn't bear to think what size / the goats and turtles were" and "12 O'Clock News" with its "signboards . . . on a truly gigantic scale," its pity for the dead "soldiers" and, as I read it, a faint sense of "self-pity" associated with alcoholism and other addictive behaviour. In another section of "Rainy Season; Sub-Tropics" entitled "Strayed Crab," the crab-speaker describes itself with astonishing directness as being "the color of *wine*," sending this reader back immediately to that other, obsolete sense of the word "scale," the very first listed in the *OED*, the sense of "a drinking bowl or cup." This "Strayed Crab," who favours "the oblique, the indirect approach, and I keep my feelings to myself," describes a nearby toad as being "at least *four times my size* and yet so *vulnerable*." We've already met this "Giant Toad" in the first section of "Rainy Season; Sub-Tropics," in which the toad-speaker prefigures the line used later by the "Giant Snail," "I am too big, too big by far. Pity me." This "Giant Toad" connects once more with "12 O'Clock News" in that other addictive thing of the world, the cigarette:

Once, some naughty children picked me up, me and my two brothers. They set us down again somewhere and in our mouths they put lit cigarettes. We could not help but smoke them, to the end. I thought it was the death of me, but when I was entirely filled with smoke, when my slack mouth was burning, and all my tripes were hot and dry, they let us go. But I was sick for days.

I'll quote without comment a letter written by Bishop in November 1948 to Carley Dawson:

I don't know how to begin this letter or what to say or how to say it—but I guess the only thing to do is to take the plunge & get it over

with . . . I got to *feeling sorry for myself* at your house on Saturday &
drank up all your liquor & made myself good & *sick* & finally got
myself (under my own steam) off on Monday to a weird kind of
convalescent home here.

In his "Afterword" to *Becoming a Poet*, David Kalstone's first-rate study
of Bishop, Moore and Lowell, James Merrill quotes Kalstone's "working
notes" for the chapter he didn't live long enough to finish:

> The Real Problem for Bishop: How to turn the descriptive poem into
> a narrative—while keeping it descriptive in nature.

Something of this "Real Problem" may be seen to underlie "12 O'Clock
News," a poem of which Merrill goes on to write:

> The vast and ominous moonscape in "12 O'Clock News" is a view of
> the writer's desk. Her dexterity has never been more sinister than
> here.

Merrill's sense of the enervated evenhandedness of "12 O'Clock
News"—which he described elsewhere as "her saddest poem"—is telling.
It's as if it were somehow balanced in the scales (another key sense of
that key word), as if the effect of stasis I pointed to earlier on resulted,
yet again, from the twinned or mirrored aspect of the prose poem,
including its physical presence on the page. I'm struck in rereading
"The End of March," three poems along from "12 O'Clock News"
in *Geography III*, by the twinning and mirroring of at least one significant
fixture in the "proto-dream-house, my crypto-dream-house" presented
there:

> At night, a *grog à l'americaine*.
> I'd blaze it with a kitchen match
> and lovely diaphanous blue flame
> would waver, doubled in the window.

A few lines later, the speaker focuses on another fixture more familiar
from "12 O'Clock News":

A light to read by—perfect! But—impossible.

This, along with the evidence of a letter written by Bishop on January 23, 1979, to James Merrill, suggests that the desk in "12 O'Clock News" is set in a proto- or crypto- "dream-house":

When I think about it, it seems to me I've *rarely* written anything of any value at the desk or in the room where I was supposed to be doing it—it's always in someone else's house, or in a bar, or standing up in the kitchen in the middle of the night.

That the desk, or at least one item on it, belongs in a dreamscape is clear from Brett Millier's *Elizabeth Bishop: Life and the Memory of It*, another first-rate account of Bishop's life and work, in which Millier notes that Bishop records a dream in which she was "sleeping on a giant *typewriter*." Millier also quotes a letter from Bishop to Lowell dated January 15, 1948:

The water looks like blue gas—the harbor is always a mess, here, junky little boats all piled up, some hung with sponges and bobbles and always a few half sunk or splintered up from the most recent hurricane—*it reminds me a little of my desk.*

Millier connects this to the description, in "The Bight," of a harbor at Key West:

Some of the little white boats are still piled up
against each other, or lie on their sides, stove in,
and not yet salvaged, if they ever will be,
        from the last bad storm,
like torn-open, unanswered letters.
The bight is littered with old correspondences.

In addition to her pointing out that these "correspondences" correspond to the *"Correspondances"* of Charles Baudelaire's poem of that title, in which "L'homme y passe à travers des forêts de symboles," Millier might have pointed to the carry-over of the "correspondences" to the "*envelopes*" in "12 O'Clock News." I'll come back to Baudelaire shortly. First, though, I want to mention Brett Millier's tantalizing note on "12 O'Clock News" in which she writes that this prose poem "had been with [Bishop] in fragments of verse since her Vassar days." Bishop is herself tantalizing on this subject in an interview with George Starbuck collected in *Conversations with Elizabeth Bishop*:

> Actually that poem, "12 O'Clock News," was another that I had begun years earlier. In a different version. With rhymes, I think.

I'm indebted to Brett Millier herself, and to Dean M. Rogers of the Special Collections of Vassar College Libraries, for so graciously putting me in the way of an uncollected poem dating to at least 1950, early drafts of which are entitled both "Desk at Night" and "Little Exercise." It's a poem which refers to "a sort of landslide, / due, no doubt to erosion of the soil" on which "individual terracings shine like scales." We also find "an exhausted unicyclist" with "coarse black hair" who's "fallen on the slope." It's clear, by the way, from the drafts of "12 O'Clock News" itself, that Bishop's first instinct was to write "slope" rather than "glacis." The definition of "glacis" is revealing, though, since it refers specifically to the exposed area before a fortification, "the parapet of the covered way extended in a long slope to meet the natural surface of the ground, so that every part of it shall be swept by the fire of the ramparts" (*OED*), substantiating a reading of the underlying tendency of this prose poem towards self-protection or self-defence. A word in a similarly obscure vein as "glacis" which appears in a draft of "12 O'Clock News" is "travertine," a reference to the shale found along the Tiber, replaced in the last version by "calcareous," another sense of scale alluded to here being that of "lime-*scale*." The most intriguing note, for me, in the "*pile of mss.*" relating to "12 O'Clock News" is the little multiplication sum in the margin of the earliest page of notes, which seems to read "$25 \times 4 = 100$," perhaps a clue to the stanzaic pattern and number of lines of a possible version of the piece in verse. As we have it, the 1950 "Little Exercise/Desk at Night" poem refers to our familiar "soldiers . . . in a machine-gun nest, / in the stained and wrinkled suits designed for camouflage in the snow" and to "signboards . . . on a terrible scale." The poem ends with the key image with which "12 O'Clock News" begins:

> At the top of the terraces, is it a cemetery?
> —illegible under a dead and goose-necked moon.

IN THE NEXT CHAPTER I'll be looking at "I tried to think a lonelier Thing," a poem by that most desk-bound of poets, Emily Dickinson, whom Bishop described in an unpublished letter to Anne Stevenson, quoted by David Kalstone, as a "self-caged bird." I'll be attempting to determine the boundaries or borders between writer and reader, the extent to which the writer determines the role of the reader and, connected to that, the question of the location of the precise historical moment when we've been able to read an Emily Dickinson poem, which may have been as recently as 1998. In the meantime, I'll look very briefly at a few poems and at least one prose work related to the desk and its accoutrements in "12 O'Clock News."

The first is an influence *on* the prose poem, T. S. Eliot's "Hysteria," which I mentioned at the outset. If you recall, the speaker there describes an erotic encounter with a woman whose teeth, in an outlandish image reminiscent of some of the out-of-scale, militaristic images of "12 O'Clock News," are "accidental stars with a talent for squad-drill." At the centre of the poem is a desk of sorts, "the rusty green iron table" on which a waiter is attempting to spread a pink-and-white checked cloth, while the woman laughs uncontrollably:

> I decided that if the shaking of her breasts could be stopped, some
> of the fragments of the afternoon might be collected, and I
> concentrated my attention with careful subtlety to that end.

The heavily ironized tone here feeds directly into the Bishop poem, just as the heavily ironized tone of a prose poem by Baudelaire, "The Soup and the Clouds," feeds into the Eliot. In the Baudelaire piece, the speaker rhapsodizes on the beauty of his "darling," as Michael Hamburger translates it, who is serving him dinner, only to be brought to his senses by her saying in a *"hysterical"* voice: "Well, are you going to eat your soup or aren't you, you bloody dithering cloud-monger?" In his introduction to his translation of a selection of *Twenty Prose Poems*, Michael Hamburger suggests that "the prose poem was a medium . . . that enabled [Baudelaire] to illustrate a moral insight as briefly and as vividly as possible. Being an artist and a sensualist, he needed a medium that was not epigrammatic or aphoristic, but allowed him scope for fantasy and for that element of vagueness or suggestiveness which he considered essential to beauty."

Though Bishop was familiar with Baudelaire in French and, as we've seen, alludes to him in "The Bight" both indirectly and directly ("if one were Baudelaire"), she was even more familiar with Baudelaire's great influence, Edgar Allan Poe, who determined Baudelaire's sense of the prose poem, some would argue, to a much greater degree than Baudelaire's fellow countrymen Maurice de Guérin and Aloysius Bertrand and Arsène Houssaye. As she explained in a May 5, 1938, letter to Marianne Moore, Bishop had set out quite deliberately to write a story "according to a *theory* I've been thinking up down here out of a combination of Poe's theories and reading 17th-century prose!" On May 2 she'd written to Frani Blough to describe how she'd been "doing nothing much but reread Poe" and evolving what she describes as a "'proliferal' style." That same style, based on the notion of "the formation or development of cells by budding or division," might be said to have been at the heart of her work, including "12 O'Clock News," this prose poem collected in 1976 but first published earlier, in *The New Yorker* of March 4, 1973.

I mention that date only because it precedes by a decent interval the publication in 1975 of *Stations*, a series of prose poems by Seamus Heaney, a writer already influenced by Bishop's combination of tact and tactility. Heaney's 1972 collection, *Wintering Out*, had included "Tinder," in which the lines "We picked flints / Pale and dirt-veined, / So small finger and thumb / Ached around them" would seem to derive from that image I quoted from Bishop's "The Map" of "These peninsulas take the water *between thumb and finger* / like women feeling for the smoothness of yard-goods." In another poem in *Wintering Out*, "Limbo," a woman is described as drowning her infant "Till the frozen knobs of her wrists / Were dead as the gravel," while the last image describes how "Even Christ's palms, unhealed, / Smart and cannot fish there." These last images are drawn, I suggest, from that description in "At the Fishhouses" where "If you should dip your hand in, / your wrist would ache immediately." While the prose poems in *Stations* are most immediately influenced by Geoffrey Hill's *Mercian Hymns*, many of these "trial runs across a territory" share a sense of the grand scale, the bird's-eye view, of Bishop's "12 O'Clock News," and the method of scrupulous observation followed by even more scrupulous observation:

> The drumming started in the cool of the evening, as if the dome of air were lightly hailed on. But no. The drumming murmured from beneath that drum. The drumming didn't murmur, rather hammered.

That prose poem from Heaney's *Stations* ends with "The air grew dark, cloud-barred, a butcher's apron," an image sufficiently outlandish to count as Martian, the term used of the work of Craig Raine, who has his own distinctive take on a butcher in the first poem in his 1978 collection, *The Onion, Memory*:

> How the customers laugh! His striped apron
> gets as dirty as the mattress in a brothel . . .
> At 10, he drinks his tea with the spoon held back,
> and the *Great Eastern* goes straight to the bottom.

While Raine has prepared the way for this last image by introducing the butcher as "smoking a pencil like Isambard Kingdom Brunel," some of his readers experience the difficulty David Kalstone divined as "The Real Problem for Bishop: How to turn the descriptive poem into a narrative—while keeping it descriptive in nature." As recently as a September 15, 2000, review in the *Times Literary Supplement*, Gerald Mangan writes:

> Raine's early poems, with their aimless catalogues of unrelated similes, always reminded me of gleaming rows of kitchen utensils, designed for exhibition and not for use.

Despite the profound sense of inertia with which many readers come away from the typical poem by Craig Raine, he has, at his best, learned to mimic Bishop's method of presenting a stripped-down, startling metaphor, often involving an unexpected jump in scale, as in "The boy turns to offer me / A miniature organ of cigarettes" ("Trout Farm") or "the lighthouse stands / like a salt cellar by Magritte" ("The Meteorological Lighthouse at O").

This last leads me to a poem by a second Irish poet influenced by Bishop's characteristic method. Derek Mahon's "A Lighthouse in Maine" owes much to Bishop's blend of specificity and nonspecificity, what Marianne Moore described as her "uninsistence":

It might be anywhere—
Hokkaido, Mayo, Maine;
But it is in Maine.

You make a right
Somewhere beyond Rockland,
A left, a right,

You turn a corner and
There it is, shining
In modest glory like

The soul of Adonais.
Out you get and
Walk the rest of the way.

Elsewhere, "A Garage in Co. Cork" appeals to Bishop's "Filling Station," his "mound of never-used cement" echoing her "*cement* porch behind the pumps," her "pumps" echoed in his image of "a god . . . changing to petrol *pumps* an old man and his wife." In "Achill," there are several direct references to "12 O'Clock News," including a comparison of the "sun" to a "pearl bulb" and the line "I glance through a few thin pages and turn off the light." In the "Key West" section of "The Hudson Letter," we find not only an epigraph drawn from Bishop but a direct allusion to her as a "shy perfectionist with her painter's eye" and the line "I keep on my desk here a coarse handful of Florida sea-moss." In "The Drawing Board" (as we must now think of the poem formerly titled "Table Talk," with its nod in the direction of Coleridge), Mahon gives another version of the writer's desk from "12 O'Clock News," in which the table does the talking:

> I pray for a wood-spirit to make me dance,
> To scare your pants off and upset your balance,
> Destroy the sedate poise with which you pour
> Forth your ephemeral stream of literature.

That "poise" leads me to the "Angle*poise*," as it appears in "The Globe in North Carolina," where it "rears like a moon to shed its savage / radiance on the desolate page." It's one of these very lamps which features so prominently as a fixture on the desk of the narrator of Salman Rushdie's 1981 novel *Midnight's Children*, a novel about a critical moment in the history of a "backward country," one which the narrator describes from a "superior vantage point" while writing in an "Anglepoised pool of light"—an echo of the "gooseneck lamp" in "12 O'Clock News."

I'll end with another version of the lamp which appears in "In Prison," the story Bishop was claiming in 1938 to have written in her "proliferal" style based on Edgar Allan Poe and Sir Thomas Browne:

> The room I now occupy is papered with a not unattractive
> wallpaper, the pattern of which consists of silver stripes about an
> inch and a half wide running up and down, the same distance from
> each other. They are placed over, that is, they appear to be inside of,
> a free design of flowering vines which runs all over the wall against a
> faded brown background. Now, at night, when the lamp is turned
> on, these silver stripes catch the light and glisten and seem to stand
> out a little, or rather, in a little, from the vines and flowers,
> apparently shutting them off from me.

Bishop follows this fastidious description with the very image she associates with Emily Dickinson:

I could almost imagine myself, if it would do any good, in a large silver *bird cage*! But that's a parody, a fantasy on my real hopes and ambitions.

This sense of being at once engaged and disengaged, which somehow hangs over "12 O'Clock News," is reinforced by a sentence from a 1972 letter to Louise Crane about Dickinson:

> There's an Emily Dickinson room here in the Houghton Library—I've never had the courage to go and see it.

CHAPTER 5

I TRIED TO THINK A LONELIER THING

EMILY DICKINSON

I tried to think a lonelier Thing
Than any I had seen -
Some Polar Expiation - An Omen in the Bone
Of Death's tremendous nearness -

I probed Retrieveless things
My Duplicate - to borrow -
A Haggard comfort springs

From the belief that Somewhere -
Within the Clutch of Thought -
There dwells one other Creature
Of Heavenly Love - forgot -

I plucked at our Partition -
As One should pry the Walls -
Between Himself - and Horror's Twin -
Within Opposing Cells -

I almost strove to clasp his Hand,
Such Luxury - it grew -
That as Myself - could pity Him -
Perhaps he - pitied me -

I'LL BEGIN WITH A QUOTATION from the introduction by R. W. Franklin to his 1999 reading edition of *The Poems of Emily Dickinson*:

> Although there can be various kinds of reading editions, with different technological bases or with greater intervention in the interests of editorial taste or recognized convention, the present one follows her own practice, selecting versions that focus on her latest full effort, adopting revisions and alternative readings for which she indicated a choice, and deferring to her custom in presentation and usage. The entry into her poetry is through her idiom.

One of the senses of the phrase "the end of the poem" I'll try to explore in this chapter is that of the *"latest full effort"* of a poet in respect of his or her poem, and the extent to which we may with confidence decide that we're reading the poem we're meant to be reading. It's a question that's particularly relevant to Emily Dickinson, given the publication history of her work. Many of us were brought up on the idea that we were able to read a poem such as "I tried to think a lonelier Thing," written in 1862 or 1863, only with the publication in 1955 of the variorum edition of *The Poems of Emily Dickinson*, edited by Thomas H. Johnson, or, more likely, Johnson's reading edition of 1960. We would not, in any event, have read it prior to 1945, when it was first published in *Bolts of Memory*, edited by Mabel Loomis Todd and Millicent Todd Bingham. We're now being asked to revise all of these dates, to accept that it's only with the publication in 1998 of Franklin's variorum edition, or, more likely, his 1999 reading edition from which I quoted earlier, that we may be said to be meeting Emily Dickinson on equal terms.

However large the philosophical question raised by the publication history of Emily Dickinson's poems, I'm even more interested in the larger, more general, issue of when we read any poem, the relationship between any writer and any reader and, as I mentioned in the first chapter, "the extent to which one determines the role of the other, one completing the other." This demarcation, or lack of it, between writer and reader, reader and writer, is all the more fascinating in the case of Emily Dickinson, who seemed resigned to the idea of her poems' not being read, though she had a very powerful sense of the effect a poem might have once it *has* been read:

If I feel physically as if the top of my head were taken off, I know *that* is poetry.

Many of us will be familiar with that definition, included in Martha Gilbert Dickinson Bianchi's *The Life and Letters of Emily Dickinson*. We're less familiar, perhaps, with the definition which immediately precedes it:

If I read a book [and] it makes my body so cold no fire ever can warm me I know *that* is poetry.

I'd like to offer a suggestion or two on the hinterland of this unlikely image, and try to relate it to the numerous references to ice, snow and frost which appear in Dickinson's own poems, linking it to the phrase "Polar Expiation" we find in line 3 of "I tried to think a lonelier Thing," and suggesting that the poem is ghosted by the fate of Sir John Franklin, who, according to the April 1851 number of *Harper's*, "in command of the *Erebus* and *Terror*, having on board one hundred and thirty-eight souls, set sail from England on the 19th of May, 1845, in search of a northwest passage. On the 26th of July, sixty-eight days afterward, they were seen by a passing whaler moored to an iceberg near the centre of Baffin's Bay; since which time no intelligence of their fate has been received." I'll also try to connect this poem to Ralph Waldo Emerson's essay "Fate."

I'VE JUST USED THE OPENING LINE, "I tried to think a lonelier Thing," as the title of the poem, appealing to a convention as old as poetry in English. In the case of Emily Dickinson, her poems are conventionally numbered rather than named, so that what I entitled "I tried to think a lonelier Thing" appears as #570 of the 1,789 poems attributed to her by Franklin in 1998–99, a fact which may be rather disconcerting to readers who were familiar with it as #532 of the 1,775 attributed to her by Johnson in 1955–60. 1,775? 1,789? No matter how you look at it, that's a lot of poems. In the poem we thought we knew as #530 in Johnson, coming two before "I tried to think a lonelier Thing," Dickinson comments on her own creativity:

You cannot put a Fire out -
A Thing that can ignite
Can go, itself, without a Fan -
Upon the slowest Night -

You cannot fold a Flood -
And put it in a Drawer -
Because the Winds would find it out -
And tell your Cedar Floor -

Part of the difficulty facing any editor of Emily Dickinson is the fact that the "Flood" of poems was indeed folded, into little booklets or fascicles, and "put in a Drawer," these fascicles often including variant texts of the poems. It's worth saying from the outset that the texts of the poem we might entitle "I tried to think a lonelier Thing" may be said to be identical in both Johnson and Franklin except in two respects, that of the number assigned it and the physical duration of that characteristic Dickinsonian notation we first meet at the end of line 2. In the case of Franklin, this appears as a spaced hyphen, rather than the en or em dash with which we'd grown accustomed from Johnson. In his introduction, Franklin asserts this spaced hyphen to be "appropriate to the relative weight of her dashes in most of the poems." *Most?* This sounds rather like the imposition of an orthodoxy of the very kind against which Johnson was reacting fifty years earlier when he wrote in *his* introduction that "Dickinson used dashes as a musical device, and though some may be elongated end stops, any 'correction' would be gratuitous."

But I'm getting a little ahead of myself. Let me go back to the very first word of the poem, "I," a first word (or some version of it, such as "I'd," "I'll," "I'm," "I've") held in common by a staggering 159 of Emily Dickinson's 1,789 poems. (I adopt Franklin's numbering here, because I'm cheered by the thought that there are now fourteen more Emily Dickinson poems than I'd hitherto supposed.) That almost one in ten of her poems should begin with the personal pronoun shouldn't seem odd, I suppose, of a poet so preoccupied by her own singularity, both in the sense of "living alone or apart from the herd" and being "above the ordinary in amount, extent, worth or value" (*OED*):

I'm Nobody! Who are you?
Are you - Nobody - too?
Then there's a pair of us!
Don't tell! they'd advertise - you know!

The second stanza of this poem, one of her most famous, turns to the subject of fame:

How dreary - to be - Somebody!
How public - like a Frog -
To tell one's name - the livelong June -
To an admiring Bog!

This poem, which appears as #260 in Franklin and #288 in Johnson, is preceded in both editions by "A Clock stopped," a poem to which I'm going to return so often you may wonder if I shouldn't have made it the focus of my talk, and which I transcribe here from Franklin:

A Clock stopped -
Not the Mantel's -
Geneva's farthest skill
Cant put the puppet bowing -
That just now dangled still -

An awe came on the trinket!
The Figures hunched—with pain -
Then quivered out of Decimals -
Into Degreeless noon -

It will not stir for Doctor's -
This Pendulum of snow -
This Shopman importunes it -
While cool - concernless No -

Nods from the Gilded pointers -
Nods from the Seconds slim -
Decades of Arrogance between

The Dial life -
And Him

I quote this poem in its entirety because, unlike "I tried to think a lonelier Thing" or "I'm Nobody! Who are you?," it includes several significant variant readings. The first has to do with the spelling of the word "can't," which Johnson gives as "can't," Franklin as "cant." "I have silently corrected," writes Johnson in his introduction, "obvious misspellings," a category into which "cant" would certainly seem to fall. In *his* introduction, Franklin quotes Dickinson's 1854 letter to her brother, Austin:

I spelt a word wrong in this letter, but I know better, so you need'nt think you have caught me.

In this very sentence, she misspells "needn't," of course, in keeping with her frequent misplacing of contractions (hav'nt, did'nt) or ignoring them, as in "cant." But this "cant" has another resonance, I think, having to do with its *OED* definition "to bring or put (a thing) into an oblique position, so that it is no longer vertical or horizontal," a definition quite appropriate in the context of a poem about a "Degreeless noon," about a "Dial life" being out of true, about a clockwork "No" at the end of a line resounding in the "Nods from the Gilded pointers - " and the "Nods from the Seconds slim - " at the beginnings of the next two lines. One of the reasons why we might notice that "No" has to do with Dickinson's own system of "Gilded pointers," the hyphens and dashes I mentioned earlier on, which prod us to and fro, offering us alternative readings from word to word and line to line. The stubby little hyphen following the "Gilded pointers" in Franklin's text is physically a little less "pointerly," perhaps, than the longer dash in Johnson, but, as if to make up for it, Franklin adds a dash between "hunched" and "with" in the line "The Figures hunched—with pain - " where Johnson made do with a comma between "hunched" and "with pain." This allows us to read the line more fully in the sense both of the "Figures hunched" (a) *because of* "pain" and (b) *in the company of* "pain."

Another, more significant, difference in the Franklin and Johnson texts occurs in the lines "It will not stir for Doctor's - / This Pendulum of snow - ," where Franklin gives us "Doctor's," Johnson "Doctors." Here

Franklin chooses not to rationalise the mispunctuated "Doctor's" in favor of a line which would be more immediately intelligible—"It will not stir for Doctors"—for reasons he sets down, once again, in his introduction:

> If the orthography, capitalization, punctuation, and usage should seem problematical, they are nonetheless Dickinson's, not the editor's or the publisher's, not, except indirectly, society's—agents with whom she conducted no negotiation toward public norms for her poetry.

It's in this sense, then, that Franklin offers us "versions *that focus on her latest full effort*" without exactly presenting us with one—without, at least, presenting us with anything like what we might have thought of as an exact version, without presenting us with anything like what we might have thought of as a reading edition, certainly not one in which the reader won't play a more active role than is thought in many quarters to be appropriate.

I'll come back to that a little later. Just now, I want to try to move past the first word of "I tried to think a lonelier Thing," on which I seem to be "dangling still" like "This Pendulum of snow" in "A Clock stopped." *This Pendulum of snow.* It brings to mind the phrase "thy rope of sands," from George Herbert's "The Collar," which, along with Herbert's other great techno-theological poem "The Pulley," lies somewhat behind "A Clock stopped." *This Pendulum of snow.* The capitalization of "Pendulum" rather than "snow" seems particularly perverse of Emily Dickinson, given that "snow" may sometimes stand for poetry (and poetry publication), as we remember from #709 in Johnson, #788 in Franklin:

> Publication - is the Auction
> Of the Mind of Man -
> Poverty - be justifying
> For so foul a thing
>
> Possibly - but We - would rather
> From Our Garret go
> White - unto the White Creator -
> Than invest - Our *Snow* -

Having been given a little cant ("a sudden movement which tends to, or results in, tilting up or turning over," *OED*) by the phrase "so foul a thing," I'm finally tilting up and turning over towards the end of line 1 and its "lonelier Thing / Than any I had seen," followed, of course, by the "gilded pointer" of the hyphen, a very particular kind of "pointer" we might recognise from "Through the straight pass of suffering," as Franklin has it in #187, having straightened out the strait in "Through the strait pass of suffering," as Johnson had it in #792:

Through the strait pass of suffering—
The Martyrs—even—trod.
Their feet—upon Temptation—
Their faces—upon God—

A stately—shriven—Company—
Convulsion—playing round—
Harmless—as streaks of Meteor—
Upon a Planet's Bond—

Their faith the everlasting troth—
Their Expectation—fair—
The Needle—to the North Degree—
Wades—so—thro' polar Air!

The "gilded pointer" I'm thinking of is the "Needle—to the North Degree—" which we might connect with the "needle" to which Dickinson refers in her June 7th, 1862, letter to Thomas Wentworth Higginson, responding to his inability to steer a course through her poems:

The Sailor cannot see the North—but knows the *Needle* can

We might connect that "see" with the "lonelier Thing / Than any I had *seen*," the "polar Air!" of "Through the strait pass of suffering" with "Some *Polar* Expiation" here in line 3 of "I tried to think a lonelier Thing." *Some Polar Expiation*. In what sense might expiation, "the action of ceremonially purifying from guilt or pollution," be "polar"? One sense of "polar," recorded by the *OED* as first appearing in the 1850 edition of Sir

William Grove's *On the Correlation of Physical Forces*, has to do with the description of molecules "regularly or symmetrically arranged in a definite direction (as though under the action of a magnetic force)," and would seem to connect with the magnetic force attracting the compass needle. Another sense, first appearing in the 1862 edition of the Grove, has to do with "forces acting in two opposite directions" and mentions "cases where a dual or polar character of force is manifested." This sense would account partly for the idea of the *"Duplicate"* in line 6, "and Horror's *Twin* - / Within *Opposing Cells*" in lines 14–15, the duality at the heart of the poem by the poet whom I described earlier as "singular." The main sense of the word "cells" with which we tend to associate Emily Dickinson is that referred to by her beloved Wordsworth:

Nuns fret not at their convent's narrow room;
And hermits are contented with their *cells*

Let's linger for a moment on the image of Dickinson as a "hermit" in her cell in the house in Amherst, Massachusetts, the house described by Diana Fuss in her brilliant essay on "Interior Chambers: The Emily Dickinson Homestead," published in 1998 in *differences: A Journal of Feminist Cultural Studies*. After reminding us that "the domestic interior as private haven, where an individual could withdraw from public view, was a relatively new cultural ideal when Dickinson began writing her poetry," Fuss suggests that "for Dickinson, interiors are public places" and extends this to a reading of the poems based on the idea that Dickinson's "poetic vision [is] frankly at odds with conventional understandings of space," and that "even the poet's celebrated notion of Circumference . . . operates as a sign less of an increasingly elusive exteriority than an infinitely expanding interiority." With Gaston Bachelard and *The Poetics of Space* as her own Baedeker, Fuss conducts us from room to room of the Dickinson homestead, reminding us of various features of the house and their sociological and psychological implications. Let me first detach and then try to draw together two of these features. The first is the Franklin stove, named after its inventor, the one and only Benjamin Franklin, who set out to design a freestanding cast-iron fireplace that could be situated away from a wall, thereby more effectively heating a room. Emily Dickinson had been familiar with the Franklin stove from her student days at Mount Holyoke Female Seminary, which she'd attended in 1847–48, and where it was a feature of each student's room. Now, as Diana Fuss reminds us, the impact of the installation in 1855 in the Dickinson homestead of a number of Franklin stoves was considerable:

> The improved heating arrangements dramatically reconfigured social relations within the home, decentralizing the family and creating new zones of privacy. More than any other revolution of the domestic interior, the Franklin stove made it possible for individual members *within* the family to seek privacy *from* the family.

The second feature of the Dickinson homestead to which I want to draw your attention also dated from the 1855 renovation—"a hallway with five exits that," as Diana Fuss tells us, "Dickinson called the 'Northwest Passage.' " What I want to try to suggest here is that much of Emily Dickinson's sense of "Some Polar Expiation" may be traced directly to a near version of that phrase, some Polar *Expedition*, particularly one undertaken by Benjamin Franklin's namesake, Sir John Franklin (1786–1847), the English rear admiral and explorer whose disappearance was the subject of that April 1851 *Harper's* article I quoted earlier:

> As month after month passed away without bringing any tidings, an anxious and painful sympathy sprung up in the public mind, and the British Government determined that searches for the missing vessels should be made in three different quarters by three separate expeditions fitted out for that purpose. One quarter, however, that region known as Boothia, where there was a probability of success, was beyond the scope of these expeditions, and Lady Franklin determined to organize an expedition to explore that region.

It wouldn't be clear what happened to Sir John Franklin until eight years after this 1851 *Harper's* article. I turn to the *Encyclopaedia Britannica* for the end of the story:

> In 1859 Capt. Leopold McClintock, sent by Lady Franklin, finally disclosed the fate of the expedition. Besides skeletons and various articles in King William Island, and reports from an eskimo in

Boothia, a record was found telling the history of the expedition up to April 25, 1848. In 1845–46 they had wintered at Beechey Island, having ascended the Wellington channel to latitude 77 degrees, and returned by the west side of Cornwallis Island. They had navigated Peel and Franklin straits but had been stopped by ice coming down McClintock channel (then unknown). An addendum dated April 25, 1848, signed by J. Fitzjames and F.R.M. Crozier, said that the ships were deserted on April 22, 1848, having been beset since Sept. 1846. Franklin died on June 11, 1847, preceded by 24 officers and men. The record stated that they would start the next day for Back river. Strength must have failed; an Eskimo woman said that they fell down and died as they walked. Franklin's expedition is credited with having discovered the northwest passage, as the point the ships reached was within a few miles of the known waters of America.

The northwest passage here refers to the sea route along the northern coast of North America between the Atlantic and Pacific oceans. The "Northwest Passage" which Emily Dickinson may be "credited with having discovered" in the Dickinson homestead is connected, I think, to "the strait *pass* of suffering," in which we met "A stately - shriven - Company - / Convulsion - playing round - / Harmless - as streaks of Meteor - / Upon a Planet's Bond - ." That poem was written in 1861, two years after the fate of Sir John Franklin was discovered and made public, and its focus on "faith" and "expectation" in that image of "The Needle" that "Wades - so - thro' polar Air!" relates to Emily Dickinson's own faith in, and expectation of, her poems' being discovered and made public. As we saw earlier, that faith and expectation wouldn't be well founded in, or met by, Thomas Wentworth Higginson, which is precisely why, a year later, she'd appeal to the same image I quoted earlier:

The Sailor cannot see the North—but knows the Needle can

This image of the needle is one which readers of Sir John Franklin's great 1824 text, *Narrative of a Journey to the Shores of the Polar Sea in 1819, 20, 21 and 22*, would have been familiar, particularly if they'd got as far as the "appendix containing geognostical observations, and remarks on the aurora borealis." They'd have been even more familiar with it had the publishers got as far as publishing it, had they "not been induced," as they tell us in a footnote, "to omit the greater part of the Appendix . . . from a conviction that its contents, besides being uninteresting to the general reader, would so greatly enhance the price of the work as effectually to retard its general circulation and utility." Even so, there's a page and a half on "the action of the Aurora upon the compass-*needle*" by Sir John Franklin.

In another poem written in either 1861 or 1862, #290 in Johnson, #319 in Franklin (R. W., that is, not Sir John nor Benjamin), Emily Dickinson uses the aurora borealis as an emblem of unrecognized "Majesty":

> Of Bronze—and Blaze—
> The North—Tonight—
> So adequate—it forms—
> So preconcerted with itself—
> So distant—to alarms—

The poem ends with an assured sense of Emily Dickinson's "Majesty" being recognized by posterity:

> My Splendors, are Menagerie—
> But their Competeless Show
> Will entertain the Centuries
> When I, am long ago,
> An Island in dishonored Grass—
> Whom none but Beetles—know.

I quote Johnson's version of this poem, by the way, because the end of Franklin's reads:

> When I, am long ago,
> An Island in dishonored Grass -
> Whom none but *Daisies*, know -

By this stage, I'm beginning to wonder about the wisdom of Franklin's approach. "Whom none but Daisies, know" may be "the latest full effort," but is it the *best* effort? Does it convey to the same extent "An

Omen in the Bone / of Death's tremendous nearness"? I think not. "Beetles" is surely a lot more engaging than "Daisies." I wonder if Franklin (R. W.) has, in his use in his introduction of that phrase "the latest full effort" an unconscious memory of another little poem on the aurora borealis, one he lists as #1,002:

Aurora is the *effort*
Of the Celestial Face
Unconsciousness of Perfectness
To simulate, to Us.

By coincidence, Johnson had also listed this poem as #1,002, reminding us only of how rarely Franklin and himself are in sync, despite each's avowal of a chronological presentation of the poems. In the case of Emily Dickinson, of course, the sense of "chronological" often has to do less with the dating of a poem by its year of composition than by the year it was stitched into one of those fascicles. Here's Dorothy Huff Oberhaus, writing in the introduction to her study of *Emily Dickinson's Fascicles: Method and Meaning*:

> In his 1955 variorum, Thomas H. Johnson attempted to identify the poet's original arrangement; then Ralph W. Franklin in his 1967 *Editing of Emily Dickinson* and a series of subsequent articles revised Johnson's ordering and added a number of missing poems. But the poet's original arrangement was not restored until 1981 with the publication of Franklin's *Manuscript Books of Emily Dickinson*. Guided by such evidence as stationery imperfections, smudge patterns, and puncture marks where the poet's needle had pierced the paper to bind them, Franklin restored the fascicles to their original state.

While it may be that the ordering of the poems in Franklin's edition reflects the ordering of the original forty fascicles, it's not necessarily the end of the story, certainly not in terms of the contextualization of an individual poem. It would seem that, while there's no consistency in the texts immediately preceding "I tried to think a lonelier Thing,"

Johnson and Franklin seem to be once again in sync with "Two Butter-flies went out at Noon." Here's the version we remember as #533 in Johnson:

> Two Butterflies went out at Noon—
> And waltzed upon a Farm—
> Then stepped straight through the Firmament
> And rested, on a Beam—
>
> And then—together bore away
> Upon a shining Sea—
> Though never yet, in any Port—
> Their coming, mentioned—be—
>
> If spoken by the distant Bird—
> If met in Ether Sea
> By Frigate, or by Merchantman—
> No notice—was—to me

One could be forgiven for thinking that the disappearance of Sir John Franklin and his crew might underlie the imagery of this poem, and the idea of the survival of a catastrophe is certainly something it holds in common with the poem as printed by Franklin:

> Two Butterflies went out at Noon
> And waltzed opon a Farm
> And then espied Circumference
> And caught a ride with him -
> Then lost themselves and found themselves
> In eddies of the sun
> Till Gravitation missed them -
> And both were wrecked in Noon -
> To all surviving Butterflies
> Be this Fatuity
> Example - and monition
> To entomology -

Apart from the first two lines, the versions of "Two Butterflies went out at Noon" are absolutely different. There's no hint from R. W. Franklin, in his reading edition, that such divergent texts might exist for *one* poem. We recognize how Franklin might have come to settle on this version as "her latest full effort," particularly since it includes the reference to what Diana Fuss referred to as Dickinson's "celebrated notion of Circumference," the "entomology" which might connect us to the "Beetles/Daisies" dilemma, the idea that both butterflies "were wrecked in Noon" connecting us to the "Degreeless noon" of "A Clock stopped," yet it doesn't quite account for why Johnson's version seems to have vanished without trace like the members of the polar expedition to whom, as I mentioned earlier, it may allude.

For those of you concerned that my suggestion that Dickinson subliminally connects "expiation" and "expedition" might be a shade outlandish, I would suggest that such outlandish near versions are common in her writing. By way of example, we need look no further than the poem Franklin prints immediately before "I tried to think a lonelier Thing"—the poem which begins "A precious - mouldering pleasure - 'tis - / To meet an Antique Book - " and ends with the lines:

Old Volumes shake their *Vellum* Heads
And tantalize just so

Even more outlandish than the "Volumes/Vellum" play is Dickinson's play on the relationship between the personal pronoun "I" and the word "eye." Since we don't seem to be making much progress through this poem, we might as well retrace our steps and go back to lines 1 and 2:

I tried to think a lonelier Thing
Than any *eye* had seen

LET ME TRY to bring together some of these farflung images having to do with the polar and the poetical, the private and the public, the relationship between reader and writer. I'll begin with another case of that slippage between "I" and "eye," in the first line of #633 in Franklin's edition, which brings us back rather neatly to the subject of the fascicles and, as Dorothy Huff Oberhaus termed it, "where the poet's needle had pierced the paper to bind them":

> I *saw* no Way - The Heavens were *stitched* -
> I felt the Columns close -
> The Earth reversed her Hemispheres -
> I touched the Universe -

The fact that the *"Heavens"* are stitched connects Dickinson's verse (the word appears twice in that single stanza, in *"reversed"* and *"universe"*) with the sky, the sky literally and metaphorically. The heavens, seen or unseen, are the province of the astronomer and the theologian, as is evident from #957 in Franklin:

> When the Astronomer stops seeking
> For his Pleiad's Face -
> When the lone British Lady
> Forsakes the Arctic Race -

It's difficult not to think of that "lone British Lady" as Lady Franklin, underwriting the series of expeditions including the one by Captain McClintock which disclosed the fate of her husband in his "Arctic Race," making that fate front-page news in September 1859. I was very happy to discover that, in his discussion of "When the Astronomer stops seeking" in his study of *Emily Dickinson's Reading*, Jack L. Capps contends that the poem derives from Dickinson's reading of that 1851 article in *Harper's* which I quoted earlier. The story of the "Voyage in Search of Sir John Franklin," as the article was entitled, is one Dickinson must have followed with keen interest, as the imagery of a poem written in 1860 would suggest:

> As if some little Arctic flower
> Upon the polar hem -
> Went wandering down the Latitudes
> Until it puzzled came
> To continents of summer -

To firmaments of sun -
To strange, bright crowds of flowers -
And birds, of foreign tongue!
I say, As if this little flower
To Eden, wandering in -
What then? Why nothing,
Only, your *inference* therefrom!

The word "inference" is rendered in italics by Franklin, as befits its extraordinary status. I describe it as "extraordinary" because if we extend the subject matter of this poem having to do with a work of art, a flower embroidered on a *"hem,"* a work of art coming "puzzled" into an indeterminate context, "Eden," in which its significance as a simile or metaphor (*"as if"*) remains to be "puzzled," there does seem to be remarkable *"Latitude"* allowed the reader in the typical Emily Dickinson poem, a remarkable allowance for the extent to which the reader addressed as "you" may make "your *inference* therefrom," a remarkable allowance for the terms of the covenant between writer and reader who's offered the choice between "Daisies" and "Beetles" *in the same text*, then between substantially differing versions of "Two Butterflies went out at Noon." I'm prompted to use this word "covenant" partly because of Emily Dickinson's appeal here to "Eden," since Eden is the site of the Covenant of Works and the Covenant of Grace, the two relations which are represented as subsisting between God and man, before and since the Fall, both of which are connected to the promise of eternal life. It's precisely because of events in Eden that "Some Polar *Expiation*" is required to free man from death, the "cool - concernless No - " which "nods" towards the "Why *nothing*, / Only, your *inference* therefrom!" In order to "puzzle" a way through this pack ice towards what our "inference" might be, let me stay for a moment with the *"polar* hem" on which the flower was, like the poems in Emily Dickinson's fascicles, stitched with a needle. ("We seemed completely *hemmed* in on every side," the *Harper's* article notes, "by heavy packed ice.") The Pole represents constancy, the force in which, as we saw earlier, we might have "faith" and "expectation," with which we might have a covenant. In the second stanza of "When the Astronomer stops seeking," Emily Dickinson uses this very term:

When the Astronomer stops seeking
For his Pleiad's face -
When the lone British Lady
Forsakes the Arctic Race -

When to his *Covenant* Needle
The Sailor doubting turns -
It will be amply early
To ask what treason means -

The fascicles upon which Emily Dickinson uses her own version of "Covenant *needle*" are connected to a near version of that word, the needle-like *icicles* such as we find in Johnson #768 or Franklin #493:

Icicles upon my soul
Prickled Blue and cool

That poem includes not only references to "Sleet" and "frost" but another play on "I" and "eye," as is the case yet again in Johnson #853, Franklin #961:

When One has given up One's life
The parting with the rest
Feels easy, as when day lets go
Entirely the West

The Peaks, that lingered last
Remain in Her regret
As scarcely as the Iodine
Upon the Cataract -

Emily Dickinson, herself beset by sight problems, connects the cataract of the eye, "an opacity of the crystalline lens," with the cataract, "a waterfall" (perhaps a frozen one), so that there is no "Partition," to borrow a word from line 12 of "I tried to think a lonelier Thing," between the "I" of the first person singular and the landscape. The word "cataract" has a particular resonance for Dickinson, of course, since its primary meaning is "flood-gates," specifically the "flood-gates of heaven," holding back a "Flood" of the sort "you cannot fold . . . and put . . . in a Drawer." Where does that leave the reader in his or her "inference"? Let's see. The personal pronoun "I" is connected to the landscape, often a snowy one, which is connected, we recall, to the "Snow" of poetry, which is in turn connected to the notion of death—what she terms elsewhere "the White Exploit"—which is in turn connected to God—"the White Creator"—which is in turn connected to a notion of immortality of the soul, as is clear from Johnson #927, Franklin #958:

> Absent Place - an April Day -
> Daffodils a'blow
> Homesick curiosity
> To the *Souls that snow* -
>
> Drift may block within it
> Deeper than without -
> Daffodil delight but
> Him it duplicate -

The "Absent Place" mentioned there may be another version of Eden, a place notable for its placelessness. That idea of the placeless place is extended by Emily Dickinson in Johnson #963, Franklin #824, a poem which, in line 1, presents us with a mirror image of a key phrase in line 4 of "I tried to think a lonelier Thing":

> A *nearness* to *Tremendousness* -
> An Agony procures -
> Affliction ranges Boundlessness -
> Vicinity to Laws
>
> Contentment's quiet Suburb -
> Affliction cannot stay
> In Acres - It's Location
> Is Illocality -

Meanwhile, the idea that this "Absent Place" is somewhere where "Drifts may block *within* it / Deeper than *without*" is connected to #451 in Johnson, #450 in Franklin:

> The *Outer* - from the *Inner*
> Derives its Magnitude -
> 'Tis Duke, or Dwarf, according
> As in the Central Mood -

Now, if we were to try to sing those four lines, we might quickly come up with another sense of the line "Him it duplicate," just as we get to the end of line 4 of "I tried to think a lonelier Thing" with a sense that, like so many of Emily Dickinson's poems, it might duplicate a *hymn*. The "Tremendousness" in line 4 seems to refer not only to Death but to another Him, God the Maker, who will sit in judgement on the "Souls that snow," determining whether or not they will find Immortality in the Kingdom of Heaven. (The *Harper's* article, by the way, refers to the Arctic snow and ice as being *"everlasting."*) This business of entering the Kingdom of Heaven is a difficult prospect, as Christ is recorded as pointing out in Matthew 7:13–14:

> Enter by the narrow gate, since the road that leads to destruction is wide and spacious, and many take it; but it is a narrow gate and a hard road that leads to life.

Dickinson alludes to this passage in Johnson #234, Franklin #249:

> "You're right 'the way *is narrow*' -
> and 'difficult the Gate' -
> And 'few there be' - Correct again -
> That 'enter in thereat' -

The "narrow way" is, I think, related to "the strait/straight pass of suffering," the poem in which "The Needle - to the North Degree - / Wades - so - thro' polar Air!," as well as "A *narrow* Fellow in the Grass" who resulted in the Fall of Man which now requires "Some Polar Expiation."

(You'll notice that the phrase "An Omen in the Bone" in line 3 is picked up by the last stanza of "A narrow Fellow": "But never met this Fellow / Attended or alone / Without a tighter Breathing / *And Zero at the Bone*," both suggesting the chill of death.) In lines 5–7 of "I tried to think a lonelier Thing," it looks very much as if Emily Dickinson is combining Matthew 7:3–14 with Matthew 19:24, another passage having to do with heaven and a needle:

It is easier for a camel to go through the eye of a needle, than for a rich man to enter the kingdom of heaven.

Trying to make sense of lines 5–7 is difficult, like looking for a needle in a haystack, yet another idea operating just under their surface, as is clear both from the phrase "*probed* Retrieveless things" and from one meaning of "Haggard," "a hay-yard" in which the harvest is stored, in which some "comfort springs" for the "good seed" of Matthew 13:24:

The kingdom of heaven may be compared to a man who sowed good seed in his field.

This comfort is "haggard" in a more conventional sense, that deriving from the meaning of the word as a "wild (female) hawk caught when in her adult plumage," that of "in early use applied to a 'wild' expression of the eyes, afterwards to the injurious effect upon the countenance of privation, want of rest, fatigue, anxiety, terror or worry," all par for the course for the explorer of the end of the earth, or the poem. According to the *OED*, John Tyndall had referred to "the *haggard* expression upon the countenance of our guide" in his *The Glaciers of the Alps*, a book published in 1860, two or three years before this poem was written. If for no other reason, we know that we're dealing here with a quite unconventional sense of "comfort" from the discomfiting, unresolved nature of these lines, just three of them in a stanza in which we've already come to expect four. I want to suggest that this lack of resolution is mirrored not only by the form but by the figure of the "Duplicate" there in line 6, a term we recognize from the last line of "Absent Place - an April Day - "—"Him in *Duplicate*." This idea of the "duplicate" may have been taken by Dickinson from a passage in Ralph Waldo Emerson's "Fate," published in *The Conduct of Life* in 1860 (once again, two or three years before this poem was written), in which Emerson writes:

> Man is the arch machine of which all these shifts drawn from himself are toy models. He helps himself on each emergency by copying or *duplicating* his own structure, just so far as the need is.

This notion of a man and a "Duplicate" connects with another sense of the word "cell," one also used by Emerson earlier on in "Fate," when he writes "Now and then one has a new *cell* or camarilla opened in his brain"—a "cell" in the biological, anatomical or botanical sense. (Emerson also describes these discrete cells as "vesicles," of which the term "fascicles" may be an unconscious echo.) One may explore these cells, with their "cell-walls" (this last term first used, according to the *OED*, in the late 1840s), by means of the microscope praised in Johnson #185, Franklin #202:

> "Faith" is a fine invention
> For Gentlemen who *see*!
> But Microscopes are prudent
> In an Emergency

That "Faith" brings us back to what I described earlier as Emily Dickinson's "faith in, and expectation of, her poems' being discovered and made public," a process that requires a second reader, a "Duplicate" of the first reader, who happens to be the writer, of the poem, as in the "pair of us" in "I'm Nobody! Who are you?" That "I tried to think a lonelier Thing" might be a poem "about" the process of reading is suggested by its being positioned just after "A precious - mouldering pleasure - 'tis - / To meet an Antique *Book* - " and just before "Two Butterflies went out at Noon," a poem in which the "Butterflies" are set against the "reading" of butterflies—"entomology." The sense of "Circumference" in the lines "Two Butterflies went out at Noon / And waltzed upon a Farm / And then espied *Circumference* / And caught a ride with him - " is the sense of immortality, be it of the soul or the poem. As she writes in Johnson #827, Franklin #820:

The only news I know
Is Bulletins all Day
From Immortality.

The immortality of the poem requires not only a reader but a reader able to make "judgements," to distinguish the good seed from the bad, the wheat from the chaff, the sheep from the goats. This reader will have made a "covenant" with the writer, one which will involve his or her taking an active role in the process of remaking the poem, one for whom there will be no "Partition" between private and public, inner and outer, corridor and Northwest Passage, Franklin stove and Franklin expedition. This reader is one capable of the "double consciousness" for which Emerson argues so memorably in "Fate":

> One key, one solution to the mysteries of human condition, one
> solution to the old knots of fate, freedom, and foreknowledge, exists;
> the propounding, namely, of the double consciousness. A man must
> ride alternately on the horses of his private and public nature, as the
> equestrians in the circus throw themselves nimbly from horse to
> horse, or plant one foot on the back of one and the other foot on the
> back of the other.

The word "key" used there by Emerson appears here subliminally in the "Duplicate" in line 6, since it is of a key that the term "duplicate" is most commonly used. I keep coming back to that second "key" stanza, to the "key" word "Duplicate," because it's in that stanza, once again, on another "key" word—"springs"—that the poem signals to its explorer/ prober/reader that he or she must enact the very leap of faith which, it seems more and more, is the poem's "subject." The poem itself "springs / From the belief that Somewhere" there is a "Creature" capable of that very leap of faith, of meeting pity with pity, as seems to be suggested by the end of the poem. Dickinson uses the word "pity" in the opening line of Johnson #588, Franklin #394, written in 1861 or 1862:

> I cried at *pity* - not at Pain -
> I heard a woman say

"Poor Child" - and something in her voice
Convinced me - of me -

So long I fainted, to myself
It seemed the common way,
And Health, and Laughter, curious things
To look at, like a Toy -

This "like a Toy" sends us back to a phrase in Emerson's "Fate" I quoted earlier—"Man is the arch machine of which all these shifts drawn from himself are *toy* models," some powered by "springs" in another sense, some by batteries with "opposing Cells" in the sense of positive and negative. It turns out that "Fate" will have had an influence on several images in "When One has given up One's life," including "as when day lets go / Entirely the West," which is borrowed from Emerson's "I know not whether there be, as is alleged, in the upper region of our atmosphere, a permanent *westerly* current which carries with it all atoms which rise to that height," and "as scarcely as the Iodine / Upon the cataract," which is borrowed from "So the great man . . . is the impressionable man;—of a fibre irritable and delicate, like *iodine* to light. He feels the infinitesimal attractions. His mind is righter than others because he yields to a current so feeble as can be felt only by a needle delicately poised." This last brings us back to the "Covenant *Needle*" in "When the astronomer stops seeking." In another section of "Fate," Emerson writes:

At the conjuror's, we detect the hair by which he moves his puppet, but we have not eyes sharp enough to descry the thread that ties cause and effect.

The combination of "toy" and "puppet" imagery drawn from Emerson may also inform some of the images of the "*puppet* bowing" in "A Clock stopped":

An awe came on the trinket!
The Figures hunched - with pain -

That "pain" is picked up by "I cried at Pity - not at *Pain -* " and both derive, I suggest, from Emily Dickinson's reading of "Fate," particularly the phrase at the end of the "One key, one solution" paragraph I quoted earlier:

> So when a man is the victim of his fate . . . he is to rally on his
> relation to the Universe, which his ruin benefits. Leaving the daemon
> who suffers, he is to take sides with the Deity who secures universal
> benefit by his *pain.*

The "Deity," in other words, who has performed "the action of ceremonially purifying from guilt or pollution," the action of expiation or catharsis, in the Aristotelian sense of the purging of the emotions of pity and fear, or pity and terror, the second of which is subliminally present, I suspect, in the name of one of Franklin's ships. We certainly have a version of "fear" or "terror" in the "Horror" of line 14, two versions of "pity" in lines 18 and 19, suggesting yet again that part of this poem's subject matter has to do with the process of making art. If man is made in God's image, God is also made in man's image, reader made in the image of writer, writer in the image of reader, each striving to clasp the other's hand. One of the reasons why, in line 16, the speaker "*almost* strove to clasp his Hand" is that, as we know from Johnson #1,551, Franklin #1,581, the Deity "who secures universal benefit by his pain" has suffered a significant wound:

> Those - dying then,
> Knew where they went -
> They went to God's Right Hand -
> That Hand is *amputated* now
> And God cannot be found -

Now, that poem was written in 1882, twenty years after "I tried to think a lonelier Thing," but the "amputated" there reminds me of an aspect of this present poem to which I've managed not to allude—that it was written at the height of the American Civil War, in the same year as the bloody battles of Chancellorsville, Gettysburg, Vicksburg and Chattanooga. There's no doubt that a strand of "I tried to think a lonelier

Thing" refers to that "Horror" involving "Polar" opposites, North and South, between whom there falls a "Partition." This idea of "amputation" is, more significantly, the logical conclusion of the effects of frostbite. This frostbite may result in a body being "so cold no fire can ever warm" it, which we recall Emily Dickinson having given as one way of recognizing poetry, and it connects yet again with the idea of "Polar Expiation" at the heart of "I tried to think a lonelier Thing," a poem which, like the other 1,774, or 1,788, written by Emily Dickinson, will enjoy an afterlife long after it has seemed to have come to an end.

CHAPTER 6

I REMEMBER

STEVIE SMITH

It was my bridal night I remember,
An old man of seventy-three
I lay with my young bride in my arms,
A girl with t.b.
It was wartime, and overhead
The Germans were making a particularly heavy raid on Hampstead.
What rendered the confusion worse, perversely
Our bombers had chosen that moment to set out for Germany.
Harry, do they ever collide?
I do not think it has ever happened,
Oh my bride, my bride.

IN MY DISCUSSION of Emily Dickinson's "I tried to think a lonelier
Thing," I mentioned Gaston Bachelard's great study *The Poetics of Space*,
in which Bachelard muses to such wonderful effect on the house from
garret to cellar, the significance of the hut, the house and the universe, on
nests, shells, corners, miniature, the phenomenology of roundness, on
the concepts of "intimate immensity" and "the dialectics of outside
and inside," these last two particularly appropriate to so many poems by
Dickinson:

There is a solitude of space
A solitude of sea
A solitude of death, but these
Society shall be
Compared with that profounder site
That polar privacy
A soul admitted to itself—
Finite infinity.

In my discussion of Stevie Smith's "I Remember," a poem which appeared in her 1957 collection *Not Waving But Drowning*, I'll appeal once again to Bachelard for an elucidation of what one might call *The Poetics of Airspace*, a notion which seems to be central to this strange little poem of sexual politics which belongs, most immediately, to a line of English lyric running back to Edward Thomas and Thomas Hardy. I'll appeal as well to the "finite infinity" of Emily Dickinson and Elizabeth Bishop, the second of whom was, I'm convinced, familiar with *The Poetics of Space* while she was writing the poems of *Geography III*. I'll be trying to make sense of some of the ideas raised by Giorgio Agamben in his unfortunately titled *The End of the Poem: Studies in Poetics*, a book published in English in 1999, the same year I embarked on this series of essays under their strikingly similar rubric. And I'll be combining some of Agamben's ideas about limits with some of Bachelard's in an attempt to address the sense of the phrase "the end of the poem" I'll be concentrating on here—that's to say the function of gender in the writing or reading of a poem, the question of whether there is indeed an "end" in gender.

It's a question raised by the opening of "I Remember":

It was my bridal night I remember,
An old man of seventy-three
I lay with my young bride in my arms,
A girl with t.b.

It's only by the time we get to lines two and three, in which the personal pronoun is linked syntactically with the phrase "An old man of seventy-three," that we recognise that the speaker of the poem is, or was, a man.

But there's something a little odd about that first line, something about that phrase "my bridal night" which will strike many readers as being a very unlikely usage for a male speaker, a speaker who's more likely to use a phrase such as "my wedding night." The seeming psychological unverifiability of the word "bridal" in the mouth of this male speaker, particularly when he describes himself shortly thereafter as lying "with my young *bride* in my arms," reminds us that the poem was written by a woman, a woman who also happens to have been "a girl with t.b."

As Frances Spalding writes in *Stevie Smith: A Critical Biography*:

> At the age of five she contracted tubercular peritonitis. This disease, most often caused by unpasteurized milk, would have brought bowel disorders, sickness and a disinclination to eat . . . She was sent to a children's convalescent home at Broadstairs . . . Stevie remained at Broadstairs for three years, returning home, it is said, only in the summer holidays.

I'll be trying to determine whether such biographical information as the fact that Stevie Smith had t.b., information which many would view as falling into the same category as the gender of the writer, is submissible as evidence in the reader's remembering and dismembering of the poem. I use these words together at the prompting of Stevie Smith herself, writing in an uncollected poem published in the *Poetry Review* of September 1984:

> Henry Wilberforce as a child
> Was much addicted to the pleasures of the wild;
> He observed Nature, saw, *remembered*,
> And was by a natural lion *dismembered*

The connection between re- and dismembering might be said to be the subject of the poem in hand, despite the fact that the words have different roots—"remember" stemming from *rememorari*, "to be mindful of once more," "dismember" from *dismembrare*, "to take apart limb by limb." The term "member" is used most often in the "body" sense, I expect, in the euphemistic phrase "the male *member*," a sense which has a particular resonance under the circumstances I mentioned earlier, in which a female poet is re*member*ing a male speaker, allowing him to speak through her in the act of ventriloquism of which every single poem is an example. In other words, the "I" in "I Remember" would be an invention, an instance of voice-throwing, even if it were written by a man, and I'll be suggesting that what's at stake here is less the veracity of the gender of the speaker than, as I've already hinted, its verifiability.

Let me linger for a moment or two over that phrase "I remember." I want to consider the effect of our meeting that phrase twice, first as the title of the poem, and second as the phrase which ends line 1, and the subtle shifts of meaning between its first and second usage. In the first case, the phrase announces the subject of the poem to be an act of recollection, of remembrance. By the time we meet the phrase "I remember" at the end of line 1, its burden has shifted ever so slightly, in at least two directions. The first reading might be paraphrasable as "It was my bridal night *as I recall*." We'd be more inclined towards this reading, of course, were there a comma between "night" and "remember," but, as we'll discover as we proceed through the poem, Stevie Smith seems to pay scant regard to conventional punctuation. At the end of line 2, for example, we might decently expect a comma after "seventy-three," just as we might decently expect a full stop at the end of line 4, after "t.b." It's precisely because of the lack of punctuation that this first sense of "It was my bridal night *as I recall*" is completely allowed for. The second sense of the first line might be paraphrasable as "It was my bridal night (*rather than anything else before or since*) which I recall." Now, if we were presented with an "is" rather than a "was," we might have more confidence in reading the first two lines in the sense of "It *is* my bridal night which I, I who am *now* an old man of seventy-three, remember." I myself don't go down that road, again partly because of the lack of a full stop at the end of line 2.

The general air of uncertainty, the sense of conflicting readings hanging around the opening of this poem, is heightened by the vocabulary. I'm thinking of the words "confusion" and "collide," which we'll meet in lines 7 and 9. One might, indeed, find a metaphor for metaphor itself in the image of an impending midair collision at the heart of "I Remember," while the syntactic fragmentation pointed up by the very lack of punctuation is mimetic of the fallout from such a midair collision, after which there might well be recollection and remembrance of *disjecta membra*.

The aspect of "recollection" implicit in the phrase "I remember" is faintly ghosted by William Wordsworth's famous phrase in the preface to *Lyrical Ballads*:

> I have said that poetry is the spontaneous overflow of powerful feelings: it takes its origin from emotion *recollected* in tranquillity.

More significant, I suspect, is the sense of "remembrance" outlined by John Keats in his famous letter to John Taylor of February 27th, 1818:

> Poetry should surprise by a fine excess, and not by singularity. It should strike the reader as a wording of his own highest thoughts, and appear almost as a *remembrance*.

I'm emboldened in this suggestion that Keats's "remembrance" lies behind the phrase "I remember" by two biographical echoes of Keats's life and one further literary resonance to be found in this poem. The biographical echoes are of Keats's own demise from consumption, or t.b., picked up in the phrase "a girl with *t.b.*" there in line 4 and, in line 6, "a particularly heavy raid on Hampstead" being a particularly heavy pointer in the direction of Keats's homes at 1, Well Walk, *Hampstead*, in which Keats wrote that "remembrance" letter to Taylor, or Wentworth Place, *Hampstead*, in which he wrote "An Ode on a Grecian Urn," with its first line's "Thou still unravished bride of quietness." And it's to this line, I suggest, that Stevie Smith ever so faintly alludes, in this poem about ravishment, or nonravishment, when she uses the word "bride" *four* times in an eleven-line poem, including twice in the last line:

> Oh my bride, my bride.

But I've leapt ahead of myself. I want to continue to muse on this phrase "I remember," which carries with it even more literary baggage, including a poem by Thomas Hood to which I'll return much later. The best-known instance of the phrase "I remember" in twentieth-century poetry has to do with a railway station in Gloucestershire:

Yes. I remember Adlestrop—
The name, because one afternoon
Of heat the express-train drew up there
Unwontedly. It was late June.

The steam hissed. Someone cleared his throat.
No one left and no one came
On the bare platform. What I saw
Was Adlestrop—only the name

Stevie Smith has learned a great deal not only from the Edward Thomas of "Adlestrop," with its brilliant presentation of active inaction, significant insignificance, in which "no one left and no one came," but also from the Edward Thomas of the sly, sidewise dramatisation of sexual politics in "As the Team's Head-Brass," a poem which underlies "I Remember" in even more significant ways:

As the team's head-brass flashed out on the turn
The lovers disappeared into the wood.
I sat among the boughs of the fallen elm
That strewed the angle of the fallow, and
Watched the plough narrowing a yellow square
Of charlock. Every time the horses turned
Instead of treading me down, the ploughman leaned
Upon the handles to say or ask a word,
About the weather, next about the war.

We recognise already the significant enjambments on the word "turn" at the end of line 1, the word "turned" at the end of line 6, of "As the Team's Head-Brass." As my friend Giorgio Agamben puts it, in *The End of the Poem*:

But the verse is, in every case, a unit that finds its *principium individuationis* only at the end, that defines itself only at the point at which it ends. I have elsewhere suggested that the word *versure*, from the Latin term indicating the point at which the plow turns around at the end of the furrow, be given to this essential trait of the verse, which—perhaps on account of its obviousness—has remained nameless among the moderns.

That Thomas is engaged by the prosodic nature of this "point at which the plow turns around at the end of the furrow" is clear not only from his subject matter but from his dramatisation of the decasyllabic blank verse in which the poem is written in his description of the rhythm of the conversation between speaker and ploughman, with the repetition of the key word "ten" at the end of two successive lines:

One minute and an interval of *ten*,
A minute more and an interval of *ten*.

Stevie Smith uses a device similar to Edward Thomas's at the end of line 7 of "I Remember," allowing the line to "turn" on the word "perversely," a word in which "verse" is, of course, embedded. Much more striking is the extent to which Smith borrows Thomas's method of allowing the halting dialogue between speaker and ploughman to carry the poem:

"Have you been out?" "No." "And don't want to, perhaps?"
"If I could only come back again, I should.
I could spare an arm. I shouldn't want to lose
A leg. If I should lose my head, why, so,
I should want nothing more . . . Have many gone
From here?" "Yes." "Many lost?" "Yes, a good few.
Only two teams work on the farm this year."

In addition to borrowing the hint of Thomas's *disjecta membra* ("I could spare an arm. I shouldn't want to lose / A leg") in "I lay with my young bride *in my arms*," Stevie Smith draws upon Thomas's combination of commonplace and comic tones into lines 9–11 of "I Remember":

Harry, do they ever collide?
I do not think it has ever happened,
Oh my bride, my bride.

The idea of whether "they ever collide" reminds us of the threat of the horses "treading me down" in "As the Team's Head-Brass," while the erotic charge of these lines owes a great deal to the connection Thomas draws between the headlong energy of the lovers and the headlong energy of the plough-team:

> Then
> The lovers came out of the wood again:
> The horses started and for the last time
> I watched the clods crumble and topple over
> After the ploughshare and the stumbling team.

As Edna Longley points out in her 1973 edition of Thomas's *Poems and Last Poems*, both the subject matter and method of "As the Team's Head-Brass," so influential on "I Remember," were themselves influenced by Thomas Hardy's "In Time of 'The Breaking of Nations' ":

> Only a man harrowing clods
>   In a slow silent walk
> With an old horse that stumbles and nods
>   Half asleep as they stalk.

One of the constants, the things that "go onward the same / Though Dynasties pass" in Hardy's poem is the constant couple who prefigure Thomas's "lovers [who] came out of the wood":

> Yonder a maid and her wight
>   Came whispering by:
> War's annals will cloud into night
>   Ere their story die.

Now, I want to suggest that, in addition to this couple, there's another couple from another poem by Thomas Hardy who lie behind Harry and his bride, a couple very definitely about to "collide." I'm thinking of those fated lovers, the *Titanic* and her iceberg, in Hardy's "The Convergence of the Twain":

In a solitude of the sea
Deep from human vanity,
And the Pride of Life that planned her, stilly couches she.

With great economy and precision, Hardy sets down the "steel chambers," "the mirrors meant / to glass the opulent," the "jewels" strewn about this sea-bed boudoir:

Dim moon-eyed fishes near
Gaze at the gilded gear
And query: "What does this vaingloriousness down here?"

Well: while was fashioning
This creature of cleaving wing,
The Immanent Will that stirs and urges everything

Prepared a sinister mate
For her—so gaily great—
A Shape of Ice, for the time far and dissociate.

We might remember that "The Convergence of the Twain," written shortly after the loss of the *Titanic* on April 15th, 1912, is shot through with a sense of the impending loss, in November of that year, of Hardy's first wife, Emma Gifford. Gradually, the two "dissociate" sides of this metaphor move to the point at which they'll come together:

And as the smart ship grew
In stature, grace, and hue,
In shadowy silent distance grew the Iceberg too.

Alien they seemed to be:
No mortal eye could see
The intimate welding of their later history,

Or sign that they were bent
By paths coincident
On being anon twin halves of one august event,

Till the Spinner of the Years
Said "Now!" And each one hears,
And consummation comes, and jars two hemispheres.

Stevie Smith carries across the idea of the possibility of this "intimate welding" of the *Titanic* and the iceberg from "The Convergence of the Twain" in the question raised of the German and British bombers:

Harry, do they ever collide?

I've already mentioned how Stevie Smith's use of direct speech in "I Remember" owes something to Edward Thomas. I think it owes just as much, in that respect, to another poem by Thomas Hardy, "Channel Firing," the poem immediately preceding "The Convergence of the Twain" in *Satires of Circumstance*. "Channel Firing," written in April 1914, is a poem about the impact of British "gunnery practice out at sea" immediately prior to the outbreak of World War I. Like "I Remember," it's a poem drawing on the imagery of a night offensive:

That night your great guns, unawares,
Shook all our coffins as we lay;
And broke the chancel window-squares,
We thought it was the Judgement-day
And sat upright.

When I proposed earlier that the speaker of "I Remember" "is, or *was*, a man," I was influenced partly by the fact that the speaker of "Channel Firing" is addressing us from the grave, the grave in which, as he says of himself and his neighbours, "down we lay again":

"I wonder,
Will the world ever saner be,"
Said one, "than when He sent us under
In our indifferent century!"

Stevie Smith's allusion to "Channel Firing" and "The Convergence of the Twain" is signalled by the near version of "Hardy" in the name

"Harry" itself. The name "Harry"? It's a name that has a particular relevance, I think, in the context of a war poem, calling up other "Old Ghosts":

I can call up old ghosts, and they will come,
But my art limps,—I cannot send them home.

As Frances Spalding, in her *Critical Biography*, writes of Stevie Smith:

She blends dialogue from *Henry IV Part I*—
    Glendower: I can call spirits from the vasty deep;
    Hotspur: Why, so can I, or so can any man;
    But will they come when you do call for them?
—with a passage from De Quincey's *Confessions of an English Opium Eater* in which he reports a child's admission that phantoms come when he calls for them and sometimes, too, when he does not call.

In using the name "Harry" as the name of the phantom-protagonist of "I Remember," Stevie Smith at once conjures up, and cuts down to size, the patriotic associations of Henry IV and, more important, Henry V, Harrys much invoked by the British during World War II. Another couple of Harrys spring to mind, these two appearing in other poems by Stevie Smith. There's the "Harold" of "Harold's Leap," dead, but listening, one assumes:

Harold, are you asleep?
Harold, I remember your leap,
It may have killed you
But it was a brave thing to do.

Then there's the "Harry" of "The Wedding Photograph":

Goodbye Harry I must have you by me for a time
But once in the jungle you must go off to a higher clime
The old lion on his slow toe
Will eat you up, that is the way you will go.

In the way that this "old lion" is related to the "natural lion" that dismembered Henry Wilberforce, the "Harry" of "The Wedding Photograph" is related to the "Harry" who remembered his "bridal night." I'll come back to the Harrys of "Harold's Leap" and "The Wedding Photograph" a little later, when I return to the subject of gender. In the meantime, let me leave my discussion of Thomas Hardy with two comments. The first is that Thomas Hardy was precisely "seventy-three" when he married his much younger second wife, Florence Dugdale. The second is that the subject matter of "The Convergence of the Twain" is referred to indirectly, by way of a popular 1955 book which dramatised the foundering of the *Titanic* on the berg. The book is Walter Lord's *A Night to Remember*, adapted for the 1958 movie of the same title, which appears almost intact in line 1, "It was my bridal *night* I *remember*." In the case of the poem, "I Remember," it's not the "consummation," as Hardy puts it, of the relationship between the *Titanic* and the berg but the almost inevitable *lack* of consummation between the "young bride" and the "old man of seventy-three" which lends a particular poignancy to the end of the poem:

> I do not think it has ever happened,
> Oh my bride, my bride.

LET ME TAKE THAT PHRASE "the end of the poem" as my cue and return, as promised, to Giorgio Agamben and his brief but brilliant chapter on the subject, from which I'd like to quote at length. Agamben proposes that "the possibility of enjambment constitutes the only criterion for distinguishing poetry from prose" and, in poetry which uses rhyme, that "the poem is an organism grounded in the perception of the limits and endings that define—without ever fully coinciding with, and almost in intermittent dispute with—sonorous (or graphic) units and semantic units." He continues:

> We have seen how the poem tenaciously lingers and sustains itself
> in the tension and difference between sound and sense, between
> the metrical series and the syntactical series. But what happens
> at the point at which the poem ends? Clearly, here there can

be no opposition between a metrical limit and a semantic limit. This much follows simply from the trivial fact that there can be no enjambment in the final verse of a poem. This fact is certainly trivial; yet it implies consequences that are as perplexing as they are necessary. For if poetry is defined precisely by the possibility of enjambment, it follows that the last verse of a poem is not a verse.

Agamben has already quoted Dante's *De vulgari eloquentia* as a partial source of this idea of the tension between metrical and semantic limits:

> And here you must know that this word [*stanza*] was coined solely for the purpose of discussing poetic technique, so that the object in which the whole art of the *canzone* was enshrined could be called a stanza, that is, a capacious storehouse or receptacle for the art in its entirety.

He then goes on to identify the "crisis for the poem," proposing how "at the point in which sound is about to be ruined in the abyss of sense, the poem looks for shelter in suspending its own end in a declaration, so to speak, of the state of poetic emergency."

I want to try now to combine Agamben's system, in which the "capacious storehouse or receptacle" is breached, in which the "sound is about to be *ruined*," in which the poem "looks for *shelter*," with Bachelard's concepts of "intimate immensity" and "the dialectics of outside and inside." I'll then try to relate these ideas not only to "I Remember" but to a number of other poems by Stevie Smith, as well as one or two by Emily Dickinson and Elizabeth Bishop. I'll begin with the Emily Dickinson poem I quoted earlier, "There is a solitude of space," with its reference to "That polar privacy / A soul admitted to itself." This is one of numerous poems by Dickinson in which the soul and the sea are connected, the sea coming to stand for society or, in some instances, eternity:

> Exultation is the going
> Of an inland soul to sea,

Past the houses—past the headlands—
Into deep Eternity—

Bred as we, among the mountains,
Can the sailor understand
The divine intoxication
Of the first league out from land?

It's tempting to think that "Exultation is the going" (#76 in Johnson, #143 in Franklin), with its images of the "inland soul" and "the first league out from land," might lie directly behind Stevie Smith's most famous poem:

Nobody heard him, the dead man,
But still he lay moaning:
I was much further out than you thought
And not waving but drowning.

Poor chap, he always loved larking
And now he's dead
It must have been too cold for him his heart gave way,
They said.

Oh, no no no, it was too cold always
(Still the dead one lay moaning)
I was much too far out all my life
And not waving but drowning.

Let me pause for a moment with that line "Poor chap, he always loved larking" to remember that Philip *Larkin* had published *The Less Deceived* in 1955, two years before *Not Waving but Drowning* appeared in 1957. Larkin's collection contains a poem entitled "I remember, I remember," with its famous last line (" 'Nothing, like something, happens anywhere' ") embodying something of what I earlier termed "active inaction, significant insignificance." More significant, the poem represents a failed sexual encounter *en plein air*:

I'll show you, come to that,
The bracken where I never trembling sat,

Determined to go through with it; where she
Lay back, and "all became a burning mist."

I'll come back to Larkin and the idea of the encounter *en plein air* a little later. Let me stay with "Not Waving but Drowning" and suggest that
another strong—perhaps even stronger—contender for the title of Dickinson poem ghosting it is "Two Swimmers wrestled on the spar—" (#201 in
Johnson, #227 in Franklin):

Two Swimmers wrestled on the spar—
Until the morning sun—
When One—turned smiling to the land—
Oh God! the Other One!

The stray ships—passing—
Spied a face—
Upon the waters borne—
With eyes in death—still begging raised—
And hands—beseeching—thrown!

Whether or not there's a direct influence of either of these Emily
Dickinson poems on "Not Waving but Drowning" is hard to tell. What's
easier to relate is the large number of instances in Stevie Smith of a
sea/soul system of imagery which is reminiscent, to say the least, of Dickinson's system, particularly in those Bachelardian senses of "intimate immensity" and "the dialectics of outside and inside." This is true of one of
Smith's very earliest poems, "On the Death of a German Philosopher,"
in which the subject matter of the relationship between individual and
society/eternity, soul and sea, is made quite explicit:

He wrote *The I and the It*
He wrote *The It and the Me*
He died at Marienbad
And now we are all at sea.

The only thing one may say with confidence about this philosopher who has "set out" *from* "Germany" is that he's a Hegelian, like the Gaston Bachelard of "the *dialectics* of outside and inside."

Let me try to relate that idea of "the dialectics of outside and inside" to several other Stevie Smith poems, poems in which an indeterminacy of location reflects other indeterminacies, in which characters are, if not "all," then somewhat, "at sea." In "Advice to Young Children," for example, she writes:

> "Children who paddle where the ocean bed shelves steeply
> Must take care they do not
> Paddle too deeply."
>
> Thus spake the awful aging couple
> Whose heart the years had turned to rubble.

One member of this "awful aging couple" is, I suspect, a version of "an old man of seventy-three" in "I Remember," the "rubble" being one likely outcome of what happens when "bombers . . . collide" and a building is destroyed. Such has been the impact of some collision, some erosion, some Hardyesque "intimate welding," on this "awful aging couple," that they have only one "heart" between them. Their bodies are without boundaries, they may not tell each other apart. It is as if they have regressed to that state in which the child has not recognized his or her individuality, a recognition of which Bachelard writes, in an uncommonly cluttered passage:

> Jean-Paul Sartre, writing on Baudelaire, quotes a sentence from Richard Hughes's *A High Wind in Jamaica* that deserves lengthy commentary: "Emily had been playing house in a nook right in the bows . . ." It is not this line, however, that Sartre discusses, but the following: ". . . and tiring of it [she] was walking rather aimlessly aft . . . when it suddenly flashed into her mind that she was *she* . . ."

This passage comes from Chapter 6 ("Corners") of *The Poetics of Space*, a book published in French in 1958, translated into English in 1964, published in paperback in 1969. It's a book with which I believe Elizabeth

Bishop was familiar while she was writing the poems of *Geography III* (1977), poems which, to say the least, contain an astonishing number of echoes of images and ideas (nests, shells, keys, "Saint Robinson" Crusoe, miniatures, the "proto-dream-house") found in Bachelard's book. I'm not about to fill out this idea on this occasion, but I do want to suggest that Bishop, in "In the Waiting Room," for example, draws on the central idea of that Richard Hughes passage quoted by Bachelard, "that she was *she*," combining it with the central idea of Chapter 10 ("The Phenomenology of Roundness"), that "the world is round around the round being":

> I said to myself: three days
> and you'll be seven years old.
> I was saying it to stop
> the sensation of falling off
> the round, turning world
> into cold, blue-black space.
> But I felt: you are an *I*,
> you are an *Elizabeth*,
> you are one of *them*.

Towards the end of "In the Waiting Room," Bishop brings together "outside and inside" by drawing on sea imagery:

> The waiting room was bright
> and too hot. It was sliding
> beneath a big black wave,
> another and another.

It's in Chapter 8 of *The Poetics of Space* that Bachelard addresses the idea of "intimate immensity," attempting to demonstrate what he describes as "the correspondence between the immensity of world space and the depth of 'inner space,'" and appealing to the work of Philippe Diolé, author of *Le plus beau désert du monde*:

> As it happens, he has had long, delightful experience of deep-sea diving and, for him, the ocean has become a form of "space" . . .

And when we have read his earlier books and shared with him this conquest of the intimacy of water, we come to the point where we recognize in this space-substance, a one-dimensional space. One substance, one dimension. And we are so remote from the earth and life on earth, that this dimension of water bears the mark of limitlessness.

It's some sense of this "mark of limitlessness" (mediated by Matthew Arnold and Emily Dickinson, of course, rather than Gaston Bachelard!) which has Stevie Smith so often present us with characters who are "all at sea." The speaker of "Fish, Fish," for example, announces, "I shall be happy then / in the watery company of his kingdom." The speaker of "Our Bog Is Dood" considers it "sweetest of all to walk alone / Beside the encroaching sea, / The sea that soon should drown them all, / That never yet drowned me." The speaker of "Look!," a version of the character we meet in "Not Waving but Drowning," is resigned to being "becalmed in a deep sea," to "give signals, but they are not answered." This speaker has an erotic experience with "a fish so transparent in his inner organs / that I know he comes from the earthquake bed / Five miles below where I sail, I sail." The word "bed" is repeated a few lines later in the poem:

Now
Into my hand he comes, the travelling creature,
Not from the sea-*bed* only but from the generations,
Faint because of the lighter pressure,
Fainting, a long fish, stretched out.

We may remember that, along with the word "shelves," the word "bed" also occurred in the first line of "Advice to Young Children" ("Children who paddle where the ocean *bed shelves* deeply") and that, together, the "shelves" and "bed" point to the absence of bounds between furnished interior and outer depths. This image of children positioned on a borderline is echoed in the paddling imagery of poems such as "Oblivion" ("I trod in a sweet and milky sea, *knee deep*, / That was so pretty and so beautiful, growing deeper") and "Venus When Young Choosing Death" ("I stood *knee-deep* in the sea / I saw gods coming towards me"). Then, in

"The Sea-widow," a poem which bears striking similarities to "I Remember," both in its vocabulary and its dramatisation of voices carrying across a void, death is once more associated with the sea:

How fares it with you, Mrs Cooper my bride?
Long are the years since you lay by my side.
Do you wish I was back? Do you speak of me dearest?
I wish you were back for me to hold nearest.
Who then lies nearer, Mrs Cooper my bride?
A black man comes in with the evening tide.
What is his name? Tell me! How does he dare?
He comes uninvited. His name is Despair.

AS I MOVE TOWARDS THE CONCLUSION of my discussion of "I Remember," I myself begin to despair as I face something of what Giorgio Agamben described as the "crisis for the poem" and "the state of poetic emergency" as the poem, or essay, comes to a finish. *The* Finish *of the Poem*? Maybe I should adopt that as my title, now that Agamben has beaten me to the post? There are at least four reasons, however tenuous or precarious, why the word "finish" might be relevant to a discussion of "I Remember." Not least of these is Stevie Smith's positioning of the word "Finis," the Latin word for "end" which is at the root of "finish," as the last word of "Tenuous and Precarious," a poem which first appeared in her *Selected Poems* of 1962. I mention the date because, while the cod Latin humour of "Tenuous and Precarious" is likely to draw on René de Goscinny's *Asterix the Gaul* (1961) or Stephen Sondheim's *A Funny Thing Happened on the Way to the Forum* (1962), it's so much of a piece with the humour of the slightly later British film comedy *Carry On Cleo* (1964) that I can hear it spoken only by the likes of Sidney James or Kenneth Williams:

Tenuous and Precarious
Were my guardians,
Precarious and Tenuous.
Two Romans.

My father was Hazardous,
Hazardous,
Dear old man,
Three Romans.

The poem continues in this vein, listing "my brother Spurious," "my husband . . . Perfidious," "Surreptitious, our son," "our cat Tedious," until, in the last stanza, the identity of the speaker is revealed:

My name is Finis,
Finis, Finis,
I am Finis,
Six, five, four, three, two,
One Roman,
Finis.

This use of the word "Finis" is a brilliant way of resolving the "crisis for the poem" in that last stanza. It's the moment where finite and infinite combine in what Emily Dickinson, at the end of "There is a solitude of space," terms "Finite infinity." I notice, by the way, that Franklin decides, for reasons best known to himself, to drop the phrase "Finite infinity" as the final line of "There is a solitude of space," the poem he gives as #1,696, so we have to go back to #1,695 in Johnson to find "Finite infinity" properly rhyming and chiming with the words "sea," "be" and "privacy" in lines 2, 4 and 6 of what Dickinson surely meant to be an eight-line poem. In other words, the rhyme serves to finish the poem in a second sense of "finish" I think appropriate here, the sense given by the OED as "to perfect." Stevie Smith uses a similar device in "I Remember," where the full rhymes on "seventy-three" and "t.b." in lines 2 and 4 are mirrored in the rhymes on "collide" in line 9 and "bride" in line 11. Although the couplet is at the heart of the poem, the fact that lines 5 and 6 ("overhead/Hampstead"), along with lines 7 and 8 ("perversely/Germany"), are rhymed with such knowing gaucheness suggests that there may be a certain awkwardness in the lovemaking of Harry and the "young bride." The fact, moreover, that the poem has an odd number of lines may suggest that the coupling of the lovers is doomed to be unsatisfactory, that they are sexually incompatible, that they will not "finish" in a third sense of the word which I seem not to be able to find in my edition of the *OED*, but which occurs in that phrase "Nice guys finish last." It may be that Harry, the "old man of seventy-three," is all too aware of the vagaries of the "Finis"/penis when he thinks back wistfully, "I do not think it has ever happened / Oh my bride, my bride."

Now, I can't mention the "Finis"/penis nexus without coming back, at last, to my question of whether there's an "end" in "gender," whether or not there's a strict demarcation of male and female subject matter or methods, whether it's appropriate or otherwise that Stevie Smith, a female, is attempting to ventriloquize Harry, a male. As I proposed earlier, I think it's largely immaterial whether or not this poem was written by a man or a woman, all that matters being the psychological verifiability of the voice. This verifiability is no less difficult for the male ventriloquizing a male or a female ventriloquizing a female. The extent to which gender *is* material has to do with whether it is likely either to clutter or to clear the way towards that psychological verifiability, and it is no more or less significant than any other biographical consideration, including the idea of the "veracity" of experience. In the case of Stevie Smith, for example, it's not inappropriate to be reminded of her wartime experience in London, as described here by Frances Spalding:

> On her walks in Grovelands Park Stevie watched the Home Guard practise bringing in the wounded. At night she, like everyone else, had to make her way through dark streets. In the mornings the air was sometimes filled with dust from bomb-damaged buildings. The nearest that the Blitz came to Palmers Green was when a V1 fell on Carpenter Gardens on 7 July 1944, about half a mile from Avondale Road.

Frances Spalding then quotes from Stevie Smith's 1949 novel, *The Holiday*, which is set during the war:

> Everything in this world is in fits and splinters, like after an air raid when the glass is on the pavements; one picks one's way and is happy in parts.

Frances Spalding has already quoted a passage from *The Holiday* which includes a phrase which might readily stand as a précis of "I Remember":

> People say people were heroic in the raids. They were certainly good humoured and plucky and uncomplaining, but is it heroism *to endure the unavoidable?*

If the "unavoidable" which must be "endured" in "I Remember" is the sexual "consummation" between "an old man" and a "young bride," then the sense of unease which is traditionally felt by a female is carried over ever so faintly into the voice of the male speaker in a way which, like the phrase "my bridal night," may not ring true for some readers. More significantly, a sense of what Frances Spalding, on the very next page, refers to as "Stevie's own sexual ambivalence," may account for the ambivalence and ambiguity of the situation we find in "I Remember." In addition to several relationships with women, Stevie Smith is reputed to have had affairs with a number of men, including George Orwell, the model for at least one character in *The Holiday*. Is George Orwell also the model for "Harry"? It is not inappropriate for some readers of "I Remember" to seize on a biographical tidbit proposed by Frances Spalding:

> Both Stevie and Orwell were by nature discreet, not given to flaunting their emotional affairs before friends. Orwell did, however, boast to Anthony Powell that he had once made love to a woman in a park as they had nowhere else to go, and male literary gossip has associated Stevie with this tale.

I want to try to relate this idea of there being "nowhere else to go," the phrase used by Frances Spalding of the circumstances of the supposed coming together *en plein air* of Stevie Smith and George Orwell, with the indeterminate siting of the consummation of the "bridal night" on which "overhead / The Germans were making a particularly heavy raid on Hampstead." That "overhead" connects "I Remember" with yet another literary source, the poem by Thomas Hood which begins "I remember, I remember / The house where I was born, / The little window, where the sun / Came peeping in, at morn," in which we meet versions of the ideas codified by Bachelard as "intimate immensity" and "the dialects of outside and inside," including that very *"house"* with its "little *window* where the *sun came peeping in."* The last stanza reads:

> I remember, I remember
> The fir trees dark and high;
> I used to think their slender spires
> Were close against the sky.

A similar lack of delineation between earth and sky whereby the "overhead" bombers are indistinguishable, if only by dint of metaphor, from the lovers below, occurs there in the "spires/ *close against the sky"* in the Thomas Hood poem.

It is not inappropriate, I suggest, to remind oneself that the work of Thomas Hood was the subject of a 1946 radio programme presented by Stevie Smith for the British Broadcasting Corporation, for which George Orwell had worked as a producer and for which, in 1942, he had invited Stevie Smith to present a selection of her poems. Two further points about George Orwell. He, too, is associated with Hampstead, where he lived during the 1930s at 3 Warwick Mansions, Pond Street. He died, in 1950, of t.b. There is, in other words, a connection in Stevie Smith's mind between the London of World War II, George Orwell/"Harry," and the Thomas Hood of the poem which begins "I remember, I remember." The Hood poem is partly mediated, of course, through the poem by Philip Larkin, with its failed sexual encounter *en plein air*, which draws directly on Hood for its title, "I remember, I remember," that repetition of the phrase itself repeated in the title and first line of the poem in hand.

Now, the speaker of the poem by Thomas Hood is a disillusioned, despairing old man, a man with a self-destructive urge:

> I remember, I remember
> The house where I was born,
> The little window, where the sun
> Came peeping in, at morn;
>
> He never came a wink too soon,
> Nor brought too long a day;

But now, I often wish the night
Had borne my breath away.

The death wish in Thomas Hood's poem is connected by the phrase "I remember" to another Stevie Smith poem, "Exeat," where it occurs in the opening line:

I remember the Roman Emperor, one of the cruellest of them,
Who used to visit for pleasure his poor prisoners cramped in
    dungeons,
So when they would beg him for death, and then he would say:
Oh no, oh no, we are not yet friends enough.
He meant they were not yet friends enough for him to give them
    death.

This instinct in Stevie Smith to "perversely" associate friendship, or sex, with death, particularly suicide, may be found in several poems. The self-destructive urge features prominently in two I quoted earlier, "Harold's Leap," in which "He leapt from one rock to the other / And fell to the sea's smother," and "The Wedding Photograph," in which the speaker exhorts her beloved:

So smile Harry smile and I will smile too
Thinking what is going to happen to you,
It is the death wish lights my beautiful eyes
But people think you are lucky to go off with such a pretty prize.

The "Harold" of "Harold's Leap" and the "Harry" of "The Wedding Photograph" have, in the guise of the speaker of "I Remember," come to understand that sense of the verb "to finish" given by the *OED* as meaning "to die." The former "Harry" and his former "young bride" have been granted the wish expressed by the speaker of that poem by Thomas Hood beginning with the line "I remember, I remember." Their "breath" has indeed been "borne . . . away." Now, the title of that Thomas Hood poem is "Stanzas," which brings me back to Dante, quoted by Giorgio Agamben, and his description of the stanza as a "capacious storehouse or receptacle." We remember that Agamben extends the room/house imagery by proposing that "the poem *looks for shelter* in suspending its own end in a declaration, so to speak, of the state of poetic emergency." To appeal once more to that phrase used by Frances Spalding in her description of George Orwell and Stevie Smith in the park, the poem has "nowhere else to go." It is *in extremis*. Part of the brilliance of "I Remember" is that we may read Harry's exasperated "Oh my bride, my bride" as coinciding precisely with the moment when the bombers do indeed collide, the moment when sexual ravishment does indeed occur but is indistinguishable from the ravages of war, the moment when sexual politics and the politics of the poem are inextricably combined in what Robert Lowell once described as Stevie Smith's "unique and cheerfully gruesome voice."

CHAPTER 7

GEORGE III

ROBERT LOWELL

(This too is perhaps a translation, because I owe so much to Sherwin's brilliant Uncorking Old Sherry, *a life of Richard Brinsley Sheridan.—R.L.)*

Poor George,
afflicted by two Congresses,

ours and his own that regularly
and legally had him flogged—

once young George, who saw
his lost majority of our ancestors

dwindle to a few inglorious Tory refugee
diehards who fled for him to Canada—

to lie relegated to the ash-heap,
unvisited in this bicentennial year—

not a lost cause, but no cause.

In '76, George was still King George,
the one authorized tyrant,

not yet the mad, bad old king,

who whimsically picked the pockets of his page
he'd paid to sleep all day outside his door;

who dressed like a Quaker, who danced a minuet
with his appalled apothecary in Kew Gardens;

who did embroidery with the young court ladies,
and criticized them with suspicious bluntness;

who showed aversion for Queen Charlotte, almost
burned her by holding a candle to her face.

It was his sickness, not lust for dominion
made him piss purple, and aghast

his retinue by formally bowing to an elm,
as if it were the Chinese emissary.

George—

once a reigning monarch like Nixon,
and more exhausting to dethrone . . .

Could Nixon's court,
could Haldeman, Ehrlichman, or Kissinger

blame their king's behavior
on an insane wetnurse?

Tragic buffoonery
was more colorful once;

yet how modern George is,
wandering vacated chambers of his White House,

addressing imaginary congresses,
reviewing imaginary combat troops,

thinking himself dead and ordering black clothes:
in memory of George, for he was a good man.

Old, mad, deaf, half-blind,

he talked for thirty-two hours
on everything, everybody,

read Cervantes and the Bible aloud
simultaneously with shattering rapidity . . .

Quand on s'amuse, que le temps fuit—

in his last lucid moment,
singing a hymn to his harpsichord,

praying God for resignation
in his calamity he could not avert . . .

mercifully unable to hear
his drab tapes play back his own voice to him,

morning, noon, and night.

IN AN INTERVIEW with Richard Gilman, published in *The New York Times*
of May 5, 1968, Robert Lowell made the following assertion:

When your private experience converges on the nation's experience
you feel you have to do something.

One of the things Robert Lowell had done had been to refuse an invitation, in the early summer of 1965, to attend a White House Festival of the Arts. When it had been presented to him over the phone, Lowell's first impulse had been to accept the request to take part in the festival. Shortly afterwards, however, he wrote a letter to Lyndon Johnson which was published in *The New York Times* of June 3, 1965:

Dear President Johnson,

When I was telephoned last week and asked to read at the White House Festival of the Arts on June fourteenth, I am afraid I accepted somewhat rapidly and greedily. I thought of such an occasion as a purely artistic flourish, even though every serious artist knows that he cannot enjoy public celebration without making subtle public commitments. After a week's wondering, I have decided that I am conscience-bound to refuse your courteous invitation. I do so now in a public letter because my acceptance has been announced in the newspapers and because of the strangeness of the Administration's recent actions. Although I am very enthusiastic about most of your domestic legislation and intentions, I nevertheless can only follow our present foreign policy with the greatest dismay and distrust. What we will do and what we ought to do as a sovereign nation facing other sovereign nations seem now to hang in the balance between the better and the worse possibilities. We are in danger of imperceptibly becoming an explosive and suddenly chauvinistic nation, and may even be drifting on our way to the last nuclear ruin. I know it is hard for the responsible man to act; it is also painful for the private and irresolute man to dare criticism. At this anguished, delicate and perhaps determining moment, I feel I am serving you and our country best by not taking part in the White House Festival of the Arts.

Respectfully yours,
Robert Lowell.

In an interview with Ian Hamilton, quoted in Hamilton's magnificent *Robert Lowell: A Biography*, Blair Clark comments on this letter, using Lowell's nickname, "Cal":

You have to say that that was a very successful operation of high-level cultural publicism. Cal the public figure—he knew what he was doing. I'm sure there were people who were terribly envious of his ability to manipulate himself as a public figure. He did it without any pomposity—but he definitely believed that he *was* a public figure.

I'd like to consider here some of the manifestations in Lowell's work of that impulse described by him in his 1968 interview in *The New York Times* that "when private experience converges on the nation's experience you feel you have to do something." I'll examine several Lowell poems which have a political end, in the sense that their "aim" or "function" is political. They are written by a poet who "definitely believed that he *was* a public figure," with the ambition of effecting a significant change of opinion. Such an ambition raises several complex questions having to do with who writes a poem and, then, who reads it.

The "ideal reader" of Lowell's letter, never mind one of his poems, certainly wasn't Lyndon Johnson. On August 4, 1965, in a speech given to a large number of students assembled on the White House lawn and reported in *The New York Times* of August 5, Johnson would respond publicly to Lowell's broadside with a little broadside of his own:

Robert Lowell, the poet, doesn't like everything around here. But I like one of his lines where he wrote: "For the world which seems to lie out before us like a land of dreams." Well, in this great age—and it is a great age—the world does seem to lie before us like a land of dreams.

As Ian Hamilton points out:

The line he quotes is, of course, from Matthew Arnold's "Dover Beach." Lowell, however, had used it as an epigraph for his book *The Mills of the Kavanaughs*, and clearly Johnson's speech writer, in a hurry to supply an upbeat quote, had not adventured past the title page.

Ian Hamilton might also have pointed out that the speechwriter had got the quote wrong in the first place, that it should have read "for the world which seems / To lie before us like a land of dreams," with no "to lie *out* before us" upsetting the iambic pentameter of the line and partly obscuring the rhyme on "seems" and "dreams." This phenomenon of the co-option by politicians, and others, of poetry quotes designed to support a position is one with which many of us are depressingly familiar. The impulse of politicians to reach for poets whom they clearly don't understand has a no less depressing mirror image in the impulse of poets to reach for politicians whom they also clearly don't understand.

I'll want to say a brief word or two about translation, in the sense of "carrying over," which would seem inappropriate to the matter in hand were it not for the fact that Lowell's "George III" was first collected in his 1977 volume, *Day by Day*, in a section entitled "Translations," with the following note:

> (This too is perhaps a translation, because I owe so much to
> Sherwin's brilliant *Uncorking Old Sherry*, a life of Richard Brinsley
> Sheridan.—R.L.)

I'll be exploring the specific "carryings over" to "George III" from Oscar Sherwin's 1960 account of Richard Brinsley Sheridan and will be suggesting that, despite its overtly public theme, this poem is also deeply personal in its concerns, that it may indeed represent a near perfect convergence of "private experience" and "the nation's experience."

WHEN ROBERT LOWELL DIED, on September 12, 1977, he may have been too famous for his own good, at least for the good of some of his poems. In a review of *Day by Day* published almost exactly a month earlier, in *The New York Times Book Review* of August 14, Helen Vendler hit on a difficulty of his autobiographical method:

> One has to know (from previous work) his reading, his past and his
> present and one has to reconstruct the scenario behind this book—
> Lowell's life in Kent, his hospitalization in England, his wife's
> sickness, their temporary stay in Boston, their separation, a
> reconciliation, a further rupture, a parting in Ireland, Lowell's return
> to America.

Here Vendler recognises what is, in this instance, a reader's problem in having to appeal to an inappropriate extent to information beyond the bounds, or bournes, of the poem. We know that no poem may be read as a completely discrete construct, that no poem may be read without some autobiographical element coming into play, but we also know that part of the function of the poem is to present a construct that is *relatively* free-standing, to create a *relatively* squared-off stand of timber on the plain, or a relatively clear-cut space in what Walter Benjamin, in his essay on "The Task of the Translator," refers to as "the language forest." Despite the exhortations of every two-bit teacher of creative writing that his or her students should write about what they know, there are major stumbling blocks in blindly following such an exhortation. Chief among these is the increased difficulty, when one is writing about what one knows, in determining just how much one *doesn't* know, in weighing how much information a reader needs, in assessing how much writer and reader may take for granted. Memory may be the mother of the Muses, as Plato proposed, but Memory does not itself equal the Muses. Helen Vendler has taken her cue partly from Lowell's own professed awareness, in "Epilogue," of the problem posed by his own poems:

Those blessed structures, plot and rhyme—
why are they no help to me now
I want to make
something imagined, not recalled?
I hear the noise of my own voice:
The painter's vision is not a lens,
it trembles to caress the light.
But sometimes everything I write
with the threadbare art of my eye
seems a snapshot,
lurid, rapid, garish, grouped,
heightened from life,
yet paralyzed by fact.

I assume that the term "heightened" is borrowed from a passage in Gerard Manley Hopkins's letter of August 14, 1879, to his friend Robert Bridges:

The poetical language of an age should be the current language *heightened*, to any degree *heightened* and unlike itself.

Let me dwell for a moment on the impact of Hopkins on Lowell, particularly his early work. I'll begin with the speaker in a short story by Lowell's first wife, Jean Stafford, who gives an account of her relationship with a Lowell lookalike named Theron:

Half a year after we were married, Theron, immersed in the rhythms of Gerard Manley Hopkins the poet, was explosively ignited by Gerard Manley Hopkins the Jesuit and, as my mother would have said, he was off on a tear.

In "A Note on Gerard Manley Hopkins" published in the fall 1944 number of *The Kenyon Review*, Lowell himself describes those "rhythms" as having "the effect of a hyperthyroid injection." Now, "a hyperthyroid injection" was meant to cure the conditions of obesity or slow metabolism. The injection itself was of thyroid extract, a substance high in iodine, and was meant to make one more active. The context suggests that Lowell views Hopkins's tendency towards the "hyperthyroid injection" as being somewhat problematical, resulting in a certain rhetorical swelling, a certain rhetorical overactivity. Something of that same tendency finds its way into Lowell's own work, in ways that may be no less problematical. I think immediately of the opening lines of "The Quaker Graveyard in Nantucket":

A brackish reach of shoal off Madaket,—
The sea was still breaking violently and night
Had steamed into our North Atlantic Fleet,
When the drowned sailor clutched the drag-net. Light
Flashed from his matted head and marble feet,
He grappled at the net
With the coiled, hurdling muscles of his thighs.

That image of the "hurdling muscles of his thighs" comes straight from Hopkins's description of "Harry Ploughman" with his "hard as *hurdle* arms" and his "lank / Rope-over *thigh*." There's more than a hint of the musclebound in this writing, despite Lowell's attempt at a disclaimer by preparing for the tortuous enjambment of "Light / Flashed" in his description of the sea "breaking violently." The most significant influence on "The Quaker Graveyard in Nantucket," in terms of both content and form, is "The Wreck of the *Deutschland*," its dedication *"To the happy memory of the five Franciscan nuns exiles by the Falck Laws drowned between midnight and morning of Dec. 7th, 1875"* picked up by Lowell's dedication *"for Warren Winslow, dead at sea."* The word "shoal(s)" appears twice in "The Wreck of the *Deutschland*," and is carried over by Lowell into the first line of "The Quaker Graveyard in Nantucket" with its "brackish reach of *shoal*." Now, the Warren Winslow who perishes on that reef is addressed by Lowell as "you, my cousin," and it gives a clue to an aspect of Lowell which sets him apart from Hopkins—the fact that he was as predisposed to be well known as Hopkins was to be anonymous.

In "The Wreck of the *Deutschland*," Hopkins is writing what is in many respects a great public poem, but one which would not be published during his lifetime. In "The Quaker Graveyard in Nantucket," Lowell is writing a great public poem with the confidence that, to go back to his phrase of 1968, his "private experience converges on the nation's experience" in ways other poets might not take for granted. This confidence derives, surely, from the sense that he is a Lowell of Boston, that there are already two high-profile poets, Amy and James Russell, in his family, that the family name of his cousin, Winslow, is almost as well known as his own, traceable as it is back to the *Mayflower* Pilgrim, Edward Winslow (1595–1655), one of the founders of the colony at Plymouth. Throughout his career, Lowell would make poems from the matter of, and with, his family as much as the matter of, and with, himself.

Among the Winslows featured in his great 1959 volume, *Life Studies*, is Uncle Devereux. "My Last Afternoon with Uncle Devereux Winslow" finds the speaker remembering himself at the age of "five and a half" on his grandfather's farm:

> Our farmer was cementing a root-house under the hill.
> One of my hands was cool on a pile
> of black earth, the other warm
> on a pile of lime.

The vision of privilege offered here (of a grandfather who has not only a "farm" but a "farmer"), is presented with seeming haphazardness:

> When I sat on the tiles,
> and dug at the anchor on my sailor blouse,
> Uncle Devereux stood behind me.
> He was as brushed as Bayard, our riding horse.
> His face was putty.
> His blue coat and white trousers
> grew sharper and straighter.
> His coat was a blue jay's tail,
> his trousers were solid cream from the top of the bottle.
> He was animated, hierarchical,
> like a ginger snap man in a clothes-press.
> He was dying of the incurable Hodgkin's disease . . .
> My hands were warm, then cool, on the piles
> of earth and lime,
> a black pile and a white pile . . .
> Come winter,
> Uncle Devereux would blend to the one color.

Despite the seemingly haphazard aspect of the poem to which I've referred, this description of "My Last Afternoon with Uncle Devereux Winslow" relies heavily on some of "those blessed structures" Lowell listed earlier, notably "plot." The repetition of the image of "the black pile and the white pile" allows the poem to end, literally, with a synthesis of the two. The description of the colour of Uncle Devereux's face as "putty," which would otherwise seem a little tired, is somehow revitalised. The description, moreover, of the colour of his trousers as "solid cream from the top of the bottle" underlines a social stratification in which Uncle Devereux is exercised by ideas of the "hierarchical." A very great deal may be read into the line "Uncle Devereux stood behind me," with its suggestion that the Lowell ancestry stretches far back and is sustaining. The name "Devereux" itself brings to mind the family name of several Earls of Essex, soldiers and statesmen in the service of Elizabeth I and James I. The Bayard of "*Bayard*, our riding horse" might allude to almost any member of the distinguished family which traced itself back to a sister of Peter Stuyvesant and included Thomas Francis Bayard, U.S. ambassador to Great Britain between 1893 and 1897, or his son, another Thomas Francis Bayard, who served in the U.S. Senate between 1923 and 1929, or, most likely, their ancestor, Colonel John Bayard, the American patriot who played a major role in the Revolutionary War and was a member of Congress, one of those "two Congresses, / ours and his own," to which Lowell refers in lines 2 and 3 of "George III." It's all a bit of a blur, as befits a poem about blending "a black pile and a white pile."

In "Dunbarton," the poem immediately following "My Last Afternoon with Uncle Devereux Winslow," Lowell uses exactly the same device of allowing landscape and figure to run into one another when he describes "the clump of virgin pine" beyond the family graveyard as

> a reddish *blur*,
> like the ever-blackening wine-dark coat
> in our portrait of Edward Winslow,
> once sheriff for George the Second,
> the sire of bankrupt Tories.

The fact that an ancestor of Lowell was "once sheriff for George the Second" will surely influence how he goes about writing, and how we go about reading, a poem entitled "George III," with its opening phrase "Poor George." Now, I've taken a long time to get round to the opening phrase of "George III" because I think it's vital to come at it with as firm a sense as we can manage of Lowell's tone. For some readers, there may be an air of condescension hanging over this phrase "Poor George," a sense that the speaker is being patronising. I'm sent back, however, to three other occasions on which Lowell uses the word "poor" as the opening word of a poem. There is, of course, section 10 of "Mexico":

> Poor child, you were kissed so much you thought you were walked on;
> yet you wait in my doorway with bluebells in your hair.

Then, there's "For Sale":

Poor sheepish plaything,
organized with prodigal animosity,
lived in just a year—
my Father's cottage at Beverly Farms
was on the market the month he died.

There is, of course, a startling aspect to the opening of "For Sale," a poem collected in *Life Studies*, given that most readers would expect the phrase "Poor sheepish plaything" (particularly the "sheepish") to refer to a person rather than a place, a "Father" rather than a "Father's cottage." Once again, there's a blurring of figure and landscape. As I read it, there's a tenderness about the phrases "Poor child" and "Poor sheepish plaything" which carries over into the phrase "Poor George." The fourth occasion on which Lowell uses the word as the opening word of a poem is in "Poor Alexander, poor Diogenes," historical characters with whom Lowell shares a fellow feeling. It's as if "Poor George" were a familiar, perhaps even a familial, character.

As it turns out, the Winslows were indeed supporters not only of George II but his grandson, George III, throwing in their lot not with the American Revolutionaries but "the one authorized tyrant," as he's described in line 13. This fact alone begins to problematise what seems to be a fairly straightforward political satire, particularly since the poem was written in 1976, the bicentenary of the Declaration of Independence, as is announced there in line 10's reference to "this bicentennial year." That problematisation is encapsulated in the shift between the words "ours" and "our" in lines 3 and 6 respectively:

Poor George,
afflicted by two Congresses,

ours and his own that regularly
and legally had him flogged—

once young George, who saw
his lost majority of *our* ancestors

dwindle to a few inglorious Tory refugee
diehards who fled for him to Canada—

There is a tension between that first use of the word "our," with its
implication that the speaker is part of a group with a unified system of
values, beliefs and political allegiances, and the second "our," whereby it's
revealed that the speaker's ancestors, or some of them, are identified as "a
few inglorious Tory refugee / diehards." The speaker is at once insider
and outsider, a position Lowell relished, particularly when we remember
this archetypical Episcopalian New Englander's bout with Catholicism, a
paradox on which he would comment in "Waking in the Blue":

> In between the limits of day,
> hours and hours go by under the crew haircuts
> and slightly too little nonsensical bachelor twinkle
> of the Roman Catholic attendants.
> (There are no Mayflower
> screwballs in the Catholic Church.)

No Winslows, that's to say, until himself. One is reminded of the description by Jean Stafford of how "Theron, immersed in the rhythms of
Gerard Manley Hopkins the poet, was explosively ignited by Gerard Manley Hopkins the Jesuit and, as my mother would have said, he was off on
a tear." Stafford's use of the name "Theron" suggests that it shares a root,
in the Greek *thero*, with the word "theroid," "like or having the form of a
brute, of bestial nature or character" (*OED*). The brutishness of "Theron"
is akin to the brutishness of Caligula and Caliban, both of whom lie behind Lowell's nickname, "Cal." The term "explosively ignited" is a telling
one, and is corroborated by Lowell's own account of an incident, taken
from a draft of "91 Revere Street" and quoted by Ian Hamilton:

> Seven years ago I had an attack of pathological enthusiasm. The
> night before I was locked up I ran about the streets of Bloomington
> Indiana crying out against devils and homosexuals. I believed I could
> stop cars and paralyze their forces by merely standing in the middle
> of the highway with my arms outspread.

Years later, Lowell's third wife, Caroline Blackwood, would report a similar sighting:

> I was in a taxi in New York, and suddenly there was a frightful swerve and I looked round and there was Cal. He'd stepped right in front of my taxi. He was just weaving through the traffic, looking neither to the right nor the left—cars screaming and screeching.

Needless to say, Lowell's second wife, Elizabeth Hardwick, was also quite familiar with his mania. Once, she had been called to a hospital in Munich on an occasion when Lowell was "on a tear," and was asked about his army record:

> And I said, "Well, he didn't have an army record. He was a conscientious objector." And the lieutenant or whoever he was started screaming: "Get that son of a bitch out of here!" And I said: "But he's an American citizen. He's got no place to go."

That Lowell was "afflicted" with mental illness, as likely to present himself as having "an army record" as being a conscientious objector, once again problematises the way in which we read a poem about a king who is "afflicted" by delusion and mania, "addressing imaginary congresses, / reviewing imaginary combat troops," as we read in lines 38 and 39. I'm struck by the fact that the word "congresses" is lowercase in line 38, upper in line 2, suggesting a certain indecision. We may remember that in 1976 Elizabeth Hardwick was still a major presence in Lowell's life and that, at his death the following year, he was returning to her in the United States, having left Caroline Blackwood in Britain. He was, one might say, "afflicted by two Congresses" in the sense that "congress" may refer to "sexual union, copulation, coition." Lowell's breakdowns often involved "imaginary congresses" with young women, a fact noted by W. H. Auden when he wrote to Charles Monteith, in December 1965, with reservations about Lowell's candidacy for the Oxford Professorship of Poetry:

> His supporters should be aware, if they aren't already, that Cal has times when he has to go into the bin. The warning signals are three:

a) He announces that he is the *only* living poet b) a romantic and usually platonic attraction to a young girl and c) he gives a huge party.

Let me try to disentangle, insofar as I'm able, one of the elements which sent Lowell "into the bin," which had him "relegated to the ash-heap," to borrow a phrase from line 9. I'm thinking of the diversion of his mania into religious fervor. In a brilliantly incisive letter written to Peter Taylor in April 1949, just a few days after the episode of what Lowell called "pathological enthusiasm," Allen Tate set down his analysis of the situation:

> Cal gave up Jean, he has given up the Church (the recent reconversion was not real—he merely used the Church for a few weeks to establish his mania in religious terms), and he has given up poetry . . . I am told that everything that paranoiacs do is symbolic action, and an objectivization of the delusion. In giving up these three things Cal has given up the three defenses against disintegration: but his mother will feel that he has given up all those wicked influences.

It was surely some version of this religious mania that had lain behind Lowell's presenting himself as a conscientious objector, and his subsequent refusal to serve in the U.S. Army, for which he'd been imprisoned in 1943 in Danbury, Connecticut. The conscientious objector in Lowell may well identify with the George III "who dressed like a Quaker." Jim Peck, another C.O., would tell Ian Hamilton of Lowell's being held for a few days in West Street jail in New York:

> Lowell was in a cell next to Lepke, you know, Murder Incorporated, and Lepke says to him: "I'm in for killing. What are you in for?" "Oh, I'm in for refusing to kill." And Lepke burst out laughing.

In "Memories of West Street and Lepke," Lowell writes of the "Czar":

> there piling towels on a rack,
> or dawdling off to his little segregated cell full

of things forbidden the common man:
a portable radio, a dresser, two toy American
flags tied together with a ribbon of Easter palm.

The merging of American and Christian iconography in the "flags" and "Easter palm" speaks more to Lowell's circumstances than Lepke's (particularly since Lepke was Jewish), as does the catalogue "of things forbidden the common man." The implication here is that Lowell is himself a "common man," an idea vigorously countered by Jim Peck:

> We got three years. He got a year and a day—it had to be a year and a day to be a felony. He got parole after four months. They didn't usually grant parole to objectors—he got it because he was a Lowell.

It was, presumably, "because he was a Lowell" that he felt so spectacularly entitled, on September 7, 1943, to write directly to President Roosevelt:

Dear Mr. President:
I very much regret that I must refuse the opportunity you offer me in your communication of August 6, 1943, for service in the Armed Forces.

It's hard not to read much of what follows without wincing at Lowell's cockiness and cheek. He writes, for example, of "sending copies also to my parents, to a select number of friends and relatives, to the heads of the Washington press bureaus, and to a few responsible citizens who, no more than yourself, can be suspected of subversive activities." That "no more than yourself" is a masterstroke of putdown and patronisation, equalled only by the "like your own" in the following sentence:

> You will understand how painful such a decision is for an American whose family traditions, like your own, have always found their fulfillment in maintaining, through responsible participation in both the civil and the military services, our country's freedom and honor.
> I have the honor, Sir, to inscribe myself, with sincerest loyalty and respect, your fellow-citizen,
> Robert Traill Spence Lowell, Jr.

Lowell recalls this occasion in the second stanza of "Memories of West Street and Lepke":

These are the tranquillized *Fifties*,
and I am forty. Ought I to regret my seedtime?
I was a fire-breathing Catholic C.O.,
and made my manic statement,
telling off the state and president, and then
sat waiting sentence in the bull pen
beside a negro boy with curlicues
of marijuana in his hair.

It would seem that Lowell himself acknowledges the "manic" nature of his "statement," which he'd attached to his letter to Roosevelt and in which he underlined his assertion that "members of my family had served in all our wars since the Declaration of Independence," though he didn't mention those "inglorious Tory refugee / diehards" who supported George III. In "Memories of West Street and Lepke," Lowell rather associates himself with the radicalism of the young Wordsworth, the line "Ought I to regret my seedtime?" being a direct allusion to Wordsworth's "Fair *seedtime* had my soul and I grew up / Fostered alike by beauty and by fear." In "George III," Lowell nods in the direction of another "fire-breathing" radical poet, Byron, of whom Lady Caroline Lamb had written in her journal that he was "mad, bad, and dangerous to know." In picking up that famous sobriquet in his description, in line 14, of George III as "not yet the *mad, bad* old king," Lowell also rather deftly reminds us of Byron's great satire, *The Vision of Judgement*, with its savage depiction of George III:

In the first year of freedom's second dawn
    Died George the Third; although no tyrant, one
Who shielded tyrants, till each sense withdrawn
    Left him nor mental nor external sun;
A better farmer ne'er brush'd dew from lawn,
    A weaker king never left a realm undone!
He died—but left his subjects still behind,
One half as mad—and t'other no less blind.

Line 42, meanwhile, with its "Old, mad, deaf, half-blind," sets up another resonance, of the famous opening of Shelley's sonnet, "England in 1819," and its description of none other than George III:

An *old*, *mad*, *blind*, despised, and dying King

Lowell is at pains, therefore, to trace his lineage to poets, like Wordsworth, Byron, or Shelley—poets inclined to take a public, political position, unabashedly "telling off" a king or a president. After "telling off" Roosevelt, Lowell turned his attention to Eisenhower, writing of his "Inauguration Day: January 1953":

Look, the fixed stars, all just alike
as lack-land atoms, split apart,
and the Republic summons Ike,
the mausoleum in her heart.

With the inauguration of John F. Kennedy, an event which he attended, Lowell might have found a president whom he could come close to admiring. After a May 1962 White House dinner in honour of André Malraux, however, Lowell wrote to Edmund Wilson with a perceptive sense of the true significance of the poet to the politician:

Except for you, everyone there seemed addled with adulation at
having been invited. It was all good fun but next morning you read
that the President has sent the 7th fleet to Laos, or he might have
invaded Cuba again—not that he will. But I feel we intellectuals play
a very pompous and frivolous role—we should be windows, not
window-dressing. Then, now in our times, of all times, the sword
hangs over us and our children, and not a voice is lifted.

The next president against whom Lowell's "voice [was] lifted" was, of course, Johnson. After declining the invitation to be "window-dressing" at the 1965 White House Festival of the Arts, Lowell appealed to another "fire-breathing" poet, Andrew Marvell, and "An Horatian Ode upon Cromwell's Return from Ireland" for the rough stanzaic template of "Waking Early Sunday Morning":

O to break loose. All life's grandeur
is something with a girl in summer . . .
elated as the President
girdled by his establishment
this Sunday morning, free to chaff
his own thoughts with his bear-cuffed staff,
swimming nude, unbuttoned, sick
of his ghost-written rhetoric!

The "ghost-written" is a sly reference, I assume, to the speechwriter who suggested that Lowell had written the line "For the world which seems to lie [out] before us like a land of dreams."

I'll come back to that image of President Johnson "with his bear-cuffed staff, / swimming nude," in a little while. For the moment, let me focus briefly on that phrase "ghost-written rhetoric" and the extent to which "George III" is itself "ghost-written." As I mentioned earlier, Lowell's note to the poem in which he acknowledges that "this too is perhaps a translation, because I owe so much to Sherwin's brilliant *Uncorking Old Sherry*, a life of Richard Brinsley Sheridan." As Steven Gould Axelrod has pointed out in "Lowell's Living Name: An Introduction," an essay collected in *Robert Lowell: Essays on the Poetry*, Lowell has indeed "carried over" much of the minutiae of Oscar Sherwin's descriptions of George III into his poem. He has also partly carried over something of Sherwin's method, including writing in a tense which one might describe as the "breathless present," by which he means to suggest, as Lowell has it in line 36, "how modern George is." On pages 228, 229, 230, and 231 of *Uncorking Old Sherry*, for example, we read:

His daily behaviour becomes more odd. He sits with young Court ladies embroidering and pretends to play the fiddle . . . He bows to an oak, seizes one of the lower branches, and shakes it with the most apparent cordiality and regard—just as a man shakes his friend by the hand . . . His eyes are affected. To see his wife he pushes the candle into her face and nearly sets her on fire . . . At Windsor he sits dictating Cervantes and the Bible—at the same time and with incredible speed—to pages whom he afterwards creates Baronets and Knights of the Holy Roman Empire. He talks for thirty-two hours on end—of everybody and everything . . . He makes a page go to sleep as an anodyne for his own insomnia and then immediately picks his pockets . . . There can be no doubt now of his lunacy. On November 27 the king is removed to Kew . . . He dances a minuet with his apothecary in a new tie wig which he orders for the purpose. He fancies himself a Quaker and is dressed like one from head to foot.

On pages 322 and 323 we find further descriptions which have been "carried over" wholesale into Lowell's poem:

The Queen enters his apartment during one of his lucid intervals and finds him singing a hymn and accompanying himself on the harpsichord . . . He loves to wander through the corridors, a venerable figure with a long silvery beard, attired in a silk morning gown and ermine night cap, holding imaginary conversations with ministers long since dead . . . The belief that he is dead is one of his regular delusions. "I must have a new suit of clothes," he says one day, "and I will have them black in memory of George the Third, for he was a good man."

Lowell's use of these phrases from Sherwin will strike some readers as being inappropriate, particularly those who've never quite been able to stomach T. S. Eliot's assertion, in "Philip Massinger," that "immature poets imitate; mature poets steal." I want to go back to Walter Benjamin and that extraordinary image from his essay on "The Task of the Translator" which I quoted earlier, in the hope of finding a way of determining how, in a sense that's somewhat more profound than a mere "carrying over," Lowell might be involved here in an act of "translation":

Unlike a work of literature, translation does not find itself in the center of the language forest but on the outside facing the wooded ridge; it calls into it without entering, aiming at that single spot where the echo is able to give, in its own language, the reverberation of the work in the alien one.

When Lowell "calls into" the "wooded ridge" of Sherwin, the "echo is able to give . . . the reverberation of the work" not so much in terms of a shift in language, but a shift in context. We are not reading precisely the same phrases in Lowell as we read them in Sherwin:

Old, mad, deaf, half-blind,

he talked for thirty-two hours
on everything, everybody,

read Cervantes and the Bible aloud
simultaneously with shattering rapidity . . .

Quand on s'amuse, que le temps fuit—

This last phrase would seem to come, once again, from page 323 of *Uncorking Old Sherry*:

So pleasantly does he while away the time that sometimes his dinner is ready before he expects it. "Can it be so late?" he asks. "Quand on s'amuse, le temps vole."

It may be that, given how he replaces Sherwin's word "vole," with its double meaning of "flies" and "steals," with *fuit* (with its hint of Virgil's "*Fugit inreparabile tempus*"), Lowell is feeling ever so slightly guilty about his "theft" of Sherwin's descriptions of "George" and his recontextualising them:

George—

once a reigning monarch like Nixon,
and more exhausting to dethrone . . .

I WANT NOW TO HAVE SOME FUN spending a moment or two on the complex attitude to Richard Nixon and the presidency as an institution which emerges from this poem. I'll be attempting to further support my earlier suggestion that, despite appearances, this is a poem which brings together "private experience" with "the nation's experience." When "George III" was written, commissioned as it was for the July 4, 1976, number of *Newsweek*, it had been two years since the Watergate scandal had forced Nixon to resign. So this is not, then, a poem meant to "dethrone" him. He's already been dethroned. What, then, is its end? We might say that part of its end is to retrospectively satirize the president/king. There's something demeaned and diminished about that objective. We've already seen, to use a phrase of Helen Vendler from her essay "Last Days and Last Poems," that "George's later mania bears a strong resemblance to phases of Lowell's own illness." As Steven Gould Axelrod also points out, in "Lowell's Living Name: An Introduction," "the narrator implies through his act of empathic identification with George and Nixon a relationship between them and himself."

By way of attempting to further disentangle that end of "George III" whereby the president/king is related to Lowell himself, I'd like to go back to that image of Lyndon Johnson, "with his bear-cuffed staff, / swimming nude." Now, this vision seems to be largely dismissive of Johnson. One is reminded, however, of the generally ameliorative associations the word "bear" has for Lowell. As Ian Hamilton remarks:

> Each friend would be given a bear-name and an appropriate bear-voice . . . Lowell seems not to have been nervous that his bear-game might be boring for his friends; being made into a bear was, after all, a mark of his friendship and regard.

In "Home After Three Months Away," Lowell writes:

> After thirteen weeks
> my child still dabs her cheeks
> to start me shaving. When
> we dress her in her sky-blue corduroy,
> she changes to a boy,
> and floats my shaving brush
> and washcloth in the flush . . .

Dearest, I cannot loiter here
in lather like a polar bear.

There is, in other words, a system of imagery, including this swimming
bear, which connects Lowell and Johnson in a kind of naked intimacy.

"Home After Three Months Away" begins as follows:

Gone now the baby's nurse,
a lioness who ruled the roost
and made the Mother cry.

I want to focus on that image of the nurse to suggest the first of several
connections, having to do with family dynamics, between Lowell and
Nixon/George III. We might remember that other nurse in line 33 of the
poem:

Could Nixon's court,
could Haldeman, Ehrlichman, or Kissinger

blame their king's behavior
on an insane wetnurse?

This nurse derives partly from Sherwin's description, on page 228, of
George III's nurse:

Some there are who rumor that his wet nurse was a lunatic and that
quack medicines unhinged his balance.

But the "wetnurse" may derive also from Lowell's memories of one of his
own nurses, memories set down by him in a draft of "91 Revere Street":

When I was two years old I had a nurse who was, herself, only
eighteen or so years old and had come to Boston from Ireland . . .
Her name was Katherine. Katherine's rosary was a memorable work
of religious mass-production . . . But what I loved more than the
beads of Katherine's rosary was the silver crucifix. It was heavy,

intricate and important, as I could see from Katherine's awed and loving glance upon it. Katherine told me about Jesus and I regret to recall that my feelings were highly egocentric; I saw, with despair, that I was second fiddle even in my nurse's affections.

The unstated burden of that last phrase is that the child was "second fiddle" not only in his mother's affections but *"even* in my nurse's affections." Lowell continues:

And then suddenly the rosary disappeared and the house was disturbed by the mystery . . . I smiled and smiled and smiled, very much in the way my father smiled and smiled and smiled . . . A day or so later the rosary was found, hidden under a corner of the rug . . . However, it was noticed that the Christus was missing and also, with embarrassment, that the chain of the rosary had been chewed. I returned to my denying smile but later Mother saw me pushing a piece of paper down the register. "You will burn up the house" she said. But two days later she again saw me pushing a whole handful of paper strips down the register. "You are setting the furnace on fire," she said. I smiled and smiled, to her intense displeasure. "Yes, I know," I said. "That's where Jesus is."

Lowell's association of abandonment, often with a sexual tinge, and some form of religious mania was a feature of his adult life. We might recall Allen Tate's comment on his giving up Jean Stafford, the Church, and poetry:

In giving up these three things Cal has given up the three defenses against disintegration: but his mother will feel that he has given up all those wicked influences.

Lowell's "empathic identification with George," as described by Steven Gould Axelrod, must have been further underpinned by the constant recurrence, in *Uncorking Old Sherry*, of the name of George's wife, Charlotte, since this was, of course, the name of his own mother, the domineering, distant Charlotte Winslow:

She was hysterical even in her calm, but like a patient and forbearing strategist, she tried to pretend her neutrality. One night she said with murderous coolness, "Bobby and I are leaving for Papa's." This was the ultimatum to force father to sign a deed placing the Revere Street house in Mother's name.

It might be said that Lowell's constantly arguing parents had enacted their own version of the War of Independence, with the house standing in for the "Colonies," as is clear from that extract from "91 Revere Street." Earlier in "91 Revere Street," Lowell makes a direct comparison between his family and the family of George III when he writes of Mordecai Myers, "my Grandmother Lowell's grandfather," that he was "a man like mad George III's pomaded, disreputable son, 'Prinny,' the Prince Regent." One "disreputable" aspect of the Prince Regent was his tendency to get "dead drunk," a tendency to which Lowell himself often succumbed, adding another sense to Jean Stafford's description of him being "off on a tear." Images relating alcohol to his family abound. We remember, in "My Last Afternoon with Uncle Devereux Winslow," how young Robert Lowell asserts himself:

> "I won't go with you. I want to stay with Grandpa!"
> That's how I threw cold water
> on my Mother's and Father's
> watery martini pipe dreams at Sunday dinner.

Devereux Winslow's father oversees a world in which "shandygaff" and "a decanter of Scotch" are permanent fixtures. Lowell describes his "five and a half" year-old self as "a stuffed toucan / with a *bibulous* multicolored beak," and positions himself "*on the tiles*," as if to prefigure that tendency to go "off on a tear." Another image I quoted earlier, from "Dunbarton," identifies "Edward Winslow, once sheriff for George the Second," with an "ever-blackening *wine-dark* coat." The very title of *Uncorking Old Sherry*, with its drink-based pun, must have given Lowell pause, particularly since the book lives up to that title and offers detailed descriptions of the drinking exploits of Richard Brinsley Sheridan, often in the company of such movers and shakers as the Prince Regent:

He spends an autumn at Brighton in riotous entertainment. He frolics like a boy, not like a man of fifty-five. On one occasion when there is a phantasmagoria at the Pavilion and all are shut in perfect darkness, he seats himself upon the lap of Madame Gerobtzoff, a haughty Russian dame, who makes a row enough for the whole town to hear. The Prince of course is delighted with all this, but at last Sheridan makes himself so ill with drinking that he gets in a perfect fever. Creevey feels his pulse and finds it going tremendously and gives him some hot white wine of which he drinks a bottle and his pulse subsides almost instantly . . . On another occasion he attends an immense assembly at Lady Caroline's, is one of the select few who sup downstairs with Lady Melbourne and the Prince and who do not separate until six in the morning. Next day he is completely and hopelessly drunk.

Now, the Lady Caroline in question here is Caroline of Brunswick, a niece of George III, first cousin and wife to the Prince Regent, later Queen to King George IV. But Lowell, as he read *Uncorking Old Sherry*, must have been reminded of another "Lady Caroline." I'm thinking not of Lady Caroline Lamb but of Lowell's third wife, Lady Caroline Blackwood. Caroline Blackwood happened to belong to the line of Richard Brinsley Sheridan, which was why, when her child by Robert Lowell was born, on September 28th, 1971, he was named "Robert *Sheridan* Lowell":

Little Gingersnap Man, homoform,
flat and sore and alcoholic red,
only like us in owning to middle-age.
"If you touch him, he'll burn your fingers."
"It's his health, not fever. Why are the other babies so pallid?
His navy-blue eyes tip with his head . . . Darling,
we have escaped our death-struggle with our lives."

The choice of imagery in "Robert Sheridan Lowell," collected in Lowell's 1973 volume, *The Dolphin*, may seem to be fairly arbitrary, yet it connects tellingly with other poems. The fact that the newborn's eyes are "navy blue" brings back the seafaring Lowell/Winslow dynasty, including the child-poet's "sky-blue corduroy" and Uncle Devereux's "blue coat," "his coat . . . a blue jay's tail." That faint association with Uncle Devereux is fleshed out by the translation of the description of him, in "My Last Afternoon with Uncle Devereux Winslow," as being "like a ginger snap man in a clothes-press" to the description of Sheridan Lowell as "flat" and a "Little Gingersnap Man." One comes away from "Robert Sheridan Lowell" with a profound sense of Lowell's concern about the heritage of his child, particularly the health-heritage of a child who is "alcoholic-red" and prone to "fever" just as Richard Brinsley Sheridan was prone to "fever." The assertion (spoken at the end of the poem by, one assumes, Lowell) that " 'we have escaped our death-struggle with our lives' " doesn't ring entirely true. In "George III," however, there seems to be an underlying acceptance of the ongoing engagement of "private experience" with "the nation's experience," a "death-struggle" from which one does not always "escape." The poem is charged with autobiographical elements which propel it more forcefully than any merely political impulse. Though it may seem to be terminally "threadbare," "George III" is a brilliantly effective political poem in that it seems equal to both private and public engagements—it is, to borrow a phrase from the end of "Dolphin," "an eel-net made by man for the eel fighting." It's the perfect embodiment of the exhortation of the "Lowell motto: *Occasionem cognosce*," mentioned by Lowell in "Sailing Home from Rapallo," which might translate as "Be alert to opportunity" or "Take your chance."

CHAPTER 8

L'ANGUILLA / THE EEL

EUGENIO MONTALE

I
The eel, the North Sea siren,
who leaves dead-pan Icelandic gods
and the Baltic for our Mediterranean,
our estuaries, our rivers—
who lances through their profound places,
and flinty portages, from branch to branch,
twig to twig, thinning down now,
ever snaking inward, worming
for the granite's heartland, threading
delicate capillaries of slime—
and in the Romagna one morning
the blaze of the chestnut blossoms
ignites its smudge in the dead water
pooled from chiselings
of the Apennines . . .
the eel, a whipstock, a Roman candle,
love's arrow on earth, which only
reaches the paradise of fecundity
through our gullies and fiery, charred streams;
a green spirit, potent only
where desolation and arson burn;
a spark that says everything

begins where everything is clinker;
this buried rainbow, this iris, twin sister
of the one you set in your eye's target center
to shine on the sons of men,
on us, up to our gills in your life-giving mud—
can you call her *Sister?*

II

If they called you a fox,
it will be for your monstrous hurtle,
your sprint that parts and unites,
that kicks up and freshens the gravel,
(your black lace balcony, overlooking
the home for deformed children, a meadow,
and a tree, where my carved name quivers,
happy, humble, defeated)—
or perhaps only for the phosphorescent wake
of your almond eyes,
for the craft of your alert panic,
for the annihilation of dishevelled feathers
in your child's hand's python hug;
if they have likened you to the blond lioness,
to the avaricious demon of the undergrowth
(and why not to the filthy fish
that electrocutes, the torpedo fish?)
it is perhaps because the blind
have not seen the wings
on your delectable shoulder-blades,
because the blind haven't shot for
your forehead's luminous target,
the furrow I pricked there in blood,
cross, chrism, incantation,—and
prayer—damnation, salvation;
if they can only think of you
as a weasel or a woman,
with whom can I share my discovery,

where bury the gold I carry,
the red-hot, pot-bellied furnace raging
inside me, when, leaving me,
you turn up stairs?

Montale: *L'anguilla; Se t'hanno assomigliato.*
Translated by Robert Lowell

IN HIS INTRODUCTION to *Imitations* (1961), in which this translation (some would say, this travesty) of Eugenio Montale's "L'anguilla" first
appeared, Robert Lowell acknowledges his tendency to overstep the
mark:

> Boris Pasternak has said that the usual reliable translator gets the
> literal meaning but misses the tone, and that in poetry tone is of
> course everything. I have been reckless with literal meaning, and
> labored hard to get the tone. More often this has been *a* tone, for *the*
> tone is something that will always more or less escape transference
> to another language and cultural moment. I have tried to write alive
> English and to do what my authors might have done if they were
> writing their poems now and in America.

There's more than a faint air of cultural imperialism, not to speak of personal imperiousness, hanging over that last sentence ("to do what *my* authors might have done if they were writing their poems *now and in
America*"), emphasised perhaps by the echo of the haughty note struck by
the speaker of T. S. Eliot's "Little Gidding" and his "History is *now and
England.*" A little later in his introduction to *Imitations*, Lowell goes on to
propose the following:

> I believe that poetic translation—I would call it an imitation—must
> be expert and inspired, and needs at least as much technique, luck
> and rightness of hand as an original poem.

I want to go further than Lowell and propose (1) that the "poetic translation" is itself an "original poem," (2) that the "original poem" on which it's based is itself a "translation" and (3) that both "original poem" and "poetic translation" are manifestations of some ur-poem. I shy away from this last idea, of course, since it smacks of a Platonism I can't quite stomach. Yet I do find this notion of the ur-poem useful on a metaphorical level, if only because I don't know of another single metaphor that's equal to the complexity of the activity of translation. The "activity of translation" is a form of criticism, surely the most exiguous form of close reading we're ever likely to experience, with one exception. That exception is the form of close reading which occurs simultaneously with what might be termed "close writing." That's why I'll be trying to combine that idea of the ur-poem with a general theory of what I call the stunt-reader and the stunt-writer (I know you're wondering if I have in mind "close reading" or "close *rodeoing*"), and bringing all this back to the business of translating "The Eel." I'll have been checking the decisions Robert Lowell made from word to word and from line to line against a number of the many other versions of the poem, including those by William Arrowsmith, John Burnside, Jonathan Galassi, George Kay, Edwin Morgan, John Frederick Nims, Tom Paulin, Jeremy Reed and Charles Wright, in an attempt to consider the phrase "the end of the poem" in the senses both of the extent to which a poem may indeed be drawn from one "language and cultural moment" to another and the extent to which certain critical judgements may or may not be "off limits."

THE FIRST CRITICAL JUDGEMENT I'LL FOCUS ON, however, relates to the literal sense of the phrase "the end of the poem." We see that Lowell presents, under the title of "The Eel," a poem in two parts. The only trouble is that Eugenio Montale's "The Eel" is a poem *in one part*, ending with the phrase Lowell translates as "can you call her *Sister*?" Lowell acknowledges that he was "reckless with literal meaning." He was also reckless with delineating the end of the poem when he found, in *The Penguin Book of Italian Verse*, edited by George Kay (1958), a translation of "Se t'hanno assomigliato" following on from that of "L'anguilla" without an evident break. As Jamie McKendrick has pointed out, in an unpublished essay which he's been kind enough to let me see:

> *Imitations* prints both Italian titles, separated by a semi-colon, after his translation, which would suggest that by the time of printing, Lowell had been made aware of his initial mistake—Alfredo Rizzardi and Renato Poggioli, whom he acknowledges for their help with the Italian, would surely have noted it. But by that stage, I suspect he was committed to the version as it stands.

Let's stick, for the next few minutes or so, and mostly for fun, with this resulting "second part" of "The Eel":

> If they called you a fox,
> it will be for your monstrous hurtle,
> your sprint that parts and unites,
> that kicks up and freshens the gravel,
> (your black lace balcony, overlooking
> the home for deformed children, a meadow,
> and a tree, where my carved name quivers,
> happy, humble, defeated)—

That piling-on of three adjectives in "happy, humble, defeated" is a device we've seen before now in Lowell, as in the "frizzled, stale and small" of the end of "Waking in the Blue." It's a device picked up by Seamus Heaney, a poet much under Lowell's influence, in "The Tollund Man," collected in *Wintering Out* (1972), in which Heaney defined himself as being "lost, unhappy, and at home." We find a version of that trademark triadism in "Casualty," a poem collected in *Field Work* (1979), in which Heaney describes the drinking man who is the subject of the poem:

> I loved his whole manner,
> Sure-footed but too sly,
> His deadpan sidling tact,
> His fisherman's quick eye
> And turned observant back.

This drinking man who is also a fisherman is described with all Heaney's usual economy and force:

> He had gone miles away
> For he drank like a fish
> Nightly, naturally
> Swimming towards the lure
> Of warm lit-up places,
> The blurred mesh and murmur
> Drifting among glasses
> In the gregarious smoke.

The net-imagery alone ("mesh," "drifting") connects this fisherman with the Robert Lowell of Heaney's "Elegy," again collected in *Field Work*:

> your dorsal nib
> gifted at last
>
> to inveigle and to plash,
> helmsman, netsman, *retiarius*.

The "netsman, *retiarius*" images are drawn directly from the last line of "Dolphin," "an *eel*-net made by man for the *eel*-fighting." By the end of "Elegy," Heaney has positioned himself as the natural heir to Lowell, the pair of poets standing under the laurel:

> you found the child in me
> when you took farewells
> under the full bay tree
> by the gate in Glanmore,
>
> opulent and restorative
> as that lingering summertime,
> the fish-dart of your eyes
> risking, "I'll pray for you."

Lowell's ability to ride "the swaying tiller of [himself]" is contrasted in "Elegy" with Heaney's "fear of water," Lowell's "bold" with Heaney's "timorous" impulses. The description of "the fish-dart of [Lowell's] eyes" and his propensity for drinking "America / like the heart's / iron vodka" connects him with the fisherman of "Casualty":

> To get out early, haul
> steadily of the bottom,
> dispraise the catch, and smile
> as you find a rhythm
> working you, slow mile by mile,
> into your proper haunt
> somewhere, well out, beyond . . .

That this fisherman with an interest in "rhythm" is a version of the "bold" Robert Lowell is underscored for me by what I, in my innocent way, consider to be the fact that Lowell's "carved name quivers" there, subliminally, in the "Low" of "*slow* mile by mile" finished off by the "well" of "*well* out, beyond . . . ," a near version of "Robert" being encoded in the "*proper* haun*t*" of the intervening line. "Why not go out on a limb?" Will Rogers asked. "That's where the fruit is." For a poem that occupies some version of literary limbo, this second section of "The Eel" would seem to have had a considerable impact on "Casualty," a notion supported by the fact that the Lough Neagh fisherman is after a very specific fish:

> In the pause after a slug
> He mentioned poetry.
> We would be on our own
> And, always politic
> And shy of condescension,
> I would manage by some trick
> To switch the talk to *eels*
> Or lore of the horse and cart
> Or the Provisionals.

Now, there are at least two other Heaney poems, also collected in *Field Work*, which focus on the interface of erotics and the animal kingdom and which seem to draw directly on this second section of "The Eel." The first is "The Skunk," the marital love poem which, as we know, is already indebted to Lowell's "Skunk Hour":

> It all came back to me last night, stirred
> By the sootfall of your things at bedtime,
> Your head-down, tail-up hunt in a bottom drawer
> For the black plunge-line nightdress.

That "black plunge-line nightdress" is of the same stuff as the *"black lace balcony"* in the second section of "The Eel," which is an interpolation by Lowell, there being no lingerie in the original.

A second erotic/animal poem in *Field Work* into which Heaney has borrowed vocabulary and imagery from Lowell's version of "Se t'hanno assomigliato" is "The Otter." Here we may compare Lowell's "your sprint that parts and unites, / that kicks up and freshens the gravel" with the following lines in Heaney:

> Turning to swim on your back,
> Each silent, thigh-shaking *kick*
> Re-tilting the light,
> Heaving the cool at your neck.
>
> And suddenly you're out,
> Back again, intent as ever,
> Heavy and frisky in your *freshened* pelt,
> Printing the *stones*.

It's no accident that "The Otter" is set in Italy, its opening announcement that "the light of Tuscany wavered" itself reminiscent of a key image in part one of Lowell's "The Eel" in which "in the Romagna one morning / the blaze of the chestnut blossoms / ignites its smudge in the dead water." Heaney has already used Lowell's term "dead-pan," from line 2 of part one of "The Eel," in his description of the Lough Neagh fisherman's *"deadpan* sidling tact."

So profound is the influence of Lowell on *Field Work* that the old "chestnut" from "the blaze of chestnut blossoms" appears in the title poem of *Field Work*, again in the context of sexual longing:

But your vaccination mark is on your thigh,
an O that's healed into the bark.

Except a dryad's not a woman
you are my wounded dryad

in a mothering smell of wet
and ring-wormed *chestnuts*.

We notice that this occasion of sexual longing coincides, as in part two of
Lowell's "The Eel," with an image of "a tree" in which something is
"carved." The word "wet" would also have occurred in close proximity to
"a tree, where my carved name quivers, / happy, humble, defeated" had
Lowell accurately translated the phrase *"felici, umidi e vinti"* not as "happy,
humble, defeated" but "happy, *wet* and won," as Jonathan Galassi has it in
his magisterial *Collected Poems 1920–1954* of Montale. Lowell has, in other
words, mixed up *umile*, "humble," with *umidi*, "wet," a not unreasonable
misreading, perhaps, in the context of a poem abounding in "delicate capillaries of slime."

One final instance of the profound impact on Heaney of Lowell's
version of "The Eel" combines that "slime" from part one with a rework-
ing of the image from part two of "the filthy fish / that electrocutes,
the torpedo fish." This occurs in "The Guttural Muse," and describes a
tench:

Once called the "doctor fish" because his *slime*
Was said to heal the wounds of fish that touched it.

The speaker of "The Guttural Muse" is, once again, positioned as a "timorous" outsider, separated from the "bold" members of "a young crowd"
who "leave the discotheque." Like the speakers of "Casualty" and "Elegy,"
the speaker of "The Guttural Muse" finds himself "wanting to *swim* in
touch with soft-mouthed life," to "find a rhythm / working you" as it does
the "Casualty" out on Lough Neagh, his poetic and fishing "line lifted,
hand / over fist." He also wants to put himself in the position of the
"helmsman," Robert Lowell, "that hand. Warding and grooming / and
amphibious."

LET ME TAKE MY CUE from Heaney's image of "that hand," an image connected to the "swaying tiller" of Lowell himself, and relate it to a phrase in Lowell's introduction to *Imitations*, that phrase about "rightness of hand" in his disquisition on how a translator in the act of translation "must be expert and inspired, and needs at least as much technique, luck and *rightness of hand* as an original poem." This gubernatorial metaphor is an apt one, surely, for the alternating process of going with and, insofar as it's possible, going against the flow. The "helmsman" is acutely aware of having given himself over to a force of nature which is likely, from moment to moment, to overwhelm him. However much he might imagine himself to be its master, he is at the mercy of that force. Here's Eugenio Montale on the subject of how at least one "original poem" got written:

"Iris" is a poem I dreamed and translated from a non-existent
language: I am perhaps more its "medium" than its author.

Montale's metaphor for writing an "original poem" is that it is "translated." We are familiar with this same argument from other writers, most famously Paul Valéry, asserting in "Variations on the *Eclogues*" that "writing anything at all . . . is a work of translation exactly comparable to that of transmuting a text from one language into another," and Octavio Paz, in his essay on "Translation: Literature and Letters":

On the one hand, the world is presented to us as a collection of
similarities; on the other, as a growing heap of texts, each slightly
different from the one that came before it: translations of
translations of translations.

One of the reasons I've just spent as long as I have on the subject of the influence on Heaney of part two of Lowell's version of "The Eel" is to substantiate the idea expressed here by Octavio Paz that all texts might properly be thought of as "translations of translations of translations," often to an extent which is shocking to the conscious mind of the writer who has given him- or herself over to the unconscious. Paz continues:

Each text is unique, yet at the same time it is the translation of another text. No text can be completely original because language itself, in its very essence, is already a translation—first from the nonverbal world, and then, because each sign and each phrase is a translation of another sign, another phrase. However, the inverse of this reasoning is also entirely valid. All texts are originals because each translation has its own distinctive character. Up to a point, each translation is a creation and thus constitutes a unique text.

As I suggested earlier, I myself would be inclined to lose the phrase "up to a point" and assert that a translation is necessarily a new thing. One need look no further for proof of this assertion than the evidence of ten translations of the opening lines of "L'anguilla/The Eel." The Italian reads as follows:

> L'anguilla, la sirena
> dei mari freddi che lascia il Baltico
> per giungere ai nostri mari

These translations of the opening of the poem are presented in the alphabetical order of the names of their translators:

> The eel, coldwater
> siren, who leaves the Baltic behind her
> to reach these shores of ours
>
> (Arrowsmith)

> The eel—that siren
> of cold seas
> who steals into our estuaries
>
> (Burnside)

The eel, siren
of cold seas, who leaves
the Baltic for our seas

(Galassi)

The eel, the siren
of cold seas who leaves the Baltic
journeying to reach our seas

(Kay)

The eel, the North Sea siren,
who leaves dead-pan Icelandic gods
and the Baltic for our Mediterranean

(Lowell)

The eel, the sea siren
That leaves behind her cold Baltic waters
In order to sport in our seas

(Morgan)

The eel, the
siren of sleety seas, abandoning
the Baltic for our waters

(Nims)

Northern muscle the eel
- greyblack all slimy
it flexes through our warm sea

(Paulin)

The eel, cold-water
siren, that leaves the Baltic
and journeys to our seas

(Reed)

The eel, siren
of the cold seas, who leaves her Baltic playground
for our warm waters, our estuaries

(Wright)

The variety of possible readings represented by these translations
would seem to substantiate another observation by Octavio Paz in his essay "Translation: Literature and Letters":

In theory, only poets should translate poetry; in practice, poets are
rarely good translators. They almost invariably use the foreign poem
as a point of departure toward their own.

This idea of the poem in the source language being "a point of departure
toward their own" poem in the target language is a complex one, particularly since there's some question as to whether or not a poet may ever
think of a poem as being his or her "own," more particularly if they are,
in Montale's own term, a "medium." I'll return to this in a while. In the
meantime, we can see that there is indeed a tendency for translators to
tinge, or taint, the poem for which they are a medium, in the way that
storage in an oak cask will tinge, or taint, a red wine with tannin.

Let me shift metaphor for a moment and suggest that we can also see that there is a tendency for translators to favour one strand of a poem over another, to pull on one thread of the complex weave, sometimes at the risk of unravelling the whole piece. In the case of "The Eel," we can see that there's an almost irresistible urge to underscore the physicality of the setting and the subject, resulting in the interpolation of the "sleety seas" by John Frederick Nims or the "Northern muscle" that "flexes," an image by which Tom Paulin manages to combine political *"muscle"* from *"Northern"* Ireland with the erotic force hanging over the eel. Tom Paulin, more than most, seems to "use . . . the foreign poem as a point of departure towards [his] own" when he goes on to describe how the eel "flexes through our warm sea / our rivers and estuaries / then licks their bottoms / with its tongue of slime / tongue threading each muddy bum."

As the poem proceeds, it will be evident from all these manifestations of it that the erotic force embodied by the eel combines elements or principles which are both conventionally male and conventionally female. The male principle is phallic, represented most clearly in those lines translated by Lowell as "a whipstock, a Roman candle, / love's arrow on earth," by Arrowsmith as "torchlight, lash, / arrow of Love on earth," by Burnside as "the eel is torch / is whiplash / is the earth's taut arrow," by Galassi as "torch, whiplash, / arrow of Love on earth," by Kay as "torch, whiplash / arrow of love on earth," by Morgan as "the brand, the lash, / the shaft of Love on earth," by Nims as "torch and whip, / arrow of love on earth," by Paulin as "tail and fins fletched / like love's arrow," by Reed as "torch, whiplash, / earthly love-arrow," by Wright as "whiplash, twisting torch, / love's arrow on earth." The female principle is enshrined in the "fecundity" of "life-giving mud," of course, but also in the fact that the dominant gender of the eel turns out to be female, as is announced from the outset in those versions by Arrowsmith, Morgan and Wright:

> The eel, coldwater
> siren, who leaves the Baltic behind *her*
> to reach these shores of ours
>
> *(Arrowsmith)*

The eel, the sea siren
That leaves behind *her* cold Baltic waters
In order to sport in our seas

(Morgan)

The eel, siren
of the cold seas, who leaves *her* Baltic playground
for our warm waters

(Wright)

Now, Edwin Morgan's translation appeared in book form in 1959, Charles Wright's in 1978, so it's not unreasonable to suggest that Paz's phrase about "translations of translations of translations" may be read in a slightly different sense. That's to say, the ludic imagery involving the "playground" in Wright's translation has indeed been drawn across from the phrase "in order to *sport* in our seas" in Morgan's. The idea of "playground" or "sport" is nowhere in the original, and may be read more as a comment on the latitude given, or taken, by some translators in constructing their "own" poems. The proposition that there might be no distinction in kind between the act of translation and the act of writing an "original text" is hinted at by Lowell himself in his introduction to *Imitations*:

> I have been almost as free as the authors themselves in finding ways to make them ring right for me.

Yet again, I'd be inclined to lose the word "almost" and state unreservedly that translators are absolutely "as free as authors themselves to make [their translations] ring right for [them]." One can never quite lose the word "almost," of course, since one can never quite lose some ideal of constancy, or fidelity, to the source text, even when involved in what Lowell terms an "imitation," which is why I referred a moment ago to "latitude given, or taken."

I myself will take a quick slide down through Lowell's poem, if I may, looking in detail at the decisions he made, from word to word and from line to line, before ending, as threatened, with some observations on the "stunt-reader" and the "stunt-writer." Let's begin with the title, "The Eel," the phrase immediately reiterated there in the first line as if the poem were steadying itself, asserting its focus, then almost immediately sidewinding to the metaphor of "the North Sea siren," Lowell's way of coming to grips with Montale's "la sirena / dei mari freddi," "the siren / of cold seas." The other seas mentioned in the Montale poem are "il Baltico" and "nostri mari," so that the idea of "the North Sea" is extraneous, the idea of the "dead-pan Icelandic gods" completely extraneous. These gods with their blank, expressionless, impassive faces are no doubt set against the "siren" of more southern climes, though Lowell doesn't go so far as Wright and Paulin to contrast "warm waters" and "warm sea" with the "cold seas." It is these "cold seas" alone that appear in Montale, so that the first line is translated by Arrowsmith as "The eel, coldwater / siren." I notice that, like the "playground"/"sport" phenomenon carried over from Morgan to Wright and the "warm waters"/"warm sea" from Wright to Paulin, Arrowsmith's phrase "coldwater / siren" is picked up bodily by Reed as "cold-water/ siren." Now, the "siren" metaphor suggests an ominous aspect to the eel, the one appealed to in the headline of the January 6, 2002, issue of the *Trentonian* newspaper, which reads TEEN SIREN BILKS RETARDED MAN. This is an eel which might lure an unsuspecting tillerman to his death by the power of her song. I write "her" song in acknowledgement of the fact that, even without the interpolations of Arrowsmith, Morgan and Wright, the female aspect of this eel will be dominant from the outset.

The Sirens of Greek myth were sometimes represented as women, sometimes as half women and half birds, sometimes described as the daughters of the sea-god Phorcys or the river-god Achelous and, as the *Encyclopaedia Britannica* points out, "the Sirens continued to exist in folklore throughout the medieval period and later, sometimes being thought of as fish-women rather than bird-women." This aspect of the "*fish*-woman" is almost certainly carried over into Montale's "*sirena*." Readers of Eugenio Montale who came upon "L'anguilla" in his great 1954 collection, *La bufera e altro* (*The Storm, Etc.*), would have been aware of a number of poems addressed to a woman, several using fish imagery, in that same book. In Jonathan Galassi's translation of "Proda di Versilia," or "Shore of Versilia," there's an extraordinary image of domestic sensuality:

> Through the wall I saw loved shadows
> stand at the sink and massage the moray *eels*
> to force their spines into their tails,
> then hack them off

In "Personae Separatae," meanwhile, we find:

> Your form came this way,
> stayed by the ditch among the grounded *eel*-pots,
> then faded like a sigh

The "eel-pots" from "Personae Separatae" show up again in "Luce d'inverno," or "Winter Light":

> When I came out of the sky above the Acropolis
> and, for miles, found hampers of octopus and *eel*
> (the sawmarks of those teeth
> on the stunned heart!)

We've met a version of this "octopus" in "Indian Serenade," another poem from *The Storm, Etc.*:

> The octopus that works
> inky tentacles among the shoals
> knows how to use you. You belong to him
> unwittingly. You're him; you think you're you.

One sense in which the addressee of this poem might "belong" to the "octopus" is connected, I suggest, to the "inky" feature of its "tentacles." Readers of Montale would have been reminded of the title of his 1925 volume, *Ossi di Sepia*, or *Cuttlefish Bones*. Like the octopus and squid, to which it's related, the cuttlefish secretes an ink when disturbed or attacked. This sepia is, or was, used both as a water-colour pigment and for writing. It is, then, in the sense that the addressee is the object of the act of writing that she is "used," becoming indivisible from the medium in which she's represented. This indivisibility might also be said to be the "subject" of "Iris," the poem for which, if you recall, Montale described himself as a "medium," by which he was himself "used":

> But if you come back, you're not you,
> your earthly history is changed,
> you don't wait for the prow at the pier,
>
> you watch for nothing: yesterday or tomorrow;
>
> *for His work* (which is transforming
> into yours) *has to continue.*

The transformative aspect of "Iris" may be approached from several points of view. There is, to begin with, the central myth of the goddess of the rainbow, daughter of Thaumas (himself son of Pontus, the Sea) and Electra (daughter of Oceanus). Iris is therefore a sister of the Harpies, wind-deities often represented as birds with faces of women and, like the Sirens, likely to lure, or lash, men off their proper course. I use the word "lash" here in the sense in which Arrowsmith and Morgan translate the word *frusta,* "a whip," allowing it, in the case of Arrowsmith, to prepare the way for the English pun in lines which he translates as:

> brief rainbow, twin
> of that other iris shining between your *lashes*

Morgan renders these lines as:

> The brief rainbow, a twin
> To that other iris set within your brows
> Which you flash out

There is, therefore, the flicker of a "lash" in "*flash.*" The lines in Italian read:

l'iride breve, gemella
di quella che incastonano i tuoi cigli
e fai brillare intatta in mezzo ai figli
dell'uomo

The translation by Galassi reads:

brief rainbow, iris,
twin to the one your lashes frame
and you set shining virginal among
the sons of men, sunk in your mire—
can you fail to see her as a sister?

One can see immediately that Galassi has tried to approximate, in the echo of "iris" in "mire," the Italian rhymes of *cigli* and *figli*, *gemella* and *quella*, the rhymes which embody, or enact, this moment of gemellarity and sisterhood. Like Burnside, Kay, Reed and Wright, Galassi opted earlier for the translation of *frusta* as "whiplash," which, despite its connotations of a violent jolt of the neck or spinal cord, certainly prepared the ground for "lashes" in the eye sense, if "eyelashes" are indeed what we're dealing with here. The supercilious among us, who would seem to include not only Morgan, with his "brows," but Kay and Reed, who opt for "forehead," are perhaps associating the English word "supercilious," with its Latin root *supercilium*, which certainly means "brow" or "forehead," as does the Italian word *sopracciglio*. Under the *sopracciglio*, as it were, are *cigli* themselves, the "eyelashes." Readers of other poems in *The Storm, Etc.* would have recognised these "eyelashes" as belonging to a strand of imagery occurring in other poems. In "Lungomare," or "Promenade," we find *"sui lunghissimi cigli del tuo sguardo,"* translated by Galassi as "on the long, long *lashes* of your look." But Galassi himself opts for translating *ciglio* as "eyebrow" in "Verso Finistere," or "Near Finistere," where *"l'arco del tuo ciglio s'e spento"* comes across as "the arc of your *eyebrow* ended."

Not that Robert Lowell could be bothered with the niceties of either "brow" or "eyelashes," not surprisingly in the light of Elizabeth Hardwick's account of Lowell's meeting with Montale in Florence, when, as she told Ian Hamilton, they "had several sweaty, mute evenings of language difficulty and great displays of blundering affection." Lowell here takes his cue partly from the image of "love's arrow on earth," partly from the subliminal connection between the "arc" of the rainbow and the *arcum* of the bow in archery, so that, in another great display of both language difficulty and blundering affection, he sets himself at "your eye's target center." So determined is he to resist the obvious term, "bull's-eye," that he perpetrates this even greater monstrosity. The reading of the word "iris" favoured here is that given by the *OED* as "a flat, circular, coloured membrane suspended vertically in the aqueous humour of the eye, and separating the anterior from the posterior chamber; in its centre is a circular opening, called the pupil, which may be enlarged or diminished so as to regulate the amount of light transmitted to the retina." It's the "circular opening, called the pupil," which Lowell is approximating here with the phrase "your eye's target center," an image which has no doubt influenced the translation by John Burnside of the corresponding phrase as "rainbow / and perfect / twin to the bright / *pupilla* of your eye / which still remains / inviolate / amongst the sons of men."

Now that phrase, "the sons of men," which occurs in the translations by Arrowsmith, Burnside, Galassi, Kay, Lowell, Nims and Wright, is a phrase with strong biblical associations, a version of it first occurring in Job 25:5–6:

> Yea, the stars are not pure in his sight. How much less man, that is a worm? And the son of man, which is a worm.

These verses from the Book of Job contain the poetic spark of "L'anguilla," including its basic structure of comparing and contrasting the sullied with the celestial, as well as the "worm" image, itself a sister of the "serpent" we find as early as Genesis 3:14:

> Upon thy belly shalt thou go, and dust shalt thou eat all the days of thy life.

That the "serpent" of Genesis is lurking in the undergrowth here is supported by the reference to Eden in Lowell's *paradise* of fecundity." We need look no further than Genesis 9:13 for the emblem established by the Judaeo-Christian God to connect the sullied with the celestial:

I do set my bow in the cloud, and it shall be a token of a covenant
between me and the earth.

The rainbow goddess of Greek myth is directly related to this emblem from the Judaeo-Christian system, since Iris is also a messenger of
the gods, particularly Juno, sometimes using the rainbow as an information highway. Given that we also first meet the term "angels" as early as
the description of Jacob's dream in Genesis 28:12, in which there is "a ladder set up on earth, and the top of it reached to heaven: and behold the
angels of God ascending and descending on it," we might remember that
the word for a messenger in Greek is *angelos*. For reasons that will be all
too obvious, I'm very taken by the proposal by Francesco Zambon, in his
book-length study of this poem (*L'iride nel fango: L'anguilla di Eugenio Montale*), that there is a play, in the Italian title, on the relationship between *anguilla* and *angelo*, so that the eel is the bearer of its own news, as it were.
I'm also very taken by the further proposal by Zambon that *"L'anguilla* is
an anagram of *la lingua*," so that "it incarnates perfectly that idea of the
'short long poem' . . . which expresses the tendency toward an objectifica-
tion without residues of sentiment, toward 'emotion which has become
thing.'" (I should state that I'm grateful to the extensive notes and commentary by Jonathan Galassi, which pointed me in the direction of
Francesco Zambon, among other illustrious commentators on this lus-
trous poem.) Zambon's image of incarnation comes directly from Montale's 1940 essay, "Let's Talk about Hermeticism," in which he admires art
"incarnated in the means of expression." In this sense, "The Eel" partakes
of the Christian idea of the Word made flesh, connecting it with those
lines from "Iris" which I quoted earlier:

for His work (which is transforming
into yours) *has to continue.*

This work of "transforming" which involves "continuity" relies on
religious imagery, of course, but its force, and source, are primarily literary. I think of that phrase translated there by Lowell as "the paradise of
fecundity." No Italian, or non-Italian, poet may use any version of the
word *Paradiso* without nodding in the direction of Dante Alighieri. In this
case, I propose that Montale may be thinking of a very specific passage

in Book XII, translated here by Allen Mandelbaum, in which the rainbow compact between God and man and the rainbow of Greek myth are combined:

> Just as, concentric, like in color, two
> rainbows will curve their way through a thin cloud
> when Juno has commanded her handmaid,
> the outer rainbow echoing the inner,
> much like the voice of one—the wandering nymph—
> whom love consumed as sun consumes the mist
> (and those two bows let people here foretell,
> by reason of the pact God made with Noah,
> that flood will never strike the world again)

Those lines (10–18) of *Paradiso* XII are almost immediately preceded by an image, in line 8, of *"nostre serene,"* "our sirens," to which Montale surely alludes when he uses versions of both these words in the first and third lines of "L'anguilla":

> *L'anguilla, la* sirena
> *dei mari freddi che lascia il Baltico*
> *per giungere ai* nostri *mari*

The combination of celestial/slime imagery must have struck a note with the Lowell who ended one of his best-known early poems with the stadium-rocking:

> When the Lord God formed man from the sea's slime
> And breathed into his face the breath of life,
> And blue-lung'd combers lumbered to the kill.
> The Lord survives the rainbow of His will.

That "comber" is an interesting word, referring as it does to both a rolling breaker and a kind of fish, though fish don't have lungs, blue or otherwise. Fish do, however, come with a lot of baggage. Lowell, like Montale in the present poem, would have been aware of the relationship between the initial letters of the Greek words meaning "Jesus Christ, Son of God,

Saviour" (ICHTHYS) and *ichthys*, "fish," and the subsequent significance of the fish in religious iconography.

As I mentioned in the previous chapter, "The Quaker Graveyard in Nantucket" owes much to the supercharged rhetoric of *the* great modern religious poet, Gerard Manley Hopkins, in "The Wreck of the *Deutschland*." Montale is also sufficiently familiar with Hopkins, according to Laura Barile (quoted by Galassi), to have borrowed the image of "the blaze of the chestnut blossoms" from the "fresh-firecoal *chestnut*-falls" of "Pied Beauty," though Hopkins was visualising the nut (*castagna*) rather than the tree (*castagno*). This is a crucial line in the poem, a line in which there's a shift in dynamics, in which what turns out to be "a spark" of inspiration sets off a chain reaction. As such, it's a line ghosted, I suspect, by the idiomatic Italian phrase *prendere qualcuno in castagna*, "to catch someone in the act." What else is being enacted here? Well, something of the meaning of the word *castagnola*, "firecracker," seems to have strayed into Lowell's "Roman candle," his version of the Italian word *torcia*, "torch," though "a cylindrical firework, which throws out a succession of stars" (*OED*) seems a shade excessive, despite that *torcia* being linked to "*la scintilla*," "a spark," and "a green spirit, potent only / where desolation and arson burn." That "arson" is a good old-fashioned mistranslation of *l'arsura*, which means "burning heat" or "parching thirst," but Lowell may have in mind the ghost of a "fuse" hovering about that "green spirit," as in "The force that through the *green* fuse drives the flower." As Jonathan Galassi reminds us, the Dylan Thomas poem was itself translated by Montale in 1946, though Galassi doesn't enumerate the key images which seem to have made their way into "L'anguilla." These include not only "the force that drives the water through the rocks" and "my veins" (which come in there as the "delicate capillaries of slime"), but the basic argument of the Thomas poem, which is that of continuity between the natural world and the speaker:

> And I am dumb to tell the hanging man
> How of my clay is made the hangman's lime.

The English word "lime" is cognate with the Italian *limo*, or "mud," the word which Montale uses in "Il gallo cedrone," the poem immediately preceding "L'anguilla," translated by Jonathan Galassi as "The Capercaillie":

Your sob's a cry for help. Living
was sweeter than sinking into this mire,
easier to come undone in the wind
than here in the *mud*, crusted over the fire.

The line immediately before had placed the speaker "in the ditch with you" and connects both "The Eel" and "The Capercaillie" with one of Montale's very first poems, "I limoni," or "The Lemons":

But I like roads that lead to grassy
ditches where boys
scoop up a few starved
eels out of half-dry puddles:
paths that run along the banks,
come down among the tufted canes
and end in orchards, among the lemon trees.

There's a link, established early on in Montale's oeuvre, between the "lemons" (*limoni*) and the slime or "mud" (*limo*), between Edenic "orchards" and the "eels." This kind of reading might seem farfetched if one didn't meet it again and again in Montale. One or two relevant examples of wordplay spring to mind. The Italian of that line from "The Lemons," translated by Galassi as "paths that run along the banks," reads *"la viuzze che seguono i ciglioni,"* so that the *"ciglioni"* ("banks") is picked up in "The Eel" by the *"cigli"* ("eyelashes") between which "this buried rainbow, this iris, twin sister / of the one" is "set." Let's set ourselves for a moment at that word "set." The Italian word is *incastonano*, and it refers to the setting of a precious stone in, say, a ring. That *"incastonano"* glints back, echoing the *"castagni"* of the "chestnut blossoms" with their "blaze," and forward to the word *gemella*, "twin," in which is embedded the Italian word for both a "bud" and "a precious stone," that word being *gemma*. To support such an idea one need look no further, once again, than "The Capercaillie," the poem immediately preceding "The Eel" in *The Storm, Etc.*:

Now the *jewel-buds*
of the perennials glow like the grub
in the gloom. Jove is underground.

It seems that, by the end of Lowell's version of "The Eel," all of us are underground, "up to our gills in your life-giving mud," the same mud from which the eel was rumoured to spring, spontaneously, self-generatingly, its reproductive arrangements no less puzzling to Sigmund Freud than to the mud-men, Aristotle (384–322 B.C.) and Saint Basil (A.D. 330–379), he of the flabbergasted *Commentary on the Six Days of Creation.* That "The Eel" might itself be a commentary on its own creation is suggested by the fact that the poem takes the form of a sinuous, single sentence, enacting its own sinuosity and singleness. That the question raised at the end of "The Eel" about the relationship between sameness and doubleness might be seen, first of all, as a question paraphrased by the last lines of "The Force That Through the Green Fuse Drives the Flower":

And I am dumb to tell the lover's tomb
How at my sheet goes the *same* crooked *worm.*

We might remember that the introductory poem to Montale's *Collected Poems 1920–1954,* translated by Jonathan Galassi as "On the Threshold," is "In Limine." "In Limine" immediately precedes "I Limoni," "The Lemons," and suggests yet again that there is no boundary, or limen, between life in the Paradise of the *limoni* and the plashy *limo,* that the higher and lower orders of "iris" and "eel" are "the same," as comes across in version after version of the end of the poem:

among the sons
of men floundering in your mud, can you
deny a sister?

(Arrowsmith)

in all this radiant mud
—can you believe
she is anything
other than sister?

(Burnside)

                              among
the sons of men, sunk in your mire—
can you fail to see her as a sister?

                                                        (Galassi)

                              among the sons
of men plunged in your mud, can you
not take her for a sister?

                                                        (Kay)

The brief rainbow, a twin
To that other iris set within your brows
Which you flash out unclouded on the crowds
Of the children of men plunged in your muds—can you doubt
It is your sister that swims in?

                                                        (Morgan)

                              among
the sons of men, steeped in your mire—in this
not recognize a sister?

                                                        (Nims)

like brother and sister
joined in perfect vision

                                                        (Paulin)

                              among
generations immersed in mud, can you
not take her for a sister?

                                        (Reed)

vanishing rainbow, twin sister
to her you set behind your own eyelids
and let shine out over the sons of men, on us
up to our hairlines in your breathing mud . . .
and *you* can't call her sister?

                                        (Wright)

That last version by Charles Wright seems to rely heavily on Lowell, substituting "hairlines" for "gills," though nothing remotely like "gills" or "hairlines" appears in the original. Lowell is perhaps confusing the Italian word *fango*, meaning "mud" or "mire," with the English word "fang," and locating that somewhere in the area of the "gills," now that he's up to speed on the "blue-lung'd" question. The italicisation by Wright of *"you"* seems to be a direct response to Lowell's italicised *"Sister."* The resulting tone is somewhat thunderous, though something of the thunder has been stolen by the occurrence of the phrase "twin sister" five lines earlier, a repetition that is more likely than not to be unconscious.

LET ME MOVE SWIFTLY towards a conclusion here by taking my description of Lowell's repetition of the word "sister" as "unconscious" as my cue for suggesting that, as a reader, I am standing in for the "writer" of the poem. I am shadowing him or her in that first process of determining, from word to word and from line to line, the impact of those words and those lines. To the extent that I might be described as a "stunt-writer," the person through whom the poem was written was a "stunt-reader," standing in for subsequent readers, foreshadowing them, determining the impact of those words and those lines. For both stunt-reader and stunt-writer there's a strong sense of the poem as an autonomous creature, one that has a life beyond them, one which, as it bucks and bounds and comes into being under them, remains intact. Montale uses an Italian equivalent of this last word, *intatta*, to describe the iris "set . . . to shine on the sons of men." The word is translated by Arrowsmith as "unsullied," Burnside and Nims as "inviolate," Galassi as "virginal," Kay as "entire," Morgan as "unclouded," Paulin as "perfect," Reed as "brilliantly," while remaining quite untranslated by Wright and Lowell:

> this buried rainbow, this iris, twin sister
> of the one you set in your eye's target center
> to shine on the sons of men,
> on us, up to our gills in your life-giving mud—
> can you call her *Sister*?

The stunt-reader or stunt-writer of "original poem" and translation alike has one major responsibility: to stay on top of the material which moves through him or her, to be a medium, yes, but also to be a mediator, with the more active role that word "mediator" implies. One of the awe-inspiring aspects of "The Eel" is the extent to which it includes a commentary on its own process, connecting the religious imagery of the *Dominus Illuminatio Mea* (a motto all too familiar, perhaps, to the Oxford community) with "a spark" of creativity, the inspiration of God breathing on "life-giving mud" with poetic inspiration, the mediation between heaven and earth with the finding of likenesses between unlike things, between "iris" and "eel," between "eel" and "you," which is at the heart of the question at the end of the poem.

Not that we would be entirely sure that *is* the question at the end of Lowell's reading of "The Eel," where the poem seems to have got out from under him. How do we know that? I'd say we might take our cue, yet again, from the unconscious repetition of "sister" and "*Sister*," along with a syntactical bogging down in the pronoun jam of "on *us*, up to *our* gills in *your* life-giving mud— / can *you* call *her* Sister?," as indicators of a failure of the stunt-reader to take into account every twist and turn of the poem. What Lowell has missed is the turn that has somehow unseated him, for the sense of that last line, attested to by all of the other versions, is rather:

can't you call her *Sister?*

The failure of Lowell as translator at this crucial moment is no different in kind from the failure of most poets as stunt-readers of their own "original poems," when they simply are not equal to the challenge of being media and mediators. It is clearly part of the same activity. What is also clear to me is that, despite this crucial misreading by Lowell, we can divine as stunt-writers what direction the poem means to take. We recognise the ur-poem of which it wishes to be a manifestation even without appealing to Montale. For that ur-poem is no more the poem written in the Italian language through the medium of Eugenio Montale than it is the poem in English by Arrowsmith, Burnside, Galassi, Kay, Lowell, Morgan, Nims, Paulin, Reed or Wright.

Another passage from Walter Benjamin's great essay, "The Task of the Translator," from which I quoted in the last chapter, may be useful here, particularly since it avails itself of religious imagery:

> To grasp the genuine relationship between an original and a
> translation requires an investigation analogous to the argumentation
> by which a critique of cognition would have to prove the
> impossibility of an image theory. There it is a matter of showing that
> in cognition there could be no objectivity, not even a claim to it; here
> it can be demonstrated that no translation would be possible if in its
> ultimate essence it strove for likeness to the original. For in its
> afterlife—which could not be called that if it were not a
> transformation and a renewal of something living—the original
> undergoes a change.

I extend this idea that "the original undergoes a change," an idea which I found wonderfully shocking when I first encountered it, to propose that the poem has what might be described as an "immortal" aspect. Any writer, or reader, will tell you that as a poem comes into being, it often presents a sense of having had an eternal existence, that it has come from "the paradise of fecundity" and will return to "the paradise of fecundity," autonomous and intact. Lowell himself seems to imagine a poem being *"intatta,"* or "whole," or "sound," when he writes, in that sentence from the introduction to *Imitations* I quoted earlier:

I have been almost as free as the authors themselves in finding ways to *make them ring right for me.*

Seamus Heaney picks up this image of "soundness" when he writes, in his "Elegy" for Lowell:

You were our big night ferry
thudding in a big sea,

the whole craft *ringing*
with an armourer's music
the course set wilfully across
the ungovernable and dangerous.

The "ungovernable" connects yet again with Lowell's gubernatorial "rightness of hand" that's needed by a translator as much as an "original" poet. "I have been almost as free as the authors themselves" is carried across to Heaney's positioning himself with the Lough Neagh fisherman:

I tasted *freedom* with him.

The "wholeness" or indivisibility of the poem, for which the "original" poet is "free" to be a medium, has an inevitable consequence. That is, of course, the abnegation of the person of the poet who gives himself over to the "other," the indivisibility of the poem leading to the combination of *divisibility* and *invisibility* of the poet. "You're him; you think you're you," as the speaker of Montale's "Indian Serenade" has it. In "Personae Separatae," from which I quoted earlier, the speaker inquires:

are we too separate persons
in another's eyes?

There is a necessary gemellarity in seeing oneself as a twinned "little doll" in the *pupillae* of the "other," an idea to which "L'anguilla" glancingly refers, its eel having struggled free of the "eel-pots" in "Personae Separatae."

CHAPTER 9

AUTOPSYCHOGRAPHY

FERNANDO PESSOA

The poet is a faker. He
Fakes it so completely,
He even fakes he's suffering
The pain he's really feeling.

And they who read his writing
Fully feel while reading
Not that pain of his that's double,
But theirs, completely fictional.

So on its tracks goes round and round,
To entertain the reason,
That wound-up little train
We call the heart of man.

Translated by Edwin Honig and Susan M. Brown

I ENDED MY DISCUSSION of Robert Lowell's imitation of Eugenio Montale's "L'anguilla / The Eel" with a profound comment on "the indivisibility of the poem leading to the combination of *divisibility* and *invisibility* of the poet." One would be hard-pressed to find a stronger candidate for that combination of divisibility and invisibility, of heteronymity and anonymity, than the Portuguese poet Fernando Pessoa, among the first of whose seventy-five heteronyms was C. R. Anon. I want to try today to explore, albeit obliquely, the conditions of anonymity and heteronymity in the hope of further making sense of how poems get written and read, of trying to ascertain where the poem bows out and the personality of the poet, insofar as we may locate it, steps in. For Fernando Pessoa, the idea of "personality" must have played on his mind from early on, since the Portuguese word *pessoa* means, of all things, "person." Pessoa was predisposed to thinking in terms of being "a person," if not multiple "persons." *Nomen est omen*, as we say in Ireland. The fact that both *pessoa* and the English word "person" derive from the Latin word *persona*, meaning "a mask used by a player," accounts for the primary meanings of the word "person" given by the *OED*:

> A character sustained or assumed in a drama or the like, or in actual life; part played; hence function, office, capacity; guise, semblance; one of the characters in a play or story.

That Pessoa wrote in the guise or semblance of so many poets raises that much broader question about the extent to which the personality of any single poet may be thought of as being coterminous with his or her poems, of the "end" of the poet coinciding with the end of the poem, which exercised so many writers who flourished in the first years of the twentieth century, including that masked man, Yeats, and Eliot, who insisted in *Tradition and the Individual Talent* (1919) that "the progress of an artist is a continual self-sacrifice, a continual extinction of personality," that poetry "is not the expression of personality, but an escape from personality." The phenomenon, or phenomena, of Pessoa seem to suggest that each and every poem invents both its writer and its reader, and that both writer and reader are engaged in an endless round of negotiations from which no true peace may ever result.

THE NOTION THAT "AUTOPSYCHOGRAPHY" is itself a poem about the contract between reader and writer which will question ideas of the autonomy of the author is announced by the seeming neologism of the title, which splices together the words "autobiography" and "psychology," allowing us to linger over the separate components of those words. To linger over those separate components is pretty much what I propose to do in this chapter. A lot of my time will be taken up with this first component, "auto," and a wide range of concepts associated with it. "Auto" derives from the Greek term for "the self," and immediately connects with that aspect of the meaning of Pessoa's own name which includes the notion of the person as a discrete, individual, independent being—the self-governing "autonomy" to which I referred. I want to return later to this notion of selfhood in political terms, to the fact that Portugal became a republic in 1910. But let me leave the idea of the "autonomic" almost as soon as I mention it and leap to the idea of the "autonymic." "Autonym" is a very specific term for "a book published under the author's real name," so that the "auto" component in "*Auto*psychography" taunts us with the idea of the "real," the "genuine," the "true," particularly when the first lines of the poem will announce:

> *O poeta é um fingidor.*
> *Finge tão completemente*
> *Que chega à fingir que é dor*
> *A dor que deveras sente.*

This is translated by Edwin Honig and Susan M. Brown as:

> The poet is a faker. He
> Fakes it so completely,
> He even fakes he's suffering
> The pain he's really feeling.

We recognise the *vera*, or "truth," there in "*que deveras sente*," a phrase translated by Simon Pleasance as "that he really feels":

> The poet is a pretender.
> He feigns so completely
> That he manages to feign pain
> The pain that he really feels.

Simon Pleasance's choice of the word "feign," combined with the "really," conjures up Touchstone's observation in *As You Like It* that "the truest poetry is the most feigning," a phrase which would surely serve as the motto of the historical personage of Fernando Pessoa, an historical personage who is extremely difficult to locate. As Pessoa writes in *The Book of Disquiet*:

> I envy—but I'm not sure that I envy—those for whom a biography could be written, or could write their own. In these random impressions, and with no desire to be other than random, I indifferently narrate my factless autobiography, my lifeless history.

Had Pessoa written something other than a "factless autobiography," we might have more than the sketchiest sense of him. In his introduction to his great 2001 edition and translation of *The Book of Disquiet*, Richard Zenith gives us some of the background:

> Fernando Antonio Nogueira Pessoa was born in Lisbon in 1888, died there in 1935, and did not often leave the city as an adult, but he spent nine of his childhood years in the British-governed town of Durban, South Africa, where his stepfather was the Portuguese consul. Pessoa, who was five years old when his natural father died of tuberculosis, developed into a shy and highly imaginative boy, and a brilliant student. Shortly after his seventeenth birthday, he returned to Lisbon to enroll in the university but soon dropped out, preferring to study on his own at the National Library, where he systematically read major works of philosophy, history, sociology and literature (especially Portuguese) in order to complement and extend the traditional English education he had received in South Africa. His production of poetry and prose in English during this period was intense, and by 1910 he was also writing extensively in Portuguese. He published his first essay in literary criticism in 1912, his first piece of creative prose (a passage from *The Book of Disquiet*) in 1913, and his first poems in 1914.

Pessoa's own account of what happened to him in 1914 is included in an extraordinary letter written in 1935 to Adolfo Casaias Monteiro:

The day that I finally gave up—it was on the 8th of March, 1914—
I walked over to the high chest of drawers and, taking a sheet of
paper, I began to write, standing, as I always do when I can. And I
wrote some thirty poems in a row, in a sort of ecstasy, the nature of
which I cannot define. This was the triumphal day of my life, and I
can never know another like that. I began with the title: *The Keeper of
Sheep* . . . And what followed was the apparition in myself of
someone I immediately named Alberto Caeiro. Pardon the absurdity
of the phrase: my master had sprung up in me.

Let's focus for a moment on that "sort of ecstasy, the nature of which
[Pessoa] cannot define" and see if we can't manage a definition which incorporates both the "auto" and "graphy" elements from "Autopsychography." I'm thinking of the term "*auto*matic *writing*," a practice Pessoa
would embrace formally for much of his life, with a particularly large
number of visitants in 1916–17, at exactly the same time W. B. Yeats was
giving himself over to the automatic writing of Georgie Hyde-Lees,
whom he had married in October 1917. As Richard Zenith points out in
his edition of *The Selected Prose of Fernando Pessoa*, Pessoa's interest in spir-
itualism was almost as longstanding as Yeats's:

> From 1912 to 1914 Pessoa lived with his aunt Anica, who was an
> enthusiast of the occult sciences and the probable catalyst of her
> great-nephew's automatic writing, which began in 1916. In 1915–16
> Pessoa translated and published four books by three authors of the
> Theosophical Society—C. W. Leadbetter, Annie Besant, and Helena
> Blavatsky—whose ideas prompted an "intellectual crisis," according
> to the draft of a letter to Mário de Sá-Carneiro. Though impressed
> by the concept of "higher, superhuman knowledge that pervades
> Theosophical writings," Pessoa could not reconcile Theosophy's
> "ultra-Christian" character with his own "fundamental paganism."

We'll return to another example of binary opposition when we come
to the "double" aspect of "reason" and "heart" later in the poem. For the
moment, I'll stay with another connection between W. B. Yeats and Fernando Pessoa, in the shifting shape of Aleister Crowley, whom Pessoa fi-

nally met in Lisbon in 1930, after reading him for a number of years. As Richard Zenith notes:

> Aleister Crowley (1875–1947), who billed himself variously as Master Therion, 666, and The Great Beast, was a talented, mischievous, much adored, and much reviled English occult master. He was initiated into the Hermetic Order of the Golden Dawn (whose most famous member was William Butler Yeats) in 1898, cofounded the Astrum Argentum, or Order of the Silver Star, in 1906, and became head of the Ordo Templi Orientis in 1921. This last group, of German origin, employed tantric sex rituals, to which Crowley added animal sacrifices and drug use. Blasted by the English press after one of his disciples died in a proto-hippie commune in the early twenties, perhaps from the ritual consumption of cat's blood, Crowley faded from view and died in relative obscurity, but by the end of the century most of his many books (including some poetry) were back in print and various occult groups had taken up his teachings.

Unless one belongs to one of those "occult groups," it's most likely that one will remember Aleister Crowley for his run-in with that "most famous member" of the Order of the Golden Dawn. In Chapter 9 of *W. B. Yeats: A Life*, R. F. Foster describes, with all his customary pithiness, the struggle between Yeats and MacGregor Mathers for control of the Golden Dawn, a struggle which came to a head in early 1900:

> On 17 April 1900 Mathers sent an envoy to break into the Isis-Urania Temple at 36 Blythe Road, Hammersmith, and take possession of the magical "properties" there. The emissary was the 25-year old Aleister Crowley. As yet uninitiated in the Order, he had attached himself to Mathers and embarked on a career in occultism where both his fame and his fabulism (as "the wickedest man in the world") would eventually eclipse those of his mentor. He was ejected when [Florence] Farr called a police constable, but sent notices claiming the right to take over proceedings. Guard duty was taken over by Edmund Hunter, who appealed to WBY (a friend and ally through Celtic ritualism as well as membership of the Second Order); on

19 April they changed the locks and awaited Crowley's next assault. He arrived before midday, wearing full highland dress plus the "mask of Osiris." The inhabitants of Hammersmith may have been more surprised than WBY, who believed he had been warned of this intervention by occult divination and astral communications ("a clear proof of the value of systematic training even in these subtle things," he pointedly told Russell). Less subtly, Hunter was a proficient boxer and his reputation had gone before him, which may have been a more decisive factor in the ejection of Crowley. But the wickedest man in the world was also discomfited to encounter WBY, whom he had met the year before and cordially hated—an antipathy sealed by WBY's unenthusiastic response to Crowley's poems (their author put it down to "bilious" jealousy).

Crowley's account of his showing Yeats the proofs of a number of lyrics entitled "Mysteries, Lyrical and Dramatic" is included in *The Confessions of Aleister Crowley*:

I had by this time become fairly expert in clairvoyance, clairaudience and clairsentience. But it would have been a very dull person indeed who failed to recognize the black, bilious rage that shook him to the soul. I instance this as a proof that Yeats was a genuine poet at heart, for a mere charlatan would have known that he had no cause to fear an authentic poet. What hurt him was the knowledge of his own incomparable inferiority.

Crowley was a poet much exercised, then, by notions of the "genuine" and the "authentic," as well as by questions of rankings. For example, he gives us this distinction on the following page of *The Confessions*:

The difference between Cambridge and Oxford is that the former makes you the equal of anybody alive; the latter leaves you in the invidious position of being his superior.

The Cambridge-educated Crowley, who nonetheless managed to think of himself as being the superior of just about everyone, is a poet with whom

Pessoa held much in common. As John Symonds writes, in his introduction to the 1973 edition of *White Stains*:

> There was not one Crowley but a multiplicity of them. He imagined himself to be someone different every moment: Crowley the English gentleman and fellow of Trinity, Crowley the World Teacher, Crowley held in the grip of the Highest Truth, Crowley wallowing in filth and humbug, and so on.

White Stains had been printed in 1898 in an edition of one hundred copies, most of which were destroyed in 1924 by British Customs, possibly because of such gems as "Necrophilia" and "A Ballad of Passive Paederasty." It was published anonymously, or heteronymously, as "the literary remains of George Archibald Bishop, a neuropath of the second empire." In 1913, Crowley published *The Book of Lies* or, to give it its full title, *The Book of Lies, which is also falsely called "Breaks," the wanderings or falsifications of the one thought of Frater Perdurabo (Aleister Crowley) which thought is itself untrue.* His best-known poem is "Hymn to Pan," which begins:

> Thrill with lissome lust of the light,
> O man! My man!
> Come careering out of the night
> Of Pan! Io Pan!

The poem, which was included in Crowley's *Magick in Theory and Practice*, seems to be less theoretical than practical:

> I am numb
> With the lonely lust of devildom.
> Thrust the sword through the galling fetter,
> All-devourer, all-begetter;
> Give me the sign of the Open Eye,
> And the token erect of thorny thigh
> And the word of madness and mystery,
> O Pan! Io Pan!

It ends with an appeal for sexual possession of the goat-god, though it seems that in some of Crowley's rites he had to make do with a mere goat:

I am thy mate, I am thy man,
Goat of thy flock, I am gold, I am god,
Flesh to thy bone, flower to thy rod.

Pessoa and Crowley shared the occultist's interest in the "mask," of course, but the supreme poet of the *persona* would have recognised in a poet given to wear the "mask of Osiris" or the heteronyms of George Archibald Bishop or Frater Perdurabo a very literal sense in which "the poet is a faker." For, as he was engaged in writing "Autopsychography," which is dated April 1, 1931, Pessoa must have been very conscious of one particular incident, from only six months earlier, in which he had conspired with Crowley to "fake it so completely." As Richard Zenith writes, in that note to *The Selected Prose of Fernando Pessoa* from which I quoted earlier:

In September of 1930 Crowley came to Lisbon with a girlfriend, who quarreled with him at a certain point and abruptly left Portugal. Crowley, with Pessoa's help, committed a dramatic pseudo-suicide, writing a jilted lover's note left at the Mouth of Hell, a cavernous rock formation on the seacoast west of Lisbon, where Crowley had ostensibly taken a flying mortal leap. He had in fact left Portugal by way of Spain, but Pessoa, who explained to the Lisbon papers the significance of the astrological signs and mystical words that graced the suicide note, also reported seeing Crowley, "or Crowley's ghost," the day after his disappearance.

This episode, which would surely fall into the category of a poet who "even fakes he's suffering / the pain he's really feeling," is telling in another way. The "flying mortal leap," fake or otherwise, from a cliff-top would have had a very particular literary resonance for both Pessoa and Crowley. I'm thinking, of course, of the end of *Melmoth the Wanderer*:

Through the furze that clothed this rock, almost to its summit, there was a kind of tract as if a person had dragged, or been dragged, his way through it—a down-trodden track, over which no footsteps but those of one impelled by force had ever passed. Melmoth and Moncada gained at last the summit of the rock. The ocean was beneath—the wide, waste, engulphing ocean! On a crag beneath them, something hung as floating to the blast. Melmoth clambered down and caught it. It was the handkerchief which the Wanderer had worn about his neck the preceding night—that was the last trace of the Wanderer.

This connection between the "suicide note" and Charles Robert Maturin's "handkerchief" might seem a bit farfetched were it not for the fact that, if you recall, one of Pessoa's first heteronyms was C.R., or *Charles Robert*, Anon. The Melmoth who finds the handkerchief is a nineteenth-century descendant, in some sense a "double," of the seventeenth-century Melmoth the Wanderer, a character "who has voluntarily exchanged the salvation of his soul for the knowledge and power that come with prolonged life and who," as Alethea Hayter puts it in the introduction to her 1977 edition of the text, "then desperately tries to lay his fearful burden on another victim."

Let's focus for a moment on the Melmothian Aleister Crowley's heteronym of "Master Therion." I'm less interested just now in the "Therion" element, its Greek meaning of "wild beast" not in the least inappropriate to a goat-embracer, but the description of Crowley as "Master." This appellation is widely used in occultism, of course, but I want to suggest that this very specific "Master," with his beastly inclination to "spring up," is looming large in Pessoa's mind when, in 1935, five years after meeting Crowley, he gives his account of that "triumphal" day in March 1914:

> And what followed was the apparition in myself of someone I immediately named Alberto Caeiro. Pardon the absurdity of the phrase: my *master* had sprung up in me.

My second reason for associating this passage with Crowley has to do with an allusion to Pessoa's reporting that he had seen Crowley, "or Crowley's ghost," after the "pseudo-suicide" in his description of "the *apparition* in myself" of Alberto Caeiro. We notice that the initials of two of Pes-

soa's heteronyms, Alberto Caeiro and Alvaro de Campos, share initials
with Aleister Crowley. They appeared to Pessoa in 1914, one year after the
publication of *The Book of Lies*, the title of which is echoed, surely, in
The Book of Disquiet, the earliest section of which was written shortly after
the publication of *The Book of Lies*. That Pessoa should associate an "apparition" with writing is understandable for at least two reasons, both
directly or indirectly involving Crowley, both relating to "Autopsychography." The first is that, at the time of the "pseudo-suicide," Pessoa was
engaged in translating into Portuguese the "Hymn to Pan" of Master
Therion, which is included in his *Obra Poetica*:

> *Vibra do cio subtil da luz,*
> *Meu homem e afã*
> *Vem turbulento da noite à flux*
> *De Pã! Io Pã!*
> *Io Pã! Io Pã! Do mar de além*
> *Vem da Sicilia e da Arcadia vem!*

The "Hymn to Pan" is written for the most part in couplets, except for
that opening quatrain, rhymed *abab*. That is, of course, the scheme of
"Autopsicografia":

> *E os que lêem o que escreve,*
> *Na dor lida sentem bem,*
> *Não as duas que ele teve,*
> *Mas só à que eles não têm.*

That's the Portuguese of the second stanza. I want to propose that Pessoa
has a sense, conscious or otherwise, of the template of Crowley's "Hymn
to Pan," including a near version of the god's name in his own hymn
to "pa(i)n," and his replication of precisely the same rhyme (*bem, têm*) in
virtually the same position in "Autopsicografia" as in his translation of
"Hymn to Pan" (*além, vem*). It's significant, I suggest, that the first indicator that Crowley had survived "fak[ing] it so completely" came in a letter
from him having to do with the "Hymn to Pan." As Pessoa explained, in a
letter to his biographer, João Gaspar Simões, dated October 5, 1931:

Crowley, who after committing suicide went to live in Germany wrote to me a few days ago, asking me for the translation, or rather the publication of the translation.

Pessoa had also gone to the trouble of explaining to Simões, in a letter of January 4, 1931, that Master Therion was not one of his heteronyms.

The other connection between the idea of an "apparition" and writing which would have hovered around the memory of Crowley has to do with his psychic powers, powers which Pessoa believed himself to have, and which underlie the *"psycho"* element of "Autopsychography." I want to think about this element for a little while, if I may, though not quite letting go of the "auto" and "graphy" components. I hope you'll forgive me if I cast about for a few minutes, in the hope of landing an idea about a connection between "autonomy" and "psyche" in a politico-geographical sense which somewhat informs this poem.

Now, earlier on I described "Autopsychography" as a word which appears to be a neologism. I say "appears" because the word turns out to merit an entry in the *OED*, though in a rather roundabout, and perhaps wrongheaded, way. It appears in a citation under the entry for "psychography":

Supposed "spirit-writing" by the hand or intervention of a medium.

The citation invites us to compare this usage with that of "autopsychography," directing us back to "the combinations that are more or less noncewords" which include the element of "auto." What we find there is, in fact, the word "autopsychology." This word was first used of the *Vita Nuova*, in a description of it as the "autopsychology" of Dante's youth. Who should have come up with this term, in *The Early Italian Poets Together with Dante's "Vita Nuova"* (later retitled *Dante and His Circle*), but his namesake, Dante Gabriel Rossetti?

One or two things about Rossetti of which we might remind ourselves: he was a spiritualist, an interest he developed partly from his reading of, among others, Charles Robert Maturin, a figure directly appealed to in the work of his sister, Christina, and partly from his father, Gabriele, the Italian poet and patriot, whose 1831 *Disquisitions on the Anti-Papal*

Spirit which produced the Reformation was quoted approvingly by Helena Blavatsky, particularly for its demonstration that "the art of speaking and writing in a language which bears a double interpretation is of very great antiquity." This "double" nature of things is a key element of Theosophy, a movement of which Professor Foster writes:

> This doctrine, originating in America during the 1870s, concentrated upon gaining insight into the Divine nature as a way of deducing phenomenal essence; it related readily to esoteric links with the creative process, reflecting many of [George] Russell's and WBY's beliefs in cyclical history, art as transfiguration, and art as an eternal conflict of opposites.

These elements of "cyclical history, art as transfiguration, and art as an eternal conflict of opposites" are all relevant to the central theme of "Autopsychography," with its "round and round," those who read "fully feel[ing]," the "fake" and "real," the "reason" and "heart" set against each other. Now here's Professor Foster on the specifics of Irish occultism, again from *W. B. Yeats: A Life*:

> More specifically, WBY (and, indeed, Russell and [Charles] Johnston) might be located in a particular tradition of Irish Protestant interest in the occult, which stretched back through Sheridan Le Fanu and Charles Maturin, took in WBY's contemporary Bram Stoker, and carried forward to Elizabeth Bowen: all figures from the increasingly marginalized middle class, from families with strong clerical connections, declining fortunes and a tenuous hold on landed authority. An interest in the occult might be seen on one level as a strategy for coping with contemporary threats (Catholicism plays a strong part in all their fantasies), and on another as a search for psychic control.

Allow me, if I may, to pick up on these notions of "landed authority" and "psychic control" and attempt to apply them to Pessoa, a man predisposed to thinking of himself as being possessed, since near versions of his name, the Portuguese words *possesso* and *possessão* mean, of all things, "possessed" in the psychic sense and "possession" in the colonial sense, respectively. *Nomen est omen*, as we continue to say in Ireland, and as they would most assuredly have said in the Durban of Pessoa's childhood, or the Portugal of his young manhood. It's not too much to suggest that "landed authority" and "psychic control" were issues at the time of Portugal's becoming a republic in 1910, obliging me to quote yet again Virginia Woolf's oft-quoted smart-ass remark about human character and 1910, which might have been written with Pessoa preeminently in mind:

> On or about December 1910 human character changed. All human relations shifted . . . those between masters and servants, husbands and wives, parents and children. And when human relations shift there is at the same time a change in religion, conduct, politics and literature.

Pessoa is in some sense the embodiment of the "possessed" country which undergoes a "personality" change. In Section 396 of *The Book of Disquiet* he appeals directly to imagery of the "colony" and "a profusion of selves":

> Each of us is several, is many, is a profusion of selves. So that the self who disdains his surroundings is not the same as the self who suffers or takes joy in them. In the vast *colony of our being* there are many species of people who think and feel in different ways.

In 1923 he would answer a question on the future of the Portuguese people, a response later collected in *On Portugal*:

> The future is for us to be everything. Who, if they're Portuguese, can live within the narrow bounds of just one personality, just one nation, just one religion? What true Portuguese can live within the sterile limits of Catholicism when beyond it there are all the Protestant creeds, all the Eastern religions, and all the dead and living Paganisms for us to experience, Portuguesely fusing them into Superior Paganism? Let's not leave out a single god! Let's incorporate them all! We conquered the Oceans; now we must

conquer the Heavens, leaving Earth for the Others, the Others who are eternally Others from birth, the Europeans who aren't Europeans because they aren't Portuguese. Let's be everything, in every way possible, for there can be no truth where something's lacking! Let's create Superior Paganism, Supreme Polytheism! In the eternal lie of all the gods, the only truth is in all the gods together.

The political heterodoxy which Pessoa valorizes is related to the idea of poetical heteronymity, both of these related to a spiritual "possession." Elsewhere in *On Portugal*, Pessoa describes admiringly "that universal brotherhood which theosophy predicts and which has long been the secret social doctrine of the Rosicrucians." Poetical autonomy, like political autonomy, may only be achieved through subservience to "all the gods together," what Eliot described in *Tradition and the Individual Talent* as "continual self-sacrifice." This is the selflessness we find in nature, whereby individual "selves" in the "colony of our being" so readily accept anonymity. It's revealing, I think, to read Pessoa's term "colony" (*colonia*) in the zoological sense first recorded in English in 1872 as "an aggregate of individual animals or plants, forming a physiologically connected structure." This brings us back to the "auto" component in "Autopsychography," and its primary meaning of "self."

The difficulty of locating the self, and its essential isolation, are nowhere more evident than in two of Pessoa's earliest manifestations, Alexander Search and Jean Seul. Alexander Search is represented at least once as being identical to Charles Robert Anon, an idea bodied out by the association of the endless quest of *Melmoth the Wanderer* with the name "Search." Indeed, on that day when Master Therion committed his "pseudo-suicide" at the Mouth of Hell, Pessoa must have been acutely aware of the Melmothian pact into which he himself had entered on October 2, 1907:

Bond entered into by Alexander Search, of *Hell*, Nowhere, with Jacob Satan, *Master*, though not King, of the same place.

The "King" will later be incorporated into the heteronym Ricardo *Reis*, which rather wittily represents the shift between the monarchy (*rex*) and the republic (*res publica*). The name "Search" might be translated into Portuguese as *Inquerito*, a word with a very particular resonance in Portugal, where an Inquisition was established in the 1530s and '40s, its main function to seek and destroy any heretics, alchemists and witches. The name of the ceremony at which the sentences of the Inquisition were handed down is a Portuguese term for "act of faith," *auto-da-fe*, and the *auto* component is lurking, however faintly, in the background here in the title of a poem about an inquiry into the truth, ghosted by Aleister Crowley— heretic, alchemist and witch. That Search's first name is "Alexander" brings to mind that other famous goat-embracer, *Alexander* Selkirk, the model for Robinson Crusoe. The solitary aspect of Selkirk is carried over into the self, alone, of *Seul*, whose sole sin (rather than goat-fucking) is that solitary sin.

The "auto" element in "Autopsychography" reminds us of Pessoa's numerous mentions of autoeroticism, including this 1916 communication from the spirit world:

> Command me. Margaret Mansel, your wife, You onanist! Go to
> marriage with me! No onanism [any] more. Love me. You
> masturbator! You masochist! You man without manhood! You man
> without a man's prick! You man with a clitoris instead of a prick! You
> man with a woman's morality for marriage. Beast! You are a man
> who marries himself. Man who makes marriage masturbation.

This communication to "a man who marries himself" is from Margaret Mansel, whose name is a near version of *man self*. The "self-abuse" for which Pessoa so often abuses himself is the subject of a recently published fragmentary note ("The self-division of the I is a common phenomenon in cases of masturbation"), a note alluded to by Richard Zenith in his introduction to the *Selected Poems* of Fernando Pessoa & Co.:

> Although it is just one of many possible glosses on Pessoa's
> condition, it has the virtue of revealing the extent of the poet's
> ruthless lucidity with respect to himself, and there is something
> chilling in the diagnosis when we consider that his only romantic
> liaison, largely epistolary, was prevented from going forward by the

constant interference of Alvaro de Campos, who so exasperated the beloved, Ophelia Queiroz, that she finally declared she hated him. Pessoa, in the end, preferred to remain with Alvaro and the other literary characters he had spawned single-handedly.

Zenith's unconscious use of a masturbatory image ("spawned single-handedly") has him fall in with Pessoa's own "Self Analysis," which is, by the way, how Peter Rickard translates the title of the present poem, offering this by way of a final stanza:

And so around its little track,
To entertain the mind,
Runs that clockwork train of ours,
The thing we call the heart.

Those last two lines, in Portuguese, read:

Esse comboio de corda
Que se chama o coração.

While the word for "heart," *coração*, is not etymologically related to the word for "string," *corda*, which derives from a term for "cat-gut," it resonates nonetheless with the *cor* at its heart. That *corda* brings to mind not only the terms *querido* or *querida*, nouns meaning "beloved" but related to the verbs *querer*, "to want or wish," and, of course, *inquirir*, "to inquire into," but the *Inquerito*, or Inquisition. All this is guaranteed to "amuse" or "entertain the reason" and is mimetic of the endless quest it describes, of which more in a moment. You'll notice, by the way, that the name of Pessoa's imaginary "beloved," *Queiroz*, represents another version of the name "Search," as does the name of Alberto *Caeiro*, the author of *The Keeper of Sheep*, who "had sprung up in" Pessoa on March 8, 1914. The name Caeiro is at once kept within the word for a sheep, *carneiro*, and keeps within itself the word *caro*, a word meaning, once again, "beloved." Most important, perhaps, it represents a near version of *cara* which, as luck would have it, means "face, aspect, appearance"—the perfect indicator of a heteronym of the masked personage of Pessoa.

IT'S NOT BEEN MY AIM HERE to make an Inquisition into, or inquest upon, Pessoa's main heteronyms. But, as I move towards the end of my very partial discussion of this extraordinary poem, I've barely mentioned Alberto Caeiro, the meddling Alvaro de Campos, Ricardo Reis, or Bernardo Soares, the author of *The Book of Disquiet*, whom Pessoa describes as a "semi-heteronym." As he explains:

> He's a semi-heteronym because his personality, although not my own, doesn't differ from my own but is a mere mutilation of it.

The idea of mutilation of the personality is connected, I think, to the underlying idea of the "Inquisition" by a masked torturer, and to the idea of an inquest being carried out to determine the cause of death, the logical extension of mutilation and the running down of the wind-up heart. We see that, just as the *corda* includes a *cor*, the "Autopsychography" includes an "autopsy," a play which operates in both English and Portuguese, where *autópsia* also signifies a post-mortem. This ties in with the Pessoa/Soares assertion, in *The Book of Disquiet*, that he narrates his "factless autobiography, [his] *lifeless* history." As Zenith writes, in his introduction to *The Book of Disquiet*:

> Like his semi-heteronym, Pessoa was an office-worker in the Baixa, Lisbon's old commercial district, and for a time he regularly dined at a restaurant on the Rua dos Douradores, the site of Soares's rented room and of Vasques & Co., the firm where he worked. But whereas Soares was condemned to the drudgery of filling in ledgers with the prices and quantities of fabric sold, Pessoa had a comparatively prestigious job writing business letters in English and French, for firms that did business abroad.

Even if Pessoa's life was slightly more interesting than Soares's, he was nonetheless a kind of automaton, "a human being acting mechanically or without active intelligence in a monotonous routine," reminiscent of "figures which simulate the action of living beings, as clock-work mice, images which strike the hours on a clock, etc." (*OED*). That "etc." would no doubt cover the "*comboio de corda*" mentioned here in the penultimate line and rendered by Edwin Honig and Susan M. Brown as "That wound-up little train," by Michael Hamburger as "that toy train," by Rickard as "that clockwork train" and, if I may quote the end of Richard Zenith's version:

And so around its track
This thing called the heart winds,
A little clockwork train
To entertain our minds.

E assim nas calhas de roda
Gira, à entreter a razão,
Esse comboio de corda
Que se chama o coração.

The use of the word *gira* at the pivotal point of the second line is a telling one, surely, since the first version of Yeats's *A Vision* had been published in 1927, and would have been read enthusiastically by an occultist like Pessoa, particularly one with an interest in the "gyres" of history, in the automatic writing of Georgie Hyde-Lees, in Yeats's theory of the mask. In "Tobacco Shop," Alvaro de Campos writes, in a translation by Honig and Brown:

When I tried taking off the mask,
It stuck to my face.
When I pulled it off and looked in the mirror,
I'd grown older.

The word used for face is *cara*, summoning up yet again Caeiro, whose name also conjures up *carneiro*, a word meaning both "sheep," as I mentioned earlier, and "burial niche." Another autopsy. The deathly aspect of that burial niche ghosting the name Caeiro is echoed in a near version of *campo*, a word signifying "open countryside" which is used self-reflexively by Alvaro de *Campos* in "Tobacco Shop." I'm thinking of *campa*, "gravestone." Another autopsy. Both *campa* and *campo* are echoed in that word *comboio*. The *comboio* is, in essence, a convoy, "a train of carriages or beasts carrying provisions or ammunition to a town or army, under the protection of an escort" (*OED*). It carries with it both a sense of con- and disjunction, not unlike that zoological colony with "an aggregate of individual animals or plants, forming a physiologically connected structure." This train is related to the train (*comboio*) of which Alvaro de Campos writes in "Tobacco Shop":

> Today I'm bowled over, as though hit by the truth.
> Today I'm clearheaded, as though I were going to die,
> Having no more brotherly feeling for things
> Than to say good-bye, turning this house and this side of the street
> Into a line of coaches in a long train with its whistle jerking good-
> bye
> From inside my head,
> And a nerve-wracking, bone-cracking jerk as it moves off.

Now, the word for head used here is *cabeça*, a word deriving from *caput*, the Latin for "head," and related to the word *campa*, a grave- or *head*-stone. The speaker of the poem has achieved the clarity that comes with a realization that he is "going to die," that there is no distinction between inner and outer:

> Today I'm torn between the allegiance I owe
> Something real outside me—the Tobacco Shop across the street,
> And something real inside me—the feeling that it's all a dream.

Alvaro de Campos describes himself as being "bowled over, as though hit by the truth," a concept which he to some extent embodies in the *var* component of his first name. The idea of being "hit by the truth" connects Alvaro de Campos with Bernardo Soares, since the verb *soar* means to sound, the term *soar bem* meaning specifically "to ring true." That *bem* at the end of line 6 resonates not only with the "Hymn to Pan" I mentioned earlier (*além, vem*) but the idea of an automaton as one of those "images which strike the hours on a clock, etc." In this instance, that "etc." would no doubt cover the "bell" to some extent embodied in the *campa* sounding through the name Campos, from the Latin *campana*, "a bell." The idea of what might "ring true" is a cryptocurrent in the second stanza of the Portuguese where the *bem* is rhymed with *têm* and the *so* component of *Soares* falls in that chiming fourth line:

Mas só à que eles não têm.

The *so* component in *Soares* brings us around yet again to the idea of "self," the *so* at the core of Pessoa's name, a near version of which occurs in the everyday phrase *por si só*, meaning "by himself" or "by or in itself." That *so* brings us around yet again to the pseudo-suicide, or *self*-death, of Aleister Crowley, the central component of whose first name appears subliminally there in the word *eles* in that same line.

Another thought about the influence of Master Therion, if I may be so bold: I mentioned earlier that the poem is dated April 1, 1931, a feature considered sufficiently important to be incorporated into the poem by Richard Zenith. And important it is, if we remember that April Fool's Day is the day on which, according to the *Encyclopaedia Britannica*, "all people, even the most dignified, are given an excuse to play the fool. In France, the fooled person is called a fish (*poisson d'avril*)." I think that, in addition to his multilingual awareness of that *poisson* being a near version of the French word *personne* (which can mean "anybody" or "nobody" and is yet another near version of his own name), Pessoa is interested in the idea of "play[ing] the fool" on a day on which there are no hard-and-fast boundaries between fact and fiction. The "fact" that the poem is set on April Fool's Day may force us to read it as a total "fiction," an idea proposed by Michael Hamburger when he renders the whole poem in parentheses, as if it were an aside in some longer conversation.

I'm reminded of Aleister Crowley's full description of *The Book of Lies*, "which is also falsely called 'Breaks,' the wanderings or falsifications of the one thought of Frater Perdurabo (Aleister Crowley) which thought is itself untrue." This might easily serve as a description of the method of "Autopsychography," its endless "round and round" harking back to the "everlasting" aspect of Frater *Perdurabo*, the hard *dur* at the heart of his name enduring, under duress, in the *dor* in lines 3, 4 and 6 (both words sharing the Latin root *durus*) not to speak of the *fingidor* in line 1 of "Autopsychography." The root of *fingidor* is the Latin *fingo, fingere, fixi, fictum*, "to mould, shape or form," including the sense of doing so falsely, as in "to invent, forge, fabricate, feign," and though it shouldn't be confused with the Latin verb *facio, facere, feci, factum*, which may also mean "to make, form, create, perform, carry into effect," it does seem that there's a fine enough line between the concepts of "maker" and "faker." In section 160 of *The Book of Disquiet*, a piece written on April 8th, 1931, a week after "Autopsychography," Pessoa is still preoccupied with images of revolution, a notion included once again in the "round and round" of that verb *girar*, not to speak of truth and falsity:

> The entire day, in all the desolation of its scattered and dull clouds, was filled with the news of *revolution*. Such reports, *true or false*, always fill me with a particular discomfort, a mixture of disdain and physical nausea. It galls my intelligence when someone imagines that things will change by shaking them up.

This appeal to the "intelligence" (compare the "reason" or "mind" of "Autopsychography") suggests that Pessoa might indeed mean the poem to be read in ironic terms, since any heartfelt impulse towards revolution ("That wound-up little train," "that clockwork train") would "fill [him] with a particular discomfort, a mixture of disdain and physical nausea." Pessoa continues:

> A sensitive and honest-minded man, if he's concerned about evil and injustice in the world, will naturally begin his campaign against them by eliminating them at their nearest source: his own person.

The "person" with whom Pessoa begins is himself:

> The inner justice we summon to write a fluent and beautiful page, that true reformation of enlivening our dead sensibility—these things are the truth, our truth, the only truth . . . Revolution? Change? What I really want, with all my heart, is for the atonic clouds to stop greyly lathering the sky. What I want is to see the blue emerge, a truth that is clear and sure because it is nothing and wants nothing.

The voice which is sounded here somehow rings true, allowing us to come away from "Autopsychography" with a sense that the argument that writer and reader have a contract which binds them in endless self-deception may not be Pessoa's last word on the subject, that he may be closer in spirit to the speaker of Marianne Moore's "Poetry":

I, too, dislike it.
    Reading it, however, with a perfect contempt for it, one
        discovers in
      it, after all, a place for the genuine.

CHAPTER 10

POETRY

MARIANNE MOORE

I, too, dislike it: there are things that are important beyond all this
   fiddle.
   Reading it, however, with a perfect contempt for it, one
      discovers in
   it after all, a place for the genuine.
      Hands that can grasp, eyes
      that can dilate, hair that can rise
         if it must, these things are important not because a

high-sounding interpretation can be put upon them but because they
   are
   useful. When they become so derivative as to become
      unintelligible,
   the same thing may be said for all of us, that we
      do not admire what
      we cannot understand: the bat
         holding on upside down or in quest of something to

eat, elephants pushing, a wild horse taking a roll, a tireless wolf
   under
   a tree, the immovable critic twitching his skin like a horse that
   feels a flea, the base-

ball fan, the statistician—
  nor is it valid
    to discriminate against "business documents and

school-books"; all these phenomena are important. One must make
  a distinction
    however: when dragged into prominence by half poets, the result
    is not poetry,
  nor till the poets among us can be
    "literalists of
      the imagination"—above
        insolence and triviality and can present

for inspection, "imaginary gardens with real toads in them," shall we
  have
    it. In the meantime, if you demand on the one hand,
    the raw material of poetry in
      all its rawness and
      that which is on the other hand
        genuine, you are interested in poetry.

THOUGH I'LL BE LOOKING AT IT in a sidelong way, my subject in this
chapter is revision, the process by which the poet attempts to determine
when a poem is finished, to determine, for the moment, when it has come
to an end. I'll be considering this idea of the poem being "finished"—in
the dual sense of "ended" and "ornamented"—in several pieces by Marianne Moore, including the two main versions of her poem "Poetry," and
looking at ways in which readings of her own name are brought into play
by a poet constantly exercised by notions of insufficiency and excess, by
less or more, more or less.

Along the way, I'll try to be mindful of Fernando Pessoa's assertion
that a poet's work is never done. Here's Pessoa holding forth in a provocative note on "The Art of Translation":

There can be no doubt that many poems—even many great poems—would gain by being translated into the very language they were written in. This brings up the problem as to whether it is art or the artist that matters, the individual or the product. If it be the final result that matters and that shall give delight, then we are justified in taking a famous poet's all but perfect poem, and, in the light of the criticism of another age, making it perfect by excision, substitution, or addition. Wordsworth's "Ode on Immortality" is a great poem, but it is far from being a perfect poem. It could be rehandled to advantage.

Pessoa doesn't specify where "Ode: Intimations of Immortality from Recollections of Early Childhood" might be "rehandled to advantage," though some readers may feel that the poem does rather nag us with the thesis that "The Child Is Father of the Man":

> But there's a Tree, of many, one,
> A single Field which I have looked upon,
> Both of them speak of something that is gone:
>   The Pansy at my feet
>   Doth the same tale repeat:
> Whither is fled the visionary gleam?
> Where is it now, the glory and the dream?

In "Virginia Britannia," a poem about transplantation and the dulling of a "visionary gleam," Moore sets down versions of that English pansy in the fertile soil of the New World:

> Narrow herring-bone-laid bricks,
>   a dusty pink beside the dwarf box-
> bordered *pansies*, share the ivy-arbor shade
>   with cemetery lace settees, one at each side,
>   and with the bird: box-bordered tide-
>   water gigantic jet black *pansies*—splendor; pride—
> not for a decade
>   dressed, but for a day, in over-powering velvet; and

gray-blue-Andalusian-cock-feather pale ones,
    ink-lined on the edge, fur-
      eyed, with ocher
on the cheek.

In the final line of "Virginia Britannia," Moore openly acknowledges the presence of Wordsworth in her allusion to the elements of the natural world that "are to the *child* an *intimation* of what *glory* is," borrowing quite specific vocabulary from the "Ode." Wordsworth has been present throughout, however, not only palpably in the pansies but impalpably in the description of the "Indian- / named Virginian / streams in counties named for English lords," since at least one Virginia county which goes *unnamed* here is Cumberland, founded in 1749. To mention the English county in which Wordsworth was born twenty-one years later in a poem already freighted with Wordsworth would have been heavy-handed in the extreme. Other impalpable, but all-pervasive, influences of "Ode: Intimations of Immortality from Recollections of Early Childhood" on "Virginia Britannia" are the rhyme scheme and, insofar as we may distinguish it from the rhyme scheme, the stanza pattern. Wordsworth's many indented lines and short couplets ("The Pansy at my *feet* / doth the same tale *repeat*") are echoed in Moore's "herring-bone-laid" lines about the "herring-bone-laid bricks" that

        . . . share the ivy-arbor *shade*
    with cemetery lace settees, one at each *side*,
    and with the bird: box-bordered *tide-*
    water gigantic jet black pansies—splendor; *pride*—
not for a *decade*
    dressed, but for a day, in over-powering velvet . . .

The term "over-powering" is yet another indicator of Moore's anxiety about the extent to which her poem continues to be in dialogue with Wordsworth's (her "splendor" sending us back to his "splendor in the grass," her "day" back to his "I love the Brooks which down their channels fret, / Even more than when I tripped lightly as they; / The innocent brightness of a new-born *Day* / Is lovely yet"), while managing to make its own shape in the world. Just as Wordsworth comments on his own metrics and the repetition intrinsic to verse ("The Pansy at my *feet* / Doth the same tale *repeat*"), so does Moore specify the stanzaic pattern as "box-bordered," a stanza interpreted as an exterior garden "room" delineated by boxwood, and "herring-bone," the pattern not only of the "bricks" but of "the one-brick- / thick serpentine wall built by / Jefferson." This herring-bone, or zigzag, is used by Moore as a stanzaic model in many poems, including, not surprisingly, "The Fish." She's prepared the ground for the pattern by already using the word "zigzag" in an earlier stanza, in the phrase "A fritillary *zigzags* / toward the chancel-shaded resting-place," the term "resting-place" being another interpretation of "stanza." The "zigzag," meanwhile, is one of the most common elements in Moorish, or Islamic, art and architecture.

"Islamic art," as the *Oxford Companion to Art* reminds us, "is above all an art of ornament." I've already suggested that Moore is concerned here that she might be too overtly Wordsworthian. Now I want to suggest that she's also conscious that she might be too overtly ornamental, too *Moorish*, which is why she moves immediately from the idea of the "overpowering velvet" pansy to the "gray-blue *Andalusian*-cock-feather one," indicating a disavowal of her own name. We remember that the art and architecture of Andalusia, including the Alhambra palace in Granada, is overwhelmingly Moorish in influence. Not only do Moorish designs include the zigzags I mentioned earlier but, as was noted in the third edition of the *Encyclopaedia Britannica*, "the greatest peculiarity in the Moorish architecture is the horse-shoe arch." It's no wonder, then, that Moore should allude to a "gold *horseshoe*" six lines after the "fritillary zigzag" in "Virginia Britannia."

Now, I know that this kind of reading may sometimes seem a little fritillarian (in the *dicey* sense which underlies both the butterfly and the flower so familiar to this audience), perhaps a little fiddle-headed, but what can I do? I'm sitting at a desk I acquired from the gentleman who looks after surplus furniture at Princeton. His name is Sam Formica. On the desk are two books. One is *The Botany of Desire: A Plant's-Eye View of the World* by Michael Pollan. The other is Archie G. Walls's *Geometry and Architecture in Islamic Jerusalem*. An Archie Walls who specializes in Islamic architecture, including "the great horseshoe *arch*" and writes of how "in the drawing it can be seen that the zeniths of the *arched* recesses in the *qibla wall* are lower than those in the side *walls*," a Pollan who specializes in pollination, a *Formica* who oversees formica? It's humorous in a parlour-gamish way, in the *Nomen est omen* mode I'm fond of playing with.

But the relationship between a writer's name and his or her work is a rather different matter, one of which Moore is aware, as we might remember from one of her very earliest poems:

> If you will tell me why the fen
> appears impassable, I then
> will tell you why I think that I
> can get across it if I try.

I'm certain that Moore's choice of the word "fen" here is related to the reading of her own name as "marsh," the second sense in which it appears in the *OED*, and is appropriate to the writer's attempt to "get across" her own self, particularly when the word "I" appears four times in as many lines. It is also the first word of "Poetry," of course, set apart even more by the comma immediately following it.

The "fen" or "marsh" introduces another major theme, that of a "soft" interior, often in contrast to a "hard" surface, which might be said to dominate Moore's work, and which also might be said to be the critical opposition in "Poetry," in which interior "genuine" is set against exterior "fiddle":

> I, too, dislike it: there are things that are important beyond all this
> fiddle.

Now, I want to try, as I finally begin to read the poem, to connect this word "fiddle" to a faintly pejorative sense of "Moorish," that of the unnecessarily ornate filigree-work we've seen disdained in "Virginia Britannia," in which "the live oak's darkening *filigree*" has "become part of the ground," just as the "clouds, expanding above / the town's assertiveness, dwarf it, dwarf arrogance / that can misunderstand / importance." The "importance" in "Virginia Britannia" is directly related to the "important" in the first line of "Poetry," and its importance will grow as the poem continues. The connotations of "fiddle" are numerous. It conjures up the verb "to fiddle" meaning "to make aimless or frivolous, to act idly or frivolously," the "fussy trifling" of "fiddling," the "nonsense" of "fiddlededee" or "fiddlesticks," the "trifling talk or action" of "fiddle-faddle," as used by Charles Darwin, recorded in his *Life and Letters*: "Describing species of birds and shells, &c, is all *fiddle-faddle*." I've already used the term "fiddle-headed," one meaning of "fiddle-head" being "the ornamental carving at the bows of a vessel, the termination of which is a scroll turning aft or inward like the head of a violin." Moore is carrying over pejorative ideas of that "ornamental carving" and "scroll" work into the "fiddle" of this first line:

> I, too, dislike it: there are things that are important beyond all this
>   *fiddle*.

The word "fiddle" also brings with it the association of Nero, the irresponsible artist "fiddling" while Rome burns, along with the U.S. slang sense of "fiddle" first recorded in 1874, three years before Moore's birth, "a swindle, or an imposture," as in the term "to fiddle the books." Both of these readings include notions of accountability, or lack of it, which are relevant, I think, to "Poetry." I mentioned the "fiddle-head" in respect of the ornamental carving, connecting it to Moorish architecture, but it may also have an association for Moore with the fiddlehead fern, a plant which occurs in "Spenser's Ireland," the poem immediately following "Virginia Britannia" in her 1941 volume, *What Are Years?*:

> If in Ireland
>   they play the harp backward at need,
>   and gather at midday the seed
> of the *fern*, eluding
> their "giants all covered with iron," might
>   there be fern seed for unlearn-
> ing obduracy and for reinstating
> the enchantment?

Here the ornate is glimpsed as a possible defense against "obduracy" because it is itself a form of "obduracy," helping in the process of "unlearning" it, in the way that the "assertiveness," "arrogance" and "misunder[stood]" sense of relative "importance" that informed the building of Jamestown, the town of "Virginia Britannia," need to be "dwarf[ed]" by the ornate "vines." Jamestown has a pivotal place in Moore's imagination, as is clear from "Enough," a poem collected in 1959's *O To Be a Dragon*:

> Some in the *Goodspeed*, the *Susan C.*,
> others in the *Discovery*,
>
> found their too earthly paradise,
> a paradise in which hope dies,
>
> found pests and pestilence instead,
> the living outnumbered by the dead . . .
>
> With nothing but the feeble tow
> to mark the site that did not flower,
>
> could the most ardent have been sure
> that they had done what would endure?
>
> It was enough; it is enough
> if present faith mend partial proof.

The hero of Jamestown, Captain John Smith, is literally emblematic of the urge to "endure," the "obduracy" at once valorized and vilified, it seems, by Moore. Let's go back to that stanza in "Virginia Britannia" which begins with "A fritillary zigzags," which mentions the metropolis of Powhatan, Werewocomoco:

>   We-re-wo-
>   co-mo-co's fur crown could be no
>   odder than we were, with ostrich, Latin motto,
> and small gold horse-shoe:
>   arms for an able sting-ray-hampered pioneer—
>   painted as a Turk, it seems—continuously
>   exciting Captain Smith

Even without Moore's footnote, we might figure out that the "ostrich and horseshoe" appear as the "crest in Captain John Smith's coat of arms, the ostrich with a horseshoe in its beak—i.e., invincible digestion—reiterates the motto, *Vincere est vivere,*" though we probably wouldn't know, even if we were permanent members of the Oxford community, that with regard to Powhatan's "fur crown," the "deer-skin mantle" presented by Powhatan to Captain Newport when crowned by him and Captain John Smith is "now in the Ashmolean."

In addition to the Moorish iconography of the horseshoe to which I've already alluded, it's telling that at least one race of ostrich is the *Struthio camelus camelus* of Moorish North Africa, this being the "sparrow-camel" which is the subject of "He 'Digesteth Harde Yron.' " "He 'Digesteth Harde Yron' " comes four poems before "Virginia Britannia" in *What Are Years?* and includes a reference to the zigzaggish or serpentine motif I mentioned earlier, when Moore writes of the bird:

> whose comic duckling head on its
> great neck revolves with compass-needle nervousness
> when he stands guard,
>
> *in S-like foragings* as he is
> preening the down on his leaden-skinned back.

The militaristic imagery of "stands guard" and "foragings" reminds us of the first use of "zigzag" in English, when it was applied to "a trench leading to a besieged place, constructed in a zigzag direction so as not to be enfiladed (or raked) by the defenders" (*OED*). Another sense of "zigzag," related and relevant here, is that of a "collector's name for a shell, or a moth, with zigzag marking," presumably based on an urge to camouflage, to conceal, to deceive, to "fiddle." Moore alludes to such a moth in "Armor's Undermining Modesty":

> It was a moth almost an owl,
>   Its wings were furred so well,
> with backgammon-board wedges interlacing
> on the wing

Those "backgammon-board wedges" would give a zigzag effect, no doubt, to the moth's wing, the "backgammon board" connecting the moth with the "fritillary" that "zigzags" from "Virginia Britannia," particularly when Gerarde's *Herball* of 1597 gives the following etymology:

> It hath been called Frittillaria, of the table or boord upon which men plaie at chesse, which square checkers the flower doth very much resemble, some thinking that it [the chessboard] was called Fritillus.

It's in this very poem, "Armor's Undermining Modesty," that Moore writes:

> Even gifted scholars lose their way
> through faulty etymology.

Another term hovering about the "fiddle" at the end of line 1, which I seem not to be able to get beyond, is another "armored" creature, the "fiddler" crab, "as it is sometimes called from the rapidity with which it works its elbows," according to W. B. Lord in *Crab, Shrimp & Lobster Lore* (1867). Let me go back to, and stay with for a moment, the musical associations of "fiddle" to try to get a grip on Moore's complex filigree work in which the strands of, in this instance, music, fern-seed, and iron are connected. We may remember those lines from "Spenser's Ireland" in which they're quite explicitly linked:

> If in Ireland
> they play the *harp* backward at need,
> and gather at midday the *seed*
> of the *fern*, eluding
> their "giants all covered with *iron*," . . .

Precisely the same strands of music, fern seed, and iron are brought together in "The Jerboa," an animal "silvered to *steel* by the force / of the large desert moon," though the instrument in this case is a "Bedouin flute," as befits a poem set in Moorish North Africa:

> By fifths and sevenths,
> in leaps of two lengths,

like the uneven notes
of the *Bedouin* flute, it stops its gleaning
   on little wheel castors, and makes *fern-seed*
     footprints with kangaroo-speed.

Its leaps should be set
to the flageolet;
   pillar body erect
     on a three-cornered smooth-working Chippendale
       claw—propped on hind legs, and tail as third toe,
       between leaps to its burrow.

The *"three*-cornered" and the "tail as *third* toe" in this zigzaggish stanza about "a Sahara field-mouse" connects us neatly with another major element in Moorish design, the trefoil, "an ornament with an opening divided by cusps so as to present or suggest the figure of a three-lobed leaf" (*OED*). In addition to zigzag trefoil, among the many varieties of trefoil are bird's-foot trefoil and hare's-foot trefoil, and Moore may carry over something of those evocative names to her "fern-seed footprints." The "fern" is a near version of the "fen" we saw earlier, and is therefore a subliminal version of the poet herself, just as the historical figure of Marianne Moore "present[ed] and suggest[ed] the figure of a three-lobed leaf" in sporting her famous tricorn or "three-cornered" hat, which, as Charles Molesworth puts it in his excellent *Marianne Moore: A Literary Life*, was "an article that was eventually to become her trademark." The "three-lobed" motif continues into the basic three-beat line of "The Jerboa."

The "burrow" towards which the jerboa leaps is a cuniculus, a rabbit-hole in the shape of a wedge, just as the shape "The Jerboa" makes on the page, like so many Moore poems that do not present themselves as good old zigzags, is that of a wedge. At the same time as she was developing her signature tricorn hat, while she was a student at Bryn Mawr, Marianne Moore was also working on her signature, as Charles Molesworth informs us:

> Style—in dress, religion, writing, and social behaviour—was a
> constant preoccupation. At one point, Moore spends parts of several

letters discussing and illustrating her "new" signature. This involved making a small loop in the downward "v" of the initial letter of both her first and last names.

In other words, Moore was acutely aware of the zigzaggish wedge shapes in her own written name. In "Marriage" she writes:

> turn to the letter M
> and you will find
> that "a wife is a coffin,"
> that severe object
> with the pleasing geometry
> stipulating space not people

Now, the term "cuniculus," or versions of it such as "cuniculine," was also used of the mine, the device used with the purpose of undermining one's enemy, often in tandem with a zigzag. No wonder, yet again, that in a poet of such complete complexity we should find a poem I quoted earlier, entitled "Armor's *Undermining* Modesty":

> Knights we've known,
>
> > like those familiar
> > now unfamiliar knights who sought the Grail, were
> > *ducs* in old Roman fashion
> > without the addition
> > of wreaths and silver rods, and armor gilded
> > or inlaid.

The "silver rods" is a direct reference to the process of filigree work, the "art which consists of curling, twisting and plaiting fine, pliable threads of metal and uniting them at their points of contact with each other and with the groundwork by means of gold or silver solder and borax" (*Encyclopaedia Britannica*), as in the aforementioned "Virginia Britannia" 's "live oak's darkening *filigree*," while the "armor gilded / or inlaid" reminds us of the Moorish mastery of the forging of steel arms and armor (Damascus being as well known for its swords as its damask). The "armor" also brings us back to those Irish "giants all covered with iron," giants whom those who are in the business of gathering "at midday the seed of the fern" are also in the business of "eluding."

The impulse to put on arms and armor is a tricky one, one which must be balanced. In "Critics and Connoisseurs," a poem having to do with "an attitude of self-defense" (with a little "fen" in the heart of "self-defense"), which focuses on "a swan under the willows in Oxford," Moore writes of "a mere childish attempt to make an imperfectly bal- / lasted animal stand up," balancing the line-break on the "bal-" of "ballasted" and allowing the "lasted" its double meaning of duration and obduracy. "The Jerboa" is stable because it is "propped on hind legs, and tail as third toe" as it stops to check on its surroundings, to check if it's under threat, to check itself. This idea of keeping one's balance under adversity is another central theme in Moore's work, and may certainly be seen as the subject matter of "Poetry," in which the "fiddle" is balanced by "a place for the genuine."

There's a constant assessment of what is "Enough," as in the poem of which the full title is "Enough: Jamestown, 1607–1957." This is not to be confused with "Enough: 1969," with its final exhortation to "Stand for truth. It's enough." The two sections of "The Jerboa" are subtitled "Too Much" and "Abundance," as if to suggest that "Abundance" and "enough" are appropriate, while "Too Much" or "excess" are inappropriate. There's an extraordinary litany of "lavishness," which denotes "unlimited bounty; extravagance; prodigality" (*OED*) in "Marriage," which includes our old friend the fiddlehead fern, of which so much has been heard in the past while:

> Unhelpful Hymen!
> a kind of overgrown cupid
> reduced to insignificance
> by the mechanical advertising
> parading as involuntary comment,
> by that experiment of Adam's
> with ways out but no way in—
> the ritual of marriage,
> augmenting all its lavishness;
> its *fiddle-head ferns,*

lotus flowers, opuntias, white dromedaries,
its hippopotamus—
nose and mouth combined
in one magnificent hopper—
its snake and the potent apple.

The opuntia, or prickly pear, is yet another example of the self-protected, this time from the vegetable kingdom, a kingdom in which there is occasional excess:

Etymologically, the word *extravagance* means to wander off a path or cross a line—orderly lines, of course, being Apollo's special domain. In this may lie a clue to the abiding power of the tulip, as well as, perhaps, to the nature of beauty. The tulip is a flower that draws some of the most exquisite lines in nature and then, in spasms of extravagance, blithely oversteps them. On the same principle, syncopation enlivens a regular, four-four measure of music, enjambment the stately line of the iambic pentameter.

The etymologist here is Michael Pollan, in *The Botany of Desire*, who continues:

Great art is born when Apollonian form and Dionysian ecstasy are held in balance, when our dreams of order and abandon come together.

The subject of a lack of such "balance" is one on which the speaker of "Armor's Undermining Modesty" would like to take those "knights we've known" to task:

I should, I confess,
like to have a talk with them about excess,
and armor's undermining modesty
instead of innocent depravity.
A mirror-of-steel uninsistence should countenance
continence

Yet again, Moore associates "steel" with "excess," which she associates with the "fiddle-head fern," which she associates with music, or a like art, such as poetry. It's in "Armor's Undermining Modesty" that we find a virtual recapitulation of the first line of "Poetry," a line I seem unable to move beyond:

> Even gifted scholars lose their way
> through faulty etymology.
> *No wonder we hate poetry,*
> and stars and harps and the new moon.

The "harps" are no doubt Irish harps, one of those mentioned in "Spenser's Ireland," which "they play . . . backward at need." Let's remind ourselves of the end of "Spenser's Ireland," where Moore announces:

> I'm troubled. I'm dissatisfied. I'm Irish.

She is, in other words, suffering from a Moore's malady, "Moore's Maladies" being the irreverent term for the *Irish Melodies* of Thomas Moore (1779–1852), among the best known of which is "The *Harp* That Once Through Tara's Halls." This "harp" is related to the lyre, is perhaps offered "In Lieu of the Lyre." In her poem of that title Moore returns to the subject of balance:

> "a force is at rest because *balanced* by some other force"

The other items mentioned in addition to the harp, the "stars" and the "new moon" are features of Moorish domes and arches, while the arch itself is the epitome of "a force at rest because balanced by some other force." As the *Encyclopaedia Britannica* reminds us, the arch "depends essentially on the mechanical properties of the wedge," that most "Mooreish" of shapes. The "star" is also quite "Mooreish," since it is with the image of "The Steeple-Jack" busily "gilding the solid- / pointed *star*, which on a steeple / stands for hope" that one of Moore's most famous poems ends. The "gilded" might be seen as yet another instance of excessive covering, just as the armor in "Armor's Undermining Modesty" is "*gilded* or inlaid," the process of inlaying being another metalworking technique in which the Moors were adept.

Another thought or two on the name "Moore." It is itself a near version of that word "armor" I've just used, of the kind worn by those Irish "giants all covered with iron" who are "elud[ed]" by the Irish. Another "game" Moore plays with her own name is also directly related to "excess," and is, of course, the word "more," a variant spelling of the proper name "Moore." To have "more" than enough is to be "in excess," so that Moore is predisposed to be mindful of such notions as "less" and "more." I've looked briefly at the strange concatenation of imagery involving iron, fern-seed and music or other arts, including the "lyric" arts. Let me go back, by way of the iron of the "gilded" armor, to find another image of excess. The armor is that of John Smith, a "smith" being the quintessential worker in iron. That's why his coat of arms gives us the "ostrich with a horseshoe in its beak," since the horseshoe denotes the smith in his smithy. There is, in other words, a climate of emblematization of proper names. But the excess of "Mo(o)re" is indicated in other ways, specifically through the image of the ostrich. In "He 'Digesteth Harde Yron,' " Moore writes of

> Six hundred *ostrich*-brains served
> at one banquet, the *ostrich*-plume-tipped tent
> and desert spear, jewel-
> gorgeous ugly egg-shell
> goblets, eight pairs of *ostriches*
> in harness, dramatize a meaning
> always missed by the externalist.

The "meaning" of these ostriches, a herd of which has a walk-on part in "The Jerboa," has to do not only with excess but, yet again, obduracy. The ostriches in "The Jerboa" have "*hard* feet," one in "He 'Digesteth Harde Yron' " has "a foot *hard* / as a hoof." But they also have to do with works of art, incorporated as they are into "jewel- / gorgeous ugly egg-shell / goblets" by Fabergé, even the "ostrich-plume-tipped tent." The "tipped" has other resonances, of course, since it's a word associated with "scales," bringing us back to the idea of balance between the "fiddle" and the "genuine" there in line 3, towards which we now seem to be moving.

Among the various definitions of "genuine" are "real, true, not counterfeit; unfeigned; not embellished or rendered specious; plain, direct," and I want to suggest that there's another sense of "Moorish" which hangs about Moore's idea of the tension between artistic interiority and exteriority.

Let me begin by focussing on those lines from "Armor's Underlying Modesty" which I quoted earlier, including the advice Moore would offer those "knights" on the subject of "excess":

> A mirror-of-steel uninsistence should countenance
> continence

The outlandish rhyme of "countenance" and "continence" draws particular attention to both words. The primary meaning of "continence" has to do with "restraint," as the father in "Silence" has it:

> "The deepest feeling always shows itself in silence;
> not in silence, but *restraint*."

"Countenance" meanwhile goes in two directions, meaning both "appearance" and "*mere* appearance" in the sense of "feigned." It's not inappropriate, I think, to connect the "mirror-of-steel" in which the "countenance" appears (particularly when it appears in turn in a poem which includes the line "No wonder we hate poetry"), with Hamlet's description of the end of art being "to hold, as 'twere, the mirror up to nature, to show virtue her own feature, scorn her own image." This is a mirror in which, as the last line of "Armor's Undermining Modesty" has it, in an appropriately balanced phrase or two,

> There is the tarnish; and there, the imperishable wish.

That "tarnish" brings to mind another relevant word, "varnish," one meaning of which is "to embellish or adorn." It's a version of this word, with this meaning, which Shakespeare puts in the mouth of the *Moor* of Venice:

> I will a round *unvarnished* tale deliver
> Of my whole course of love . . .

This aspect of Moorishness embodied by Othello, that of the *black*amoor, is connected to two images of pansies. One of these occurs in a poem entitled "Propriety," which immediately precedes "Armor's Undermining Modesty" in *The Complete Poems of Marianne Moore* and in which a Moorish zigzag or herring-bone is echoed in "the fish-spine / on firs" before the relative weights of "Brahms and Bach" are set in the scales. The final, balancing image suggests that

> both are the
> unintentional pansy-face
> uncursed by self-inspection; *blackened*
> because born that way.

These black pansies which are disinclined to look in "a mirror-of-steel" are reminiscent of the "jet-*black* pansies" by the "herring-bone-laid bricks" in "Virginia Britannia." This sense of Moorishness is carried over by Marianne Moore into the "live oak's *darkening* filigree"—a filigree which is, in other words, "tarnished." What Moore sees as being truly tarnished, of course, are the reputations of the "discoverers" of Virginia, for those images of the "jet black pansies" and the "gray-blue-Andalusian-cock-feather pale ones, / ink-lined on the edge" are followed immediately by a scathing commentary on the disgrace of slavery:

> The at first slow, saddle-horse quick cavalcade
> of buckeye-burnished jumpers
> and five-gaited mounts, the work-mule and
> show-mule and witch-cross door and "strong sweet prison"
> are a part of what has come about—in the *Black*
> idiom—from "advancin' back-
> wards in a circle"; from taking the Potomac
> cowbirdlike, and on
> the Chickahominy establishing the *Negro*,
> inadvertent ally and best enemy of
> tyranny.

Another way of describing such a movement as " 'advancin' back- / wards in a circle,' " or moving "cowbirdlike" or, indeed, going "like the

uneven notes / of the Bedouin" while making "fern-seed foot-prints,"
would be an arabesque, "a species of mural or surface decoration
in colour or low relief, composed in flowing lines of branches, leaves,
and scroll-work fancifully intertwined" (OED). This would serve as the
perfect description of "the live oak's darkening filigree / of undulating
boughs, the etched / solidity of a cypress indivisible / from the now
aged English hackberry" which is planted four-square in the midst of
"Virginia Britannia." This is "the now tremendous vine-encompassed
hackberry / starred with the ivy flower" which gives the shade to the
"chancel-shaded resting-place" toward which "a fritillary zigzags," the
"chancel" originally referring to the *cancelli* or "bars of lattice work"
(these based on Moorish *mashrabeyya* or "interlacing grilles") set up by the
"discoverers." I've used this word "discoverers" twice now, both times in
quotes, for we might remember that the name of one of the ships in
"Enough: Jamestown, 1607–1957" is the *Discovery*. I suspect that something of the double-edged nature of that discovery in which "the victims
of a search for gold / cast yellow soil into the hold" is carried over by
Moore into line 2 of "Poetry":

> Reading it, however, with a perfect contempt for it, one *discovers* in
> it, after all, a place for the genuine.

The singsongish rhyme of "in" and "genuine" at the ends of lines 2
and 3 throws some doubt over whether the discovery here is of fool's gold
or the real thing, the discovery of the real thing being the alchemist's
dream. While the "chem" element of "alchemy" derives from the Egyptian term for the "black earth" of Egypt, the *al* is the Arabic definite article, testimony to the impact of the Moors on that pseudoscience to which
Moore alludes in "An Octopus":

> the cavalcade of calico competing
> with the original American menagerie of styles
> among the white flowers of the rhododendron surmounting rigid
>   leaves
> upon which moisture works its *alchemy*,
> transmuting verdure into onyx.

The quintessential alchemical transmutation is also described by Moore in "Sojourn in the Whale," where Ireland itself is addressed:

> You have been compelled by hags to spin
> *gold* thread from straw

The "cavalcade of calico" in "An Octopus" brings to mind the "cavalcade" Moore describes in "Virginia Britannia" where she describes "jumpers" (horses, that's to say) as being "burnished," or "made bright and shining as by friction, polished" (*OED*). This is the polish of the fish "whose scales turn aside the sun's sword by their *polish*" ("An Egyptian Pulled Glass Bottle in the Shape of a Fish"), the sense of "finish" of which Moore has already written in "An Octopus":

> Neatness of *finish*! Neatness of *finish*!
> Relentless accuracy is the nature of this octopus
> with its capacity for fact.

"Relentless accuracy" and "capacity for fact" are features of a poet whose own name, with its *m*, *r* and double *o*, is a near version of that "mirror" held up to nature, giving back things as they are, but who resists any ideas of "finish" and "finality." Such ideas are not resisted by Clive Driver, the editor of *The Complete Poems of Marianne Moore*, who notes that "the text conforms as closely as is now possible to the author's final intentions," the phrase "as is now possible" meaning, I expect, that Moore is no longer with us and therefore no longer able to refinish a poem such as "Poetry," which is usually printed in the three-line version I've just been discussing. But "the definitive edition of the work of one of America's greatest and best-loved poets," which incorporates "all the final revisions" made by Moore, may not be quite so definitive or final as one might expect, quite apart from Pessoa's contention that any and every poem has the potential of being made "perfect by excision, substitution, or addition." The version of the poem which appears in *The Norton Anthology of Poetry* (fourth edition, 1996) is the twenty-nine-line version, with the note that "Moore later cut the poem to three lines only," including the phrase from line 1 ("there are things that are important beyond all this fiddle") on which I've spent almost all of this chapter. We can see why she might have felt that, yet again, the twenty-nine-line version is overwrought, a mere restatement of the first three lines, just as "Ode: Intimations of Immortality" might be perceived as a mere restatement of its three-line epigraph. We can see that Moore might have felt that much of the long version (what shall we call it—the dance mix?) of "Poetry" appeals to much that is Mooreish. The "hair that can rise, if it must" is a familiar image of the protective hackle, one partly mediated in this case through Emily Dickinson's remark on her being able to recognize the "genuine" article in poetry "if I feel physically as if the top of my head were taken off." The "elephants" will eventually be "pushing" their way into "Elephants," a poem from the 1944 collection *Nevertheless*:

> Uplifted and waved till immobilized
> wistaria-like, the opposing opposed
> mouse-gray twined proboscises' trunk formed by two
> trunks, fights itself to a spiraled inter-nosed
>
> deadlock of dyke-enforced massiveness.

The very title of the collection, *Nevertheless*, reminds us of Moore's constant weighing of "the opposing opposed" which we meet once again in the "on the one hand" and "on the other hand" of lines 25 and 28. The "tireless wolf under / a tree" is a perfect example of the "opposing opposed" in that if a wolf is "under a tree" it's less likely to be "tireless" than *tired*. This is a version of the "loping wolf" from the "Lawrence pottery with loping wolf design" found in "Virginia Britannia," while the "baseball fan" is a version of Moore herself, the fan who writes in "Hometown Piece for Messrs. Alston and Reese":

> A neat bunt, please; a cloud-breaker, a drive
> like Jim Gilliam's great big one. Hope's alive.
>
> Homered, flied out, fouled? Our "stylish stout"
> so nimble Campanella will have him out.

There's a double-edged quality to that "neat," I think, particularly when we remember Moore's skepticism about "*neatness* of finish," just as "stylish" brings back her constant anxiety about representing "Style," as in the poem of that title:

> There is no suitable simile. It is as though
> the equidistant three tiny arcs of seeds in a banana
> had been conjoined by Palestrina.

This imagery almost exactly replicates that of "The Jerboa" with its "fern-*seed* / footprints" and its leaps "set / to the flageolet; / pillar body erect / on a *three*-cornered smooth-working Chippendale / claw," another quintessentially Moorish trifoliate arc(h). The "style" also reminds us of a note in which Moore explains the source of the phrase " 'literalists of / the imagination' " in lines 21–22. It comes from W. B. Yeats's *Ideas of Good and Evil*, and an observation of Yeats on Blake:

> The limitation of his view was from the very intensity of his vision;
> he was a too literal realist of imagination, as others are of nature;
> and because he believed that the figures seen by the mind's eye,
> when exalted by inspiration, were "eternal existences," symbols of
> divine essences, he hated every grace of *style* that might obscure
> their lineaments.

It would seem that the longer version of "Poetry" represents the "grace of style that might obscure [the] lineaments" of the Mooreish architecture of the poem. The phrase "literal realist" is echoed in the title of the poem immediately following "Poetry" in *The Complete Poems of Marianne Moore*, a poem entitled "Pedantic Literalist":

> What stood
> erect in you has withered. A
> little "palm-tree of turned wood"
>   informs your once spontaneous core in its
>   immutable production.

In addition to the Moorish feel of that little "palm-tree of turned wood," this poem is exercised by the Mooreish imbalance between the "withered" surface and the "once spontaneous core," between "imaginary gardens" (the garden a central feature of Moorish architecture, of course) and "real toads." The tension between surface and core is one Moore detected not only in her own work—the alchemical "Black Earth" with the "beautiful element of unreason under it"—but that of her Bryn Mawr classmate H.D., whose poem "Sea Poppies" will be the subject of my next chapter. In her 1925 review in *The Dial* of H.D.'s *Collected Poems*, Marianne Moore might easily be writing of herself, adopting as she does the terms "beauty" and "unreason" from "Black Earth":

> We have in these poems an external world of commanding *beauty*—
> the erect, the fluent, the unaccountably brilliant. Also, we have that
> inner world of interacting reason and *unreason* in which are
> comprehended the rigor, the succinctness of hazardous emotion.

CHAPTER 11

SEA POPPIES

H.D.

Amber husk
fluted with gold,
fruit on the sand
marked with a rich grain,

treasure
spilled near the shrub-pines
to bleach on the boulders:

your stalk has caught root
among wet pebbles
and drift flung by the sea
and grated shells
and split conch-shells.

Beautiful, wide-spread,
fire upon leaf,
what meadow yields
so fragrant a leaf
as your bright leaf?

AS I ATTEMPT to read H.D.'s "Sea Poppies," I'll be thinking of the rubric "the end of the poem" in terms of depth rather than duration, trying to pry below the surface of the poem to the crab world which lies submerged far, or not so far, below. This very phrase "crab world" was used by H.D. of Marianne Moore's *Selected Poems* of 1935, and is quoted by Barbara Guest in *Herself Defined: The Poet H.D. and Her World*:

> I do like Marianne Moore's poems, but they leave me a little stricken or shriven or shriveled, somehow. It is a very "crab" world, collecting junk from under the sea from old hulks; it sometimes reminds me of myself—much that is exquisite.

One of Moore's "'crab' world" poems H.D. might have been thinking of is "Sea Unicorns and Land Unicorns," in which we find:

> Britannia's sea unicorn with its rebellious child
> now ostentatiously indigenous to the new English coast;
> and its land lion oddly tolerant of those pacific counterparts to it,
> the water lions of the west.

I'll be trying to find a way into the submarine imagery by which H.D. was reminded of herself, imagery which informed so many of her early poems, and attempting a Freudian reading of several poems, including "Sea Rose," "Sea Violet," "Sea Lily" and "Sea Iris," all published in her 1916 collection, *Sea Garden*, paying particular attention to certain images and their "counterparts." Along the way, I'll be relying quite heavily on H.D.'s own account, in *Tribute to Freud*, of her relationship with "the famous doctor" as well as letters just published in Susan Stanford Friedman's wonderful *Analyzing Freud: Letters of H.D., Bryher, and Their Circle*, which reflect H.D.'s own forays into the "deep" in what she described as the "long and slimy process . . . of un-UNKing the UNK."

I'LL BEGIN, though, with a distinctive aspect of the "'crab' world" as described by a namesake of H.D., R. F. Doolittle, in his 1984 study of *The Plasma Proteins*:

Certain crustacea have an extracellular protein, casually referred to as "fibrinogen," that can be gelled directly by a transglutaminase without concordant proteolysis; in contrast, fibrin formation in vertebrates involves the thrombin-catalyzed release of peptides from the amino-terminal segments of the alpha and beta chains. Some other invertebrates possess a system based on limited proteolysis, but gel formation in those creatures involves a protein called "coagulogen" that bears no resemblance to vertebrate fibrinogen.

In a word or two, there are quite different systems of blood-clotting, and, indeed, different kinds of blood, in vertebrates and such invertebrates as the "crabs" with their external "husks" that live in the proximity of Moore's "old hulks." While the real world may not allow a "land" phenomenon to find a "counterpart" in a "sea" phenomenon, it's precisely the interchangeability of the words "hulk" and "hull," both referring to ships, and the interchangeability of the words "hull" and "husk," both referring to fruit or grain, that underlie the first stanza of "Sea Poppies":

Amber *husk*
fluted with gold,
fruit on the sand
marked with a rich *grain*.

These words "fruit" and "grain" send us back to a major source for H.D.'s image-trove, since they both derive from a poem supercharged with the details of harvesting by a poet H.D. read in what she described to Thomas B. Swann as "the usual school routine":

Season of mists and mellow *fruit*fulness,
Close bosom-friend of the maturing sun,
Conspiring with him how to load and bless
With *fruit* the vines that round the thatch-eaves run;
To bend with apples the mossed cottage-trees,
And fill all *fruit* with ripeness to the core

Keats's notion of a "core," or kernel, is inextricably bound up with H.D.'s notion of a "husk," which it informs, while the piling of "fruit" upon "fruit" upon "fruit" leads to the great hoard of grain in the second stanza of "To Autumn":

> Who hath not seen thee oft amid thy store?
> Sometimes whoever seeks abroad may find
> Thee sitting careless on a *granary* floor,
> Thy hair soft-lifted by the winnowing wind;

Having determined the provenance of the "fruit" and the "grain," we recognise almost immediately the provenance, or part of it, of the "poppies" themselves:

> Or on a half-reaped furrow sound asleep,
> Drowsed with the fume of *poppies*, while thy hook
> Spares the next swath and all its twined flowers.

The "fume" of poppies is an "odour or odorous exhalation (either fragrant or offensive) emitted from a substance, flower etc" (*OED*), which prepares the way for the "fragrant" leaf of the final stanza of "Sea Poppies." But "To Autumn" has otherwise "marked with a rich grain" H.D.'s poem. For instance, the "treasure" of line 5 is influenced by the obsolete sense of "store" as "treasure" in Keats's "Who hath not seen thee oft amid thy *store?*" The "stalk" of line 8 is derived partly from the "stubble-plains" found in the third stanza of "To Autumn," and may partly inspire H.D.'s strange use of the word "shriveled" in her review of Marianne Moore. In the second stanza of "To Autumn," moreover, we come upon these lines:

> And sometimes like a gleaner thou dost keep
> Steady thy laden head across a brook;
> Or by cider-press, with patient look,
> Thou watchest the last oozings hours by hours.

I suspect that Keats's use of the word "oozings" is a harking back to Shakespeare's "our poesy is as a gum that *oozes* from whence 'tis nourished." Since there's always a possibility that the "gum that oozes" might become the "fossil resin of extinct coniferous trees that flourished along the Baltic coast in Tertiary times, from 60,000,000 to 70,000,000 years ago," as the *Encyclopaedia Britannica* describes true "amber," it's hardly coincidental that we find amber in line 1 of "Sea Poppies." Since these are "*Sea* Poppies," however, that amber may also be a form of ambergris, described by my trusty *Encyclopaedia Britannica* as "a concretion (whether normal or pathological is still debated) formed in the intestinal tract of the sperm whale." Ambergris is often "cast up on shores," which would account for its being "fruit *on the sand*" or "treasure / spilled near the shrub-pines / to bleach *on the boulders*." Indeed, as the *Encyclopaedia Britannica* points out, the process of bleaching is integral to the development of ambergris:

> Fresh ambergris is soft in consistency, black in colour, and has a disagreeable odour. *Exposed to sun, air and sea water*, however, the material hardens, its colour *fades to a light gray*, and it develops a subtle and pleasing fragrance.

One of the main uses of ambergris that has been allowed to "bleach on the boulders" is, of course, in the fragrance industry, where "introduced into fine perfumes, ambergris adds to the scent of essential flower oils its own suave and long-lasting bouquet." This association of the amber of line 1 with ambergris would highlight the centrality of the perfume of the "Sea Poppies" that have "so *fragrant* a leaf."

In addition to the "fume of poppies" in "Ode to Autumn," H.D. may be drawing on at least two other occasions in Keats where poppies are associated with an alteration of the state of consciousness. One is "the magic bed of sacred ditamy, and *poppies* red" in lines 554–55 of Book I of *Endymion*, by which Endymion embarks on a dream-vision:

> Moreover, through the dancing *poppies* stole
> A breeze, most softly lulling to my soul,
> And shaping visions all about my sight
> Of colours, wings, and bursts of spangly light;
> The which became more strange, and strange, and dim,
> And then were gulfed in a tumultuous swim—
> And then I fell asleep.

There is, in other words, an association of the dream world with the "swim" of the ocean, of the "Morphean" with the "fount" as in—guess what?—the "Morphean fount" of line 748 of Book I of *Endymion*. We remember that Morpheus is a son of Somnus, the god of sleep, and that one of the reasons "Sleep" might be "quiet in his *poppy* coronet," as he's described in line 348 of Keats's "Sleep and Poetry," is that there's also a connection between sleep and what we might term "Opiatery," given that opiates such as morphine are derivative of plain old land poppies. These two Keatsian instances of the association of poppies with a shift in state of consciousness, specifically a dream state, underlie these "Sea Poppies" of H.D.

This is particularly the case of the poppies in *Endymion*, which offer a portal to an erotic scene in which

> I e'en dared to press
> Her very cheek against my crowned lip,
> And, at that moment, felt my body dip
> Into a warmer air—a moment more,
> Our feet were soft in flowers. There was store
> Of newest joys upon that alp. Sometimes
> A scent of violets, and blossoming limes,
> Loitered around us; then of honey cells,
> Made delicate from all white-flower bells;
> And once, above the edges of our nest,
> An arch face peeped—an Oread as I guessed.

This Oread, or mountain nymph, does a little more than "peep" into one of H.D.'s best-known poems, itself cunningly entitled "Oread":

> Whirl up, sea—
> whirl your pointed pines,
> splash your great pines
> on our rocks,
> hurl your green over us,
> cover us with your pools of fir.

This poem was published in 1914, a good twenty-two years before Meret Oppenheim covered a cup, saucer and spoon with fur and called it *Luncheon in Fur*, but there's a connection between the two works of art, I think, if only in that slippage between "fir" and "*fur*" in the last line of "Oread." The resulting impact is not unlike that of *Luncheon in Fur*, which Robert Hughes describes, in *The Shock of the New*, as "a self-contradictory image of astounding power." Hughes continues:

> *Luncheon in Fur* has also retained a long, secret life as a sexual emblem. The action it implies, the artist bringing her lips to a hairy receptacle full of warm fluid, makes Oppenheim's cup the most intense and abrupt image of Lesbian sex in the history of art.

A similarly "self-contradictory" system is at work in "Oread," where the "pines," "great" and "pointed" as they are, represent a transposition—an anagram, to boot—of "penis," also no doubt "great" and "pointed," in a world of indeterminacy of sea and land. That indeterminacy is emblematic of H.D.'s own sexual indeterminacy, so that the "Sea Poppies" exhibit conventional male and female characteristics, "your *stalk* has caught *root*" belonging to the conventionally male system, the "split conch-shells" to the conventionally female. Indeed, it should come as little surprise that the word "concha" is given in the *OED* as "another term for vulva." The "wet" is a conventional indicator of female arousal, though it may also suggest a post-orgasmic male member, as in the "poppies hung / dew-dabbled on their stalks" in line 683 of Book I of *Endymion*, that word "stalks" reappearing in "your *stalk* has caught root" in line 8 of "Sea Poppies." The indeterminacy of conventional male and female imagery is there in that phrase from *Endymion* I quoted earlier where "There was store / Of newest joys upon that alp," where the very unconventionality of the use of the word "alp," with its suggestion of the "mounting" male, might alert us to the fact that the word is also an anagram of the word "lap," once used to refer specifically to "the female pudendum" (*OED*), and now the object of Keats's poppy-induced reverie. Not that Keats has exclusive rights to the erotics of poppydom. Another of H.D.'s influences here may be Robert Burns, Imagiste, who writes so memorably in "Tam o' Shanter":

> But pleasures are like *poppies* spread—
> You seize the flow'r, its bloom is shed;
> Or like the snow falls in the river—
> A moment white—then melts forever.

We may remark on the fact that H.D. uses the word "spread" of the "beautiful, wide-*spread*" poppies, and decide that it's mere coincidence, but there's at least one poem by Burns which is resolutely central to the entire flower system of H.D. I'm thinking of "A Red, Red Rose":

> O my luve is like a red, red rose,
> That's newly sprung in June.

The sense in which "my luve" is "*like* a red, red rose" connects Burns and H.D. in at least two important ways. First, there's the physical resemblance between the petals of the flower and the foliated female lap. Second, there's a connection between the transitory nature of beauty in the flower and the transitory nature of the beauty of the beloved. These often combine the exhortation "Let us crown ourselves with rosebuds, before they be withered" from the Wisdom of Solomon with Horace's "Carpe diem." We see it in Shakespeare's first sonnet:

> From fairest creatures we desire increase,
> That thereby beauty's rose might never die.

We see it in Sonnet 18:

> Rough winds do shake the darling buds of May,
> And summer's lease hath all too short a date.

We see it in Spenser:

> Gather therefore the Rose, whilst yet is prime,
> For soon comes age, that will her pride deflower:
> Gather the Rose of love, whilst yet is time.

We see it in Herrick:

> Gather thee rosebuds while ye may,
> Old Time is still a-flying.
> And this same flower that smiles today
> Tomorrow will be dying.

We see it in Blake:

> O Rose, thou art sick!
> The invisible worm
> That flies in the night,
> In the howling storm,
>
> Has found out thy bed
> Of crimson joy,
> And his dark secret love
> Does thy life destroy.

The idea of "defloration," the "worm / That flies in the night" that "Has found out thy bed / Of crimson joy," partly informs the violent imagery of the "drift *flung* by the sea / and *grated* shells / and *split* conch-shells" in "Sea Poppies," all the detritus of a "howling storm." The word "flung" also occurs in the sixty-four-word "Sea Rose," though it's only one of an astonishing thirteen instances of shared vocabulary with "Sea Poppies":

> Rose, harsh rose,
> marred and with stint of petals,
> meager flower, thin,
> sparse of *leaf*,
>
> more precious
> than a *wet* rose
> single on a stem—
> you are *caught* in the *drift*.
> Stunted, with small *leaf*,
> you are *flung on the sand*,
> you are lifted
> in the crisp *sand*
> that *drives* in the wind.
>
> Can the spice-rose
> drip such acrid *fragrance*
> hardened in a *leaf*?

That phrase "Rose, harsh rose" which opens "Sea Roses" is an irreverent rewriting of the opening of Yeats's "To the Rose upon the Rood of Time":

Red Rose, proud Rose, sad Rose of all my days!

It is, less obviously, an allusion to Burns via Yeats, an allusion H.D. makes quite clear when she throws her voice through Eurydice, as in the wonderfully angry poem of that title:

At least I have the flowers of myself
and my thoughts, no god
can take that.
I have the fervour of myself for a presence
and my own spirit for light;
and my spirit with its loss
knows this:
though small against the black,
small against the formless rocks,
hell must break before I am lost;
before I am lost,
hell must open *like a red rose*
for the dead to pass.

The positioning of the speaker who identifies her "self" with "flowers" as "small against the black, small against the formless rocks" is completely consistent with the positioning of the "Sea Rose" that is "stunted, with *small* leaf / . . . flung on the sand" and the "Sea Poppies" that are "spilled near the shrub-pines / to bleach on the *boulders*."

Let's stay with that "treasure / spilled near the shrub-pines" for a moment. We remember Robert Burns, Imagiste, and his great lines in "Tam o' Shanter" about the "snow" that "falls in the river." This "snow" is pretty clearly a seminal discharge, particularly when it is "a moment white— then melts forever." There's more than a faint whiff of the seminal, particularly if we think of Onan, who "spilled his seed on the ground," in this image of the "treasure / *spilled* near the shrub-pines." We notice that the pubic "shrub" of the "shrub-pines" is obscuring another "penis." That penis reappears as a "stalk" and a "root." This root is bifurcated, to say the least. To begin with, it signals what one might call the subject matter of "Sea Poppies"—the endurance of the seemingly frail. This endurance is what has "hardened" in the leaf of the "Sea Rose" which is "more precious / than a wet rose / single on a stem," that "stem" another version of the "stalk" or "root." Both "Sea Rose" and "Sea Poppies" are poems which are less persuaded by the passing of things than their persistence. It is to this sense of persistence that Burns's "Red, Red Rose" testifies:

> As fair art thou, my bonnie lass,
> So deep in luve am I;
> And I will love thee still, my dear,
> Till a' the seas gang dry.
>
> Till a' the seas gang dry, my dear,
> And the rocks melt with the sun:
> O I will love thee still, my dear,
> While the sands o' life shall run.

The "sands o' life" are related to the "crisp *sand* / that drives in the wind" of "Sea Rose" and the "*sand* / marked with a rich grain" in "Sea Poppies." Also to the "sand-bank" in "Sea Violet":

> The white violet
> is scented on its stalk,
> the sea-violet
> fragile as agate,
> lies fronting all the wind
> among the torn shells
> on the *sand-bank*.

That "stalk" on which the "Sea Violet" is set is connected to the stalk that "has caught root" in line 8 of "Sea Poppies." I promised that that "root" was "bifurcated," and I'd better deliver on my promise. I want to try to connect it to another use of the word "root" by H.D. It occurs in her description of why, in 1933, she became an "analysand" of Sigmund Freud:

> I wanted to dig down and dig out, *root* out my personal needs, strengthen my purposes, reaffirm my beliefs, canalize my energies.

The rationalizing of the force of water implicit in H.D.'s "canalizing" metaphor is an extension of the sea imagery connected with the unconscious mind. In *Tribute to Freud*, her publication of 1956, H.D. writes of her profound sense of duality:

> Then in later life, there were 2 countries, America and England as it happened, separated by *a wide gap in consciousness and a very wide stretch of sea.* The sea grows narrower, the gap in consciousness sometimes seems negligible; nevertheless there is a duality, the English-speaking peoples are related, brothers, twins even, but they are not one. So in me, 2 distinct racial or biological or psychological entities tend to grow nearer or to blend, even, as time heals old breaks in consciousness.

This passage might serve as the main plank of a Freudian interpretation of "Sea Poppies," particularly now that we're all but overwhelmed by the "tumultuous swim" of its "stalk/root" system of imagery. Let's stick with that system for the moment and try to bring to bear some of H.D.'s own later adventures in Freudian analysis on these early poems. The "stalk that has caught root" is one for which one must "dig down and dig out." Whatever else it is, it is not "one root of the white sort" that we find in "Sea Violet":

> but who would change for these
> who would change for these
> one root of the white sort?

The "white sort" is a conventional male root, I expect, one that is "a moment *white*—then melts forever." These are more likely to be female flowers, their names, like Lily, Iris, and Poppy itself, the names of women who might be apostrophized—"Rose, harsh rose," "Violet, your grasp is frail." The "violet" is a flower on which "the famous doctor," in *The Interpretation of Dreams*, so memorably presents a view:

> *"Violets"* was ostensibly quite asexual; but, very boldly, as it seemed to me, I thought I could trace a secret meaning for the word in an unconscious link with the French word *"viol"* ["rape"]. To my surprise the dreamer gave as an association the English word "violate." The dream had made use of the great chance similarity between the words *"violet"* and *"violate"*—the difference in their pronunciation lies merely in the different stress upon their final syllables—in order to express "in the language of flowers" the dreamer's thoughts on the violence of defloration (another term that employs flower symbolism) and possibly also a masochistic trait in her character. A pretty instance of the "verbal bridges" crossed by the paths leading to the unconscious.

I've already used one "verbal bridge," the word "root," to connect H.D. and Freud, whom she sees as a kind of father figure. In *Tribute to Freud*, she is at great pains to lay out their shared heritage (might one say, their *roots*?), announcing that, like her father's second wife, Freud is "a Moravian actually by birth." A few paragraphs later, H.D. describes her mother, as remote a parent as one might encounter:

> But one can never get near enough, or if one gets near, it is because one has measles or scarlet fever.

This association of "redness" with female affection (or lack of it) is telling, surely, in the context of "Sea Poppies" and "Sea Roses" and "Sea Violets." The strongest sense we get of H.D.'s father is that he's even more remote than the mother:

> Provided you do not speak to him when he is sitting at his table, or disturb him when he is lying down, you are free to come and go.

Freud might have seen, in this line, a "verbal bridge" between the words "free" and "go" and the name "Godfree," as in Edward Godfree.

(We've seen another unconscious allusion to the name in those lines from "Eurydice," "At least I have the flowers of myself / and my thoughts, no *god* / can take that.") Edward Godfree was the name by which the poet Richard Aldington was christened in 1892. He had met H.D. in London in 1911 and they were married in 1913. By the time "Sea Poppies" was written, that marriage was under severe strain, largely because of Aldington's philandering. In that phrase from *Tribute to Freud* about one being "free to come and go," H.D. has neatly conjoined her by then ex-husband, Richard Aldington, and her astronomer father, head of the Flower Observatory at the University of Pennsylvania. The fact that he was an astronomer accounts partly for his topsy-turvy behaviour:

> He has some mysterious habits, this going out at night and sleeping on the couch in his study by day.

H.D. describes the "only picture that was hanging in his study":

> The original picture was by Rembrandt, if I am not mistaken. The half-naked man on the table was dead so it did not hurt him when the doctors sliced his arm with a knife or a pair of scissors. Is the picture called *A Lesson in Anatomy?*

Almost immediately, H.D. conjoins her father and Freud:

> It does not really matter what the picture is called. It is about doctors. There is a doctor seated at the back of the couch on which I am lying. He is a very famous doctor. He is called Sigmund Freud.

I want to suggest that, long before she met the "famous doctor," H.D. had made another "verbal bridge" between her father's "couch" and its near version, "conch," as in the "split *conch*-shells." It is, after all, the father (and to a lesser degree the mother) whose privacy must not be violated, or "violeted." They live within a self-protected "shell." Some version of that very shell is alluded to shortly afterwards in a passage from *Tribute to Freud* which, if you'll forgive me, I'll quote at some length:

I had accepted as part of my racial, my religious inheritance, the
abstract idea of immortality, of the personal soul's existence in some
form or other, after it had shed the outworn or outgrown body. The
Chambered Nautilus of the New England poet, Oliver Wendell
Holmes, had been a great favourite of mine as a school-girl; I did not
think of the poem then, but its metres echo in my head now as I
write this. *Till thou at length are free*, the last stanza ends, *Leaving thine
outgrown shell by life's unresting sea!* And *Build thee more stately
mansions, O my soul* is another line, and with the Professor, I did feel
that I had reached the high-water mark of achievement; I mean, I felt
that to meet him at 47, and to be accepted by him as analysand or
student, seemed to crown all my other personal contacts and
relationships, justify all the spiral-like meanderings of my mind and
body. I had come home, in fact.

It's telling, I think, that H.D. appeals to the image of "the *high-water
mark* of achievement," the high-water mark being the point at which

> your stalk has caught root
> among wet pebbles
> and drift flung by the sea
> and grated shells
> and split conch-shells.

Those "conch-shells" have been "split" because they've been "outworn or
outgrown," in other words, as if they, too, were discarded "husk[s] /
fluted with gold." That "husk." Years after writing "Sea Poppies," again in
Tribute to Freud, H.D. would make a direct connection between that
"husk" and her Professor, on whose behalf she's rather concerned:

> One day, I was deeply distressed when the Professor spoke to me
> about his grandchildren—what would become of them? He asked
> me that, as if the future of his immediate family were the only
> future to be considered. There was, of course, the perfectly secured
> future of his own work, his books. But there was a more imminent,
> a more immediate future to consider. It worried me to feel that he
> had no idea—it seemed impossible—really no idea that he would

"wake up" when he shed the frail locust-husk of his years, and find himself alive.

This "locust-husk" seems to go in two directions at once. One direction leads to the comparatively ameliorative associations of the "shell" which has been "outworn or outgrown" so that the true being may be "free," as a cicada throws off successive outer casings before reaching maturity, or as Oliver Wendell *Holmes* might bring one, by another "verbal bridge," *"home*, in fact." The other leads towards the pejorative associations of fragility. We notice that H.D. refers to the word "frail locust-husk" of Freud, just as the "Sea Violet" is *"frail* on the edge of the sand-hill." The association of the male "stalk" with the "fragile" and the "frail" go back to her association of the fragile nature of the relationship between daughter and father, wife and husband. It is from the sleeping-place of the "couch" that one would "wake up," or come to consciousness, after a poppy-induced dream, to make sense of all those "spiral-like meanderings of [my] mind and body."

Indulge me, if you will, in a few more "spiral-like meanderings" of my own as I try to "grasp" "the edge of the sand-hill" and connect it to H.D.'s father and one or two other father and mother figures, whom she herself conjoins, usually quite directly, as in the case of her apostrophizing Robert Frost at the end of "Sea Violet":

Violet
your grasp is frail
on the edge of the sand-hill,
but you catch the light—
frost, a star edges with its fire.

We recall that "Sea Poppies" was published just three years after the appearance, in 1913, of Frost's first book, *A Boy's Will*, two after the publication in 1914 of *North of Boston*. Another male New England poet, like Oliver Wendell Holmes, Frost is conjoined with an astronomer father who spends his nights trying to "catch the light" of "star" after "star," where "a star edges with its fire." The words "edge" and "edges" are used within three lines in "Sea Violet," and bring us neatly to that most cutting-edge of the Imagists, a poet with whom both Frost and H.D. were friendly. I'm thinking of F. S. Flint, who's referred to quite directly in "Sea Lily," another poem in *Sea Garden*:

> Myrtle-bark
> is flecked from you,
> scales are dashed
> from your stem,
> sand cuts your petal,
> furrows it with hard edge,
> like *flint*
> on a bright stone.

We see traces of "flint" in the "wet *pebbles*" of "Sea Poppies," while a near version of the name occurs in the phrase *"stint* of petals" in "Sea Rose," along with the valorization of the flintiness that's *"hardened* in a leaf." It had been F. S. Flint who, in the March 1913 number of *Poetry*, had outlined the main ideas of the Imagist movement ("direct treatment of the 'thing,' use of absolutely no word that did not contribute to the presentation, to compose in the sequence of the musical phrase, not in the sequence of the metronome"). In April 1914, *Poetry* carried a poem in which the "metronome" had been chipped away to the "metro" in Ezra Pound's "In a Station of the Metro":

> The apparition of these faces in the crowd;
> petals on a wet, black bough.

Like Flint, his co-founder of the Imagist movement, Pound appears in "Sea Poppies" in a less than obvious guise. He comes in by way of a common synonym for words and phrases such as "wet pebbles / and drift *flung by the sea*" and *"grated* shells" and indeed *"split* conch-shells." They've all been pulverized or *pound*ed. We see further examples of pounding in the "Sea Rose" that is *"flung on the sand"* by the pounding wind and waves and the "Sea Lily" whose "scales *are dashed* / from [your] stem" and the "Sea Iris" so buffeted that "one petal like a shell / is broken." That "petal" has fallen from "a wet, black bough," surely, the "wet" also influencing the "wet pebbles" of "Sea Poppies." In *Tribute to Freud*, H.D. would write of an occasion in 1911 when she found, on a visit to Paris with her first main female lover, Frances Gregg, a ring with a serpent-and-thistle motif which had hitherto seemed to exist only in the mind of her other lover, Ezra Pound:

> Under the glass, set in a row with other seal-rings, was a little grey-agate oval. It was a small ring with rather fragile setting, as far as one could judge, but the design was unmistakable. On the right side, as in the original, was the coiled upright serpent; on the left, an exquisitely chased stalk, with the spiny double leaf and the flower-head, our thistle.

H.D. has already drawn on this system and its vocabulary in her description "the white violet / is scented on its *stalk*, / the sea-violet / *fragile* as *agate*," where Pound is conjoined with Richard Aldington. The notion of the pounding by heavy artillery, of "shells" in a military sense, must be somewhere in the background of those "grated shells," particularly when the word "front" is used of the "Sea Violet" which

> lies *fronting* all the wind
> among the torn shells
> on the sand-bank.

This viole(n)t imagery leads me to date "Sea Violet" even later than "Sea Poppies." Neither appears in the April 1915 publication of *Some Imagist Poets*, in which "Sea Lily," "Sea Iris" and "Sea Rose" are presented as a group. If "Sea Violet" does turn out to be earlier, its imagery would be extraordinarily prescient of the experience of the most immediate male poet in H.D's experience, the aforementioned Richard Aldington, to whom she was of course married. Or by whom she was "marred," as we might deduce from the "word bridge" which we find in "Sea Rose":

> Rose, harsh rose,
> *marred* and with stint of petals

Though Aldington would not actually enlist until 1916, nor go to the Western Front until 1917, he knew in 1915 that he would be called up. In any event, it's inevitable that something of the precarious nature of post–June 1914 Europe and the precarious nature of the Aldingtons' relationship would find their way into the fractured imagery of all these flower poems. "Richard" appears there at the end of "Sea Rose" in the near-anagram of "acrid" and "hard" in "*acrid* fragrance / *hard*ened," while in "Sea Poppies" the "amber husk / fluted with gold, / fruit on the sand" is "marked with a *rich* grain." One of my reasons for thinking "Sea Poppies" was written in late 1915 or early 1916 is that it may derive something of its force from the poppy imagery of "In Flanders Fields," the great poem by John McCrae which was written in response to the death of a fellow soldier by shrapnel from "grated *shells* / and split conch-*shells*" (that double use of "shells" drawing so much attention to itself):

> Take up our quarrel with the foe:
> To you from failing hands we throw
> The torch: be yours to hold it high.
> If ye break faith with us who die
> We shall not sleep, though poppies grow
> In Flanders fields.

"In Flanders Fields" was published in the December 8, 1915, issue of *Punch* and, if it was indeed read by H.D., may have influenced some of the imagery and vocabulary of "Sea Violet," its insistence on "failing hands" perhaps carried over into the "your *grasp* is *frail*" and "the sea-violet / *fragile* as agate, / lies fronting all the wind," with its slightly awkward positioning of "lies," picking up, perhaps, on "now we *lie* / in Flanders fields." It's just possible that the word "mark" in line 3 of "In Flanders Fields," "the crosses, row upon row / that mark our place" may inform the phrase "*marked* with a rich grain" in line 4 of "Sea Poppies." More likely, as I've suggested before, is that "Rich" Aldington is himself an even greater influence here, given his tendency to marital infidelity ("break[ing] faith" in a much more direct sense) and cover-up which may inform the phrase "*lies fronting*" in "Sea Violet." Aldington's sexual inconstancy, his being a "reed in the wind" seems to lie behind the opening of "Sea Lily":

> *Reed,*
> slashed and torn
> but doubly rich.

I KNOW YOU'RE BEGINNING TO WONDER if I'm now going backwards rather than forwards in my reading of "Sea Poppies," but I want to begin to draw things to a close, perhaps even reach a conclusion, by focussing on the word "exquisite" in one of the "doubly rich" Aldington poems included in his 1915 collection, *Images*, which includes an image of H.D.:

> Like a gondola of green scented fruits
> Drifting along the dark canals of Venice,
> You, O exquisite one,
> Have entered into my desolate city.

I think it's more than coincidental that H.D. uses the word "exquisite" in her strange review of Marianne Moore's *Selected Poems*:

> I do like Marianne Moore's poems, but they leave me a little stricken or shriven or shriveled, somehow. It is a very "crab" world, collecting junk from under the sea from old hulks; it sometimes reminds me of myself—much that is *exquisite*.

H.D. has transferred herself, through Aldington's description of her, to the mother figure of Moore. It's helpful to remind ourselves that this review was written in 1935, only a few months after H.D. had completed her extensive psychoanalysis with Freud. In a letter to Bryher dated October 28, 1934, and included in *Analyzing Freud: Letters of H.D., Bryher, and Their Circle*, H.D. is ecstatic about a recent communication:

> I have had my first real fan letter from a woman—Marianne of all people! Write this in letter[s] of gold—"And I hope you will never doubt from such worms as myself the admiration which the shining face of your courage evokes!" I am positively limp!!!!

The four exclamation marks that follow "limp" signal an awareness of the overstatements from all involved, including Moore's categorization of herself as a "worm." An "invisible *worm* / that flies in the night," perhaps? Perhaps a worm from a "worm-eaten hulk," since the term "worm-eaten" does seem to be applied to a "hulk" with monotonous regularity. Something of the "worm-eaten hulk" syndrome is transferred by H.D. to her description, the following year, of Moore's poetry as "collecting junk from under the sea from old *hulks*." The "limp" is an unconscious response to the valorization of the "hardened" in several of these sea-flower poems, and connects with the "shriveled" nature of the "hulk/hull/husk" nexus I mentioned earlier. It's the unconscious association of "husk" with "shriveled" that accounts for H.D.'s description of her response to Moore as "shriveled." That association with "Sea Poppies," in particular the phrase "husk / fluted with gold," also accounts for H.D.'s exhortation to Bryher to "write this in letter[s] of *gold*." As we've seen, the "husk / fluted with gold" is transferred to the description of the "locust-*husk*" of Freud, which is in turn transferred to the "shriveled" Moore. Mama Moore is conjoined with Papa Freud, both related to Richard Aldington, who compares himself, in "Childhood," one of the poems included in *Some Imagist Poets* of 1915, to "a chrysalis / in a match-box" with "*shriveled* wing."

Let's look at those other two adjectives, "stricken" and "shriven," which H.D. uses in the phrase "stricken or shriven or shriveled." It's difficult not to think that H.D. doesn't quite understand the word "shriven," a word meaning "confessed" or "absolved," from the verb "to shrive," with the transitive meaning of "to impose penance upon; hence, to administer absolution to; to hear the confession of," and the intransitive meaning of "to make one's confession and receive absolution and penance." Or perhaps H.D. understands only too well the meaning of "shriven," using it at once transitively and intransitively, absolving and being absolved, declaring herself "free" of "Godfree." She is, after all, the analysand who's concerned less with her own security than the "perfectly secured future" of the "famous doctor," just as she's less concerned with the "crab world" of Marianne Moore than that she "reminds me of myself." So much for "shriven." What about "stricken"? As you know, it's a word used variously to describe being "advanced in years," "wounded in the chase," "struck with a blow," "afflicted with disease," "smitten with love," and reflects H.D.'s complex relationship with her classmate from Bryn Mawr of whom she continues, in that October 1934 letter to Bryher:

I was terrified of M.M.—and she wrote THE most beautiful letter. Now I repeat: I have YOU to thank for all this, Fido!

The faithful "Fido" is, as I've mentioned, Bryher. I've not mentioned that Bryher was the pseudonym of Winifred Ellerman, the heiress to a shipping fortune who was, after 1919, H.D.'s female lover, though H.D. was also involved with Kenneth Macpherson, one of Bryher's two husbands, himself bisexual. Such is the pressure per square inch in the murky underwater world in which we've spent the last fifty minutes that it should come as no great shock to discover that Bryher had, in 1933, herself published a poem dedicated "to M.M." and entitled "Nautillus," so coming "home, in fact" not only to Moore (perhaps even influencing her poem "The Paper Nautilus," written eight years later), but to H.D.'s version, in the "grated shells / and split conch-shells," of the *Chambered Nautilus* which she would later associate with the "high-water mark" of her work with Freud.

Before we leave Marianne Moore and Freud, let me suggest that they are connected yet again in H.D.'s mind by the word "junk," which she uses in her 1935 review of Moore ("collecting junk from under the sea") and in a 1936 letter to Bryher:

> It is a long and slimy process, this, of un-UNKing the UNK or debunking the *junk*.

Yet again, the "UNK," or "unconscious," is connected to the world of "junk," both below the water and at the high-water mark, the "un-UNKing" of which by "the famous doctor" would become the "crown of my achievement." The doctor might well have gone to town on the associations of that "crown," particularly since it's a version of a hat, on which Freud holds forth in *The Interpretation of Dreams*:

> A woman's hat can very often be interpreted with certainty as a genital organ and, moreover, as a *man's*.

Freud amends this later in *The Interpretation of Dreams*:

> Other, less transparent cases had led me to believe that a hat can also stand for female genitals.

It must have been difficult for Freud to know which way to jump if and when he heard H.D.'s account of her father's background, as she describes it in a passage from *Tribute to Freud* which I quoted from earlier:

> He comes from those Puritan fathers who wear high peaked hats in the Thanksgiving numbers of magazines. They fought with Indians and burned witches. Their hats were like the hats the doctors wore, in the only picture that was hanging in his study. The original picture was by Rembrandt, if I am not mistaken. The half-naked man on the table was dead so it did not hurt him when the doctors sliced his arm with a knife or a pair of scissors. Is the picture called *A Lesson in Anatomy?*

It might have been an account of this scene that led Freud to conclude, as H.D. reported in a letter to Bryher of November 24, 1934, that she wore two hats:

> I have gone terribly deep with papa. He says, "you had two things to hide, one that you were a girl, the other that you were a boy." It appears that I am that all-but extinct phenomina [*sic*], the perfect bi-.

She is, in other words, "doubly rich," as in the "doubly rich leaf" of "Sea Lily" or the "double leaf" in Pound's grey-agate ring with the "double leaf" in its "exquisitely chased stalk, with its spiny double leaf and the flower-head, our thistle." There's that "exquisite" again, connected subliminally with the "exquisite" mother figure of Moore. The "chased" is a wonderful touch, referring as it does to the "grooved, or indented" stalk, like the "*fluted*" "Sea Poppies," and the stalk by which one might no longer be "chaste," or "pure from unlawful sexual intercourse." The "flower-head" is another humdinger of a word-bridge, given that H.D.'s father was the *head* of the *Flower* Observatory at the University of Pennsylvania, and that another type of "flower-head" is associated with Freud:

> To be accepted by him as analysand or student, seemed to *crown* all my other personal contacts and relationships.

The first meaning of "crown" given by the *OED* is "an ornamental fillet, or similar encircling ornament for the head, worn for personal adornment, or as a mark of honour or achievement; a coronal or wreath of leaves or *flowers*." The two "papas," Charles Doolittle and Sigmund Freud, are interchangeable, just as the two "poppies," Aldington and Pound, are interchangeable. Let's think more about the "double leaf." It's "spiny," or "having the characteristics of a thorn or thorns; resembling a thorn in form or qualities." The word "thorn" has a powerful resonance for H.D. For example, the pseudonym "Thorne" is used of the Macpherson/ Bryher characters in *Borderline*, Macpherson's 1930 film, largely because of the obvious association of the thorn with the word "briar," a homophone for Bryher. As early as the poems of *Sea Garden*, however, H.D. was mindful of the "thorn," through a system of imagery deriving to some extent from those lines spoken by Theseus in Act I, Scene i of *A Midsummer Night's Dream*:

> But earthlier happy is the rose distill'd,
> Than that which withering on the virgin thorn
> Grows, lives and dies, in single blessedness.

The "withering" is brought across into the "husk" in "Sea Poppies," the "Sea Rose" that is "marred and with stint of petals" rather than "a wet rose, single on a stem," that "single" deriving from the phrase "in *single* blessedness." The "rose distill'd" is one used in the perfume industry, as is appropriate in the context of the "fragrance" in "Sea Rose" and the "so fragrant a leaf" in "Sea Poppies." The rose/thorn iconography will connect Bryher, Freud and H.D. in an interesting way, since her sense of Bryher/briar lies behind H.D's poem "The Master," an account of her disagreement with Freud over the matter of whether or not she had fallen afoul of the dreaded penis envy:

> I was angry with the old man
> with his talk of man-strength,
> I was angry with his mystery, his mysteries,
> I argued till day-break;

This is in itself an engaging scenario, since it places analyst and analysand in the conventional roles of male and female lovers anticipating the dawn that will part them. The speaker goes on to assert of the woman:

> there is purple flower
> between her marble, her birch-tree white
> thighs,
> or there is a red flower,
>
> there is a *rose* flower
> parted wide.

The "parted wide" is echoic of the end of "Sea Poppies":

> Beautiful, *wide*-spread,
> fire upon leaf,
> what meadow yields
> so fragrant a leaf
> as your bright leaf?

We see a version of the "double leaf" in the last couplet of "Sea Poppies," a couplet appealing to the perfect rhyme of "so fragrant a *leaf*" and "as your bright *leaf*," the end of the poem already sign-posted by the "fire upon leaf." This use of a couplet allows H.D. to overcome the difficulty set out by Barbara Hernstein Smith in her excellent *Poetic Closure: A Study of How Poems End*:

> Closure in the "pure" imagist poem was usually weak, but that was part of its intended effect. The image itself, the presentation of the raw data, the sensory experience of the poet recreated in the reader—that was the object of the objectivity. If it was successful, presumably the recreated experience would be sufficient and stable enough—but in the way any sense impression would be, with a lingering "after-image." Like the *haiku* by which it was influenced, the imagist poem did not assert the speaker's motives or personality except in what has been described [by Earl Miner] as "a tone of

melancholy and restrained plaintiveness." And it usually did not assert anything else either.

This form of "anti-closure" that "Sea Poppies" exhibits is far less obviously assertive than the strident end of "The Master," with its *mastur*batory climax:

> O God, what is it,
> this flower
> that in itself had power over the whole earth?
> for she needs no man,
> herself
> is that dart and pulse of the male,
> hands, feet, thighs,
> herself perfect.

The much younger poet of "Sea Poppies" is less strident, but no less assertive, in her delight in the tenacity of "the flower of [her]self" in the midst of the tenuous and the transitory, a delight she would have shared with Marina Tsvetayeva, whose long "Poem of the End" will be the subject of my next chapter.

I'll end here with a further brief treatise on the masturbatory theme I introduced earlier, following a lead from my colleague Michael Cadden and focussing less on the term "masturbates" than on "*mistress*bates." The Mistress Bates I have in mind is Katharine Lee *Bates* (1859–1929), a professor of English at Wellesley College, where she would enjoy a twenty-five-year "romantic friendship" with a certain Katharine Coman. In addition to having been a founder of the New England Poetry Club in 1915, the year in which "Sea Poppies" seems to have been written, Katharine Bates would have been in H.D.'s mind for other reasons, just as she would have been in the mind of any literate, or even illiterate, American. The positioning of "beautiful" in the last stanza of "Sea Poppies" is one indicator of H.D.'s debt to the author of "America the Beautiful."

> O *beautiful* for spacious skies,
> For *amber* waves of *grain*,

For purple mountain majesties
Above the *fruited* plain!

H.D. appeals not only to the vocabulary of "America the Beautiful," first published in 1895 and revised in 1911, but to its valorization of "freedom" and "self-control":

America! America!
God shed His grace on thee
And *crown* thy good with brotherhood
From *sea* to shining *sea*!

CHAPTER 12

POEM OF THE END

MARINA TSVETAYEVA

Closely, like one creature, we
start: there is our café!

There is our island, our shrine, where
in the morning, we people of the

rabble, a couple for a minute only,
conducted a morning service:

with things from country markets, sour
things seen through sleep or   spring.
The coffee was nasty there
entirely made from oats (and

with oats you can extinguish
caprice in fine race-horses).
There was no smell of Araby.
Arcadia was in

that coffee.

But how *she* smiled at us
and sat us down by her,
sad and worldly in her wisdom
a grey-haired paramour.

Her smile was solicitous
(saying: you'll wither! live!),
it was a smile at madness and being
penniless, at yawns   and love

and—this was the chief thing—
at laughter   without reason
smiles   with no deliberation
and our faces   without wrinkles.

Most of all   at youth
at passions   out of this climate
blown in from some other place
flowing from some other source

into that dim café
(burnous and Tunis) where
she smiled at hope and flesh
under old-fashioned clothes.

(My dear friend   I don't complain.
It's just another scar.)
To think how she saw us off,
that proprietress in her cap

stiff   as a Dutch hat . . .

Not quite remembering, not quite
understanding, we are led away from the festival—
along our street!   no longer ours   that
we walked many times, and no more shall.

Tomorrow the sun will rise in the West.
And then David will break with Jehovah.
—What are we doing?—We are *separating*.
—That's a word that means nothing to me.

It's the most inhumanly senseless
of words: *sep   arating*. (Am I one of a hundred?)
It is simply a word of four syllables and
behind their sound lies; emptiness.

Wait! Is it even correct in Serbian or
Croatian? Is it a Czech whim, this word.
Sep   aration! To *sep   arate!*
It is insane   unnatural

a sound to burst the eardrums, and spread out
far beyond the limits of longing itself.
Separation—the word is not in the Russian
language. Or the language of women. Or men.

Nor in the language of God. What are we—sheep?
To stare about us as we eat.
Separation—in what language is it,
when the meaning itself doesn't exist?

or even the sound! Well—an empty one, like
the noise of a saw in your sleep perhaps.
Separation. That belongs to the school of
Khlebnikov's   nightingale-groaning

swan-like . . .
                    so how does it happen?
Like a lake of water running dry.
Into air. I can feel our hands touching.
To separate. Is a shock of thunder

upon my head—oceans rushing into
a wooden house. This is Oceania's
furthest promontory. And the streets are steep.
To separate. That means to go downward

downhill   the sighing sound of two
heavy soles   and at last a hand receives
the nail in it. A logic that turns
everything over. *To separate*

means we have to become
single creatures   again

we who had grown into one.

Translated by Elaine Feinstein

ONE SENSE OF THE PHRASE "the end of the poem" on which I'll be musing today corresponds to the fifteenth definition of the word "end" given
by the *OED*—that's to say the "object for which a thing exists; the purpose
for which it is designed or instituted." The notion that poetry might
be "designed or instituted" to make some impact in the world is
one to which pundits (and poets) return again and again, particularly
in times of strife. I'll be concentrating on section 10 of Marina
Tsvetayeva's "Poem of the End," a long, difficult poem of fourteen sections written in 1924 about the impact on her of private strife—the termination of an adulterous relationship. Given that Tsvetayeva had also
endured the public strife of the Russian Revolution and its aftermath, and
that her history is inextricably linked with that of the Soviet state, something of that public history may inform "Poem of the End," if only tangentially. *Only* tangentially? My own conviction is that the tangential is
most likely to be on target, most likely to hit the butt. I'm using the word
"butt" here in the combined senses of "a mark for archery practice; terminal point; that towards which one's efforts are directed; an end, aim,
object" (*OED*). I'm reminded, in this regard, of the work of the contemporary Northern Irish poet, Medbh McGuckian, and the epigraph to her
1994 collection, *Captain Lavender*, which comes from Pablo Picasso's observation of 1944:

I have not painted the war . . . but I have no doubt that the war is in
. . . these paintings I have done.

I mention that "Poem of the End" is a "long poem," a definition of
which might be a poem that resists coming to a close, or drawing its own
conclusion. In my final three chapters I'll be trying to link the sense that a
poem might have its own agenda to the question of how we know when it's
over and done with. My theory is that, as it comes into being, the poem is
marking and measuring itself against a combination of what it might now
be and what it might yet become. I'll be trying to connect that concept to
an aspect of translation I touched on in my discussion of Montale's "The
Eel"—that of the poem as "autonomous creature"—and arguing, so far as
it's possible, for setting a boundary between the purpose for which the
poem might be "designed and instituted" and the purpose for which the
poet imagines he or she might be "designed and instituted." My conclusion,
insofar as I have a sense of it at this juncture, will be that the idea of anything "designed and instituted" by a poet will almost certainly run counter
to what I believe to be the "object for which" poetry exists.

For today, though, I'll be trying to raise the ghosts of several Russian
poets—Konstantin Balmont, Andrey Bely, Alexander Blok—whose pres-
ences inform this section of "Poem of the End" in somewhat unlikely
ways. I'll be making a suggestion or two about Tsvetayeva's critique of
what would become known as structuralist linguistics and structuralist
poetics, ideas in which she may have been influenced by Roman Jakobson,
a devotee of both Ferdinand de Saussure and the Russian Futurist Velimir
Khlebnikov. Velimir Khlebnikov was a man with an agenda, a promoter of
poetry that has "a palpable design upon us." I borrow the phrase from
Keats's famous letter to John Hamilton Reynolds:

We hate poetry that has a palpable design upon us—and if we do not
agree, seems to put its hand in its breeches pockets.

That sense of the phrase "the end of the poem" which underscores its
having a design upon us is often associated with a position we might describe as extreme, "endmost, situated at either of the ends (of a line, series, or scale)." Such extremism heralds the end of the poem in another
interpretation of the phrase I've not touched on so far—that's to say the

"termination of existence" of the poem, and the beginning of propaganda, "any association, systematic scheme, or concerted movement for the propagation of a particular doctrine or practice" (*OED*).

THE PARTICULAR DOCTRINES or practices with which Marina Tsvetayeva was forced to contend for the larger part of her writing life were those of Bolshevism and Communism. The Russia into which she was born in 1892 would be changed forever in 1917, a year which saw the February Revolution, the abdication of Tsar Nicholas II, the October Revolution, and the Civil War. In October 1917, Tsvetayeva happened to be visiting her friend Maximilian Voloshin in the Crimea. She describes her return by train to Moscow, translated here by Jamey Gambrell in her recently published edition of Tsvetayeva's *Earthly Signs: Moscow Diaries 1917–1922*:

> The news is vague. I don't know what to believe. I read about the
> Kremlin, Tverskaya Street, the Arbat, the Metropol Hotel,
> Voznesensky Square, the mountains of corpses . . . Not a thought—
> about the children. If S. is no longer, then neither am I, and neither
> are they. Alya won't live without me, she won't want to, won't be
> able to. As I won't without S.

The "S." in question was Sergei Efron (known familiarly as Seryozha), Tsvetayeva's husband and father of their two children, Alya and Irina. Efron had been drafted into the Imperial, or White, Army. I'll let Jamey Gambrell pick up the story:

> Tsvetayeva made another trip south, this time with her husband,
> who had joined the White Army. She returned to revolutionary
> Moscow in late November, planning to move to Koktebel with the
> children, to be closer to Efron. But by that time travel was no longer
> possible. Tsvetayeva would have no word of her husband for three
> years, and it was four before they met again.

The emotional and physical duress under which Tsvetayeva lived is all but unimaginable, even when, in "Attic Life," she gives us an all-too-clear insight into her day-to-day existence in 1919–20:

I live with Alya and Irina (Alya is six, Irina is two years and seven months) on Boris and Gleb Lane across from two trees, in an attic room that used to be Seriozha's. There's no flour, no bread, under the desk there's about twelve pounds of potatoes, the leftovers of a bushel "loaned" by our neighbours—that's the entire pantry . . . My day: I get up . . . I split wood. Start the fire. In icy water I wash the potatoes, which I boil in the samovar. Cleaning is next. "Alya, take out the basin!"

The nitty-gritty of the day is given in excruciating detail, including the tedious expedition to the "Prague cafeteria," the Generalov store ("to see if by chance there's bread for sale") and Prechistenka Street (to pick up an "enriched meal"); having come home again,

Straight to the stove. The coals are still smouldering. I blow on them. Warm them up. All meals go into one pot: a soup that's more like kasha. We eat. (If Alya has been with me, the first order of business is to untie Irina from the chair. I started tying her up after the time she ate half a head of cabbage from the cabinet when Alya and I were out.)

This detail must have had a particular poignancy for Tsvetayeva when, later in the year 1919, she installed Alya and Irina in an orphanage just outside Moscow, since she was no longer able to care for them by herself, despite having taken a job in the People's Commissariat of Nationalities. When Alya became ill, Tsvetayeva brought her home to take care of her, leaving Irina in the orphanage. In February 1920, however, Irina died of malnutrition. As it happens, one of the last entries in Tsvetayeva's account of "Attic Life" was made just before Irina's death, and it gives a thumbnail sketch of the poet Konstantin Balmont and the dreadful circumstances under which they all lived:

Balmont—in a woman's crisscrossed Scottish shawl—under the covers—frightful cold, steam rising like a stake—a plate of potatoes fried in coffee grinds nearby.

This image of the "plate of potatoes fried in coffee grinds" seems far removed from the comparatively upbeat opening of section 10 of "Poem of the End":

Closely, like one creature, we
start: there is our café!

There is our island, our shrine, where
in the morning, we people of the

rabble, a couple for a minute only,
conducted a morning service.

The translation of these lines by Elaine Feinstein is surely quite awkward. Quite apart from Feinstein's disavowal of the formal structure of Tsvetayeva's lines, the insistent rhymes clear even to a nonspeaker of Russian such as myself, the two instances of "morning" in such quick succession (lines 4 and 6) seem less conscious than unconscious.

David McDuff doesn't fare much better:

A combined and united
shiver.—Our milkbar!

Our island, our shrine
where in morning time

—Riff-raff! Couple for minutes!—
we'd celebrate matins.

McDuff does at least introduce the idea of a "shiver," which Feinstein has rendered confusingly as "start," too easily read in the "beginning" sense rather than in the sense of "sudden movement," that "shiver" somewhat reminiscent of a sexual shudder. Feinstein has no doubt hoped to capture the erotic frisson of the scene in the phrase "morning *service*" with its association of "the action of covering a female animal." McDuff also attempts to replicate the rhyme of the second couplet ("shrine/ time"), and the dyslexic rhyme of the third ("minutes/matins"), but the phrase "where in morning time" seems quite uncolloquial in English, while the "our island, our shrine" phrase seems to have been taken bodily from Feinstein's earlier translation. The "shrine" is, in any case, more accurately translated as "temple," with its associations in both English and

Russian of the body as the "temple of the Holy Spirit" (John 2:18), the cathedral replaced by "our café." Or "our milkbar," as McDuff has it. This is a completely anachronistic concept, a feature more of Philadelphia or Pimlico in 1963 than Prague in 1923, the time to which "Poem of the End" looks back. We remember that the connection between "Prague" and a "café" was already fixed in Tsvetayeva's mind when she made that daily pilgrimage to the *"Prague cafeteria"* in Moscow in 1919 and 1920, and much of the bleakness of those years informs the opening of "Poem of the End."

The comparative enthusiasm with which "our café" is introduced soon gives way to the fact that the coffee was "nasty there / entirely made from oats," as Feinstein puts it, or in the case of McDuff:

The coffee here was pigswill,—
Oats, terrible stuff!

(Oats can disable
A trotter's verve!)

This "trotter" is an unfortunate word choice, given that "trotter" is as likely to send us in the direction of "a pig's foot" (particularly when it follows so hard on the heels of *"pig*swill") as in the direction of "a horse especially bred and trained to the trot" (*OED*), a horse which follows so hard on its own heels. The "horse" in Feinstein harkens back to the "morning service," with its stud-farm resonances, while McDuff's "trotter's verve" is almost as disastrously hackneyed as the description of fish as "the finny tribe." No less awkward, in its own way, is Feinstein's

with oats you can extinguish
caprice in fine race-horses.

Apart from any other considerations, this seems to be a misunderstanding by Tsvetayeva herself of the effect on a horse of oats, which is to make it even more frisky. To say of a horse that it "is feeling its oats" is to say that it is more than usually rambunctious, more than usually capricious. The "caprice" has to do with the goatlike tendencies of a horse, its propensity to *caper* codified in the equestrian terms "caper" and "capriole." There are latent associations of the sexual licentiousness of a goat. In the case of Feinstein's translation, the goatish associations combine with the notion of the "sowing of wild oats," a suggestion of profligacy that would not be inappropriate of Tsvetayeva. In her own biography of the poet, *A Captive Lion: The Life of Marina Tsvetayeva*, Feinstein writes again and again of Tsvetayeva's infidelities, which had begun in 1914, only two years after her marriage to Efron:

> Marina's most passionate erotic involvement in the years between 1914 and 1916 was with a woman; Sophia Parnok . . . Marina made no attempt to hide her love affair, and began traveling around Russia with Sophia, staying occasionally at places of historic interest and making love wherever they slept. Unsurprisingly, Seryozha found not only the affair but also the attendant gossip bitterly humiliating . . . Part of his determination to join the war undoubtedly came from his wish to escape from the pain of the situation. For six months in 1915, after Seryozha joined the ambulance train in March, Marina and Sophia lived together openly as a couple, even though Marina continued to feel as if she still belonged to her husband in some other, more enduring way.

This would not preclude her relationship, in 1916, with Osip Mandelstam, which, as Feinstein tells us, "was probably the only love affair with a man of the many Marina embarked upon with such intensity during this period, that was physically consummated." Elsewhere, Feinstein proposes that this laissez-faire attitude has to do with Marina's social class:

> Sexual liberty, assumed as natural among the Russian upper classes of the time, was taken up by the intelligentsia before the Revolution, but Seryozha had always been unusually psychologically dependent on his wife's love, which had to replace that of a much-loved mother. Salomea Halpern married (according to Vera Traill) with her husband's agreement to allow her to sleep with whomever she chose, but Marina and Seryozha had no such understanding.

We should remember that the Salomea Halpern mentioned here had been the Princess Andronnikova before the Revolution, so moved in somewhat more exalted circles than the upper-middle-class Tsvetayevas. (Salomea appears as "Salominka" in a number of Mandelstam's poems, including "Tristia," published in 1922, two years before "Poem of the End." Small world, as they say, till you have to clean it.) The fact that the Tsvetayevas were indeed upper middle class before the Revolution partly ironizes the phrase "people of the / *rabble*" in Feinstein's translation, the "*riff-raff*" in McDuff's. There's an implication, moreover, that the speaker and her lover might once have been "*fine* race-horses" but have been spoiled by excess, perhaps even an excess of deprivation of appropriate food. In that sense, Tsvetayeva is right about the adverse effects of long-term overfeeding of oats to horses, animals whose stomachs are adapted to eat the more humdrum grass and hay. Let's stay with the "coffee," though, and the figure of Konstantin Balmont, forced to eat "a plate of potatoes fried in *coffee* grinds." For Konstantin Balmont hangs over "Poem of the End" like a Christ. I don't use that comparison lightly, at least no more lightly than Tsvetayeva herself, who writes, towards the end of section 10 of "Poem of the End," how "at last a hand receives / the nail in it." Balmont is associated with a "stake," if you recall, in that description of his lying "under the covers—frightful cold, steam rising like a *stake*—a plate of potatoes fried in coffee grinds nearby." The imagery of Calvary, including the lead-up to the crucifixion of Christ, with the "Judas" who is unfaithful to the Christ who will become a "whipped . . . condemned man," has been central to section 9 of the poem, translated here by David McDuff:

> —Forgive me, I didn't mean it!
> The sob of those *whipped* inside out.
> Thus at four o'clock in the morning
> *Condemned men* wait to be shot,
>
> With a smile, ironic, teasing
> The corridor's *Judas*, at chess.
> It's true: we are pawns in a chess-game,
> And someone is playing at us.
>
> Who? *Thieves*? The *gods* in heaven?
> The peephole is filled by an eye.
> The clank of a red corridor.
> The board is lifted away.

Imagery associated with Konstantin Balmont is picked up in the next stanza, which echoes the tobacco-sharing scene immediately following the "plate of potatoes fried in coffee grinds" in "Attic Life":

I ask for a smoke. He gives me his pipe, and orders me not to distract myself while I smoke. "This pipe requires a great deal of concentration, so I advise you not to talk, since there are no matches in the house." I smoke, that is, I draw with all my might—the pipe seems stopped up—1/10 of a drag comes through with every draw—for fear it will go out I not only don't talk, I don't think—and—after a minute, relieved: "Thank you—I've had enough!"

This is echoed, consciously or unconsciously, in "Poem of the End":

A drag on the coarse tobacco.
Spit. They've had it, then. Spit.
Over this paving is chequered
A straight road to the pit

And the blood. The eye, secret:
The dormer eye of the moon . . .
. . . .
And straining, squinting, sidetracked:
"How far you've already gone!"

The association of Konstantin Balmont with this moment where the close of section 9 cross-fades into the opening of section 10, with its extension of imagery associated with the passion of Christ ("spit," "blood") forces us to reread the opening of section 10 less as a sexual shudder than as a death-throe. In a poem so preoccupied with the tension between faith and faithlessness, the name Konstantin, with its associations of *constancy*, is particularly resonant. Even more resonant when the name of the man with whom Tsvetayeva had the affair in Prague in 1923 was *Konstantin* Rodzevitch. A little more background information would be useful here, I think. We remember that Tsvetayeva had been separated from her husband in 1917 and would not see him again until 1922. In the interim, Efron had fought for the White Army, the army Tsvetayeva commemorated in

her cycle of poems written between 1917 and 1921 under the title *Swans'*
Encampment, or *The Demesne of the Swans*:

This man was White   now he's become Red.
Blood has reddened him.
This one was Red   now he's become White.
Death has whitened him.

In July 1921 Tsvetayeva received a letter from Seryozha, their first
communication since 1917. After the defeat of the White Army, he had
moved to Prague to study Byzantine art. Tsvetayeva resolved to move to
Berlin to meet him, though "resolved" is perhaps too strong a word, since
it was ten months later before she set out. Here's Jamey Gambrell, writing
in her introduction to *Earthly Signs*, to take up the story:

In May 1922 Tsvetayeva and Alya left Russia for Berlin to rejoin
Efron, who was living in Prague. She plunged into the whirlwind of
Berlin's émigré literary life, quickly arranging the publication of two
collections, *Psyche* and *Craft* (both in 1923). Before she could even be
reunited with her husband she became involved with her publisher,
Abram Vishniak. During the same period she struck up an intense
friendship with the poet Andrei Bely (who wrote enthusiastically
about her versification) and began an epistolary romance with Boris
Pasternak that would last more than a decade. After two months in
Berlin, the family moved to a small village outside Prague with no
running water.

The fact that they had so little money forced Efron to live in student
hostels, while Tsvetayeva and Alya roomed in that small village with no
running water. Their being apart allowed for Tsvetayeva to broaden her
range of contacts in Prague. We know from the diary of Vsevelod Kho-
dasevich, for example, that on November 23, 25 and 29 of 1923 Tsvetayeva
met with him and Roman Jakobson, the founder of the Moscow Linguistic Circle who would later found the Linguistic Circle of Prague, of whom
more anon. That Tsvetayeva and Efron were living apart also gave her the
opportunity to embark on the affair at the heart of "Poem of the End." In
the fall of 1923 Efron would write to Max Voloshin:

Marina is a woman of passions . . . Plunging headfirst into her hurricanes has become essential for her, the breath of life. Nearly always (now as before)—or rather always—everything is based on self-deception. A man is invented and the hurricane begins. If the insignificance and narrowness of the hurricane's arouser is quickly revealed, then Marina gives way to a hurricane of despair. A state which facilitates the appearance of a new arouser.

It turned out that the "new arouser," Konstantin Rodzevitch, was a friend of Efron. As Elaine Feinstein describes him in *A Captive Lion*:

In Prague in 1923, Rodzevitch was thought by many to have been a White officer. He had, in fact, served with the Red Navy for a time but (accurately) judged that things would go better for him in émigré circles if he allowed the impression to stand that he had fought on the White side. Although his father, Boris Kazimirovich, had been a general in the Tsarist army, after the Revolution his son had served on a ship in the Bolshevik military flotilla on the Dnieper. After being captured by the White Army, sentenced to death, then reprieved, Konstantin was persuaded to join the Whites. A haphazard way of forming an allegiance, it was in many ways typical of the man.

That haphazardness was also typical of the woman with whom Rodzevitch formed an "allegiance" in the fall of 1923. In "Poem of the Mountain," a companion piece to "Poem of the End" which is devoted to the rapturous beginning of the affair between Rodzevitch and herself, Tsvetayeva writes of the mountain's participation in their impromptu lovemaking:

How far from schoolbook Paradise
it was: so *windy*, when
the mountain pulled us down on our
backs. To itself. Saying: lie here!

The violence of that pull bewildered us.
How? Even now I don't know.

Mountain. Pimp. For holiness.
It pointed, to say: here.

Something of the complicity of the "pimp" mountain is to be found in the "grey-haired paramour," the "proprietress" of the café with her "solicitous" smile who appears as a kind of Madam, complete with her "cap / stiff   as a Dutch hat," a contraceptive *Dutch cap* slipped in there as "she saw us off." The "schoolbook Paradise" mentioned in "Poem of the Mountain" recurs in the image of the "*Arcadia* that was in / that coffee" in section 10 of "Poem of the End." The "fall" of the lovers on the Edenic mountain, from which they're "seen off" by a female God ("But how *she* smiled at us"), prepares the way for the Judaeo-Christian imagery which culminates in the crucifixion and the "*sep   aration*" which follows the breaking of the pact between God and man, lover and lover, in a world in which what seemed steadfast is suddenly shaky:

Tomorrow the sun will rise in the West.
And then David will break with Jehovah.
—What are we doing?—We are *separating*.
—That's a word that means nothing to me.

The figure of David means a great deal to Tsvetayeva, one with very specific literary connotations, as is clear from the following passage from her memoir *Captive Spirit*, in which she recalls her earliest encounters, in 1910, with the symbolist poet Andrey Bely:

I often used to see him . . . in Musaget, but saw him, rather than talked to him; most often his back would be turned to me, as he danced to and fro with a stick of white chalk in his hand in front of the blackboard, which would instantly be peppered—it was as if they flew out of his coatsleeves!—with the commas, half-moons and zigzags of rhythmic schemes, which I found so reminiscent of our geometry lessons at school that I found myself yielding to a perfectly natural instinct for self-preservation (what if he were to suddenly turn round and call me out to the blackboard?) and letting my attention stray from Bely's dancing back to the immobile faces of Staatsrat Goethe and Dr Steiner who stared at us from the wall with enormous eyes that were perhaps, come to think of it, not staring at us at all. That is how I still remember him: the early Bely dancing before Goethe and Steiner, *as once David danced before the ark of the covenant*. In the life of a symbolist everything is a symbol. There is nothing that is not symbolic.

Yes, but of what? The fact that Bely is connected with the image of David dancing before the ark of the covenant is difficult enough to interpret—is, indeed, open to misinterpretation. We recall that, in the account of the episode given in 2 Samuel 6:14–21, the sight of David "wearing a linen loincloth" and "leaping and whirling round before Yahweh" fills Michal, daughter of Saul, "with contempt." In this instance, Bely is not so much "making an exhibition of himself under the eyes of his servant-maids, making an exhibition of himself like a buffoon," as Michal accuses David, but, as David retorts, "dancing for Yahweh, not for them." The supernatural power in question here is the power of poetry, its "rhythmic schemes" outlined to a "servant-maid" (Tsvetayeva) by a David (Bely) who's not even "wearing a linen loincloth" to cover his "stick of white chalk." The whiteness of this chalk is worth lingering over. The name "Bely" was a pseudonym, taken by Boris Aleksandrovich Bugayev, and it means "white." This whiteness connects Bely not only to the two *White* Guards (Efron and Rodzevitch) who are duking it out in the heart of the poem but another poet, Velimir Klebnikov, who has a walk-on part—though it turns out to be a central role—in "Poem of the End":

> *Separation*—in what language is it,
> when the meaning itself doesn't exist?
>
> or even the sound! Well—an empty one, like
> the noise of a saw in your sleep perhaps.
> *Separation*. That belongs to the school of
> Khlebnikov's   nightingale-groaning
>
> swan-like . . .

I'M GOING TO SPEND much of the rest of my time trying to disentangle these lines, translated by David McDuff as:

> Not even a sound. Just a hollow
> Rasp, like a saw, say, through sleep.
> Separation is simply the Khlebnikov
> School's nightingales that weep
>
> Like swans . . .

These swans carry a lot of weight on their broad shoulders. We remember the series of poems written between 1917 and 1921 under the title *Swans' Encampment*, or *The Demesne of the Swans*, in which the birds are associated with the White Army, an association which once more connects Efron and Rodzevitch. But the swan is also associated with Alexander Blok, as Robin Kemball points out in the introduction to his new edition of Marina Tsvetayeva's 1922 volume *Milestones:*

> No account of *Milestones* would be complete without some reference to the décor and its trappings—the birds, the skies, and the waters which play such a prominent part in the early poems of the cycle: doves, pigeons, eaglets, ravens and raven chicks, swans and cygnets, such as Mandelstam as her "young eaglet" (poem 13) or Alya as her "cygnet" (poem 19). Her first description of Blok's name is that of "a bird cupped in the palm" (poem 41) and later she sees in him the "snowy swan," calling "with a long-drawn sigh, with a swanlike cry" (poem 42).

Alexander Blok is on Tsvetayeva's mind here for a very specific reason. Along with Konstantin Balmont, he had been one of the targets of the manifesto published in 1912 under the title "A Slap in the Face of Public Taste":

> To the readers of our First New Unexpected. *We* alone are the *face* of *our* time. Through us the horn of time blows in the art of the world. The past is too tight. The Academy and Pushkin are less intelligible

than hieroglyphics. Throw Pushkin, Dostoevsky, Tolstoy etc., etc. overboard from the ship of Modernity. He who does not forget his *first* love will not recognize his last. Who, trustingly, would turn his last love toward Balmont's perfumed lechery? Is this the reflection of today's virile soul? Who, faint-heartedly, would fear tearing from warrior Bryusov's black tuxedo the paper armor-plate? Or does the dawn of unknown beauties shine from it? Wash your hands which have touched the filthy slime of the books written by the countless Leonid Andreyevs. All those Maxim Gorkys. Krupins, Bloks, Sologubs, Remizovs, Averchenkos, Chornys, Kuzmins, Bunins, etc. need only a dacha on the river. Such is the reward fate gives tailors. From the heights of skyscrapers we gaze at their insignificance! We *order* that the poet's *rights* be revered: To enlarge the *scope* of the poet's vocabulary with arbitrary and derivative words (Word-novelty). To feel an insurmountable hatred for the language existing before their time. To push with horror off their proud brow the Wreath of cheap fame that You have made from bathhouse switches. To stand on the rock of the word "we" amid the sea of boos and outrage. And if *for the time being* the filthy stigmas of your "common sense" and "good taste" are still present in our lines, these same lines *for the first time* already glimmer with the Summer Lightning of the New Coming Beauty of the Self-sufficient (self-centered) Word. [Italics in original.]

That "Slap in the Face of Public Taste" was of course the manifesto of the Russian Futurists, a document co-authored by David Burliuk, Alexander Kruchenykh, Vladimir Mayakovsky, and Velimir Khlebnikov—the group to which Tsvetayeva refers, in McDuff's translation, as "the Khlebnikov / School's nightingales that weep / Like swans." The "swan-like cry" of Blok would seem to have ameliorative connotations, given the high regard in which Blok was held by Tsvetayeva, and it's odd to see it used pejoratively here, a comedown for those poets who once conventionally sang like "nightingales." In English, the word "swan" is cognate with the Latin *sonare*, an ironic comment on the bird's making no *sound* whatsoever beyond the occasional hiss. We see a version of this "self-sufficient" hiss in Khlebnikov's famous poem of 1910, "Incantation by Laughter":

O laugh it up you laughletes!
O laugh it out you laughletes!
That laugh with laughs, that laugherize laughingly
O laugh it out so laughily
O of laughing at laughilies—
    the laugh of laughish laugherators.

Part of Khlebnikov's ambition here was to find "a touchstone for the transformation of all Slavic words one into another, for the free fusion of all Slavic words. Such is the self-valuing word without relation to life or use." The last description comes from Roman Jakobson's *Modern Russian Poetry*, a study published in Prague in 1921, two years before Tsvetayeva moved there and two years before she met Jakobson. Khlebnikov's influence on Jakobson is well documented. Undocumented is what I propose to be their joint influence on Tsvetayeva. I've already pointed to the iconography of the passion of Christ which underscores section 10 of "Poem of the End." That iconography is combined with elements from the Futurist manifesto in quite striking ways. The "riff-raff" and "rabble" with whom Tsvetayeva associates Rodzevitch and herself are drawn partly from the mob that spat on Jesus on his way to Golgotha, partly from the mob responsible for "the sea of boos and outrage" which would be likely to meet the Futurist manifesto. This is the mob which overrules Pontius Pilate, who washes his hands of the responsibility for the death of Jesus. The Futurist manifesto draws on that specific imagery (*"Wash your hands which have touched the filthy slime of the books written by the countless Leonid Andreyevs"*) and combines it with a version of the crown of thorns which was placed mockingly on the "King of the Jews" in the call "to push with horror off their proud brow *the Wreath of cheap fame that You have made from bathhouse switches.*" The "switches" have nothing to do with light fixtures, by the way, but a "massage instrument made of twigs," as is only slightly clearer from C. M. Bowra's translation of this same sentence, which makes it seem as if the "switches" are toilet brushes:

To tear with horror from their proud heads the crowns of worthless fame made of bathroom brushes.

One way or another, these switches might be used "to strike, hit, beat, flog, or whip" a person "nailed against the shameful stake," as Tsvetayeva has it in a poem of May 1920:

> Nailed against the shameful stake
> Of the inveterate Slavic conscience,
> My forehead marked, at my heart a snake,
> I testify that I am guiltless.

In addition to drawing on her associations of the Christ/Balmont with his "shameful stake," Tsvetayeva's poem also draws on the iconography of the Futurist manifesto when she identifies herself and her beloved with Christ. We remember that the co-signatories of the manifesto position themselves "on the rock of the word 'we' amid the sea of boos and outrage." The "rock of the word" is an allusion to *petra*, the word with which the great punster, Christ, had such fun when he made Peter the "*rock* on which I will build my church." The church is also associated with a ship, "the *ship* of Modernity" which ventures out "amid the *sea* of boos and outrage." Khlebnikov & Co. are Christ-like in setting themselves above and beyond the jeering mob:

> From the *heights* of skyscrapers we gaze at their insignificance!

They recognize that they will almost certainly not be seen as the redeemers they undoubtedly are, despite the fact that their lines "glimmer with the Summer Lightning of the New Coming Beauty of the Self-sufficient (self-centered) Word." The "Summer Lightning" is picked up by Tsvetayeva in her storm imagery:

> To *separate*. Is a shock of thunder
>
> upon my head—oceans rushing into
> a wooden house. This is Oceania's
> furthest promontory.

I like to think that this vision of "Oceania" may derive from the house in the "small village outside Prague" suddenly acquiring "running water."

On a more serious note, the source of the "shock of thunder" is partly the "summer lightning," as I've suggested, partly the description of "darkness over all the land" and "the veil of the Sanctuary . . . torn in two from top to bottom" (Matthew 27:45–51) at the crucifixion of Christ on Golgotha. The "thunder" sends us back to "Poem of the Mountain":

> The mountain was like thunder!
> A chest drummed on by Titans.
> (Do you remember that last house
> of the mountain—the end of the suburb?)

The positioning of the mountain at "the *end* of the suburb" suggests that it, too, is a version of Golgotha, the hill "outside the gate" of Jerusalem. There's a return to this mountain imagery, and the specific vocabulary of those lines from "Poem of the Mountain," in section 11 of "Poem of the End":

> All at once to lose all—
> No purer way.
> Suburb, last port of call:
> End of our days.

That's from the translation by David McDuff. And a good thing we have it, too, since Elaine Feinstein's translation of "Poem of the End," published in *Marina Tsvetayeva: Selected Poems*, simply doesn't include section 11. We can see from McDuff's translation that there are quite specific echoes of the vocabulary of the Futurist manifesto, including "the dacha on the river" carried over to "Dachas, a third of you empty and bare, / You'd do better to burn, and not be there!" and the all-pervasive iconography of Good Friday. This includes a musing on "the seam that sews the dead to the earth / Is the one by which I'm sewn to you," which sends us back to the image of Christ's "undergarment [being] seamless, woven in one piece from neck to hem" (John 19:23), and "The execution's today, / In the suburbs a draught to our brains," which extends the crucifixion imagery of section 10:

> *To separate.* That means to go downward

downhill   the sighing sound of two
heavy soles   and at last a hand receives
the nail in it . . .

Even the mark of this nail in the hand is derived partly from the Futurist manifesto, in which, if you recall, "the filthy *stigmas* of your 'common sense' and 'good taste' are held in such disdain by the Messiahs who embody the 'New Coming Beauty of the Self-sufficient Word.'" This last idea stems, of course, from the opening of the Gospel of John:

> In the beginning was the Word: the Word was with God and the Word was God.

Tsvetayeva's extended meditation on the word "separation" alludes to "the language of God":

> It's the most inhumanly senseless
> of words: *sep   arating*. (Am I one of a hundred?)
> It is simply a word of four syllables and
> behind their sound lies: emptiness.
>
> Wait! Is it even correct in Serbian or
> Croatian? Is it a Czech whim, this word.
> *Sep   aration*! To *sep   arate*!
> It is insane   unnatural
>
> a sound to burst the eardrums, and spread out
> far beyond the limits of longing itself.
> *Separation*—the word is not in the Russian
> language. Or the language of women. Or men.
>
> Nor in the language of God. What are we—sheep?
> To stare about us as we eat.

These "sheep" remind us of the conventional system of imagery whereby the people are "sheep" and Christ the pastor, or shepherd. The poem continues:

Separation—in what language is it,
when the meaning itself doesn't exist?

or even the sound! Well—an empty one, like
the noise of a saw in your sleep perhaps.

I quote these stanzas at length because their mimesis of a "long-drawn sigh, a swanlike cry" such as Tsvetayeva associated with Alexander Blok (who was, as I mentioned earlier, one of the targets of the Futurist manifesto) is a significant element in their effectiveness. One of Tsvetayeva's great achievements in "Poem of the End" is to make manifest at least one of the ideas included in the manifesto. In that sense, she out-Khlebnikovs Khlebnikov. The ideal of *zaumny yazyk*, generally rendered as "trans-sense," which includes onomatopoeic effects and neologisms (like Khlebnikov's "laughletes") is managed rather elegantly in the musing on the sound of *"sep   arating,"* that sound itself managed rather elegantly in McDuff's English version:

Not even a sound. Just a hollow
Rasp, like a *saw, say,* through sleep.
Separation is simply the Khlebnikov
School's nightingales that weep

Like swans.

This description of labored breathing is even more poignant when we remember that, in 1924, the "swan" Efron had contracted tuberculosis.

Just as important as these stanzas' enactment of, and commentary upon, this basic tenet of Futurism is their enactment of, and commentary upon, one of the basic tenets of structuralism. I'm thinking of the "separation" between signifier and signified described in Ferdinand de Saussure's 1916 *Cours de linguistique générale*, in which he defined a language as "a series of differences of sound combined with a series of differences of ideas." Tsvetayeva's ruminations on the word *"sep   arating"* (written two years later) are textbook examples of Saussure's analysis of the dichotomy between signifier and signified, asserting as they do that there is no real link between the "meaning" and the "sound":

It's the most inhumanly senseless
of words: *sep   arating* . . .

It is simply a word of four syllables and
behind their sound lies: emptiness.

Or again:

Separation—in what language is it,
when the meaning itself doesn't exist?

or even the sound!

Tsvetayeva may even have in mind the further groundbreaking dichotomy proposed by Saussure between *langue* and *parole*, the dichotomy between the elements of language and the rules for their combination (like grammar and syntax), and the use people make of language, its utterance. The notion of the function, or lack of it, was also an important element in the world-picture of Khlebnikov, who, as you'll recall, favored the "free fusion of all Slavic words" and "the self-valuing word without relation to life or *use*." It's one further reason why Khlebnikov is summoned up at this moment in the poem. The main reason, which I touched on earlier, is Khlebnikov's influence on Roman Jakobson, who had just recently moved to Prague. While Jakobson was himself at this point best known as a Slavicist, he would later extend Saussure's notion of a binary split to phonology and grammatical structure, and something of this vision of "separation" may already have been in his mind in 1923 when, as I mentioned earlier, he met Tsvetayeva on a number of occasions.

I hesitate to return to my rather antiquated belief in *Nomen est omen*, but I do think that Jakobson is predisposed to follow in the footsteps of the biblical figure of Jacob, the icon of duality. Jacob is the twin of Esau, is married to two wives (Leah and Rachel), and is the father of twelve sons who become the leaders of the twelve tribes of Israel. As the son of Isaac and the grandson of Abraham, he is the embodiment of Israel and prefigures the Christ at the time of whose death the veil of the sanctuary is "torn in two." We've had an allusion to the fate of Jacob's son Joseph in section 9 of "Poem of the End" where we found the image of "a straight road to the pit / and the blood," which reminds us of his brothers' throwing him into a well and convincing their father that a wild animal has killed Joseph by covering his coat with the blood of a goat. The bloody coat of many colors is cut from the same cloth as the seamless garment over which the soldiers will cast lots at Golgotha, the "twenty shekels of silver" for which his brothers sell Joseph to the Ishmaelites taken from the same purse as the "thirty pieces of silver" for which Judas will betray Christ:

> Only don't tremble
> Faced with your open wound's lip.
> To the suburbs, the suburbs
> Seams that rip.

The "single creatures" who had until recently "grown into one" are going their separate ways, just as the spirit and body of Christ will part company on Golgotha. Something of the tension between the ideas of the "end" and the "ongoing" may be included in the little play on the Russian word for "end" (*konyets*) which is built into the unnamed but "ongoing" *Konstantin*. "Ongoing," of course, until his perfidy is revealed:

> "Here?" Like a conspiracy,
> A look. Of those trodden down.
> "Can we climb the mountain?"
> For the last time, we can.

These lines from section 11 of "Poem of the End" (translated by David McDuff, untranslated by Elaine Feinstein) call to mind a richly telling letter from Tsvetayeva to Pasternak written on May 25th, 1926, and included in *Letters: Summer 1926 (Boris Pasternak, Marina Tsvetayeva, Rainer Maria Rilke)*:

> "Poem of the Mountain" came earlier and shows a masculine face, at first impassioned, of highest intensity from the very start, whereas "Poem of the End" is a build-up of feminine grief, imminent tears,

me when I lie down, not me when I get up. "Poem of the Mountain"—a mountain as seen from another mountain. "Poem of the End"—a mountain on top of me, me under a mountain.

SOMETHING OF THIS FEELING of being overwhelmed, of having come to "the limits of longing itself," would have Tsvetayeva determine, on August 31, 1941, that she had "reached a dead end" in the town of Yelabuga. The list of disasters which had befallen her since her time in Prague seventeen years earlier makes for distressing reading. Here's Jamey Gambrell:

> In November 1925, the family moved to France; for the next fourteen years Tsvetayeva would live in and around Paris . . . The family lived in poverty, and Tsvetayeva's day-to-day life in France, as in Czechoslovakia and post-revolutionary Moscow, was a study in contrasts: the everyday grind of cooking, cleaning, and child care under much less than comfortable circumstances was intercut with exalted flights of poetic creation.

The duality of Tsvetayeva's life may even be the larger subject of "Poem of the End," a duality which continued through the 1930s. Sergei Efron changed his political allegiance and became enthusiastically pro-Soviet, going so far as to work for the secret police. When he was questioned by French authorities in 1937 about his possible involvement in the murder of a Soviet defector, Efron fled to Moscow. Shortly afterwards, Alya followed him. Tsvetayeva and her fourteen-year-old son, Georgy (or Mur), who had been born in 1925, returned to Russia in June 1939. In August 1939, Alya was arrested. In October 1939, Efron was also arrested, by the secret police for whom he had worked. When the Germans invaded in June 1941, Tsvetayeva and Mur were evacuated to Yelabuga. She tried to get a job washing dishes in the nearby town of Christopol. On August 31, she hanged herself from a nail used to tether horses, no doubt horses in which caprice had been "extinguished." Mur, who was sixteen at the time, would be drafted into the Soviet army in 1943 and killed in 1944. In the meantime, Tsvetayeva was buried in Yelabuga cemetery, though, as David McDuff puts it, "the exact location of her grave is unknown." This was a far cry from Tarusa, the small town outside Moscow where she had spent her summers as a child. It's the place mentioned in Medbh McGuckian's poem, "Little House, Big House":

> I should like to lie in Tarusa under matted winter grass,
> Where the strawberries are redder than anywhere else.

It was in Tarusa that Alya, who was released only in 1955, after seventeen years in Soviet camps, would be buried in 1975. According to Viktoria Schweitzer, in her study *Tsvetayeva*,

> Long before her death, contemplating the fact that she was unlikely to be buried in her beloved Tarusa, she had asked for a stone with an epitaph:

> *Here Marina Tsvetayeva would have liked to lie.*

CHAPTER 13

DOVER BEACH

MATTHEW ARNOLD

The sea is calm to-night.
The tide is full, the moon lies fair
Upon the straits;—on the French coast the light
Gleams and is gone; the cliffs of England stand,
Glimmering and vast, out in the tranquil bay.
Come to the window, sweet is the night air!
Only, from the long line of spray
Where the sea meets the moon-blanch'd land,
Listen! you hear the grating roar
Of pebbles which the waves draw back, and fling,
At their return, up the high strand,
Begin, and cease, and then again begin,
With tremulous cadence slow, and bring
The eternal note of sadness in.

Sophocles long ago
Heard it on the Aegean, and it brought
Into his mind the turbid ebb and flow
Of human misery; we
Find also in the sound a thought,
Hearing it by this distant northern sea.

The Sea of Faith
Was once, too, at the full, and round earth's shore

Lay like the folds of a bright girdle furl'd.
But now I only hear
Its melancholy, long, withdrawing roar,
Retreating, to the breath
Of the night-wind, down the vast edges drear
And naked shingles of the world.

Ah, love, let us be true
To one another! for the world, which seems
To lie before us like a land of dreams,
So various, so beautiful, so new,
Hath really neither joy, nor love, nor light,

Nor certitude, nor peace, nor help for pain;
And we are here as on a darkling plain
Swept with confused alarms of struggle and flight,
Where ignorant armies clash by night.

"TO BE A PROFESSOR OF POETRY is tantamount to declaring that one is not a poet." This acerbic little aperçu by A. Dwight Culler, from the introduction to his 1961 edition of *Poetry and Criticism of Matthew Arnold*, is one upon which I've been maggoting these past four years. I'm reminded of it today in particular because, though "Dover Beach" was published in 1867, just as Arnold was coming to the end of the Professorship of Poetry at Oxford, the poem was almost certainly written in 1851. This was five fruitful years before he took up the appointment in 1857 and entered a period of what Culler would no doubt delineate as poetic fallowness. I'll be trying today to determine why Arnold might have suppressed this poem, if "suppressed" is the word, for more than fifteen years. I'll be trying to connect it to an idea expressed in his inaugural lecture, "On the Modern Element in Literature," given in November of 1857, in which Arnold had written of the requirement that literature bring "intellectual deliverance":

But first let us ask ourselves why the demand for an intellectual deliverance arises in such an age as the present, and in what the deliverance itself consists? The demand arises, because our present age has around it a copious and complex present, and behind it a copious and complex past; it arises, because the present age exhibits to the individual man who contemplates it a vast multitude of facts awaiting and inviting his comprehension. The deliverance consists in man's comprehension of this present and past. It begins when our mind begins to enter into possession of the general ideas which are the law of this vast multitude of facts. It is perfect when we have acquired that harmonious acquiescence of mind which we feel in contemplating a grand spectacle that is intelligible to us; when we have lost that impatient irritation of mind which we feel in the presence of an immense, moving, confused spectacle which, while it perpetually excites our curiosity, perpetually baffles our comprehension.

In addition to the two instances of "vast multitudes," which are echoed in the "vast edges drear" of line 27, these images of a "confused spectacle" seem to be associated with, if not drawn directly from, lines 35–37 of "Dover Beach":

And we are here as on a darkling plain
Swept with *confused* alarms of struggle and flight,
Where ignorant armies clash by night.

The "baffles" in "perpetually baffles" is an obscured version of "battles" fought in obscurity, not on "the cliffs of England," as it happens, but at Epipolae. This was the scene of a night encounter between the Athenians and Spartans during the Peloponnesian War which was famously documented by Thucydides and redocumented by Thomas Arnold—the editor of Thucydides' *The Peloponnesian War* (1835), the head of Rugby School, and the father of Matthew.

I'll be trying today to map the butts and bounds of that "confused spectacle" at the end of "Dover Beach" and trying, moreover, to determine the extent to which it might represent Arnold's own family drama (in his relationships to his father and to his wife), the drama of his society, and the drama of reading a poem. The main sense of the phrase "the end of the poem" I'll be hoping to encompass is that of the "function" of the poem, the "demand for an intellectual deliverance" which Arnold proclaimed as being "emphatically, whether we will it or no, the demand of the age in which we ourselves live," just as the Peloponnesian War demanded the "intellectual deliverance" of Thucydides. The word "deliverance" has very particular religious connotations, of course, having to do with the sense of "salvation" attending the word in Matthew 6:13:

> And lead us not into temptation but *deliver* us from evil. For thine is the kingdom, and the power, and the glory, for ever. Amen.

That "for ever" informs the *"eternal* note of sadness" we find at the end of the first stanza of "Dover Beach," just as it does the *"perpetually* baffles" in "On the Modern Element in Literature." I'll be saying a word or two on the "eternal" and "perpetual" aspects of a poem, its endlessness or "Immortality," to which Arnold to some extent subscribes when he engages in this notion of "intellectual deliverance." As he writes a little later in "On the Modern Element in Literature":

> Let us consider one or two of the passages in the masterly introduction which Thucydides, the contemporary of Pericles, has prefixed to his history. What was his motive in choosing the Peloponnesian War for his subject? Because it was, in his opinion, the most important, the most instructive event which had, up to that time, happened in the history of mankind.

Arnold's use of the word "instructive" is instructive here, because it introduces the notion of the possibility of one's "conveying knowledge" (*OED*), of shedding light on the "darkling plain" in what is essentially a religious sense, the sense of *"Dominus illuminatio mea."* The word "darkling" in the "darkling plain" connects "Dover Beach" to Keats, Samuel Johnson, and the Shakespeare of *Antony and Cleopatra* and, preeminently, *King Lear*, in what turn out to be rather interesting ways. I'll be appealing to several other texts for help in making sense of "Dover Beach," including Shakespeare's Sonnets 18, 106 and 138; Wordsworth's "Calais, August, 1802," "September, 1802. Near Dover" and "It is a beauteous evening, calm and free"; Yeats's "The Nineteenth Century and After"; Frost's "Once By the Pacific"; Bishop's "At the Fishhouses"; and Glyn Maxwell's "The Sea Comes In Like Nothing but the Sea."

LET'S LOOK AT HOW "DOVER BEACH" comes in, which is nothing like the conventional iambic pentameter, though we recognise a fine specimen of iambic pentameter in the first nine words of the poem:

> The sea is calm to-night. The tide is full . . .

The thwarting of the iambic pentameter, its not being allowed to run its course on one line, is the first indicator that the thwarting of received ideas, or the refutation of the expected, may be a theme of this poem. It's as if the conventional shape of the line in English will fall short of describing the scene in which "the tide is full, the moon lies fair," will not be equal or adequate to the task. The idea of "adequacy" is one on which Arnold dwells in "On the Modern Element in Literature":

> Next comes the question: Is this epoch adequately interpreted by its
> highest literature? Now, the peculiar characteristic of the highest
> literature—the poetry—of the fifth century in Greece before the
> Christian era, is its *adequacy*; the peculiar characteristic of the poetry
> of Sophocles is its consummate, its unrivalled adequacy; that it
> represents the highly developed human nature of that age—human
> nature developed in a number of directions, politically, socially,
> religiously, morally developed—in its completest and most
> harmonious development in all these directions; while there is shed
> over this poetry the charm of that noble serenity which always
> accompanies true insight.

The "serenity," or "clear, fair, or calm weather" (*OED*) again seems to be associated with, if not directly drawn from, the opening of "Dover Beach":

> The sea is *calm* to-night.
> The tide is full, the moon lies *fair*
> Upon the straits . . .

Another meaning of "fair," given by the *OED* as "equitable," with its associations with such terms as "adequacy" and "harmonious acquiescence," which we've already met in "On the Modern Element in Literature," underpins this first line in an almost invisible way. It becomes visible only when one remembers Arnold's background in Greek and Latin, his classical scholarship to Balliol, and divines in the words "adequacy" and "acquiescence" near versions of the Latin word *aqua*. The aquatic is then associated with the calm, or *quiescence*, in "acquiescence," and these images of water and quiet combine in the opening line:

> The *sea* is *calm* to-night.

In addition to sending the reader back to the opening line of Wordsworth's "It is a beauteous evening, *calm* and free," a poem composed "on the beach near Calais," that "calm" reminds us of that phrase Arnold uses of "human nature" in "On the Modern Element in Literature" having to do with a version of the "*harmonious* acquiescence" which morphs into "the completest and most *harmonious* development." The meaning of "completest," meanwhile, is itself completed in the very next phrase:

> The tide is *full*, the moon lies fair
> Upon the straits . . .

Let's pause for another moment or two on that "fair." It brings with it several pieces of extra but essential baggage, the first of which is in the back of the mind of most readers of poetry in English:

> *Fair* stood the wind for France.

This comes from Michael Drayton's "The Ballad of Agincourt," and prepares the ground for lines being drawn between "the *French* coast" and "the

cliffs of England" and the battle "where ignorant armies clash by night."
The other two pieces of baggage having to do with the word "fair" are
even more obscure, I'd venture, though they're both packed by William
Shakespeare. The first is an incidence of the word "fair" in Sonnet 106:

> When in the chronicles of wasted time
> I see descriptions of the *fair*est wights,
> And beauty making beautiful old rime,
> In praise of ladies dead and lovely knights . . .

That word "wights" is one that would have had a powerful resonance
for Matthew Arnold in 1851, the year in which he twice visited Dover just
after his marriage to Frances Lucy *Wight*man. The sense of "wight" in the
proper name Wightman is not that in Sonnet 106, of course, where it
means "a living being in general; a creature," but "strong and courageous,
esp. in warfare" (*OED*). Let's think about whether or not all's "fair" in love
and war between those two old enemies, England and France. Well,
they're not quite equally drawn up, are they? On one side "the cliffs of
England stand." One might expect "the coast of France" to be equal and
opposite. But no, it's "the *French* coast." Arnold resists "the coast of
France" partly because it too obviously resonates with the line "Fair stood
the wind for *France*," partly because it too obviously resonates with
the line "The coast of France—the coast of France how near!" from
Wordsworth's "September, 1802. Near Dover." His main reason, I suggest,
is that the phrase would rather less obviously resonate with the name of
Frances Lucy Wightman. An early version of the lines which now read
"On the French coast the light / Gleams and is gone" had read "the cliffs
of the light / Shines [*sic*] and is gone," where there's a syntactical paral-
lelism between "the cliffs of the light" and "the cliffs of England" that's
now been lost. What hasn't been lost is the other component in Frances
Wightman's name, the "light" of *Lucy* which now "gleams and is gone,"
the "light as opposed to dark" (*OED*) which is yet another sense of the
"fair" that would befit the "*fair*est *Wight*man." I'll return to enlightenment
later in my discussion of this poem. Before we leave Sonnet 106, we might
remark on the two "lovely (k)nights" in "Dover Beach" also, one at the
end of the first line, one at the end of the last ("the sea is calm to-*night*,"
"where ignorant armies clash by *night*"). Also relevant to Arnold's con-

sciousness of Sonnet 106 is the punning, paradoxical nature of the phrase "lies fair," pun and paradox being the staple of so many of the Sonnets, including 138, in which we find "Therefore I *lie* with her and she with me, and in our faults by *lies* we flatter'd be," and 18, in which we find:

> Sometime too hot the eye of heaven shines
> And often is his gold complexion dimm'd;
> And every *fair* from *fair* sometime declines,
> By chance or nature's changing course untrimm'd.

Now, the earlier draft of "Dover Beach" in which the singular "shines" was matched with the plural "cliffs of the light" is a case of "the eye of heaven *shines*" pushing itself forward into the poem, probably unbeknownst to the author, before being checked by his conscious mind and changed to "the light / *gleams* and is gone." The "gleams" is echoed by the "glimmering," both of these echoic of the *"dimm'd/untrimm'd"* nexus in Sonnet 18. Another instance of phrases carried over from Sonnet 18 will be found later in "Dover Beach," where the lines "But thy eternal summer shall not fade" and "When in eternal lines to time thou grow'st" combine in that *"eternal* note of sadness." The "eternal" also nods and winks in the direction of Wordsworth's "It is a beauteous evening, calm and free":

> Listen! The mighty Being is awake,
> And doth with his *eternal* motion make
> A sound like thunder—everlastingly.

We can see how Arnold repeats Wordsworth's "Listen! The mighty Being is awake" in his *"Listen!* you hear the grating roar . . ." Which brings me to a third Shakespeare text, one even better known than Sonnets 18 and 106, that informs "Dover Beach." I'm thinking here of *King Lear*, a play in which a crucial scene is set in "the country near Dover":

> How fearful
> And dizzy to cast one's eyes so low!
> The crows and choughs that wing the midway air
> Show scarce so gross as beetles; halfway down
> Hangs one that gathers samphire, dreadful trade!

This description is given to the blinded Gloucester by his faithful son, Edgar, who "lies fair" to the old man. Edgar paints a vivid picture of the view from the "cliffs of England":

> The murmuring surge,
> That on th'unnumber'd idle pebble chafes,
> Cannot be heard so high.

The vocabulary and subject matter of this passage are echoed by Arnold as he goes about his own scene-setting:

> Listen! you hear the grating roar
> Of *pebbles* which the waves draw back, and fling,
> At their return, up the *high* strand,
> Begin, and cease, and then again begin,
> With tremulous cadence slow, and bring
> The eternal note of sadness in.

The main point of contact between "Dover Beach" and *King Lear* is their presentation of *paysages moralisés* in which the heath in a storm represents the "naked" Lear's psychological turmoil or the coming and going of the waves on "Dover Beach" that "bring / The eternal note of sadness in." That "note of sadness" is itself echoic of the note of "villainous *melancholy*" from which Edmund takes his cue and which presides over the entire play, as do the "packs and sects of great ones / that ebb and flow by th'moon" (Act V, Scene iii, lines 18–19). We'll meet that very vocabulary in the "*melancholy*, long, withdrawing roar" in line 25 of "Dover Beach," the "*ebb and flow* / Of human misery" in lines 17–18, and "the *moon* lies fair / Upon the straits" and "the sea meets the *moon*-blanch'd land" in lines 2–3 and 8 respectively. The "blanch'd" in line 8 is itself derivative of the name of one of King Lear's dogs, "Tray, *Blanche*, and Sweetheart," an element of that last name having already appeared in line 6 in the phrase "*sweet* is the night air." That "blanch'd" means "white" is a pun once-removed on the first element of the surname of Frances Lucy *Wight*man, with whom, as we recall, Arnold spent his honeymoon in 1851.

I PROMISED SOME NEWS of "family drama" in my reading of this poem, and I'll focus first on the drama involving Frances Lucy Wightman. For it's hard not to read the poem as a description of lovemaking, perhaps that of "ignorant" newlyweds who "clash by night." The vocabulary of the poem may be erotically construed, moving as it does from "full" through "lies . . . upon" and "stand" and "spray" and the rhythm of "begin, and cease, and then begin again" and "withdrawing" to "the eternal note of sadness" that corresponds to what is sometimes known as post-coital tristesse. The "full" aspect of the tide is the point of contact between it and the "Sea of Faith," which

> Was once, too, at the *full*, and round earth's shore
> Lay like the folds of a bright girdle furl'd.

The erotic charge of the "folds" and "furl'd," combined with the "girdle," immediately brings to mind Lear's rant on female sexuality from Act IV, Scene vi, lines 120–28:

> The fitchew nor the soiled horse goes to't
> With a more riotous appetite.
> Down from the waist they are Centaurs,
> Though women all above;
> But to the *girdle* do the Gods inherit,
> Beneath is all the fiend's.

The "*bright* girdle" is connected to those elements of "*fair*ness" and "*white*ness" associated with Frances *Lucy Wight*man. The "girdle" itself is connected to those "shingles" we'll meet in line 28, the word "shingles" referring at once to the "small roundish stones; loose waterworn pebbles such as are found collected upon the seashore" (a word cognate with the Norwegian *singl*) and the "eruptive disease often extending round the middle of the body (whence the name); usually accompanied by violent neuralgic pain" (*OED*). It's hard, once again, not to read into this idealized vision of womanhood, which turns out to be "drear" in reality, something of a sexual "pain" for which there can be no "help." The frankness of these lines may have been one reason why Arnold didn't publish them for fifteen years, taken aback as he must have been by the Learean self-exposure of his own "*naked* shingles."

That derivation of "shingle," from *cingulum*, a "girdle," would have been as familiar to Matthew Arnold as to his father, Thomas, and introduces the other family drama enacted here, the extent to which a father and child, as much as husband and wife, may be "true to one another." It's one of the main themes of *King Lear*, as we've seen, and it underpins "Dover Beach" in ways that are largely subliminal but nonetheless striking. The idea of being "true to one another" is intimately connected to the idea of inheritance, and I want to propose that the line "But to the girdle do the Gods *inherit*" connects with Matthew Arnold's own failure to inherit the *God* of his father, and the system of organized religion which Thomas Arnold so earnestly supported. I'll want to suggest that the break between the positions of Arnold *père et fils* accounts only partly for the "suppression" of "Dover Beach," since the main reason for Matthew Arnold's disquiet must have stemmed from the poem's being antithetical to the poet's views as set down in essays such as "On the Modern Element in Literature."

Let's begin with the relationship between father and son, insofar as we may disentangle it (in the case of "Dover Beach," at least) from the relationship between husband and wife. I've already mentioned Thomas Arnold's interest in the battle of Epipolae as described by Thucydides, a description praised by Matthew Arnold for its "intellectual deliverance." Here's part of that description in a translation by Richard Crawley:

> The Athenians now fell into great disorder and perplexity, so that it was not easy to get from one side or the other any detailed account of the affair. By day certainly the combatants have a clearer notion, though even then by no means of all that takes place, no one knowing much of anything that does not go on in his own immediate neighbourhood; but in a night engagement (and this was the only one that occurred between great armies during the war) how could any one know anything for certain?

This is the "certitude" which is lacking in lines 32–34 of "Dover Beach," despite the fact that, as Thomas Arnold points out in a footnote to his edition of the Greek text of *The Peloponnesian War*, there's a moon:

They saw one another as men naturally would by *moon*light; that is, to see before them the form of the object, but to mistrust their knowing who was friend and who was foe.

The "moon" itself, which once lay "fair / upon the straits" and "blanch'd" the land, may no longer be relied upon. An excess of light has, paradoxically, contributed to the unreliability of one's vision. Even more alarming is the unreliability of that most dependable of modes, language itself:

> The victorious Syracusans and allies were cheering each other on with loud cries, by night the only possible means of communication, and meanwhile receiving all who came against them; while the Athenians were seeking for one another, taking all in front of them for enemies, even although they might be some of their now flying friends; and by constantly asking for the watchword, which was their only means of recognition, not only caused great confusion among themselves by asking all at once, but also made it known to the enemy, whose own they did not so readily discover, as the Syracusans were victorious and not scattered, and thus less easily mistaken.

The treachery of language is an element we recognise from *King Lear*, in which Cordelia, for example, bandies words with her father. She refuses to give him the conventional shibboleth which would ensure her passing safely into her inheritance:

> *Cordelia*: Why have my sisters husbands, if they say
> They love you all? Happily, when I shall wed,
> That lord whose hand must take my plight shall carry
> Half my love with him, half my care and duty:
> Sure I shall never marry like my sisters,
> To love my father all.
> *Lear*: But goes thy heart with this?
> *Cordelia*:   Ay, my good Lord.
> *Lear*: So young, and so untender?
> *Cordelia*: So young, my Lord, and true.

Arnold carries over this "true" into lines 29–30 of "Dover Beach":

> Ah, love, let us be *true*
> To one another!

Arnold has neatly combined the "true" from Cordelia's tart words for Lear in Act I, Scene i, with the "let's" from Lear's tender words for Cordelia in Act V, Scene iii:

> No, no, no, no! Come, *let's* away to prison;
> We two alone will sing like birds i' th' cage:
> When thou dost ask me blessing, I'll kneel down,
> And ask of thee forgiveness: so we'll live,
> And pray, and sing, and tell old tales, and laugh
> At gilded butterflies . . .

The religious vocabulary ("blessing," "forgiveness") is of a piece with the religious vocabulary of lines 33–34 of "Dover Beach":

> Hath really neither *joy*, nor *love*, nor *light*,
>
> Nor certitude, nor *peace*, nor *help for pain*

Arnold here appeals to the "tremulous cadence slow" of Shakespeare, the iambic tolling of "and pray, and sing, and tell old tales" resounding through "neither joy, nor love, nor light / Nor certitude, nor peace, nor help for pain." That speech of Lear to Cordelia in Act V is the same one which ends with the image of the "packs and sects of great ones / That ebb and flow by th' moon." We've already seen how that vocabulary ("ebb and flow," "moon") has found its way into "Dover Beach." In line 35, Arnold yet again relies on a word drawn from *King Lear*, since "a darkling plain" derives partly from that startling line that comes from the mouth of the Fool in Act I, Scene iv, lines 234–37:

> For you know, Nuncle,
> The hedge-sparrow fed the cuckoo so long,
> That it's had it head bit off by it young.
> So out went the candle, and we were left *darkling*.

I want to propose that Matthew Arnold's "suppression" of this poem has to do largely with his embarrassment over the fact that, in "Dover Beach," he bites off the head of his father. Thomas Arnold had a profound influence on his son. Some of the key ideas in Matthew Arnold's world-picture may be traced directly to his father. For instance, the notion that Thucydides was a "modern," proposed by Arnold *fils* in "On the Modern Element in Literature," had been proposed by Arnold *père* in the preface to his edition of *The Peloponnesian War*:

> I must beg to repeat what I have said before, that the period to which Thucydides refers belongs properly to *modern* and not to ancient history . . . The history of Greece and Rome is not an idle inquiry about remote ages and forgotten institutions, but a living picture of things present, fitted not so much for the curiosity of the scholar, as for the instruction of the statesman and the citizen.

Arnold *fils* again echoes Arnold *père*'s idea of "instruction" in that excerpt from "On the Modern Element in Literature" I quoted earlier, when he describes the Peloponnesian War as "the most *instructive* event which had, up to that time, happened in the history of mankind." What's "instructive," of course, for Arnold *père* is set down unabashedly in his preface to *The Peloponnesian War*:

> And those who vainly lament that progress of earthly things which, whether good or evil, is certainly inevitable may be consoled by the thought that its sure tendency is to confirm and purify the virtue of the good: and that to us, holding in our hands not the wisdom of Plato only, but also a treasure of wisdom and of comfort which to Plato was denied, the utmost activity of the human mind may be viewed without apprehension, in the confidence that we possess a charm to deprive it of its evil, and to make it minister for ourselves certainly, and through us, if we use it rightly, for the world in general, to the more perfect triumph of good.

A key phrase here is "if we use it rightly." Arnold *père*'s argument, one taken up by Arnold *fils*, is that art has a "function," that of preparing the way for "the more perfect triumph of good." It's an idea he puts forth in "On the Modern Element in Literature," in his rather bumptious view of the impact of Horace on the "best" men:

> The best men in the best ages have never been thoroughly satisfied with Horace. If human life were complete without faith, without enthusiasm, without energy, Horace, like Menander, would be the perfect interpreter of human life: but it is not; to the best, to the most living sense of humanity, it is not; and because it is not, Horace is inadequate.

PERHAPS I SHOULD ACKNOWLEDGE my own feelings of inadequacy before this tricky subject of the extent to which the family drama of Arnold *père* being countered by Arnold *fils*, or Arnold *fils* being countered by his own poem, might be symptomatic of their age. Whereas Sophocles "saw life steadily, and saw it whole," the likes of Horace, or Lucretius, or Virgil, are deemed not to be "adequate interpreter[s]" of their ages. I want to suggest that it's precisely Arnold's sense that the world-picture espoused by his father, and himself, is no longer "commensurate with its epoch" that had him "suppress" "Dover Beach." Life may no longer be viewed "steadily" or "whole" and Arnold will think of himself as failing, like poor Horace, to offer a piece of literature that is "interpretative and fortifying." That image of "fortifying," used in Arnold's lecture of 1857, is derived, I suggest, from the 1853 translation by Frederick Henry of Martin Luther's hymn:

> A mighty *fortress* is our God,
> A bulwark never failing.
> Our helper He amid the flood
> Of mortal ills prevailing.

This is, if you recall, the hymn sung to a seal by the speaker of "At the Fishhouses," Elizabeth Bishop's remake of "Dover Beach," in which she slyly alludes to the Arnoldian "*melancholy* stains" of rust on ironwork before presenting another metaphorical seascape something akin to a *paysage moralisé*:

It is like what we imagine knowledge to be:
dark, salt, clear, moving, utterly free,
drawn from the cold hard mouth
of the world, derived from the rocky breasts
forever, flowing and drawn, and since
our knowledge is historical, flowing, and flown.

This derives partly from Arnold's "ebb and *flow*," partly from the "cadence slow" of both the end of "Dover Beach" and Wordsworth's "Calais, August, 1802" ("when truth, when sense, when liberty were *flown*"). "The world" of "Dover Beach" is a world that offers no comfort, a world to which Virgil himself would not be adequate:

> Over the whole of the great poem of Virgil, over the whole *Aeneid*, there rests an ineffable *melancholy*: not a rigid, a moody gloom, like the *melancholy* of Lucretius; no, a sweet, a touching sadness, but still a sadness; a *melancholy*, which is at once a source of charm in the poem, and a testimony to its incompleteness.

The element of "withdrawing" in the "melancholy, long, withdrawing roar" of the Sea of Faith looks forward to a term which Arnold applies to Lucretius:

> Yes, Lucretius is modern; but is he adequate? And how can a man adequately interpret the activity of his age when he is not in sympathy with it? Think of the varied, the abundant, the wide spectacle of the Roman life of his day; think of its fullness of occupation, its energy of effort. From these Lucretius *withdraws* himself, and bids his disciples to *withdraw* themselves; he bids them to leave the business of the world, and to apply themselves "*naturam cognoscere rerum*—to learn the nature of things"; but there is no peace, no cheerfulness for him either in the world from which he comes, or in the solitude to which he goes.

This idea of recession from the "fullness" to the "melancholy, long, withdrawing roar" of the Sea of Faith ushers in the twentieth century, as is rather neatly hinted at by Yeats in his four-line remake of "Dover Beach," "The Nineteenth Century and After":

Though the great song return no more
There's keen delight in what we have:
The rattle of pebbles on the shore
Under the receding wave.

We can see how "no peace" in the phrase "but there is no peace, no cheerfulness" is carried over into "The Modern Element in Literature" from the phrase *"nor peace*, nor help for pain" in line 34 of "Dover Beach." The phrase "nor help for pain," meanwhile, prepares the way for a description of Lucretius in the same lecture:

> The predominance of thought, of reflection, in modern epochs is
> not without its penalties; in the unsound, in the over-tasked, in the
> over-sensitive, it has produced the most *painful*, the most lamentable
> results; it has produced a state of feeling unknown to less
> enlightened but perhaps healthier epochs—the feeling of depression,
> the feeling of *ennui*.

The idea with which Arnold doesn't come to terms in "On the Modern Element in Literature" is that if an epoch "Hath really neither joy, nor love, nor light, / Nor certitude, nor peace, nor help for pain," then the literature of that epoch, to be "commensurate" or "adequate" to it, is likely to have "neither joy, nor love, nor light, / Nor certitude, nor peace, nor help for pain." Rather than accept the intrinsic logic of his own argument, or the argument of the poem "Dover Beach," Arnold continues to hanker after the possibility of salve, of salvation, of "enlightenment," of "elucidation."

In "Once By the Pacific," yet another remake of "Dover Beach," Robert Frost has his own take on there being, or not being, light:

> The shattered water made a misty din.
> Great waves looked over others coming in,
> And thought of doing something to the shore
> That water never did to land before.
> The clouds were low and hairy in the skies,
> Like locks blown forward in the gleam of eyes.

Frost's sexualization of the "great waves" that "thought of doing some-thing to the shore / That water never did to land before" is of a piece with Arnold's, the "gleam of eyes" taking up "the light / *Gleams* and is gone." Frost picks up immediately on the next phrase in Arnold, "the cliffs of England," with two parallel cliffs:

> You could not tell, and yet it looked as if
> The shore was lucky in being backed by *cliff*,
> The *cliff* in being backed by continent;
> It looked as if a night of dark intent
> Was coming, and not only a night, an age.
> Someone had better be prepared for rage.
> There would be more than ocean-water broken
> Before God's last *Put out the Light* was spoken.

"It looked *as if*," Frost writes, mimicking the structure of Arnold's "for the world, *which seems* / To lie before us" and "we are here *as on* a darkling plain."

For a twenty-first-century poet like Glyn Maxwell, the urge to make connections, however strong, may not be satisfied with the same ease as Wordsworth was able to connect, in "It is a beauteous evening, calm and free," "the Sea" with "the mighty Being":

> the mighty Being is awake,
> and doth with his eternal motion make
> a sound like thunder—everlastingly.

For Maxwell, it's an altogether different story, whereby concerns about proving the existence of God have been overtaken by concerns about proving the existence of *man*:

> The sea comes in like nothing but the sea,
> but still a mind, knowing how seldom words
>
> augment, reorders them before the breaker
> and plays them as it comes. All that should sound

is water reaching into the rough space
the mind has cleared. The clearing of that mind

is nothing to the sea. The means whereby
the goats were chosen nothing to the god,

who asked only a breathing life of us,
to prove we were still there when it was doubted.

This echoes precisely the "retreating" in Arnold of "the Sea of Faith" and its being replaced by nothing more than "the *breath* / Of the night-wind," just as the idea of Eternity is replaced by "the eternal note of sadness" in the "melancholy, long, withdrawing roar." The word "with-drawing" occurs just one line before the word "retreating," and I want to propose that this near-redundancy may represent a little nub of indeter-minacy which may be an indicator of a subliminal presence in the word "withdrawing." The presence is that of Darwin, a version of whose name is found in "with*drawing*." Now, I'm well aware that Charles Darwin's *On the Origin of Species by Means of Natural Selection, or the Preservation of Favoured Races in the Struggle for Life* was not published until 1859, some eight years after it's generally accepted "Dover Beach" was written. How-ever, it would still be another eight years before the poem was published, and it's not beyond the bounds of possibility that the word "struggle" from Charles Darwin's subtitle might have found its way into the awk-ward penultimate line of the poem:

And we are here as on a darkling plain
Swept with confused alarms of *struggle* and flight,
Where ignorant armies clash by night.

It's more likely, I suppose, that the notions of Erasmus Darwin, the grandfather of Charles, might more substantially inform "Dover Beach." Erasmus was, after all, one of the first proponents of the idea of evolu-tion, the "unrolling" which is central to much of the sea imagery of the poem. Here's that celebrated passage from Erasmus Darwin's *Zoonomia*, a book published in 1794:

The world itself might have been generated, rather than created; that is, it might have been gradually produced from very small beginnings, increasing by the activities of its inherent principles, rather than a sudden evolution of the whole by the Almighty fiat. What a magnificent idea of the infinite power of THE GREAT ARCHITECT! THE CAUSE OF CAUSES! PARENT OF PARENTS! ENS ENTIUM! For if we may compare infinities, it would seem to require a greater infinity of power to cause the causes of effects, than to cause the effects themselves.

The "fiat" to which Erasmus Darwin refers is the *Fiat Lux* which has now been overwhelmed by "a darkling plain." Let's focus on the word "darkling" once again. This is a far cry from the all-but-literal use of the word in Keats's "Ode to a Nightingale," another poem much taken with "the eternal note":

> *Darkling* I listen; and for many a time
> I have been half in love with easeful Death,
> Call'd him soft names in many a mused rhyme,
> To take into the air my quiet breath;
> Now more than ever seems it rich to die,
> To cease upon the midnight with no pain . . .

That "breath" partly inspires "the *breath* / Of the night-wind" in lines 25–26 of "Dover Beach," while "no pain" is reflected in the "*nor* help for *pain*" in line 34.

Another text lying behind the "darkling" plain is *Antony and Cleopatra*. I'm thinking of the lines Cleopatra speaks over the dying Antony in Act IV, Scene xv, lines 9–11:

> O sun,
> Burn the great sphere thou mov'st in, *darkling* stand
> The varying shore o' the world.

Again, the vocabulary of this death scene, more love scene, informs the love scene, more death scene, of "Dover Beach," in phrases such as "the cliffs of England *stand*," "round earth's *shore*" and "naked shingles of the *world*." The fact that the word "world" appears in such quick succession, in lines 28 and 30, is an indicator to me of another little nub of indeterminacy where Arnold simultaneously resists and embraces the allusion to *Antony and Cleopatra* at this moment of intimacy between himself and Lucy:

> Ah, love, let us be true
> To one another! for the *world*, which seems
> To lie before us like a land of dreams,
> So various, so beautiful, so new,
> Hath really neither joy, nor love, nor light

Notice, by the way, the little variation on the "varying" in Shakespeare in Arnold's "so *various*."

The word "darkling" has one further source, I suggest, in Samuel Johnson's *Vanity of Human Wishes*:

> Must helpless man, in ignorance sedate,
> Roll *darkling* down the torrent of his fate?

That man is "helpless" is echoed in the fact that there is "nor *help* for pain," the "ignorance sedate" is echoed in the "*ignorant* armies," while the image of the "torrent" is echoed in the first word of the penultimate line:

> *Swept* with confused alarms of struggle and flight,
> Where ignorant armies clash by night.

The "clash" here comes to refer not only to "the loud but broken sound of the collision of weapons" but "the conflict or collision of contrary arguments or opinions" (*OED*), so that Matthew Arnold's professed "demand for an intellectual deliverance" as the end of the poem is repudiated by the end of the poem itself.

CHAPTER 14

HOMAGE TO CLIO

W. H. AUDEN

Our hill has made its submission and the green
    Swept on into the north: around me,
From morning to night, flowers duel incessantly,
    Color against color, in combats

Which they all win, and at any hour from some point else
    May come another tribal outcry
Of a new generation of birds who chirp
    Not for effect but because chirping

Is the thing to do. More lives than I perceive
    Are aware of mine this May morning
As I sit reading a book, sharper senses
    Keep watch on an inedible patch

Of unsatisfactory smell, unsafe as
    So many areas are: to observation
My book is dead, and by observations they live
    In space, as unaware of silence

As Provocative Aphrodite or her twin,
    Virago Artemis, the Tall Sisters
Whose subjects they are. That is why, in their Dual Realm,
    Banalities can be beautiful,

Why nothing is too big or too small or the wrong
   Color, and the roar of an earthquake
Rearranging the whispers of streams a loud sound
   Not a din: but we, at haphazard

And unseasonably, are brought face to face
   By ones, Clio, with your silence. After that
Nothing is easy. We may dream as we wish
   Of phallic pillar or navel-stone

With twelve nymphs twirling about it, but pictures
   Are no help: your silence already is there
Between us and any magical center
   Where things are taken in hand. Besides,

Are we so sorry? Woken at sunup to hear
   A cock pronouncing himself himself
Though all his sons had been castrated and eaten,
   I was glad I could be unhappy: if

I don't know how I shall manage, at least I know
   The beast-with-two-backs may be a species
Evenly distributed but Mum and Dad
   Were not two other people. To visit

The grave of a friend, to make an ugly scene,
   To count the loves one has grown out of,
Is not nice, but to chirp like a tearless bird,
   As though no one dies in particular

And gossip were never true, unthinkable:
   If it were, forgiveness would be no use,
One-eye-for-one would be just and the innocent
   Would not have to suffer. Artemis,

Aphrodite, are Major Powers and all wise
   Castellans will mind their p's and q's,

But it is you, who never have spoken up,
 Madonna of silences, to whom we turn

When we have lost control, your eyes, Clio, into which
 We look for recognition after
We have been found out. How shall I describe you? They
 Can be represented in granite

(One guesses at once from the perfect buttocks,
 The flawless mouth too grand to have corners,
Whom the colossus must be), but what icon
 Have the arts for you, who look like any

Girl one has not noticed and show no special
 Affinity with a beast? I have seen
Your photo, I think, in the papers, nursing
 A baby or mourning a corpse: each time

You had nothing to say and did not, one could see,
 Observe where you were, Muse of the unique
Historical fact, defending with silence
 Some world of your beholding, a silence

No explosion can conquer but a lover's Yes
 Has been known to fill. So few of the Big
Ever listen: that is why you have a great host
 Of superfluous screams to care for and

Why, up and down like the Duke of Cumberland,
 Or round and round like the Laxey Wheel,
The Short, The Bald, The Pious, The Stammerer went,
 As the children of Artemis go,

Not yours. Lives that obey you move like music,
 Becoming now what they only can be once,
Making of silence decisive sound: it sounds
 Easy, but one must find the time. Clio,

Muse of Time, but for whose merciful silence
    Only the first step would count and that
Would always be murder, whose kindness never
    Is taken in, forgive our noises

And teach us our recollections: to throw away
    The tiniest fault of someone we love
Is out of the question, says Aphrodite,
    Who should know, yet one has known people

Who have done just that. Approachable as you seem,
    I dare not ask you if you bless the poets,
For you do not look as if you ever read them
    Nor can I see a reason why you should.

THERE WAS ONE RATHER SIGNIFICANT OMISSION from the long list of poems influenced by "Dover Beach" with which I concluded my last chapter. I'm thinking of W. H. Auden's "September 1, 1939," in which Auden extends the sea imagery of "Dover Beach":

> *Waves* of anger and fear
> Circulate over the bright
> And darkened lands of the earth

The dark/light motifs of "Dover Beach" and the associated vocabulary ("armies clash by night," "the world, which seems / to lie before us," "the moon lies fair," "nor love, nor light") also informs the end of "September 1, 1939":

> Defenceless under the *night*
> Our *world* in stupor *lies*;
> Yet, dotted everywhere,
> Ironic points of *light*
> Flash out wherever the Just

Exchange their messages:
May I, composed like them
Of Eros and of dust,
Beleaguered by the same
Negation and despair,
Show an affirming flame.

The dating of the poem not only in the title ("September 1, 1939") but also after the last line (*September 1939*) is a double reminder of the significance of the date, the outbreak of World War II. Indeed, Auden goes much further than Arnold and refers quite explicitly to Thucydides, the historian of the Peloponnesian War, whose description of the night battle at Epipolae is the backdrop for the end of the Arnold poem:

Exiled *Thucydides* knew
All that a speech can say
About Democracy,
And what dictators do.

More delicately, Auden echoes both the content and cadence of "Ah, love, let us be true / To one another!" in the final line of the penultimate, eighth stanza of "September 1, 1939":

We must *love one another* or die.

We remember that's how the line read when the poem was first published, in October 1939, though it was changed by Auden to "we must love one another *and* die" and appeared as such in Oscar Williams's 1955 anthology, the *New Pocket Anthology of American Verse*. A mere two years later, in a footnote in his study of *The Making of the Auden Canon*, Joseph Warren Beach did not mince his words on this change, saying that it was a "misprint" that "makes no sense at all." Let me resort at some length to Beach to give a little more of the context:

In the case of half a dozen poems from which one or more stanzas were omitted in revision, we enter a dubious border region where our speculations as to the author's reasons are more hazardous . . .

Perhaps the most startling instance of this is in the poem which is probably the most widely known of all his work . . . It was written after Auden's coming to live in the United States, and was provoked by the outbreak of the Second World War. It was eagerly looked to for a statement of the famous poet's reaction to that catastrophic event. It is one of the poems in which he most distinctly makes his break with the old Marxian ideology . . . So far as one can make out, there is nothing whatever in this poem, nor in the omitted stanza, that might not meet the approval of the mature Auden . . . There is no better statement of Auden's political and psychological position as exhibited in much of his subsequent writing; and this poem may be cited as marking the moment in which he distinctly showed himself a reformed thinker, at least in political theory, for his religious conversion seems to have followed on this and to have been consummated somewhat later. This eighth stanza marks the crux of the whole matter. And yet, for inscrutable reasons, he chose to cut it out of the 1945 version, and to keep it out in the 1950 version.

Since Beach made these observations, in 1957, things might appear to have become more and more inscrutable. For example, "September 1, 1939" is excluded from Edward Mendelson's 1976 edition of Auden's *Collected Poems* but included in the 1979 *Selected Poems*, both published by Vintage. Edward Mendelson points out that the *Collected Poems* honors Auden's sense, as conveyed by him to Mendelson in 1971 or 1972 ("I don't want it reprinted during my lifetime"), of what might be included or excluded, and that the *Complete Poems*, which Mendelson is in the process of editing, will contain the poem. Even so, "September 1, 1939" still occupies that "dubious border region" Beach referred to, the limbo of a poem disavowed by its author. I want to try today to understand the extent to which an author is entitled to own or disown the work that has been written through him or her. This goes back to a question I've been threatening to address but have never quite got round to addressing, a question having to do with our knowing when and why a poem has come to an end, a question related to a notion of its function in the world, and one which I want to try to explore by appealing to metaphors of predestination and free will. In the case of "September 1, 1939" Auden decided that the poem

had its own agenda, one to which he was not sympathetic, probably because it did not "show an affirming flame" in the best Arnoldian tradition.
I'm thinking of Arnold's description of how "we have to turn to poetry,"
as he puts it in "The Study of Poetry," an essay first published in 1880 as
the general introduction to *The English Poets*, edited by T. H. Ward:

> More and more mankind will discover that we have to turn to poetry
> to interpret life for us, to console us, to sustain us. Without poetry,
> our science will appear incomplete; and most of what now passes
> with us for religion and philosophy will be replaced by poetry.

This meshing of ethics and aesthetics would be echoed by W. H. Auden, M.A., in "Making, Knowing and Judging," his 1956 inaugural lecture
as Professor of Poetry at Oxford:

> Speaking for myself, the questions which interest me most when
> reading a poem are two. The first is technical: "Here is a verbal
> contraption. How does it work?" The second is, in the broadest
> sense, moral. "What kind of guy inhabits this poem? What is his
> notion of the good life or the good place? His notion of the Evil
> One? What does he conceal from the reader? What does he conceal
> even from himself?"

I want to try here to begin to understand why Auden, and so many
others in the Arnoldian tradition, feel obliged to trouble themselves with
"the notion of the good life or the good place" and the "notion of the Evil
One" when they know perfectly well that this is high-sounding claptrap, a
substitute for the demise of organized Christianity. "The strongest part of
our religion today is its unconscious poetry," wrote Arnold, again in "The
Study of Poetry." Arnold's delineation, in that same essay, of "the historic
estimate and the personal estimate, both of which are fallacious" is
echoed by Auden's minding the gap between "the romantic *lie* in the brain
/ Of the sensual man in the street" and "the *lie* of Authority / Whose
buildings grope the sky" in "September 1, 1939." The relationship between the poets and the historical period out of which they are writing,
and the extent to which one might trust one to comment on another, is

even more finally and even more forcibly put by Auden in the title poem of his 1960 collection, *Homage to Clio*:

> I dare not ask you if you bless the poets,
> For you do not look as if you ever read them
> Nor can I see a reason why you should.

Yet this, too, seems blustering, bogus, blather through a bullhorn. Isn't there some middle ground between an idea of poetry that is "adequate" in the Arnoldian sense without being a loose-box for Anglo-Catholics, lapsed or latent? I hope so, particularly since I'm vastly more taken by the observation that immediately precedes the "good life . . . good place . . . Evil One" paragraph, in which Auden speaks of a more recognisable class of poet:

> He may have something sensible to say about woods, even about
> leaves, but you should never trust him on trees.

Well, let me try to say a word or two about leaves, woods, *and* trees. I'll begin with a few details, shot in big close-up, of "leaves," and then pull back suddenly, with the help of Francis Fukuyama, Saint Augustine, and Jean Baudrillard, for the wide-angle shot of the "woods."

WE ENCOUNTER LEAF DETAILS in "Homage to Clio" as "the first step" and "the tiniest fault," the world where "nothing is too big" and, more important, "nothing . . . too small." For it's only from moment to moment, from death to death, that battles are lost and won:

> Our hill has made its submission and the green
> Swept on into the north . . .

The word "submission" is a telling one, since it includes the dual sense of "yielding to the claims of another" (*OED*), whereby the military might of the "hill" gives way to the military might of the "green," one army succumbing to another, and the sense of an "agreement to abide by a decision . . . a contract by which parties agree to submit disputed matters to arbitration; also the document embodying such a contract" (*OED*). That duality might be one of the subjects of the poem is announced in line 3 ("flowers *duel* incessantly"), while the militaristic imagery established in lines 1 and 2 continues through the poem ("*combats /* Which they all win," "*Major Powers*"). We've met the sense of "submission" as an "act of deference or homage" (*OED*) as early as the title of the poem, "*Homage* to Clio." The root of "homage" is the Latin *homo*, and the term signifies the "formal and public acknowledgement of allegiance, wherein a tenant or vassal declared himself the *man* of the king or the lord of whom he held, and bound himself to his service" (*OED*). Something of this notion of a contractual arrangement, and that second sense of the word "submission" as "the document embodying such a contract," informs Auden's use of the word in line 1. The giving over of oneself to a power beyond oneself is, of course, central to the idea of the writer (even a documentarian) as medium which Auden so readily embraced, and which lies behind the poetry/birdsong imagery of stanza 2 of "Homage to Clio":

> Of a new generation of birds who chirp
>> Not for effect but because chirping
>
> Is the thing to do . . .

This "new generation of birds" is a generation of poets whose ancestors (or at least those associated with Pembroke College, Oxford) were once described by Doctor Johnson as "a nest of singing birds." For these birds, poetry is "a way of happening, a mouth," as Auden had written in "In Memory of W. B. Yeats."

Poetry is a function of its own historical moment. And it's at this point that we should remind ourselves, I suppose, that this poem is indeed addressed "*to Clio*," the Muse of history, who is associated in Auden's symbol system with the opposite of chirping:

> . . . but we, at haphazard
>
> And unseasonably, are brought face to face
>> By ones, Clio, with your *silence* . . .

This "silence" is reminiscent of the *"silence* [that] invaded the suburbs" on the day of Yeats's death, a silence of which Yeats was unaware as "the provinces of his body revolted, / The squares of his mind were empty." History is rather provocatively associated with silence in several other instances in Auden, such as his beautiful evocation, from 1947, of "The Fall of Rome":

> Altogether elsewhere, vast
> Herds of reindeer move across
> Miles and miles of golden moss,
> *Silently* and very fast.

The most striking example of this trope of history happening "altogether elsewhere" had already been seen in Auden's 1938 poem "Musée des Beaux Arts":

> In Breughel's *Icarus*, for instance: how everything turns away
> Quite leisurely from the disaster; the ploughman may
> Have heard the splash, the forsaken cry,
> But for him it was not an important failure; the sun shone
> As it had to on the white legs disappearing into the green
> Water; and the expensive delicate ship that must have seen
> Something amazing, a boy falling out of the sky,
> Had somewhere to get to and sailed calmly on.

Yet again, the "silence" of ongoing history is interrupted by the "splash" and "cry" of the discrete event, the occasion that might ordinarily be thought of as history-making.

Let me appeal for a moment to the distinction between event and history made by Francis Fukuyama in his distressingly entitled *The End of History*, an early version of which had first been published in *The National Interest* in 1989:

> In it, I argued that a remarkable consensus concerning the legitimacy of liberal democracy as a system of government had emerged throughout the world over the past few years, as it conquered rival

ideologies like hereditary monarchy, fascism, and most recently communism. More than that, however, I argued that liberal democracy may constitute the "end point of mankind's ideological evolution" and "the final form of human government," and as such constituted "the end of history" . . . Many people were confused in the first instance by my use of the word "history." Understanding history in a conventional sense as the occurrence of events, people pointed to the fall of the Berlin Wall, the Chinese communist crackdown in Tiananmen Square, and the Iraqi invasion of Kuwait as evidence that "history was continuing" and that I was *ipso facto* proven wrong. And yet what I had suggested had come to an end was not the occurrence of events, even large and grave events, but History: that is, history understood as a single, coherent, evolutionary process, when taking into account the experience of all peoples in all times.

Something of this break between "event" and "History" seems to inform these poems of Auden, in which the "something amazing" of the fall of Icarus is negated by the ship that "sailed *calmly* on," the impact of "the fall of Rome" is made meaningless by "the herds of reindeer" that move "*silently and very fast*," and the death of Yeats is trivialized as "silence *invaded* the suburbs." These images of overwhelming insidiousness are connected once more to the opening image of "Homage to Clio," in which

> Our hill has made its submission and the green
>   *Swept* on into the north: around me,
> From morning to night, flowers duel incessantly,
>   Color against color, in combats

> Which they all win . . .

The "green" is mixed, we might recognize, on the same palette as "the *green* / Water" of "Musée des Beaux Arts," that violent en*jamb*ment of "green / Water" literally taking in the "white *legs*" of the boy. Greenness is associated in Auden with childhood, innocence, sexual yearning (one meaning of the verb "to green" being "to desire earnestly"), and sexual intercourse ("greens" in *Letters from Iceland*). The boy's "cry" from "Musée des Beaux Arts" is intercut with a slogan from one of those "silent" northern tribes—Goths, Vandals, or Huns?—and echoed in the next few lines of "Homage to Clio":

> . . . and at any hour from some point else
>   May come another tribal out*cry*
> Of a new generation of birds who chirp
>   Not for effect but because chirping
>
> Is the thing to do . . .

That notion that "chirping / Is the thing to do" echoes, once again, "Musée des Beaux Arts" and its assertion that "the sun shone / *as it had to.*" These notions of history in which "the sun shone / as it had to" and "chirping / is the thing to do" are related to a Christian idea of historical predestination which may be traced through Augustine, Aquinas and, to a negligible extent in the case of the Anglo-Catholic Auden, Calvin. It's Saint Augustine's *Confessions*, in particular, which are appealed to again and again in the Auden oeuvre, as John Fuller points out in his endlessly illuminating *W. H. Auden: A Commentary*. In "The Love Feast" of 1948, for example, Auden ventriloquizes Augustine directly in the last line:

> Who is Jenny lying to
> In her call, Collect, to Rome?
> The Love that made her out of nothing
> Tells me to go home.
>
> But that Miss Number in the corner
> Playing hard to get . . .
> I am sorry I'm not sorry . . .
> Make me chaste, Lord, but not yet.

The "birds who chirp" are somewhat reminiscent of the "cauldron of unholy loves" who "*sang* all about" Augustine's ears in Carthage, an image already given great currency by Eliot's reference to it in his notes to "The

Waste Land." But Auden had more than a passing interest in Augustine, particularly in Augustine's "duel" with the "unholy love" of Manichean "duality," as he made clear in a 1954 essay on *The Tempest*:

> As a biological organism Man is a natural creature subject to the necessities of nature; as a being with consciousness and will, he is at the same time a historical person with the freedom of the spirit. *The Tempest* seems to me a Manichean work, not because it shows the relation of Nature to Spirit as one of conflict and hostility, which in fallen man it is, but because it puts the blame for this upon Nature and makes the Spirit innocent:

However geometrically crude he may judge the Caliban/Ariel split, Auden is nonetheless much exercised by such polarities in "Homage to Clio," his repeated positioning of himself with his "book" unmistakably echoic of Prospero's positioning of himself:

> . . . More lives than I perceive
>   Are aware of mine this May morning
> As I sit reading a *book*, sharper senses
>   Keep watch on an inedible patch
>
> Of unsatisfactory smell, unsafe as
>   So many areas are: to observation
> *My book* is dead, and by observations they live
>   In space, as unaware of silence
>
> As Provocative Aphrodite or her twin,
>   Virago Artemis, the Tall Sisters
> Whose subjects they are . . .

If Auden is exercised by polarities, as I suggested earlier, it is almost always with a view to synthesising them, sometimes by allowing them to cancel each other out. We've already seen an instance of the "flowers [that] duel incessantly, / Color against color, in combats / *Which they all win.*" In this instance, the duality of Aphrodite and Artemis is at once confirmed and denied, confirmed in the epithets "Provocative" and "Virago," denied by their being "Tall *Sisters*." That capitalized "Tall" will send close readers of Auden back to the third stanza of his June 1939 poem "The Riddle":

> Bordering our middle earth
> Kingdoms of the Short and *Tall*,
>   Rivals for our faith,
> Stir up envy from our birth.

Indeed, the opening stanza of "The Riddle" reads as a limbering up for the opening stanzas of "Homage to Clio," complete with shared imagery:

> Underneath the leaves of life,
> *Green* on the prodigious tree,
>   In a trance of grief
> Stand the fallen man and wife:
> Far away a single stag
> Banished to a lonely crag
> Gazes placid out to sea,
> While from thickets round about
> Breeding animals look in
>   On *Duality*,
> And small *birds* fly in and out
>   Of the world of man.

That "stag" is perhaps a manifestation of Actaeon, the hunter who startled Artemis while she was bathing and was changed into a stag that would be dragged down by his own hunting dogs. Among these "small birds" that "fly in and out" are perhaps "The Willow-wren and the stare," the subjects of one of "Five Songs" written in 1948, which ends with a riddling exchange:

> *Did he know what he meant?* said the willow-wren—
> *God only knows*, said the stare. [Italics in original.]

In his note to this poem in *W. H. Auden: A Commentary*, John Fuller writes:

When the starling says "God only knows," we may be able to take this literally as well, a reminder of Auden's belief that "agape is the fulfillment and correction of eros."

The idea that "God only knows" is a slogan of predestination, though Auden also allows for the operation of free will, particularly when it operates in "fulfillment and correction." This was a position he outlined in his 1956 essay collected in James A. Pike's *Modern Canterbury Pilgrims*:

> As a spirit, a conscious person endowed with free will, a modern man has, through faith and grace, a unique "existential" relation to God, and few since Saint Augustine have described this relation more profoundly than Kierkegaard. But every man has a second relation to God which is neither unique nor existential: as a creature composed of matter, as a biological organism, every man, in common with everything else in the universe, is related by necessity to the God who created that universe and saw that it was good, for the laws of nature to which, whether he likes it or not, he must conform are of divine origin.

The vocabulary Auden uses here—"a creature composed of matter," "related by necessity," "laws of nature"—echoes precisely phrases from his earlier essay on *The Tempest*, in which he wrote that "Man is a natural *creature* subject to the *necessities of nature*." In other words, those "necessities of nature" have birds chirp "because chirping is the thing to do." I was struck recently by a passage in the drearily entitled *The Illusion of the End*, in which Jean Baudrillard, in a translation by Chris Turner, connects the idea of poetic language with predestination:

> The poetic form is not far removed from the chaotic form. Both flout the law of cause and effect. If, in Chaos Theory, for sensitivity to initial conditions we substitute sensitivity to final conditions, we are in the form of predestination, which is the form of fate [*le destin*]. Poetic language also lives with predestination, with the imminence of its own ending and of reversibility between the ending and the beginning. It is predestined in this sense—it is an unconditional event, without meaning and consequence, which draws its whole being from the dizzying whirl of final resolution.

Baudrillard goes on to connect this idea of "reversibility between the ending and the beginning" with a vision of history:

> What this brings us to, more or less, is a poetic, ironic analysis of events. Against the simulation of a linear history "in progress," we have to accord a privileged status to these backfires, these malign deviations, these lightweight catastrophes which cripple an empire much more effectively than any great upheavals.

This resonates rather powerfully with Auden's tendency to foreground the beautiful banalities, "the torturer's horse" from "Musée des Beaux Arts," that "scratches its innocent behind against a tree" while, in the background, the "martyrdom must run its course," or the "herds of reindeer" that upstage the "altogether elsewhere" of "The Fall of Rome." The figure of Saint Augustine is "silently" foregrounded even here, given that Augustine died in Hippo in A.D. 430, just as the Roman Empire was being "crippled" by the Vandals. This vision in which "nothing is too big or too small" is embodied in the valorization of human love in the face of twentieth-century Huns which is at the heart of "September 1, 1939," and it's a theme which reappears as late as "Aubade" of 1972. In "Aubade," Auden "silently" refers back to that suppressed "We must love one another and/or die":

> Human time is a City
> where each inhabitant has
> a political duty
> nobody else can perform,
> made cogent by Her Motto:
> *Listen, Mortals, Lest Ye Die.*

This motto turns out to be a Latin motto, taken from a passage in Eugen Rosenstock-Huessy's *Speech and Reality*, a fact for which I'm once again indebted to John Fuller:

> *Audi, ne moriamur.* Listen, lest we die; or: listen and we shall survive is an a priori that presupposes a power in man to establish relations with his neighbour that transcend their private interests.

My private interest in this passage from Rosenstock-Huessy, to whom "Aubade" is dedicated, has to do with Auden's private interest in it. For there, staring him in the face in that Latin motto, *Audi, ne* is an anagram of his own name, "I, Auden." The "Au" component in *Auden* has already been echoed in the title, "*Au*bade," and is echoed again in Saint *Au*gustine, who is named and quoted at length in the first stanza of the poem:

again, as wrote Augustine,
I know that I am and will,
I am willing and knowing,
I will to be and to know,
facing in four directions,
outwards and inwards in Space,
observing and reflecting,
backwards and forwards through time,
recalling and forecasting.

This last "backwards and forwards through time" brings me back to Baudrillard, and the "enchanted alternative to the linearity of history" he posits in *The Illusion of the End*:

Perhaps, deep down, history has never unfolded in a linear fashion; perhaps language has never unfolded in a linear fashion . . . Might we not transpose language games on to social and historical phenomena: anagrams, acrostics, spoonerisms, rhyme, strophe and catastrophe. Not just the major figures of metaphor and metonymy, but the instant, puerile, formalistic games, the heteroclite tropes which are the delight of a vulgar imagination? Are there social spoonerisms, or an anagrammatic history (where meaning is dismembered and scattered to the winds, like the name of God in the anagram), rhyming forms of political action or events which can be read in either direction?

Baudrillard goes on to make a distinction between time and historical meaning which is of a piece with Fukuyama's distinction between "Event" and "History" and, in "Aubade" and "Homage to Clio" respectively, Auden's distinction between *"sotto-voce"* and "Motto," between "silence" and "loud sound":

> And the anagram, that detailed process of unraveling, that sort of poetic and non-linear convulsion of language—is there a chance that history lends itself to such a poetic convulsion, to such a subtle form of return and anaphora which, like the anagram, would—beyond meaning—allow the pure materiality of language to show through, and—beyond historical meaning—allow the pure materiality of time to show through?

LET ME GIVE UP MY OWN "enchanted alternative to the linearity of history" and try to move towards some conclusions, insofar as they're possible in a post-Baudrillardian world, by announcing that "Homage to Clio" has long since announced itself to be an unrhymed ode, partly because of its form, partly because of its subject matter. As Edward Callan points out in *Auden: A Carnival of Intellect*, the opening of the poem is somewhat reminiscent of the opening of Horace's Ode 4.7, *Diffugere nives*, translated here by A. E. Housman, who described it as "the most beautiful poem in ancient literature":

> The snows are fled away, leaves on the shaws
> And grasses in the mead renew their birth,
> The river to the river-bed withdraws,
> And altered is the fashion of the earth.

The name of Horace has already been "silently" evoked, of course, in the near versions of that name to be seen in "*Ho*mage," and in line 5's "at any *hour* from some point else," where Auden has resisted using the word "p*lace*," by which the word "Horace" would have been completed, and introduced the slightly awkward phrase "some point else." Now, as Joseph Warren Beach put it earlier, the moment we begin to think in such terms, "we enter a dubious border region where our speculations as to the author's reasons are more hazardous." Even more hazardous, it's generally supposed, are speculations on the unconscious of the author. Yet we speculate on those, unconsciously, all the time, in ways no more or less out-landish than my speculations on the "silent" Horace and the secret ana-gram on Auden's name in "Aubade." It seems to me that all reading is, to a greater or lesser extent, involved with speculation on what's going on, consciously or unconsciously, in the writer's mind, just as all writing is in-volved with speculation on what's going on, consciously or unconsciously, in the reader's mind. I use the word "speculation," by the way, with an eye to its farflung roots in *specula*, "watch-tower," and *speculum*, "mirror."

Let me continue to try to describe the "Dual Realm" of writing and reading with an appeal to the metaphors of predestination and free will with which we've been so preoccupied today. For example, when I de-scribe "Homage to Clio" as having announced itself as an "unrhymed ode," what am I making of the fact that there is a rather obvious rhyme in lines 2 and 3, on "me" and "incessantly"? What I'm making of it is pre-cisely what Auden made of it. I'm desperately trying to ignore it. When Auden ignored it, he was ignoring it at his peril, since he was supremely aware of the relationship between setting up an expectation and either let-ting it sail through or scuttling it. For to set up a rhyme scheme as early as lines 2 and 3 seems to be going in the direction of one of Auden's favorite four-line stanza patterns, rhymed *abba*, as in "The Fall of Rome" with its "vast . . . across . . . moss . . . fast." By the time Auden got to the end of line 4, he had to make a choice. Should he find a chime for "green," for ex-ample? At least one really good contender springs to mind: "Keen," a word meaning "brave, bold, valiant, daring," as would befit duelists, or "having a very sharp edge or point," as would befit their weapons. The *OED* goes so far as to suggest that one resonance of a root for "keen," the Old Norse *koenn*, is "skilled in war" or "expert in battle," a resonance which, along with those others, would make it seem a natural choice for a poem beginning with images of warfare. But Auden will have none of it, a fact thrown into relief by his absolute avoidance of the word "keener" in favour of the phrase *"sharper* senses" in line 11. It's that decision, like the decision to avoid the phrase "some place" in favour of "some point else" that confirms for me the sense that there's something rather seriously awry with the poem.

Another indicator that the poem is engaged "in combat" with itself as it moves between lines 4 and 5 and 5 and 6 is the syllable count of line 5.

While Auden has chosen not to be overly concerned with what's going on at the end of the line, he's a little more involved with what's going on within it, setting up a pattern of an eleven- or twelve-syllable line followed by a line of nine syllables followed by an eleven- or twelve-syllable line followed by a line of nine syllables. By the time we get to line 5, where the "some point else" has won over "some place," we're up to thirteen syllables, clunking both in meaning and duration. Now, am I engaged in mind reading when I make this assertion? Or am I simply going from word to word as the author went from word to word, attempting to determine the effect of those words on subsequent readers? That's to say, the writer was reading the mind of the reader, an idea that somehow seems less problematic than its reverse. Isn't this how, to use the title of Auden's inaugural Oxford lecture, the poet makes, knows, and judges? He judges, for example, that Horace unrhymed may, on balance, be preferable to Horace rhymed. And we can work out how and why he came to that conclusion by using precisely the same method he used. That's to say, by judging the poem, as it comes into being, against what it might want to be. In this instance, Auden has gone against the wish of the poem and imposed his own authority on it, often to the disservice of the poem. For example, having given up on allowing the poem to find its way into the world by rhyme, he allows it to flop and flounder into being, trading the largely deft syllabic count of the line for the duffness of line endings such as "else," "as," "that," "there," "if," "which," "after," "they," "any," "and," and "that." When I describe these line endings as "duff," I'm balancing precisely the same elements Auden balanced, but arriving at a different conclusion. Auden was happy to allow what I consider to be aural infelicities to mar the poem as it made its way into the world, perhaps because the auditory duality of "sound" (used twice as a line ending) and "silence" (used four times as a line ending) is one of the main subjects of the poem. Maybe so.

On the subject of "subjects," let's look at that phrase in lines 18–19, "the Tall Sisters / Whose *subjects* they are." The question that springs to mind is, What is the subject of *they*? The reader has to trawl back through the range of possible subjects. Is it "observations"? No. "Areas"? No. "Senses"? Maybe. "Lives?" Maybe. Maybe we should go back to "observations"? I'm not persuaded that this tortuous syntax is an indicator of complexity, only of tortuousness. Also tortuous, for other reasons, are phrases like those lines in stanza 20 which read "Making of silence decisive sound: it sounds / Easy" where that second "sounds" sounds pretty slaphappy, just as the repetition of "know" in stanza 22 seems to happen unbeknownst to Auden:

> . . . to throw away
> The tiniest fault of someone we love
> Is out of the question, says Aphrodite,
> Who should *know*, yet one has *known* people

> Who have done just that.

The "Who should know," meanwhile, defuses, and diffuses, the iambic pentameter of the last line, "Nor can I see a reason why you should." As to why Aphrodite "should know" that "to throw away / The tiniest fault of someone we love / Is out of the question" is not at all clear.

As John Fuller points out, Auden's version of Aphrodite may have to do with a version of Aphrodite presented by Robert Graves in *The White Goddess*, where Graves identifies her with the Sea-goddess Marian, a figure he relates to the Blessed Virgin Mary, which is one reason why the "Madonna of silences" is flown in as a version of Clio. In "In Memory of Sigmund Freud," written in 1939, Auden wrote of "weeping anarchic Aphrodite," the tearful aspect of the goddess connecting with the Madonna of the tears, as distinct from the *"tearless* bird" we meet in stanza 11. We might bear in mind that in 1953, two years before "Homage to Clio" was written, the profusely weeping plaster statue of the "Madonna of Syracuse" had appeared to Antonina Jannuso in Syracuse, Sicily, an island renowned as the site of a major sanctuary to Aphrodite. In addition, 1954 had been designated a Marian year of prayer by the Vatican, marking as it did the centenary of the proclamation, in 1854, of the dogma of the Immaculate Conception of Mary. In other words, Marianism was much in Auden's mind, if not unproblematically. John Fuller quotes a 1956 letter Auden wrote to Ursula Niebuhr in which he enclosed a copy of the poem:

You were so much in my mind while I was writing it, as the only person I know who will understand my Anglican problem:—Can one write a hymn to the Blessed Virgin Mary without being "pi"? The Prots don't like her and the Romans want bleeding hearts and sobbing tenors. So here is my attempt which I submit to your severe, theological and feminine eye.

Ah. So that's what we have here. A hymn to the Blessed Virgin Mary, rather than the Gravesian "appetitive goddesses," among whom Aphrodite is included in "Sext" of 1954. As for Artemis, who doesn't make the cut in "Sext," she's also drawn largely from *The White Goddess*. A Christianized version of Artemis is given by Graves as Saint Artimedos, and that Christianization may have emboldened Auden in his blending of Clio and the Blessed Virgin Mary, particularly since Artemis is associated with childbirth. That description of Aphrodite and Artemis as "Tall Sisters" conforms also with Graves's exalted sense of the Muse which he presents in his famous self-portrait, "The Face in the Mirror":

I pause with razor poised, scowling derision
At the mirrored man whose beard needs my attention,
And once more ask him why
He still stands ready, with a boy's presumption,
To court the queen in her *high* silk pavilion.

And the Muse Queen is also related to the Queen of Heaven, according to Graves, again in *The White Goddess*:

In mediaeval poetry the Virgin Mary was plainly identified with the Muse by being put in charge of the Cauldron of Cerridwen. D. W. Nash notes in his edition of the Taliesin poems:
The Christian bards of the thirteenth and fourteenth centuries repeatedly refer to the Virgin Mary herself as the cauldron or source of inspiration—to which they were led, as it seems, partly by a play on the word *pair*, and the secondary form of that word, on assuming the soft form of its initial *mair*, which also means Mary.

Graves goes on to describe how "in mediaeval Irish poetry Mary was equally plainly identified with Brigit the Goddess of Poetry: for St. Brigit, the Virgin as Muse, was popularly known as 'Mary of the Gael' . . . Her Aegean prototype seems to have been Brizo of Delos, a moon-goddess to whom votive ships were offered, and whose name was derived by the Greeks from the word *brizein*, to enchant." Elsewhere in *The White Goddess*, Graves describes Brigit as "The High One," a description confirming her place among the "Tall Sisters." In this immediate context, Graves might have mentioned that Delos was the birthplace of Artemis, and drawn a connection between the Athenian festival of Artemis Brauronia, where "a girl of ten years old and a girl of five, dressed in saffron-yellow robes in honour of the moon, played the part of sacred bears," and the fact, had he been aware of it, that Brigit is primarily a bear goddess ("*Bergit*" being a version of her name where that connection is somewhat clearer). One of the many words for "bear" in Gaelic is *art*, a word related to the Latin *ursus* and the Greek *arctos*, and needless to say, *Art*emis.

A word here about my next chapter. It'll feature poems by three Irish poets, including Robert Graves's "Welsh Incident" and Cecil Day-Lewis's "A Failure." As it turns out, it was to Sean Day-Lewis, a son of Cecil, that Auden bequeathed, in his "Last Will and Testament" from *Letters to Iceland*, the famous Laxey Wheel. We see it mentioned there in stanza 19, within a line or two of "the children of Artemis." The Laxey Wheel, as John Fuller tells us, dependably as ever, is on the Isle of Man, "an overshot waterwheel built as a power source for local lead mines." This wheel is associated for Auden with Graves's description of "the goddess of the mill"—another version of Artemis, Artemis Calliste—"to whom the she-bear was sacred in Arcadia." This "mill" is related to the "millstone of the universe" and the Omphalos, or "navel-stone," to which Auden refers directly in stanza 7, and which has long been a key image for Seamus Heaney, the third Irish poet I'll be discussing in my final chapter, looking in particular at his poem "Keeping Going." This "navel-stone" has a particular poignancy in the context of "Homage to Clio," if it is (as Auden contends) a "hymn to the Blessed Virgin Mary," given that both Mary and the "foam-born" Aphrodite were "miraculously" conceived.

The Blessed Virgin Mary is perhaps most important to Auden in her role as Mediatrix, a shuttle diplomat between this world and the next, a role which is particularly attractive as we search for a metaphor for the negotiation of the "Dual Realm" of writing and reading. We can see how a religious vocabulary has helped us find ways of describing everything from "inspiration" to "redemption," the latter much in evidence in "The Redress of Poetry," Seamus Heaney's inaugural lecture as Professor of Poetry, in which he riffs rather brilliantly on the various meanings of "redress," including "to bring back (the hounds or deer) to the proper course." Heaney continues:

> In this "redress" there is no hint of ethical obligation; it is more a matter of finding a course for the breakaway of innate capacity, a course where something unhindered, yet directed, can sweep ahead into its full potential.

This corresponds to the relationship between predestination and free will, between free will and predestination, the endless arbitration on the arbitrary with which poets are involved from word to word and from line to line. The poem, like the soul, has a concupiscence for becoming all it might. This concupiscence is related to the idea of "anxiety" central to the theology of Reinhold Niebuhr, husband of Ursula, to whom Auden had sent a copy of the poem. Here's John Fuller, in a note on "The Age of Anxiety":

> Niebuhr saw man as living a two-dimensional existence of necessity and freedom; he is both a spirit, and a child of nature, compelled by its necessities: "In short, being both free and bound, both limited and limitless, is anxious. Anxiety is the inevitable concomitant of the paradox of freedom and finiteness in which man is involved."

That quotation from Niebuhr's *The Nature and Destiny of Man* (1941–43) resonates powerfully with Auden's idea of "fulfillment and correction," the *limiting* of readings of the poem with which the poet, as stunt reader, as I've sometimes referred to the first reader of the poem, must get involved. But, just as the hunter sometimes fails to "redress" the deer or hounds, that stunt reader sometimes comes a cropper and falls off the horse. If that's the case with "Homage to Clio," it's because the stunt reader, in the person of W. H. Auden, hasn't given the poem its head. We know that not because we're mind readers but because we've been right up there with him, falling with him as he falls.

CHAPTER 15

WELSH INCIDENT BY ROBERT GRAVES,

A FAILURE BY C. DAY-LEWIS,

KEEPING GOING BY SEAMUS HEANEY

WELSH INCIDENT

"But that was nothing to what things came out
From the sea-caves of Criccieth yonder."
"What were they? Mermaids? dragons? ghosts?"
"Nothing at all of any things like that."
"What were they, then?"
                                  "All sorts of queer things,
Things never seen or heard or written about,
Very strange, un-Welsh, utterly peculiar
Things. Oh, solid enough they seemed to touch,
Had anyone dared it. Marvellous creation,
All various shapes and sizes, and no sizes,
All new, each perfectly unlike his neighbour,
Though all came moving slowly out together."
"Describe just one of them."
                                  "I am unable."
"What were their colours?"
                                  "Mostly nameless colours,
Colours you'd like to see; but one was puce
Or perhaps more like crimson, but not purplish.
Some had no colour."

"Tell me, had they legs?"
"Not a leg nor foot among them that I saw."
"But did these things come out in any order?
What o'clock was it? What was the day of the week?
Who else was present? How was the weather?"
"I was coming to that. It was half-past three
On Easter Tuesday last. The sun was shining.
The Harlech Silver Band played *Marchog Jesu*
On thirty-seven shimmering instruments,
Collecting for Caernarvon's (Fever) Hospital Fund.
The populations of Pwllheli, Criccieth,
Portmadoc, Borth, Tremadoc, Penrhyndeudraeth,
Were all assembled. Criccieth's mayor addressed them
First in good Welsh and then in fluent English,
Twisting his fingers in his chain of office,
Welcoming the things. They came out on the sand,
Not keeping time to the band, moving seaward
Silently at a snail's pace. But at last
The most odd, indescribable thing of all,
Which hardly one man there could see for wonder,
Did something recognizably a something."
"Well, what?"
              "It made a noise."
                              "A frightening noise?"
"No, no."
        "A musical noise? A noise of scuffling?"
"No, but a very loud, respectable noise—
Like groaning to oneself on Sunday morning
In Chapel, close before the second psalm."
"What did the mayor do?"
                        "I was coming to that."

A FAILURE

The soil was deep and the field well-sited,
    The seed was sound.
Average luck with the weather, one thought,
    And the crop would abound.

If harrowing were all that is needed for
    Harvest, his field
Had been harrowed enough, God knows, to warrant
    A record yield.

He gazed from a hill in the breezy springtime:
    That field was aflow
With wave upon wave like a sea's green shallows
    Breathing below.

He looked from a gate one summer morning
    When the mists uprolled:
Headland to headland those fortunate acres
    Seemed solid gold.

He stood by the field as the day of harvest
    Dawned. But, oh,
The fruit of a year's work, a lifetime's lore,
    Had ceased to grow.

No wickedest weather could thus have turned,
    As it were overnight,
His field to so wan and weedy a showing:
    Some galloping blight

From earth's metabolism must have sprung
    To ruin all;
Or perhaps his own high hopes had made
    The wizened look tall.

But it's useless to argue the why and wherefore.
　　When a crop is so thin,
There's nothing to do but to set the teeth
　　And plough it in.

KEEPING GOING

for Hugh

The piper coming from far away is you
With a whitewash brush for a sporran
Wobbling round you, a kitchen chair
Upside down on your shoulder, your right arm
Pretending to tuck the bag beneath your elbow,
Your pop-eyes and big cheeks nearly bursting
With laughter, but keeping the drone going on
Interminably, between catches of breath.

The whitewash brush. An old blanched skirted thing
On the back of the byre door, biding its time
Until spring airs spelled lime in a work-bucket
And a potstick to mix it in with water.
Those smells brought tears to the eyes, we inhaled
A kind of greeny burning and thought of brimstone.
But the slop of the actual job
Of brushing walls, the watery grey
Being lashed on in broad swatches, then drying out
Whiter and whiter, all that worked like magic.
Where had we come from, what was this kingdom
We knew we'd been restored to? Our shadows
Moved on the wall and a tar border glittered
The full length of the house, a black divide
Like a freshly-opened, pungent, reeking trench.

Piss at the gable, the dead will congregate.
But separately. The women after dark,
Hunkering there a moment before bedtime,
The only time the soul was let alone,
The only time that face and body calmed
In the eye of heaven.
                                      Buttermilk and urine,
The pantry, the housed beasts, the listening bedroom.
We were all together there in a foretime,
In a knowledge that might not translate beyond
Those wind-heaved midnights we still cannot be sure
Happened or not. It smelled of hill-fort clay
And cattle dung. When the thorn tree was cut down
You broke your arm. I shared the dread
When a strange bird perched for days on the byre roof.

That scene, with Macbeth helpless and desperate
In his nightmare—when he meets the hags again
And sees the apparitions in the pot—
I felt at home with that one all right. Hearth,
Steam and ululation, the smoky hair
Curtaining a cheek. "Don't go near bad boys
In that college that you're bound for. Do you hear me?
Do you hear me speaking to you? Don't forget!"
And then the potstick quickening the gruel,
The steam crown swirled, everything intimate
And fear-swathed brightening for a moment,
Then going dull and fatal and away.

Grey matter like gruel flecked with blood
In spatters on the whitewash. A clean spot
Where his head had been, other stains subsumed
In the parched wall he leant his back against
That morning like any other morning,
Part-time reservist, toting his lunch-box.
A car came slow down Castle Street, made the halt,
Crossed the Diamond, slowed again and stopped

Level with him, although it was not his lift.
And then he saw an ordinary face
For what it was and a gun in his own face.
His right leg was hooked back, his sole and heel
Against the wall, his right knee propped up steady,
So he never moved, just pushed with all his might
Against himself, then fell past the tarred strip,
Feeding the gutter with his copious blood.

My dear brother, you have good stamina.
You stay on where it happens. Your big tractor
Pulls up at the Diamond, you wave at people,
You shout and laugh above the revs, you keep
Old roads open by driving on the new ones.
You called the piper's sporrans whitewash brushes
And then dressed up and marched us through the kitchen,
But you cannot make the dead walk or right wrong.
I see you at the end of your tether sometimes,
In the milking parlour, holding yourself up
Between two cows until your turn goes past,
Then coming to in the smell of dung again
And wondering, is this all? As it was
In the beginning, is now and shall be?
Then rubbing your eyes and seeing our old brush
Up on the byre door, and keeping going.

SINCE MY ELECTION to the venerable Oxford Chair of Poetry, I have
often been mistaken for a respectable public figure, and four
American universities have recently wanted to make me their guest
poet. I declined politely.

So Robert Graves begins his provocative 1963 lecture, "Nine Hundred
Iron Chariots." And so he continues:

Though my Oxford obligations are no great burden, and can be annually settled in two months or less, I grudge every hour spent away from my home among the rocks and olives of Majorca, except on important business. Yet among my latest preoccupations has been a wish to discover the mystique behind modern science: so, on being invited to spend two weeks on the M.I.T. campus as the Arthur D. Little Lecturer, I thought: "This is it! Nowhere in the world can a more massive concentration of scientific thought be found than at M.I.T. Let me pretend for once that I am a respectable public figure, and investigate."

In my final chapter, I'd like to investigate three poems by three Irish poets, all respectable public figures who held the Chair of Poetry at Oxford and who, in these three poems at least, are concerned with "mystique" and "science," with difficulty and the coming to terms with difficulty, with problems and their solutions. The poem itself is, after all, the solution to a problem only it has raised, and our reading of it necessarily entails determining what that problem was. Only then may we determine the extent to which it has, or has not, succeeded. That is the only decent end of the poem and our only decent end is to let the poem have its way with us, just as the poet let it have its way with him or her. Robert Graves goes on to give a blow-by-blow account of this shamanistic experience:

> Symptoms of the trance in which poetic composition occurs differ greatly from those of an induced mediumistic trance; though both seem directed by an external power. In a poetic trance, which happens no more predictably than a migraine or an epileptic fit, this power is traditionally identified with the ancient Muse-goddess. All poems, it seems, grow from a small verbal nucleus gradually assuming an individual rhythm and verse form. The writing is not "automatic," as in a mediumistic trance when the pen travels without pause over the paper, but is broken by frequent critical amendments and excisions. And though the result of subsequently reading a poem through may be surprise at the unifying of elements drawn from so many different levels of consciousness, this surprise

will be qualified by dissatisfaction with some lines. Objective recognition of the poem as an entity as a rule then induces a lighter trance, during which the poet realizes more fully the implications of his lines, and sharpens them. The final version (granted the truthfulness of its original draft, and the integrity of any secondary elaboration) will hypnotize readers who are faced by similar problems into sharing the poet's emotional experience.

The key to Graves's notion of "trance" is that both writer and reader are involved in it. Both are "hypnotized." Writer and reader blend into one indivisible function. Where their ends meet is itself indivisible from—might even be thought of as the definition of—the end of the poem. It's not a new idea, of course—one thinks of Ralph Waldo Emerson's assertion that "there is creative reading as well as creative writing"—but it's an idea that has not so far had the currency it might. Both writer-as-reader and reader-as-writer meet at the interface between what is recognisable and what is new, negotiating as they do the to-and-fro between familiar and strange, both operating somewhere between the primary ecstatic state and the "secondary elaboration," as Graves describes it.

That negotiation might be said to be at the heart of the "Welsh Incident," and is foregrounded as early as the first word of the title. As Graves surely knew, the word "Welsh" derives from the Anglo-Saxon *wylisc*, "foreigner," and is particularly appropriate to a poem whose subject matter is "all sorts of queer things." We need to spend a little time with the title, as I propose to do, if only because it's not the title under which the poem was first published in *Poems, 1929*, where it appeared as "Railway Carriage." The title as we have it, then, was written not *through* Graves the primary ecstatic but *by* Graves the secondary elaborator. One may begin to understand why the secondary elaborator thought he was on the right track, as it were, in changing the title when we consider that the other major change Graves made to the poem when it appeared in *Collected Poems, 1938* was in the description of the noise made by "the most odd, indescribable thing of all" and the "something recognizably a something" it did. In the first version of the poem, the something it did was to emit "a loud belch." Douglas Day notes in *Swifter Than Reason*, his study of the poetry and criticism of Graves, how the poet, "moved by an inexplicable

and uncharacteristic niceness, changed the belch to 'a very loud, respectable noise— / Like groaning to oneself on Sunday morning / In
Chapel'—thereby robbing the poem of a large degree of its humor."

What was going on in Graves's mind when he made these revisions?
The answer is at once "too much" and "not enough." In dropping the title
"Railway Carriage" we all but entirely lose the context of the dialogue of
which the poem is made up, the setting of this rambling conversation.
"Railway Carriage" may not be the most scintillating title in the history of
poetry in English, but it's certainly no less scintillating than the new title,
which threatens rather redundancy. There's surely no doubt that the setting of the poem is in Wales and that it describes, in its own way, an "incident," that's to say "something that occurs casually in the course of, or in
connection with, something else, of which it constitutes no essential part"
(OED). The word "Incident" sends us back, not unrewardingly, to our
great poet of "incidents" (including "Incident at Bruges").

William Wordsworth's sonorous blank verse will be confirmed as being a model here by the time we get to the end of the first line or two of
"Welsh Incident":

> "But that was nothing to what things came out
> From the sea-caves of Criccieth yonder."

This sends me back, not only in its prosody but its "sea-beast" imagery, to
the first description of the leech-gatherer in Wordsworth's "Resolution
and Independence":

> As a huge stone is sometimes seen to lie
> Couched on the bald top of an eminence;
> Wonder to all who do the same espy,
> By what means it could thither come, and whence;
> So that it seems a thing endued with sense:
> Like a sea-beast crawled forth, that on a shelf
> Of rock or sand reposeth, there to sun itself.

These Wordsworthian "things" ("the *things* which I have seen I now can
see no more") are distinctly un-Wordsworthian in that they offer not "Inti-

mations of Immortality" nor any kind of "help," as with the sturdy "leech-gatherer on the lonely moor" and the steadfast, all but static "Old Cumberland Beggar"—"Him even the slow-paced waggon leaves behind."

That image of the "slow-paced waggon" reminds me of another major source in "Railway Carriage," if we may continue to call it that for the moment, since I still haven't left my discussion of the title. I'm thinking, of course, of the unreliable correspondent in Robert Frost's "The Mountain," who, not unlike the old Cumberland beggar, was "a man who moved so slow / With white-faced oxen, in a heavy cart, / It seemed no harm to stop him altogether." Like "Railway Carriage," "The Mountain" is a dramatic poem, in which the poem's protagonist and the teamster-testifier keep glancing off each other ineffectually before what might be described as the poetic equivalent of a slow fade to black:

"You've lived here all your life?"

> "Ever since Hor
Was no bigger than a ———" What, I did not hear.
He drew the oxen toward him with light touches
Of his slim goad on nose and offside flank,
Gave them their marching orders and was moving.

We see immediately how Frost's poem rolls to a halt in precisely the same way as Graves's, with its "I was coming to that."

What's intriguing about the relationship between Graves and Frost is the extent to which their influence was mutual. When Frost first came to England, one of the poets by whom he was most inspired was Graves, whom he would meet in the fall of 1914, the very year in which "The Mountain" was collected in *North of Boston*. Graves would go on to edit a selection of Frost's poems, and to describe him as "the first American who could be honestly reckoned a master-poet by world standards." When he met Frost, Graves had just been commissioned as an officer in the Royal Welch Fusiliers, so that component of the title *"Welsh* Incident" has a resonance above and beyond his childhood associations with Harlech. So closely are *Fairies and Fusiliers* connected in Graves's mind that it is the title of a book of poems published in 1917, in which we read "Letter to S.S.":

> You'll see where in old Roman days,
> Before revivals changed our ways,
> The Virgin 'scaped the Devil's grab,
> Printing her foot on a stone slab
> With five clear toe-marks; and you'll find
> The fiendish thumbprint close behind.
> You'll see where Math, Mathonwy's son,
> Spoke with the wizard Gwydion
> And had him for South Wales set out
> To steal that creature with the snout,
> That new-discovered grunting beast
> Divinely flavoured for the feast.
> No traveler yet has hit upon
> A wilder land than Meirion,
> For desolate hills and tumbling stones,
> Bogland and melody and old bones.
> Fairies and ghosts are here galore,
> And poetry most splendid, more
> Than can be written with the pen
> Or understood by common men.

In an interview with Leslie Norris published in *The Listener* of May 28, 1970, Graves explained his interest in this land of "ghosts and fairies":

> My father was an Irish bard who was attached to the Eisteddfod; and he was one of the group who helped to start the Welsh Folk-Song Society. I used to go with my sister through the hill country behind Harlech; we had one of those wax phonographs and used it to collect Welsh folk-songs. Unfortunately, those were the days before cassettes and other instruments. All we had was the phonograph, and my sister, who was a musician, would note down what we had recorded—and then we had to rewax the cylinder. We had only one. It was a great pity because we lost the actual singing voices

of the people. Nowadays when you collect folk-songs you get the actual singing voice, and that's important. You get all the gracenotes.

Something of the tenderness with which Graves recounts this ethnomusicologist childhood is evident in his account of the aurality of the experiences at the heart of the "very loud respectable noise" of "Welsh Incident" or "a loud belch" in "Railway Carriage." It is related partly to "the grunting beast" in "Letter to S.S." The "aurality," or lack of it, is reminiscent of the end of "The Mountain." There, the last bit of information given by Frost's teamster-testifier is not actually heard by the protagonist, and might as well be a "belch" like the one expurgated from "Welsh Incident." The fact that the "belch" has disappeared allows for the appearance of "Welsh" in the title, of course, that full rhyme being too ludicrous had the "belch" been retained in the body of the poem.

But let me continue to ponder this title, and the "lighter trance" arguments Graves might have mustered to change it from "Railway Carriage." In his interview with Leslie Norris printed in *The Listener*, he describes the origin of the poem:

> It started when my father and I were in a train compartment of the old Cambrian railway. The train was going round that curve from Barmouth, through Llan-bedr, round into Harlech where you see the sea stretched out; and there was a policeman aboard, a Welsh policeman. He got very excited and started telling my father how he had recently seen a mermaid.

The report of a mermaid-sighting would have been dear to the heart of Alfred Perceval Graves (1846–1931), himself the author of so many poems having to do with "queer things," particularly "fairies and ghosts." I think of "The Fairy Host," a versification of a prose passage translated by Kuno Meyer from *The Book of Leinster*, with its representation of, yet again, a noisesome otherworldly troop:

> Pure white the shields their arms upbear,
> With silver emblems rare o'ercast;
> Amid blue glittering blades they go,
> The horns they blow are *loud of blast*.

These fairies are part of the little platoon sighted by William Allingham ("down along the rocky shore / some make their home"). More important in this instance, they have found their way out of a poem collected in Robert Louis Stevenson's *A Child's Garden of Verses* (1885):

> Faster than fairies, faster than witches,
> Bridges and houses, hedges and ditches.

The title of the Stevenson poem is, as you may recall, "From a *Railway Carriage*." But that coincidence is just *one* reason why Graves is inclined to drop his first title. The main reason is connected to his relationship with his father. That this relationship was troubled is clear from the tone of Robert Graves's musings in *Goodbye to All That*:

> I am glad in a way that my father was a poet. This at least saved me from any false reverence of poets, and his work was never an oppression to me. I am even very pleased when I meet people who know his work and not mine. Some of his songs I sing without prejudice; when washing up after meals or shelling peas or on similar occasions. He never once tried to teach me how to write, or showed any understanding of my serious work; he was always more ready to ask advice about his own work than to offer it for mine.

Goodbye to All That was published in 1929, and Robert Graves had to wait only a year to hear some "advice" from his father in the form of Alfred Perceval Graves's *To Return to All That*:

> In writing of [Robert] I must point out that there is much in his autobiography that I do not accept as accurate. For the change in his outlook I hold the war and recent experiences responsible. To these I impute his bitter and hasty criticism of people who never wished him harm . . . He gives me no credit for the interest I always felt and showed in his poetry. During the War I offered poems of his to editor after editor, and even arranged with Harold Munro of the Poetry Book Shop to whom I introduced Robert, for the publication of *Over the Brazier*.

A. P. Graves goes on to make much of the fact that, while serving as a Royal Welch Fusilier, Robert was wounded and reported dead in *The Times* of August 3, 1916:

> The first two doctors who had seen him had thought his case hopeless. The second of these, wanting his place in the clearing station for a more hopeful case, sent him off to the base hospital . . . He was still regarded as a hopeless case when he wrote his first letter home in the train.

And then A. P. Graves makes a throwaway remark which, like so many throwaway remarks, is bang on target:

> The journey to Rouen he has himself described as a nightmare, *and for some years after the war he was unable to go in any train without feeling violently sick.*

I want to propose that Graves's association of the "Railway Carriage" with his trauma, his father, and his father's dismissal of him in *To Return to All That* (1930), are the main reasons for his changing the title of the poem in 1938. Let me focus on the trauma for the moment, and try to connect this with a key image in another poem from *Fairies and Fusiliers*. In "Escape," Graves describes how, while he "was dead, an hour or more," he met Cerberus:

> Cerberus stands and grins above me now,
> Wearing three heads—lion, and lynx, and sow.
> "Quick, a revolver! But my Webley's gone,
> Stolen! . . . No bombs . . . no knife . . . The crowd swarms on,
> Bellows, hurls stones . . . Not even a honeyed sop . . .
> Nothing . . . Good Cerberus! Good dog! . . . But stop!
> Stay! . . . A great luminous thought . . . I do believe
> There's still some morphia that I bought on leave."
> Then swiftly Cerberus' wide mouths I cram
> With army biscuit smeared with ration jam;
> And sleep lurks in the luscious plum and apple.

He crunches, swallows, stiffens, seems to grapple
With the all-powerful poppy . . . then a snore,
A crash; the beast blocks up the corridor
With monstrous hairy carcase, red and dun—
Too late! for I've sped through!
                    O life! O sun!

The coloration of Cerberus ("red and dun") tallies with that of the one conventionally coloured "thing" in "Welsh Incident" that "was *puce* / Or perhaps more like *crimson*, but not *purplish*." The fact that one head of Cerberus is that of a "sow" relates it to the "grunting beast" of "Letter to S.S." and "the most odd, indescribable thing of all" that makes "a very loud, respectable noise" in "Welsh Incident." In *The White Goddess* (1948–75), Graves would describe how Cerberus is one of those beasts likely to visit the poet while he or she is in the ecstasy in which poems get made:

> To think with perfect clarity in a poetic sense one must first rid
> oneself of a great deal of intellectual encumbrance, including all
> dogmatic doctrinal prepossessions: membership of any political
> party or religious sect or literary school deforms the poetic sense—
> as it were, introduces something irrelevant and destructive into the
> magic circle, drawn with a rowan, hazel or willow rod, within which
> the poet insulates himself for the poetic act.

This is precisely the enclosed openness, if I may call it that, which Graves encourages the scientist to cultivate in "Nine Hundred Iron Chariots":

> He will see that the future of thought does not lie in the cosmical
> nonsense-region of electronic computers, but in the Paradisal region
> of what he will not be ashamed to call "magic."

In the case of "Welsh Incident," however, Graves has allowed himself to introduce something "irrelevant and destructive into the magic circle," namely his own "intellectual encumbrance." In an effort to make a point about "respectability," he uses the word "respectable" when the logic of the poem cries out for the word *"disrespectable,"* perhaps even *"disrespect-ful,"* which is surely how the Welsh congregation would perceive "groaning to oneself on Easter morning." As we've seen before, however, the poem survives the obstacles put in its way ("the beast [that] blocks up the corridor"), and like Graves surviving his near-death experience, like the Christ rising again from his "sea-cave" at "half-past three / On Easter Tuesday last," manages to "sp[e]ed through" to the sun.

IF POETS NAMED GRAVES are likely to be much exercised by "ghosts," so a poet named Day-Lewis is likely to be exercised by "the *day* of harvest," a phrase we meet there in the first line of the fifth stanza of "A Failure." Lest we think this farfetched, we might remind ourselves that his autobiography of 1960 was entitled *The Buried Day.* One of the main activities having to do with a "day" is winning it, of course, winning being a word derived from, or cognate with, the Middle Low German *winnen,* meaning quite specifically "to till the ground." The imagery of "A Failure" is deeply imbued with a sense of country lore.

Though Cecil Day-Lewis, who was born in 1904 in Ballintubber, County Laois, Ireland, moved to England when he was two years old, I like to think of that landscape imprinting itself on him in the way that the landscape of County Monaghan imprinted itself on another Irish poet born in 1904:

Now leave the check-reins slack,
The seed is flying fat today—
The seed like stars against the black
Eternity of April clay.

This seed is potent as the seed
Of knowledge in the Hebrew Book,
So drive your horses in the creed
Of God the Father as a stook.

Forget the men on Brady's hill.
Forget what Brady's boy may say.

For destiny will not fulfill
Unless you let the harrow play.

Forget the worm's opinion too
Of hooves and pointed harrow-pins,
For you are driving your horses through
The mist where Genesis begins.

Patrick Kavanagh's appeals to Genesis and Blake's "Proverbs of Hell" ("the cut worm forgives the plough") give "To the Man after the Harrow" an oddly literary tinge, especially if read in the light of Kavanagh's reputation for groundedness.

Day-Lewis, meanwhile, is no less au courant with the ins and outs of ploughing:

The soil was deep and the field well-sited,
    The seed was sound.

By the time we get to the end of line 2, however, there's a hint that this may not be a poem simply about ploughing. The word "sound" may be read both in the senses of "free from disease, infirmity, or injury" and "the particular auditory effect produced by a special cause" (OED), such as the sound at the heart of music and poetry:

The soil was deep and the field well-sited,
    The seed was sound.
Average luck with the weather, one thought,
    And the crop would abound.

The imagery of the poem, however matter-of-fact, points to at least one major literary influence. We might remember that "A Failure" was included in Poems 1943–1947 (1948), the first book of poems Day-Lewis published after his brilliant translation of Virgil's Georgics:

I've noticed seed long chosen and tested with utmost care
Fall off, if each year the largest

Be not hand-picked by human toil. For a law of nature
Makes all things go to the bad, lose ground and fall away.

But Day-Lewis goes beyond Virgil (*Georgics*, Book I, lines 197–200) in presenting a metaphorical landscape, one that his readers would have recognised from at least as far back as the title poem of 1931's *From Feathers to
Iron*, in which the coming to term of a child is compared to a crop coming
to fruition. Here we find lines such as "Twenty weeks near past / Since
the seed took to earth" and "Beautiful brood the cornlands, and you are
heavy; / Leafy the boughs—they also hide big fruit." In 1931, Day-Lewis
had been just as much exercised by the social ramifications of bringing another child into the world:

> What were we at, the moment when we kissed—
> Extending the franchise
> To an indifferent class, would we enlist
> Fresh power who know not how to be so great?
> Beget and breed a life—what's this
> But to perpetuate
> Man's labour, to enlarge a rank estate?

Day-Lewis is appealing here to a central tenet of Marx and Engels, the
latter of whom, in *The Origin of the Family, Private Property and the State*
(1884), identified the domestication of plants and animals as the beginning
of organized labour. While he may be having a little fun with the double
sense of "labour" that includes both "physical exertion directed to the
supply of the material wants of the community" and "the pains and efforts of childbirth," Day-Lewis is most interested in making a point having to do with "the general body of labourers and operatives, viewed in its
relation to the body of capitalists, or with regard to its political interests
and claims" (*OED*):

> Planted out here some virtue still may flower,
> But our dead follies too—
> A shock of buried weeds to turn it sour.
> Draw up conditions—will the heir conform?

Or thank us for the favour, who
Inherits a bankrupt firm,
Worn-out machinery, an exhausted farm.

By the time Day-Lewis returns to this system of imagery in "A Failure," there is more than a faint sense that the "bankrupt," the "worn-out"
and the "exhausted" are terms applicable to the political agenda that had
preoccupied his earlier self and which might now seem overly restrictive.
The word "abound" at the end of line 4 prepares the ground, as it were,
for the notion of containment it (somewhat paradoxically) contains. The
idea of a boundary is also included in the phrase "Headland to headland"
in stanza 4, since part of the OED definition of "headland" is "a strip of
land in a ploughed field, left for convenience in turning the plough at the
end of the furrows, or near the border; in old times used as a *boundary*."
"The Failure," though, of this poem has less to do with political matters
than literary—the work of art that, despite tending, comes to nothing.
These "headland" strictures of Day-Lewis's poem also have literary an-
tecedents, deriving partly from the 1942 poem by Day-Lewis's strict contemporary, Patrick Kavanagh:

A dog lying on a torn jacket under a heeled-up cart,
A horse nosing along the posied *headland*, trailing
A rusty plough.

This section of "The Great Hunger" ends with an eroticized description
"Where men are spanging across wide furrows, / Lost in the passion that
never needs a wife— / The pricks that pricked were the pointed pins of
harrows." It seems that it's the mechanism of a harrow rather than a
plough to which Day-Lewis appeals at the end of "A Failure":

But it's useless to argue the why and wherefore.
When a crop is so thin,
There's nothing to do but to set the teeth
And plough it in.

In this instance, the word "plough" may be read metaphorically. The other
way of reading it is literally, of course, and reading the phrase "to set the

teeth" metaphorically, as though it were an amalgam of "to set one's face" and "to grin and bear it," along with the slightly unfortunate resonances of "to set one's teeth on edge." There is resignation here before the turn of the wheel of Fortune, the goddess whose *"fortunate* acres / Seemed solid gold." The *fortunatus* comes directly from Book 2, lines 458–500, of the *Georgics*:

> Oh, too lucky for words, if only he knew his luck,
> Is the countryman who far from the clash of armaments
> Lives, and rewarding earth is lavish of all he needs!

The idea of "fortune" implies the existence of a system beyond one-self, be it the cycle of the seasons, the endless round of growth and decay and regrowth, or some notion of poetic inspiration. In *The Lyric Impulse*, the book based on his 1964–65 Norton Lectures at Harvard, Day-Lewis describes poetry as a "gift from the goddess." He goes on to describe what is essentially a Gravesian relationship between poet and goddess:

> The Muse, though she visit her poet but fitfully, is the ground of his being. She will not come meekly to his call; but when she does come, she possesses him entire, and her absence leaves a void which cannot be filled with other preoccupations. He may have no religious belief, may even feel no need for god, yet he is religious in the sense that he cannot live by material values; though he may not know it, he is the man in Browning's poem—the one "Through a whole campaign of the world's life and death, / Doing the King's work all the dim day long."

The "King" in question is from Browning's "How It Strikes a Contemporary," and is to be thought of partly as "our Lord the King" in the Christian world-picture. The description of him continues:

> In his old coat and up to knees in mud,
> Smoked like a herring, dining on a crust,—
> And, now the day was won, relieved at once.

That phrase "now the *day* is won" would, yet again, have had a resonance (conscious or unconscious) for Day-Lewis, and it may account for the allowing of the possibility of the poetic unconscious in the phrase *"though he may not know it."* For the "King" in "How It Strikes a Contemporary" is also a poet, specifically a version of Shelley, and the poem was written at about the same time as Browning's "Introductory Essay to the *Letters of Percy Bysshe Shelley*" (1852). It's in that essay, we may recall, that Browning makes his famous distinction between the objective and subjective poet. The latter is "rather a seer . . . than a fashioner, and what he produces will be less a work than an effluence." Now, according to Browning, the "subjective" poet is particularly likely to fail, and is described in terms which Day-Lewis seems to have taken over not only in *The Lyric Impulse* but "A Failure":

> Although of such depths of *failure* there can be no question here, we must in every case betake ourselves to the review of a poet's life ere we determine some of the nicer questions concerning his poetry—more especially if the performance we seek to estimate aright, has been obstructed and cut short of completion by circumstances—a disastrous youth or a premature death. We may learn from the biography whether his spirit invariably saw and spoke from the last height to which it had attained. An absolute vision is not for this world, but we are permitted a continual approximation to it, every degree of which in the individual, provided it exceed the attainment of the masses, must procure him a clear advantage. Did the poet ever attain to a higher platform than where he rested and exhibited a result? Did he know more than he spoke of?

The concerns of the speaker of "A Failure" are remarkably of a piece with Browning's here, "perhaps his own high hopes had made / The wizened look tall" echoing the imagery of Browning's "clear advantage," "but it's useless to argue the why and wherefore" echoing Browning's "an absolute vision is not for this world." The notion that a poet might "know more than he spoke of" is connected, I think, with the idea that the poem (the "effluence" for which the poet is a conduit) might "know more" than the poet. It's when the poet recognises that his or her field is "wan and weedy" rather than showing the "solid gold" to which it aspires that he or she is forced to counter vision with revision. At that point the poet is coming under the scrutiny of the poem, and may or may not be able to look it straight in the eyes. This is precisely the relationship subsequent readers will have with the poem—subsequent readers who may be better able for, may bring more to bear on, the poem than the first writer.

IF ONE OF A POEM'S MAIN AIMS is to continue to present itself as a problem only it has raised, a poem gladly enlists other readers in order to further itself, in order to find the equivalent of a "gutter" for its "copious blood," a "black divide" in which writer/reader and reader/writer lie down together. Like the speakers of "Welsh Incident" and "A Failure," the speaker of "Keeping Going," a speaker fairly coterminous with the historical figure of Seamus Heaney, is as much engaged by artistic dilemmas and deliverances as by Hugh Heaney's "shout[s]" and "laugh[s] above the revs." Those "revs," or "revolutions," represent one form of "turn" against which the poet, and his brother, display resolution. The other "turn" is the "attack of illness, faintness, or the like" (*OED*) from which Hugh comes to towards the end of the poem.

"Keeping Going" was collected in *The Spirit Level* (1996) and is one of a number of poems in that volume which are dedicated to friends and family of the poet. The dedication "for Hugh" is reminiscent of a dedication we saw three poems earlier in "A Brigid's Girdle," which is "for Adele." Just as "Hugh" is addressed overtly in the body of the poem as "my dear brother," the "Adele" in question is named, more covertly, in the body of "A Brigid's Girdle" in the lines:

> I heard the mocking bird
> And a delicious, articulate
>
> Flight of small plinkings from a dulcimer
> Like feminine rhymes migrating to the north
> Where you faced the music and the ache of summer
> And earth's foreknowledge gathered in the earth.

The "feminine rhyme" on "dulcimer" is "Dalsimer," the full name of Adele Dalsimer, a scholar and co-founder of the Irish Studies Program at Boston College, who would die from multiple myeloma in 2000. "A Brigid's Girdle" closes with the "revolutionary" image of "the motions you go through going through the thing" which connects the poem the-matically with "Keeping *Going.*" That "dulcimer" also connects the po-ems, given that the most famous dulcimer, accompanied by damsel, is to be found in Coleridge's "Kubla Khan," the archetypical "trance" docu-ment, at least according to Coleridge.

"A Brigid's Girdle" connects with "Keeping Going" in another, even more subliminal way. As I mentioned in my discussion of W. H. Auden's "Homage to Clio," Brigit is a version of a bear goddess who is associated with fertility. Her feast-day, February 1, corresponds to the Celtic festival of Imbolc, which, as Seamas O'Cathain tells us in *The Festival of Brigit*, his great study of the bear-goddess, is "a word whose basic meaning has much to do with the notion of milking and milk-production." The posi-tioning of Hugh Heaney "in the milking parlour . . . between two cows" is no accident. Indeed, Heaney will also be well aware of the similarity be-tween his own name in Gaelic (O'hAoine) and the genitive case, *aonaigh*, of the Gaelic word for "a fair," generally a fair involving the sale of cattle. Indeed, Hugh Heaney is continuing in the tradition of cattle-dealing es-poused by his and the poet's father, Patrick, whose spirit appears in "The Strand":

> The dotted line my father's ashplant made
> On Sandymount Strand
> Is something else the tide won't wash away.

This three-line poem, also from *The Spirit Level*, is terrifically reso-nant. The title refers not only to a strand in the sense of "the land border-ing the sea" but the transferred sense of strand as "a thread or filament," as in "strands of thought" (*OED*). Interwoven rather neatly here are the figures of James Joyce (with his trademark drover's ashplant) on Sandy-mount Strand and the drover father of the poet whose house overlooks Sandymount Strand. The "sand" is a significant element in the O'hAoine iconography, since it's still believed in some quarters that sand taken from the grave of the twelfth-century Saint Murrough O'Heaney brings luck, though only if it's "lifted" by a Heaney descendant. Murrough O'Heaney's grave is in Banagher, County Derry, and it just happens that the third-to-last poem in *The Spirit Level* is entitled "At Banagher" and con-cerns "a journeyman tailor who was my antecedent." The "strand" by which Heaney connects to his literary antecedent, James Joyce, is two-ply. The second ply is summoned up there by the word "wash" in "something else the tide won't *wash* away," a word which connects it to the process of white*wash*ing that is described so vividly in "Keeping Going":

> But the slop of the actual job
> Of brushing walls, the watery grey
> Being lashed on in broad swatches, then drying out
> Whiter and whiter, all that worked like magic.

The description of the process of whitewashing chimes with the description of Joyce's method of composition as described so memorably by A. Walton Litz in *The Art of James Joyce*, where he writes of *Work in Progress*:

> Usually the basic outline of a paragraph remained the same throughout its growth. Joyce seems to have thought of his original units as fundamental designs which could be expanded indefinitely through his techniques of amplification.

The process of whitewashing might well be described as a "technique of amplification," or "an elaboration of a basic text," as Litz also puts it. Litz also quotes Herbert Read's observation that "the closest analogy to the literary method of *Work in Progress* is perhaps to be found in the early graphic art of Joyce's own country, the abstract involved ornament of the Celts." In the way that Joyce incorporated a reference to the "Tunc" page of *The Book of Kells* in the passage about "pidgin fella Balkelly" who "augmentationed himself in caloripeia to vision so throughsighty" / and achieved the condition of "pure hueglut," Heaney's description of the "grey lashed on in broad swatches" that becomes its own "hueglut" is a brilliant description of the poem's own method of achieving brilliance. What works "like magic" in the poem is the visual artist's technique involving successive "broad thin layer[s] of colour laid on by a continuous movement of the brush." There is indeed a magical quality to the layering of the narratives of make-believe "piper's sporrans," the all-too-believable fate of the "part-time reservist" who leaves "a clean spot / Where his head had been" and "the actual job / of brushing walls." All bleed together until, like Hugh, we can't be certain if we should call a whitewash brush a piper's sporran or "the piper's sporrans whitewash brushes," just as in the poem "Widgeon" there's some confusion about the source of the "small widgeon cries" that seem to be emitted by the man who "found, he says, the voice box" of the duck.

This "Widgeon" is casting its voice, almost inaudibly this time, through "Keeping Going," resonant in that sense of the term "whitewash" meaning "to cover up, conceal, or gloss over the faults or blemishes of." I'm thinking of the near version of "widgeon" to be found in the name "Widgery," the controversial Lord Chief Justice whose report on the events of "Bloody Sunday" was famously described by John Hume, the Social Democratic and Labour Party Member of Parliament, as "whitewash." The figure of John Hume, I propose, is another ghostly presence in "Keeping Going," since Heaney and Hume were contemporaries at St. Columb's College in Derry, the school in which Heaney first came upon "that scene, with Macbeth helpless and desperate / In his nightmare." In his most recent collection, *Electric Light* (2001), Heaney gives us "The Real Names" of at least some of his fellow students who took part in these school productions and, in one passage, connects a scene from *Macbeth* with a scene of violent action from the 1950s:

> Duncan's horses, plastered in wet, surge up
> Wild as the chestnut tree one terrible night
> In Mossbawn, the aerial rod like a mast
> Whiplashed in tempest, my mother rocking and oching
> And blessing herself—
> > the breach in nature open
> As the back of the raiders' lorry hammering on
> For the Monaghan border, blood loosed in a scrim
> From the tailboard, the volunteer screaming *O Jesus!*
> *O merciful Jesus.*

The burden of these lines might be said to be that there's no delineation between art and history. The very thing that would mediate between the two, the "scrim" or "open-weave muslin or hessian fabric used in . . . the theatre to create the illusion of a solid wall or to suggest haziness, etc., according to the lighting" (*Collins English Dictionary*) is composed of "blood" just as it's the "smoky hair" in "Keeping Going" which engages in its own stagecraft in *"curtaining* a cheek." The graphic description of the wounded IRA man in the back of the lorry is reminiscent of the graphic description of the dead "reservist" in "Keeping Going" who "saw an ordinary face / For what it was" and the dead shopkeeper from the poem "Station Island" whose murderers were "barefaced as they would be in the day, / shites thinking they were the be-all and end-all." The "nightmare" in which Macbeth is "helpless and desperate" is also the *"nightmare* from which I am trying to awake," as Stephen Dedalus describes "history" (Irish history, to be precise) in *Ulysses*. This occurs in the "Nestor" chapter of the novel, where much is made of Stephen being seen as a "bullockbefriending bard" who's entrusted with Mr. Deasy's letter on "foot and mouth disease" in cattle. The other great "nightmare" in the hinterland of *Ulysses* involves Oliver Gogarty's fellow Oxford student and Martello Tower dweller, Samuel Chenevix (later Dermot) Trench, as Richard Ellmann explains in his *James Joyce*:

> What happened was that during the night of September 14 [1904] Trench began to scream in his sleep. He was convinced that a black panther was about to spring. Half waking, he snatched his revolver and shot at the fireplace beside which Joyce was sleeping. After having dispatched his prey, he turned back to sleep. While Joyce trembled, Gogarty seized the gun. Then Trench, again ridden by *nightmare*, screamed and reached again for his revolver. Gogarty called out, "Leave him to me," and shot not the panther but some pans hanging above Joyce's bed, which tumbled down on the recumbent poet. The terrified Joyce considered this fusillade his dismissal; without a word he dressed and left, having—at that hour—to walk all the way to Dublin.

This episode ghosts "Keeping Going" in an almost invisible way, in that "freshly-opened, pungent, reeking *trench*" and its near version, the *"gutter"* that's fed with "copious blood." This blood, like the "matte tacky *blood* / on the bricklayer's knuckles, like the damson stain / that seeped through his packed lunch" from "Damson," another piece from *The Spirit Level*, is associated with a heraldic moment. The word "gules," indeed, is the first word of "Damson," signifying "red, *as one of the heraldic colours"*

(*OED*). In "Keeping Going," the elaborate positioning of the "reservist" guardant, "a gun in his own face," on a field of argent confirms a tendency for the humdrum to become heraldic in a way beloved of Joyce. Now, Joyce and his ashplant, with which the character of Stephen is associated from the outset of *Ulysses*, informs "Keeping Going" in at least one further, rather more important, way. We first met Heaney meeting Joyce in 1984's *Station Island*, in the title poem of which, we remember, the speaker meets "a tall man" who "walked straight as a rush / upon his ashplant" who argues that "you lose more of yourself than you redeem / doing the decent thing."

I want to end my discussion of "Keeping Going" with an observation or two on this "trench" in which Heaney has been at war with himself for so long, a muddy ground out of which has come some of his very best poems, such as this one. It's the area presided over by what we might call, to pun on one of his titles, "The *Gutter*al Muse," in which Heaney finds himself "between two cows"—one representing an urge towards an Arnoldian "adequacy," perhaps even an Arnoldian "deliverance," and the position we saw earlier espoused by Joyce in "Station Island":

> "The English language
> belongs to us. You are raking at dead fires,
>
> rehearsing the old whinges at your age.
> That subject people stuff is a cod's game,
> infantile, like this peasant pilgrimage.
>
> You lose more of yourself than you redeem
> doing the decent thing."

The impulse towards redemption is very understandable, but even more understandable is the recognition that, as the speaker has it in the shopkeeper section of "Station Island," there is no "buying back" when it comes to those "shites thinking they were the be-all and end-all":

> "Not that it is any *consolation*
> but they were caught," I told him, "and got jail."

Allied to the ideas of redemption and consolation is the idea of "restoration," an idea we meet in section 2 of "Keeping Going":

> Where had we come from, what was this kingdom
> We knew we'd been restored to?

This "kingdom" is only partly the realm of Browning's "our Lord the King" in what I described earlier as "the Christian world-picture." Like Browning's character in "How It Strikes a Contemporary," the king is also an artist, the kingdom one we enter by the "magic" of the art of whitewashing. One of the poignancies of "Keeping Going" is the speaker's assertion—one we don't expect from a Heaney speaker—that, despite the "magic" of Hugh's calling "the piper's sporrans whitewash brushes" there's the insurmountable fact of the limitations of art:

> But you cannot make the dead walk or right wrong.

This is not to say that a poem, such as any of the three I've looked at here, doesn't have *some* efficacy in the world, doesn't effect *some* change. It must change something, as these three examples so elegantly display. One of the ways in which they do this is to clear their own space, bringing us "all together there in a foretime," if I may borrow that phrase from section 3 of "Keeping Going." This "foretime" is the "kingdom" to which we are to be *re*stored, of course, a sense of "foreknowledge" Heaney associates with a work of art in "Poet's Chair," also collected in *The Spirit Level*. This condition of a "foretime" of the poem is, yet again, a version of what I described earlier as the "problem" to which the poem is a "solution." We appeal to the "foretime" of "Welsh Incident" and recognise that, despite the wobble on "respectable," the poem triumphs over the person through whom it was written. We appeal to the "foretime" of "A Failure" and recognise that it meets its own "solid gold" standard, winning its own day. We appeal to the "foretime" of "Keeping Going" and recognise, as we emerge with Hugh from our "turn," that to carry itself forward in the world—testing itself, and us, against a sense of how it itself "was / In the beginning, is now and shall be"—*is* indeed the end of the poem.

AUTHOR'S NOTE

I'M VERY GRATEFUL to a number of people who helped me as I prepared these lectures, which are published here much as they were given, though sometimes in slightly extended versions.

I'm particularly grateful to my first readers—Michael Cadden, James Richardson, P. Adams Sitney, and C. K. Williams—all friends and colleagues at Princeton, on whom I called for frank and forthright comments. It is I, I'm afraid, who remain responsible for any lapses they were too polite to bring to my attention.

I'm also grateful to Jill Balcon, C. D. Blanton, Maria Brodsky, R. F. Foster, John Fuller, Seamus Heaney, Vicki Howard, Alan Jenkins, Hermione Lee, Peter MacDonald, Jamie McKendrick, Edward Mendelson, Ben Metcalf, Brett Millier, Gerard Quinn, Dean M. Rogers, Jon Stallworthy, Erica Wagner, Ruth Webb, and Clair Wills for their generosity and graciousness in helping me with specific matters of information and interpretation.

I'm grateful to the editors of *American Poet*, *American Poetry Review*, *Dublin Review*, *Fulcrum*, *Harvard Review*, *New England Review*, *Parnassus: Poetry in Review*, and *The Yellow Nib*, in which several of the lectures first appeared in print, and to Dorothy McCarthy of Oxford University Press, who kindly oversaw publication by the press of the inaugural lecture.

As always, I have a special word of thanks to Paul Keegan and Christopher Reid of Faber and Faber Ltd, and Jonathan Galassi of Farrar, Straus and Giroux, editors and publishers as steadfast as one might hope for, particularly in this spasmodic era.

My visits to Oxford were cheered by Joan Arthur, Paul Burns, Melanie Clancy, Jenny Houlsby, and Jo Jackson, stalwarts all of the English Faculty Office. I'm particularly grateful to Sir Walter Bodmer and the Fellows of Hertford College, among whose number I was happy to be counted while I was Professor of Poetry. I was also happy to be allowed through the gates of Hertford by the magnificent Pam Horwood and Judy Mullee.

A final word of thanks to Tom Paulin, who first raised the idea of my standing for the Professorship and who (with his wife, Giti) continued to support me in ways, intellectual and physical, too numerous to mention.

Bertha Georgie Yeats. Excerpt from "Adam's Curse" copyright © 1903 by The Macmillan Company; renewed 1931 by William Butler Yeats. Reprinted in the United States by permission of Scribner, an imprint of Simon & Schuster Adult Publishing Group, from *The Collected Works of W. B. Yeats, Volume I: Poems, Revised*, edited by Richard J. Finneran, and reprinted by permission of AP Watt Ltd on behalf of Michael B. Yeats.